West's Law School Advisory Board

JESSE H. CHOPER
Professor of Law,
University of California, Berkeley

DAVID P. CURRIE
Professor of Law, University of Chicago

YALE KAMISAR
Professor of Law, University of San Diego
Professor of Law, University of Michigan

MARY KAY KANE
Chancellor, Dean and Distinguished Professor of Law,
University of California,
Hastings College of the Law

LARRY D. KRAMER
Dean and Professor of Law, Stanford Law School

WAYNE R. LaFAVE
Professor of Law, University of Illinois

JONATHAN R. MACEY
Professor of Law, Yale Law School

ARTHUR R. MILLER
Professor of Law, Harvard University

GRANT S. NELSON
Professor of Law,
University of California, Los Angeles

JAMES J. WHITE
Professor of Law, University of Michigan

INTERNATIONAL LAW TODAY

A HANDBOOK

By

Anthony D'Amato
Leighton Professor,
Northwestern University

Jennifer Abbassi
Associate Professor, Political Science
Chair, Global Studies Program
Randolph–Macon Woman's College

AMERICAN CASEBOOK SERIES®

Mat # 40462365

West, a Thomson business, has created this publication to provide you with accurate and authoritative information concerning the subject matter covered. However, this publication was not necessarily prepared by persons licensed to practice law in a particular jurisdiction. West is not engaged in rendering legal or other professional advice, and this publication is not a substitute for the advice of an attorney. If you require legal or other expert advice, you should seek the services of a competent attorney or other professional.

American Casebook Series and West Group are trademarks registered in the U.S. Patent and Trademark Office.

© 2006 Thomson/West
      610 Opperman Drive
      P.O. Box 64526
      St. Paul, MN 55164–0526
      1–800–328–9352

ISBN–13: 978–0–314–16807–8
ISBN–10: 0–314–16807–9

Table of Contents

INTRODUCTION [p. 1]

CHAPTER 1. THE TRANSFORMATION OF INTERNATIONAL LAW [p. 3]

CHAPTER 2. THE AUTHORITY AND METHOD OF INTERNATIONAL LAW

		Page
A.	Is International Law "Law"?	13
B.	Method in International Law	29

CHAPTER 3. TREATIES AND CUSTOM IN INTERNATIONAL LAW

A.	Treaty Law	36
B.	Criticisms of Current Treaty Practice	52
C.	Customary Law	57

CHAPTER 4. THE IDENTITY AND ROLE OF THE STATE

A.	Personality	72
B.	Nationality	76
C.	State Jurisdiction	81
D.	State Succession	90

CHAPTER 5. HUMAN RIGHTS

A.	Individual Rights	101
B.	Cultural Rights	112
C.	Gender	117

CHAPTER 6. GROUP RIGHTS

A.	Collective Paradigms	121
B.	Self–Determination	127

CHAPTER 7. HUMANITARIAN INTERVENTION [p. 140]

CHAPTER 8. INTERNATIONAL CRIMINAL LAW

		Page
A.	Genocide	154
B.	War Crimes	160
C.	Crimes Against Humanity	167
D.	Universal Jurisdiction	176
E.	Prosecuting Heads of State	186
F.	The International Criminal Court	191

CHAPTER 9. TERRORISM

A.	Terrorism and State Responsibility	196
B.	Use of Force in Response to Terrorism	203
C.	Prisoner Rights	216

CHAPTER 10. THE GLOBAL ENVIRONMENT

A.	The Study of Environmental Law	224
B.	Environmental Governance	226
C.	Unilateral Environmental Action	240
D.	Trade Linkages	245

CHAPTER 11. ECONOMIC GLOBALIZATION

A.	Economic Globalization and International Law	248
B.	World Trade Organization	254
C.	Linkages: Trade and . . .	261

CHAPTER 12. EMERGING ISSUE AREAS

A.	Rights of the Child	271
B.	Health	280
C.	Biotechnology	285
D.	Internet	290

CHAPTER 13. INTERNATIONAL LAW TOMORROW
[p. 299]

INTERNATIONAL LAW TODAY

A HANDBOOK

*

INTRODUCTION

International law is one of the most rapidly growing—and rapidly changing—subjects in our colleges and law schools. This Handbook is designed to update this exciting field of study. Our reader-friendly and inexpensive format is ideal either for a stand-alone text in college courses in international politics and relations, or for a handbook to accompany any international law coursebook available on the market today.

We expect to keep this Handbook as fresh as today's headlines. We will do so by either issuing an annual supplement or, when there is sufficient new material, a new edition. Naturally, we cannot cover all the topics in this vast field. Our best judgment in selecting articles for this first edition of 2006 will not be sufficient to carry us forward. We must rely on the kindness of our readers to let us know what needs to be added to the succeeding supplements or new editions. Please send either of us an email telling us which topics need to be added or supplemented, and if possible, your recommendation for including particular articles.

Because of its importance, international law should be utterly devoid of wishful thinking. Despite its name, international law does not provide the solution to the problems of the world. International law will not always do for you what you would want it to do. Yet there is no lawful alternative: we only have one world and international law is the only law that transcends the artificial boundaries of states. We students of the subject have no choice but to ascertain and recognize the impact of international law on international politics even if, from time to time, that impact seems of minor importance. Yet it would be an error to focus on just those failings of the international rule of law that make headlines. For every failure there are hundreds of thousands of small success stories—instances of law-abiding behavior that serve to reduce international friction. In the aggregate, these small successes have served in recent years to reduce drastically the annual number of deaths due to war. One might even come up with a perhaps counterintuitive theory that the greater the total of legally regulated interactions among states, the less is the chance that interstate misunderstandings or disagreements will escalate into armed conflict!

International law is not just constraining; it is facilitative. It enables nations to do things together that none of them could have accomplished separately. Our subject has been around for three or four thousand years. It began when small city-states realized that they would be better off with neutral rules governing their relations than by constantly contesting those rules on the battlefields. International law has evolved to be a law of peace.

But we should not make the mistake of regarding rules of international law as simplistic or primitive. The rules that have evolved over the course of many centuries have done the remarkable job of placing both sides to a controversy on a level playing field and giving each side exactly equal rights and precisely equal expectations of reciprocity. Indeed, the study of the evolution of international law is at the cutting edge of game theory. As the mathematical theory of games becomes more sophisticated in its current turn toward N-person non-zero-sum games, its theorists are finding that rules that evolve in the course of N-person games are fiendishly clever mechanisms for both sides to attain reciprocal advantage. And even beyond the cutting edge of game theory is the fact that the "players" in international relations are not just the single entities we call states, but rather are composites of states plus the people in the states. People have their own interests which are not always congruent with those of their own nations (for example, human rights as asserted by a minority group within a state). How international law works out these diverse and often competing interests (or in some cases, fails to work them out) is a unique intellectual challenge.

We bid you a warm welcome into the discourse of international law.

—Anthony D'Amato
—Jennifer Abbassi

Email us at:
a-damato@northwestern.edu
jabbassi@rmwc.edu

ACKNOWLEDGEMENTS

We would like to thank the journals cited herein, that hold the copyrights jointly with their authors, for permission to republish. In the case of each excerpt from the A.J.I.L. and the Proc. A.S.I.L., the copyright is held by the American Society of International Law and is used here by permission.

Chapter 1

THE TRANSFORMATION OF INTERNATIONAL LAW

Editors' Introduction: Many cogent insights about international law have been written, and from among them we have chosen two of the very best for this introductory chapter. We stress that the two authors, Richard Falk and Philippe Sands, are talking *about* international law without telling us what it is. In effect, they are setting the stage for the next chapter which will explore the contested question whether international law is really "law."

State System. Richard A. Falk, *The Declining World Order: America's Imperial Geopolitics* (2004), exerpt.

As the Cold War ended, the Soviet Union disintegrated, the world economy flourished, constitutional democracy was robust—there existed a historical moment of unprecedented opportunity to salvage the Westphalian legacy. Salvaging would have involved a mixture of initiatives designed to promote humane global governance: especially demilitarization, the buildup of UN peacekeeping capabilities, and a "Marshall Plan" for Africa and the Caribbean. Seizing the occasion depended on American leadership, which was timid and ambivalent, retreating from any claim to promote what had earlier been called "liberal internationalism." Unlike the endings of the two world wars of the twentieth century, the end of the Cold War did not give rise to grassroots demands for global reform, nor were the leaders on the scene dedicated to achieving a peaceful settlement that addressed the major problems of world order. Instead, the prevailing mood was complacent and foolishly optimistic about the future, triumphalist in response to the outcome of the East/West struggle, economistic in its sense of what needed to be done to secure human well-being, and essentially unresponsive to the legitimate grievances of peoples in the South.

There was some recognition of the opportunities and challenges of the 1990s. George Bush in 1990–1991 temporarily aroused interest and built support during the lead up to the Gulf War by constantly referring to the possibility of establishing "a new world order," by which he meant a functioning collective security process under UN auspices. Humanitarian diplomacy was also taken seriously in this period, both in relation to the protection of the Kurdish minority in Iraq, the response to the humanitarian catastrophe in Somalia, and the effort to avoid "ethnic cleansing" in Bosnia. But for reasons too complicated to discuss here, disillusionment ensued, and the more promising implications of such initiatives never materialized. Among the more hopeful initiatives was the effort by Lloyd Axworthy, while foreign minister of Canada, to champion a shift from "national security" to "human security" as the basis for the role of the sovereign state, a conceptualization earlier given currency in an annual volume of the Human Development Report. Instead, the United States led a return to Westphalian geopolitics in its narrower state-centric ethos, a backlash against the United Nations, and a primary reliance on the world economy organized ideologically along neoliberal lines (with hypocritical self-serving exceptions to protect some private sectors from competitive pressures) to address problems of human suffering (including poverty and the AIDS epidemic) and ecological sustainability.

The opportunity to initiate comprehensive negotiations to abolish nuclear weapons was not even seriously considered during this period, nor were proposals to establish a UN volunteer peacekeeping force that could respond to humanitarian catastrophes rapidly and without even passing through the realist, geopolitical, and nationalist filters of leading states. Such states were reluctant to bear the financial or human costs of a diplomacy that could not be validated by traditional criteria associated with national security and strategic overseas interests (for example, to put the matter most starkly, oil is worth dying for, especially in a Third World setting.) As a result, the main deficiencies of Westphalia were preserved: the war system of global security and the vulnerability of the peoples of the world to various forms of oppressive governance exercised within territorial boundaries.

Nevertheless, the case for drastic global reform was being made in various arenas, and if not attainable within the Westphalian framework then possibly its realization could be achieved through the agency of transnational social forces and the emergence of post-Westphalian structures of governance. What was this case? What were these social forces? Essentially, the plausibility of post-Westphalian perspectives involved the rise to high visibility of a multidimensional normative agenda: implementation of human rights, accountability for past crimes of state, abridgements of sovereignty, the rise of humanitarian peacekeeping.

Beyond the agenda, steps were taken to achieve institutionalization: an increasing willingness of national judicial bodies to apply international legal standards as relevant; greater reliance on multilateral approaches to global security, especially under the auspices of the United Nations; and the impressive growth of regional governance, especially in Europe, with mandates to promote human rights, to sustain a social contract between citizens and market forces, and to facilitate trade and investment. Such goals by their nature could not be realized without compromising the internal autonomy of sovereign states, and this would not happen without the agency of political actors other than the state. In effect, drastic global reform, if it is to occur, will eventuate in a post-Westphalian scenario of transformed state structures and strengthened transnational, regional, and global formal and informal institutional procedures.

The most currently promising of these developments is the campaign to promote global democracy and the various movements to build comprehensive regional frameworks for democracy, human rights, and political identity, If cumulatively effective, the impact will be to view the outcome as post-Westphalian: states become subject to external and internal standards of accountability, the rule of law is extended to the foreign policy of governments, and official policies are subject to the discipline of democratic practices; and regional institutions become vital actors that adhere to frameworks that ensure constitutionalism and collective well-being within regional boundaries, but also participate in efforts to increase the quantity and quality of global public goods. World order is thus no longer state-centric, although the role of the states remains crucial, even if reconfigured in light of legal and ethnical norms. The dusk of Westphalia can be best understood in relation to the setting sun of sovereignty and the rising sun of regional and global policy horizoning, rather than by supposing that the state itself will disappear by stages, or is in the process of being marginalized.

Transformation. Philippe Sands, "Turtles and Torturers: The Transformation of International Law" 33 NYU J. Int'l L. & Pol. 527 (2000).

International law was traditionally presented as a set of rules with the object of preserving the peace and harmony of nations. But recently it has become clear that it serves a broader range of societal interests, and that it now connects with a wider range of actors and subjects. The transformation that is underway challenges some of the most basic assumptions that have dominated international legal relations for much of the past century and beyond, assumptions that continue to inform public and private views on the nature and effectiveness of international law. In this inaugural public lecture, I will focus on two recent cases to explore some of the changes which are under way: how new actors, new rules, and new international courts are transforming the landscape of international law. The two proceedings are those before the English courts relating to the request for Senator Pinochet's extradition to Spain, and those before the Appellate Body of the World Trade Organization concerning the prohibition by the United States of imports of shrimp from four Asian countries. I should say at the outset that I have chosen these two cases because they are topical and because they provide insights into some of the challenges they present for traditional assumptions about the international legal order. Also, they are cases arising in two of the new areas of international law—human rights and the environment—which seem more attuned to our new, globalized world of technology, deregulation, and "democratization."

Let us begin with the past: how international law was at the close of the last century. Two late nineteenth century decisions illustrate where we have come from. The first case comes from New York: the 1876 decision of the State Supreme Court in *Hatch v. Baez*. The court was faced with a claim from a plaintiff, Mr. Davis Hatch, that he had suffered injuries in the Dominican Republic as a result of acts done by the defendant, Mr. Buenaventura Baez, in his official capacity of President of the Dominican Republic. The court accepted that, because former President Baez was physically present in New York, he came within the territorial jurisdiction of the New York state courts. The court went on to find, however, that the former President was immune from its jurisdiction because such immunity was "essential to preserve the peace and harmony of nations," because the acts alleged sprang from the capacity in which the acts were done, and because they emanated from a foreign and friendly government. There was nothing exceptional about the decision at the time, based as it was on a traditional judicial respect for the sovereignty of a foreign state. I mention it here because it states a principle which is less easily recognisable a century later, particularly after the *Pinochet* decisions.

The second case was decided seventeen years later, in 1893, in Paris. An international arbitral tribunal gave an award in a dispute between the United Kingdom and the United States. The case concerned the exploitation or preservation of Pacific fur seals. Born within the jurisdiction of the United States, each year they migrated beyond the three-mile limit of U.S. territorial waters onto the high seas. Before they could reach the safety of the Pribilov Islands in the Bering Sea, the great majority of them were caught by British registered vessels, skinned, and sent back to London. The United States objected. It claimed a right of property and protection over these creatures, and the right to take steps even outside its territory to conserve them for the benefit of humankind. This was a radical argument at the time, and a precursor to positions taken with increasing force today. Against the argument, Great Britain claimed the right to harvest the fur seals, if necessary to extinction. It invoked long-standing rights of high seas fisheries freedom. The arguments of the United States did not prevail, and the tribunal ruled by a large majority that there was no basis in international law for the United States to seek to apply its standards of conservation to measures taking place outside its territory. The arbitral tribunal ruled that the United States had neither a property right in the fur seals, nor the right to protect the resource from extinction.

These two decisions reflect some of the most cherished assumptions of the international legal order at the close of the 19th century. It was an order in which the state was the only player, and the need to protect its sovereignty was paramount. There were relatively few rules of international law—and certainly no rules protecting fundamental human rights or the environment which could be invoked to override immunity or to claim an interest in activities beyond a state's territory. It was an order which permitted states to do that which they were not expressly prohibited from doing, and in which the existence of restrictions on sovereign rights would not easily be presumed. There were no nongovernmental organizations (NGOs) around to intervene in the proceedings, and commercial interests—in this case the fur industry—had to be channeled through the legal arguments of the British delegation. It was an order in which there existed no international organizations and no permanent international courts: arbitral tribunals were created on an ad hoc basis. If one state did not wish to settle the dispute by arbitration, there would be no such settlement. In those circumstances, the options for enforcement were limited. It was, in short, a legal order promoting a potentially Hobbesian state of nature, to be controlled by establishing a limited number of basic ground rules of inter-course while respecting the equal sovereignty of all nations. Any effort by a tribunal or other third-party institution to restrict sovereignty beyond the bare essentials necessary for intercourse would destabilize the situation because sovereigns would not tolerate such restrictions, and the whole effort to establish a minimal international legal order might perish in the process.

Over the next century there were very significant changes. Regional and global institutions were created. Treaties and other international obligations were adopted across a broad range of subject areas, establishing limits on sovereign freedoms. New standards were adopted seeking to protect and promote fundamental human rights and, more recently, conserve the environment. Gradually, new actors emerged with an international voice, of which corporations and NGOs were to become the most active. Inherent in these developments—but not explicitly conceived—were the seeds for change: the development of a new consciousness of international public law governing legal relations beyond the nation state, available to influence public and administrative law at the national level, and accessible to an emergent international civil society.

It is against this background that we can turn to the present, and consider the two late twentieth century decisions which addressed, in broad terms, very similar issues to the two late nineteenth century decisions. Both judgments share one important feature: they seemed to turn conventional wisdom on its head.

On October 16, 1998, a Metropolitan Magistrate in London issued a provisional warrant for the arrest of Senator Augusto Pinochet Ugarte. This was pursuant to a request for his extradition to Spain, on the grounds that he had committed criminal acts over which Spain had jurisdiction, including genocide, hostage taking, and torture. Senator Pinochet claimed immunity from the jurisdiction of the English courts, on the grounds that he was a former sovereign and that the acts which he was alleged to have carried out—or turned a blind eye to—had occurred whilst he had been the head of state of Chile, a friendly foreign nation. On classical grounds of international law—the preservation of the peace and harmony of nations—as well as the construction of the State Immunity Act 1978 which dealt with immunity in English law, there was every expectation that his claim to immunity would prevail. Any other conclusion would have been without precedent before the national courts of any country anywhere in the world, and at odds with the judgment that liberated Buenaventura Baez. At first instance the Divisional Court unanimously upheld Senator Pinochet's claim. On appeal to the House of Lords in November 1998 however, that ruling was overturned by three votes to two. CNN broadcast the judgment live—a first for the Law Lords—and it was watched world-wide. If you visit the archive on the CNN web site and watch and listen to the judgment being delivered, you might just be able to pick up the sharp intake of breath around the Chamber of the Lords at the moment it became apparent that the Law Lords had ruled that Senator Pinochet was not entitled to claim immunity from the English courts, since under customary inter-national law there was no entitlement to claim immunity. Within the Chamber it felt like a moment in which the traditional international legal order had been transformed. The order, which I had been brought up on, which gave primacy to the interests of the state, had been replaced by one which recognised and gave practical effect to the interests of the victims of torture. The significance of the ruling is evident from the fact that it made front-page news around the world, most of which was positive. That judgment of the Law Lords was later annulled, for other reasons, but there followed another judgment which made a similar finding on narrower grounds, namely that the loss of immunity arose not under customary international law, but rather from the coming into force in late 1988 of the 1984 Convention Against Torture, to which Chile, Spain, and the United Kingdom were all parties. The fact that the Law Lords relied on the 1984 Convention indicated a desire to respect state sovereignty as expressed through the consent to be bound by the Convention; the difficulty with this approach, as Lord Goff recognized, was that the 1984 Convention said nothing about immunity, and on that basis a loss of immunity could not be presumed. But Lord Goff was unable to persuade his fellow judges to take the traditional line, and six of the seven Law Lords ruled against the claim to immunity.

The second case is a decision of the Appellate Body of the World Trade Organization (WTO), handed down in the same week that Senator Pinochet was arrested. The decision of the WTO Appellate Body has also received attention, although less than the *Pinochet* decision, but in many respects it may prove to be equally significant, since it recognized that one country can have a legal interest in activities carried out in another country which are harmful to migratory, endangered species. This is the *Shrimp/Turtle* case, as it has come to be known. The United States had banned the import of shrimp harvested in the waters of four Asian countries—India, Malaysia, the Philippines, and Thailand—on the grounds that the shrimp had been caught in an environmentally harmful way, namely by incidentally killing sea turtles. Sea turtles are a highly migratory species that swim over vast distances. They are internationally recognized as endangered. The harvesting of the shrimp did not conform to U.S. federal regulations, requiring that the shrimp had to be harvested "using measures to reduce the incidental catch and mortality of sea turtles in shrimp trawls." The four Asian countries objected to the U.S. import ban, on the grounds that it violated WTO free trade rules. In their view, the United States was not entitled to restrict imports on the basis of an application of its environmental standards to activities taking place outside the United States, including in the territory of these four countries. On the classical principles of the Pacific fur seal arbitration, this is an argument which should have prevailed, and easily so, as it had done in earlier decisions. Contrary to the expectation of many commentators, the Appellate Body ruled that the U.S. measures in the *Shrimp/Turtle* case were "provisionally justified": since the United States had a legal interest in the prosecution of the shared but endangered natural resource represented in the declining population of sea turtles. In coming to its decision, the Appellate Body said "there is a sufficient nexus between the migratory and endangered [sea turtles] involved and the United States for the purposes of [GATT/WTO law]." The Appellate Body went on to hold that notwithstanding the finding of provisional justification, the manner in which the restriction had been applied by the United States was contrary to WTO law. But, for our purposes, the essential point is this: a legal interest now exists where previously there had been none, under general international law and within the WTO context.

What happened in the hundred or more years between *Hatch v. Baez* and the Pacific fur seal arbitration to have effected these changes in the landscape of international law? The two recent decisions have certain similar features. First, both reflect a recognition that what one state does or permits to be done within its territory can be of legitimate interest in another state, however distant. Local acts are internationalized, and national boundaries seem more permeable after both decisions. Second, both cases originated with acts which were not taken by the executive arm of the state *and* which the executive arm was not able to stop through political actions or applications before respective national courts: in the *Shrimp/Turtle* case, the U.S. import restrictions were the result of legal proceedings initiated before the U.S. federal courts by the Earth Island Institute, a U.S.-based non-governmental organization; in *Pinochet,* the extradition request was the result of the investigation and charges brought by Judge Garzón, which the Spanish government was powerless to bring to an end. Third, both decisions indicated the significant role which can be played by national and international courts where the international rules that are being applied are vague or ambiguous. A traditional approach would have sought out a clear and express rule which established limits on sovereign rights or freedoms. In the absence of such a rule, courts would be expected to apply an assumption that the international community of states had not intended to fetter sovereign freedom. In the two recent decisions, no such clear rule existed. Nevertheless, both courts overcame ambiguity in the rules and chose not to follow the path of deference.

I do not want to suggest that these two developments occurred out of the blue. They did not. They are part of a continuum, and find their roots in historical conceptions of international law—which used to be the *droit des gens*—and developments which can be traced back to the establishment of the United Nations and beyond. But both decisions mark an extension of our expectations as to the role international law can play. In a way that was not necessarily predictable, a national court and an international court have made a connection between international law and a broader set of values than those to which states have given express approval. The conditions under which this could occur are complex, and I would not wish to suggest that this lecture can provide all of the answers. But against the background of substantive and institutional changes which have taken place, particularly in the 1980s and 1990s, four factors appear to be especially relevant.

The first factor is "globalization," a buzz word for the 1990s which has particular relevance for the prospects for international law. Anthony Giddens has referred to globalization as a "stretching process," in which connections have been made between different social contexts or regions and become networked across the earth as a whole. For today's purposes, it encompasses the perception that there exists a "nexus" between the United States and, say, India with regard to sea turtles, with the consequence that what one community does to that species may be of legitimate interest to another community. Or it means that Spain is entitled to assert an interest in acts which occurred in Chile under the Pinochet regime. In a globalized world, international law recognizes these interests and finds ways to give effect to them. I do not need to spell out the broader implications of this type of connection for international law. Simply put, it means that activities which were previously treated as local (a matter of domestic concern only, to take the language of the U.N. Charter) are internationalized. This, in turn, provides conditions for new levels of law-making beyond the state, which, in turn, creates the conditions for the manifest feelings of disempowerment which give rise to demonstrations such as those which occurred in Seattle on the occasion of the WTO Ministerial Round in November 1999.

"Globalization" is itself promoted by technological innovation, a second factor for change in the international legal order. It is not only the *nature* of the changes but also their extent. We are now aware of the tremendous capacity for new technologies to produce spill-over effects over great distances. The 1986 Chernobyl accident illustrated the permeability of national boundaries in ways which had not previously been experienced, and the depletion of the ozone layer and the onset of climate change reflect our greater understanding of the impacts of new technologies over great distances. Beyond the developments in technology and scientific understanding, changes in the means of communication have had significant consequences for access to the products and processes of international law. The fax, email, and the internet have increased the speed of exchange. These technologies have made generally and easily available documentation forming part of international negotiations and decision-making processes, within minutes of their adoption. U.N.

documents—such as Security Council resolutions—which were previously available only to those with access to major libraries in London, Paris, or New York, and even then only with great difficulty, are now available to every person in the world with internet access. Oral arguments can be downloaded from the International Court of Justice website on the same day that they have been presented to the Court: the arguments made, for example, by NATO countries in the proceedings brought by Yugoslavia to challenge last year's action in Kosovo are instantly accessible, with all that implies for accountability. I am told that on the day the Court gave its judgment in that case, there were over one million hits on its website. With the decisions of most of the international courts now readily available, it is understandable that they are being relied upon more frequently before national proceedings around the world.

A third factor for change, gradually weaving its way into international legal consciousness, is "democratization." According to one view, democracy is on the way to becoming a global entitlement, reflecting the emergence of a community expectation that those who seek the validation of their empowerment—the governors—should govern with the consent of the governed. Commentators have generally addressed "democracy" issues at the national level, in terms of self-determination, the right to free expression, and the emergence of a normative entitlement to a participatory electoral process. But it is not just about elections. It includes rights of access to information, to participate in decision-making processes, and to have effective access to judicial and administrative proceedings, including redress and remedy. If participatory democracy is relevant to the national levels of governance then it is equally applicable at the international level, particularly since so many important decisions are now being taken outside national jurisdictions. There is plenty of evidence that access to information, decision-making, and remedies are now being sought in relation to the activities of international organizations and functioning of international courts and tribunals. The internet now means that more people have more information on what goes on within these various international bodies. Armed with that information, non-state actors whose interests are at issue are keen to get involved to influence their governments in the decisions which may be taken. This has led to radical changes even within such conservative bodies as the World Bank; a decade ago it would have been unimaginable that non-governmental organizations would be able to initiate international administrative proceedings to challenge acts of the World Bank. But this is precisely what has happened with the creation of the World Bank Inspection Panel in 1993. Against this background, the formal exclusion of non-state actors from the GATT and the WTO, as well as from the International Court of Justice, and the limited right of judicial review of acts of the European Commission, seem increasingly difficult to justify.

Finally, a fourth factor for change which characterizes modern society is the promotion of private enterprise and ownership as a dominant feature of societal structure, with the emphasis increasingly on the public sector playing a residual role in a deregulated society. If the frontiers of the state are to be pushed back at the national level, as Mrs. Thatcher put it back in 1977, then why should they not be pushed back also at the international level? The deregulation of capital flows, the promotion of direct foreign investment, the increase in global trade; together these and other objectives have contrived to enhance the international role of the private and corporate sectors. These players are unlikely to remain contented with a back-seat role in the making and applying of international law. We see shades of the interrelationship between state and commercial interest in the effort of foreign ministries around the world, including in this country, to play a more active role in promoting enterprise and commerce. There was understandable surprise when news leaked out, a few weeks ago, that the commercial attaché to the British Embassy in Japan turned out to be funded by British Nuclear Fuels. But in the coming world of "U.K. public limited companies," the pressures on international law to accommodate this change will undoubtedly grow. The increased role of the private sector is now also reflected in the design of international law rules. For example, the Kyoto Protocol to the U.N. Framework Convention on Climate Change which commits the United Kingdom and others to cut their emissions of carbon dioxide, provides for international trading in emissions of carbon and other greenhouse gases, with an express role for the private sector. If these instruments create rights and obligations for the private sector, then why should they be content to be excluded from the legislative process or subject to traditional intergovernmental dispute settlement processes?* There is even talk of international institutions being privatized. These and related developments coalesce around a simple theme: the enhanced role of the private sector in international affairs.

So where does this leave international law today? With new actors, new institutions, and new rules, the landscape is a very different one from that which faced the Supreme Court of the State of New York in *Hatch v. Baez* and the international arbitral tribunal in the Pacific fur seal case. The landscape is a very different one even from that which was presented to me when I first studied international law, some twenty years ago. Globalization, technology, "democratization," and deregulation have transformed our expectations of what international society is, what international law should deliver, and how it should be delivered. In particular, the recent developments in human rights and environmental law have built a stronger and more direct connection between the rules of international law and the man or woman in the street. International law emerges as a common language which cuts across boundaries and within societies.

* The protection of private property rights is reflected in the increasing number of international instruments designed to protect foreign investments as well as fundamental human rights, many of which provide for private fights of access to international adjudication.

Chapter 2

THE AUTHORITY AND METHOD OF INTERNATIONAL LAW

Editors' introduction: The term "international law" implies a system of rules that states are legally bound to uphold. But are these rules compulsory "law" per se, or merely guidelines to which states may selectively adhere? The answer, debated in the first section below, depends on how one interprets the complex give-and-take relationship between states and an individual state's motivations in the global arena. Scholars of course differ in their approaches to the study of international law, resulting in a rich variety of methods that help guide legal inquiry. The methods discussed in the second section below emphasize the role of the state, a subject to which we return in the following chapters.

A. IS INTERNATIONAL LAW "LAW"?

Affirmative. Anthony D'Amato, "Is International Law Really 'Law' "? 79 Nw. U.L. Rev. 1293 (1984).

Many serious students of the law react with a sort of indulgence when they encounter the term "international law," as if to say, "well, we know it isn't really law, but we know that international lawyers and scholars have a vested professional interest in calling it 'law.' " Or they may agree to talk about international law as a sort of quasi-law or near-law. But it cannot be true law, they maintain, because it cannot be enforced: how do you enforce a rule of law against an entire nation?

I believe that a conclusive argument can be fashioned that international law is really law, by showing that international law is enforceable in the same way that domestic law is enforceable. That kind of showing should be convincing to the most hardened skeptic of international law.

Of course, I won't make the claim that international law is always, invariably enforced. Rather, I'll suggest that we take a closer look at what we mean by enforcement, and then show that our meaning of the term is applicable equally to the domestic and to the international legal systems.

When we examine the concept of enforcement of law, the first thing we notice is that law can be enforced in many ways. For example, a parent might frown upon a child who does not brush his teeth, or might express stern disapproval. This could tend to "enforce" the law, social disapproval is not quite a satisfactory concept when we think of enforcement. It's not satisfactory because it's too easy for the child (or a nation) to decide to violate the law and pay the mild price of incurring social displeasure.

Thus, we want to narrow the concept of enforcement. Perhaps a good way to begin to narrow it is to exclude all modes of "enforcement" that are extrinsic to the legal system itself. Social disapproval, in this conception, is extrinsic to the legal system. Social disapproval is an external mechanism for enforcing (or more accurately, reinforcing) the law, but we know intuitively that it is not provided by or required by the law itself.*

When we look at the internal workings of a legal system, we find provisions for deprivations and disabilities. When a person disobeys the law, the law itself provides for his "punishment." This possibility of punishment, in turn, is supposed to deter a rational person from violating the law in the first place.

Enforcement thus consists of some form of *legally* imposed sanction. Sanctions don't have to be physical; a monetary fine is an example of a punishment that is purely financial. Physical punishments include being deprived of your freedom (for example by being incarcerated or being forced to perform some kind of community service) or physical harm (the old methods of beatings or public whippings). In the extreme, the law may impose capital punishment.

In this spectrum of legally imposed sanctions for violation of the law, we find that what the law has in fact done is to remove one or more of your entitlements. I could use the word "rights" here instead of "entitlements"—for example, your rights to life, to liberty, and to property. But the word "entitlements" is more precise, because it denotes legally recognized rights. If you claim a right that the law does not recognize (for example, a woman's claim to the right to vote before the Constitutional amendment of 1920 providing for universal suffrage), you may have a claim of right but you do not have a claim of entitlement. Since we are talking about enforcement mechanisms intrinsic to the legal system, it is more precise to speak of entitlements than to speak of rights.

In all cases of law violation, the law responds by depriving you of one or more of your entitlements. You have a legal entitlement to liberty; you lose it if you commit a crime punishable by incarceration.

---

* If the law required social disapproval to be inflicted upon any law-violator, then you would have the problem of how to force people to socially disapprove of a miscreant's behavior. This would entail an infinite regress, because we'd need other people to socially disapprove of those persons who fail to disapprove of the miscreant's behavior.

You have a legal entitlement to your bank account; you lose it if you have failed to pay your taxes or if someone obtains a judgment against you and attaches it. You have an entitlement to performance under a private contract that you make with someone else; if you fail to perform your part of the bargain, a court may decide that you have forfeited your entitlement under the contract. Some of these entitlement deprivations that you suffer because you have violated the law can be effectuated against you without any need for physical enforcement. Your bank account can be taken away from you by a bookkeeping entry made in the bank pursuant to a court order. Your marriage can be legally dissolved by a court decree without your willing compliance or participation. Thus, when we think of legal enforcement, we need not imagine the use of physical force against the person of the law-violator, although, of course, in some cases physical force is used. The deprivation of your entitlement to life, liberty, or property may be imposed by court order as a result of your conviction of a crime.

In order to deter or punish people by the threat of removal of their entitlements, people have to start out by having entitlements. Accordingly, all legal systems without exception assign certain entitlements to the people—usually but not always life, liberty, and property. With those entitlements, each person becomes vulnerable to their deprivation by law. Thus it comes about that legal systems typically enforce their rules by removing one or more entitlements of rule-violators.

How does the international legal system work in this regard? Let us begin by imagining a simple international situation. Two nations are at war with each other, but are weary of it and are interested in the possibility of peace. The problem now is how to send a peace ambassador from one nation to the other. The war between them is so total and brutal that no one "volunteers" to be an emissary, because of reasonable fear of being killed by the other side. Since we have not assumed any prior history between the two warring nations, we cannot invoke prior prescribed methods of getting the two sides to talk about peace.

Perhaps nation A might find a particularly brave person who would carry a letter saying, "don't kill the bearer of this letter, as we are attempting to set up communications with you, and we promise to give safe conduct to any person you choose to send to us who has a similar letter signed by you. Moreover, as evidence of our good faith, you can hold the bearer of this letter hostage while your emissary is en route to us, and release him upon the safe return of your own emissary." Such a letter, of course, would not guarantee that its bearer would be safe. All we know is that, in some instances, letters such as this one must have worked. Of course, we don't know much about instances where the letter didn't work, because its bearer was killed and presumably no written record of the event has survived. But in those cases where the letter did work, a primitive entitlement became established between the two nations. We could call that entitlement "limited ambassadorial immunity" or refer to the document as "a letter of safe conduct."

But one entitlement will not suffice. Suppose nation A is furious with the peace terms brought by nation B's emissary, and responds by killing the emissary. A has, of course, violated the "safe conduct" agreement. What can B do? B can, of course, kill A's emissary (the one B held as a guarantee of the safe return of its own emissary). But that act simply plunges A and B back into total war. And the next time around, a new entitlement might have a harder time getting started, because A and B will remember what happened when the first entitlement got started and then was promptly violated.

Peace would have had a better chance of getting started between A and B if there had been a second, different entitlement in the picture. Suppose, in addition to the emissaries, each nation was holding hostage a national of the other nation. Then the newly emerging entitlement of diplomatic immunity might have had a better chance to survive because of the possibility of retaliation not against the other emissary but against the hostage. Increasing the importance of the hostage would serve the cause of peace even better. That is probably why, in early wars, the king of each side would often volunteer personally to go over to the other side and be held hostage. The kings thus served as personal guarantors for the safety of the peace negotiators.

We can see that the more entitlements on the list, the better the chance that peace has to get started. The fact is that international law provides states with a long list of entitlements. Even a newly born state (such as a nation that has just received its independence from a colonial power) immediately gets a gift of these entitlements.

Our new nation receives at its birth a host of entitlements. It has not chosen any of these entitlements; it has not selected any; it has not even consented to receive any.

Instead the entitlements are simply thrust upon the new nation. The first entitlement is of fundamental importance: the entitlement of statehood, which means, in the international system, that our new nation is a geographic entity entitled to exert its own legal jurisdiction in the area within its boundaries and to claim the inviolability of those boundaries against all other states. The legal sanctity of its borders signifies that our new state is a state in a community of states, and not merely a gang of thieves subject to the untrammelled degradations of other neighboring gangs. Indeed, the new nation's receipt of the entitlement of statehood is almost a tautology: by becoming a new state, the new state can enjoy the international law definition of what a state is. A new state would hardly be a "state" without enjoying the sanctity of its borders. But the entitlement of statehood is not wholly tautological. For international law could have evolved in a manner such that a new state (like a human infant) at first does not possess the full entitlement of statehood (like a child not possessing all the rights of an adult). For example, in its early years, a state might be subject to interventions at will from neighboring states. However, that sort of system never evolved. For good or ill, the international system in fact has evolved so as to give a new nation a full, mature set of the very same entitlements that all other states have.

In sum, our new nation depends for its very identity upon the recognition of other similar states in the community of states. I am not talking about de jure recognition; rather, all that is necessary is a sense in the international community that the new state is enclosed by international boundaries, and those boundaries, like all boundaries, are lines that differentiate the internal affairs of the state from the external affairs and cannot be crossed at will by military forces in either direction. This notion of a boundary is so fundamental that the Vienna Convention on the Law of Treaties specifically excepts boundary-establishing treaties from the normal rules of rebus sic stantibus (article 62), and the World Court in its leading decision in the Continental Shelf Cases made it clear that the normal generation of customary international law cannot affect ownership of territory (in those cases, the submerged land areas) absent a showing of consent from the owner.

Our new state might, therefore, look upon the international law of the sanctity of its boundaries as a gift of a valuable entitlement. But the entitlement carries with it reciprocal duties, so that it is not necessarily a gift. Reciprocity entails that our new nation must respect the borders of all the other states. Indeed, reciprocity is inherent in the concept of defining states as separate entities. Viewed from "within" (or "subjectively"), a state may regard itself as entitled to any values or goods it wishes, even if those values and goods are located outside its borders. But a state may also view itself from "without" (or "objectively")—recognizing itself to be one state among many, deserving no more consideration than any other state. Any subjective desire is matched up against recognition of the objective desires of all states including oneself. The result of the subjective-objective dualism is an expectation of reciprocity.

From just a subjective point of view, the entitlement of sanctity of boundaries may seem more a curse than a blessing. If our new state is militarily powerful and expansionist minded, it might want to extend its boundaries at the expense of its neighbor—in other words, it might want to annex its neighbor. Obviously the desire to annex and the desire to have other nations respect the annexation are mutually incompatible when assessed "objectively"—our new state clearly would not want to be annexed by other states. Hence, the reciprocity inherent in the notion of independent states operates not so much as a limitation upon the freedom of action of our new state (even though it may seem that way from the "subjective" point of view), but rather simply as a rule of the game.*

---

* Nearly all rules of nearly all games are reciprocal; though a rule may temporarily constrain one player, that player knows that the same rule can and will operate to constrain the opposing player. It would be rather absurd for a player in a game to demand to be entitled to violate one of the rules while insisting that the rule be respected by the other side.

The rule of sanctity of boundaries, therefore, is simply imposed upon the new state at birth. The new state has become a player in the game of international relations, and the rules—which were there before the player joined the game—go with the territory. The new state may dislike particular rules, but I suspect that the new state, whatever it may say, welcomes the entirety of the rules. For if it is pressed to make a judgment whether to accept or reject the list of entitlements as a whole, the new nation would most likely accept the list. It is hard to imagine how the new nation could reject the list, because that would entail giving up its standing as a new nation. Moreover, the list of entitlements is not in its entirety onerous; after all, the list was not handed down from a handful of feuding gods on Mount Olympus, but rather evolved slowly over time to serve the collective self-interest of all the states in the international system.

So far I have mentioned only one entitlement—the basic entitlement to sanctity of boundaries. But there are more; in fact, the list is very long indeed. For the list includes every rule of customary international law. Every single norm in the international system is an entitlement, a "rule of the game," which serves to give our new nation a right against all the other states and at the same time to oblige our new state to respect that same right when it is asserted by any other state. Thus, immediately following the initial entitlement of sanctity of boundaries, would be the entitlement of diplomatic immunity (to facilitate negotiations with other states), the entitlement to enter into binding treaties with other nations, to have those treaties construed and applied according to the generally accepted rules of customary international law pertaining to the interpretation of treaties, to enjoy free use of the high seas, to claim rights over the superjacent airspace, to have jurisdiction over its continental shelf (if the new nation happens to have a continental shelf),* to have its citizens enjoy the protections of human rights law when they travel to other countries, to regulate its commercial trade with other states, to enjoy the protections of the laws of war and rules regulating the conduct of hostilities, to exert extraterritorial jurisdiction within the international rules regulating that subject, and so on through the entire list of international norms. Each specific norm works in two ways: to benefit our new nation to the extent that it has any interest in claiming any specific entitlement, and to impose upon our new nation the duty to respect the same entitlement when it is asserted against itself by other nations.

* Obviously our new nation will be physically endowed in a unique way. Nations are quite different from each other in terms of whether they border on the oceans, whether they have mineral wealth beneath their soil, and so forth. There is no "reciprocity" regarding these physical attributes in the international system any more than there is reciprocity among persons who are born with different physical attributes and talents. The "law" as it has evolved both internationally and domestically may give each unit (a state, a person) "equal protection of the law," but, so far at least (except for the communist experiment in sharing property), it does not attempt to redistribute physical assets or personal property.

Taken as a whole, these entitlements define what it is to be a "nation" (or "state") in the modern world. Interestingly, a state is more "vulnerable" to entitlement-deprivation than a person. A person is not *defined* by her legal entitlements; rather, a person can acquire entitlements when she becomes subject to a particular legal system. But states are different. A state is nothing but a bundle of entitlements. If you take away all the state's entitlements, nothing is left, whereas if you take away a person's entitlements, the person remains in a "state of nature." To be sure, if you take away a person's entitlement to life, then nothing is left. But the crucial point is that people were not born into this world with an "entitlement" to life in the legal sense; they were simply born into the world, and entitlements came later. In contrast, in the modern era at least (we don't have to go back now to primitive states in antiquity), a state is only "born" when the international community recognizes it as a state. And that recognition by the international community is simply a shorthand description of the international community's bestowing upon the new state the long list of entitlements that we call customary law.

This conclusion in turn illustrates why, as a matter of its very identity, a state should act in such a manner as to preserve its entitlements. Yet, its identity as a state, its bundle of entitlements, is dependent upon the acquiescence of all the other states in the system. Since every state has the same bundle of entitlements, the other states in the system have an obvious interest in acquiescing in the entitlements of any given state. In this manner, a new state starts out, as we have seen, with its full complement of entitlements.

But just as all the states in the international legal system have a collective interest in acquiescing to all the entitlements for any given state in the system, they also have an interest in preserving the entitlements as they have been defined in the course of the development of international customary law. For ease of illustration, let us consider the previously mentioned entitlement of diplomatic immunity. All the states in the system have an interest in the preservation of this particular entitlement. The existence of this entitlement, like other entitlements, helps define what a state is and what the international legal system is. The system would be something different, perhaps diminished, if the entitlement of diplomatic immunity were undermined.

Prior to 1979, it would have been difficult to come up with a single example of a state which directly violated the entitlement of diplomatic immunity. In nearly every case from the dawn of history down to 1979, whenever a diplomat's life or liberty was threatened, the host state immediately took action against those persons who threatened the diplomat. Safety of the other side's diplomatic representatives was something that was inviolate, even in the darkest days of the two world wars. But then in 1979, the unprecedented happened. After some radical students occupied the American Embassy in Teheran, the government of Iran took the unheard of step of ratifying the action and holding the American diplomatic personnel hostage. This was a case of a blatant violation of a hallowed international entitlement. To allow it to go unremedied would constitute a threat to the existence of the entitlement of diplomatic immunity within the international legal system.

Let us consider the strategies open to the international community to reverse Iran's action. We dismiss at the outset the absurd idea of dropping a nuclear bomb on Iran (even though some outraged Americans suggested doing so), because that would, among other horrible things, kill the very diplomatic personnel who were being held hostage. Moreover, the retaliation would be clearly disproportionate to Iran's initial act. A second strategy would be to allow the United States to violate Iran's diplomatic entitlement by arresting and detaining diplomatic and consular officials of Iran who were physically present in the United States at the time of the takeover of the American embassy in Iran. This tit-for-tat strategy deserves a closer look. In the first place, it is not always effective. As we saw previously in the idealized example of two states at total war, the tit-for-tat strategy would simply eliminate the incipient ambassadorial-immunity entitlement and plunge the states back into the chaos of total war. Today, under a more developed international legal system, the tit-for-tat strategy might not have as negative an outcome, but it nevertheless could operate to erode rather than to preserve the entitlement in question. For instance, if the United States had jailed all Iranian diplomatic and consular officials, such an action at least in theory could be interpreted not as an attempt to punish Iran for its initial act but rather as a recognition that Iran's act was correct and that in fact diplomats are not entitled to immunity. I say "in theory" because this particular example has too strong a history of diplomatic immunity behind it to be eroded so quickly by the two counterexamples we posit as coming from Iran and the United States. But generally, since the content of international law depends upon the recognition by all the states in the system of what the entitlements are, the action I have just hypothesized by the United States and Iran might well be interpreted as a new understanding of the entitlement of diplomatic immunity, i.e., that such immunity exists no longer. At least it will be an important step along the customary-law route that could lead to the destruction of this particular entitlement. Consider the following more realistic example of the same theoretical process: nation A announces a territorial sea of 300 miles from its coastline; nation B argues that A has illegally infringed upon the high seas by attempting to expropriate part of it, and in a spirit of sheer retaliation, nation B proclaims its *own* 300–mile territorial sea. Despite nation B's claim (that it was issuing its proclamation in retaliation for A's), the action it took tends to *reinforce* A's claim. Thus, rather than challenging A's claim to a 300–mile territorial sea, B has perhaps inadvertently reinforced it. A new rule for territorial seas, giving coastal states a much larger area of jurisdiction over the high seas, may well have been started by A's and B's similar proclamations. Thus, the tit-for-tat strategy, played against the background of customary international law, could not only fail to deter the original entitlement violation but in fact serve to reinforce it and make a new rule of law out of it.

As things turned out, perhaps for the reason I've just suggested as well as other reasons, the United States did not choose to retaliate by jailing Iranian consular and diplomatic officials. That very strategy was considered by the U.S. government and duly reported in the media. Instead, the United States tried a third strategic approach.

The United States "froze" approximately thirteen billion dollars of Iranian deposits in American banks and in various European banks where the United States, through American corporations, had the power to act. If it were not for the initial Iranian act of holding the American diplomats hostage, the United States would have violated the Iranian entitlement to the use of its own bank deposits abroad. Yet customary international law regarded the U.S. "freeze" as intended to preserve the diplomatic-immunity entitlement that Iran had violated. More was involved than just a temporary freeze; as I review the figures, the United States actually was involved in a taking of Iranian assets. The United States effectively confiscated much of the interest the Iranian bank assets would have earned. I've not seen any real public discussion of this aspect of the matter, but by my own reckoning, at the time the $13 billion of Iranian money was blocked, world interest rates were at approximately 15%. The Iranian assets remained blocked for slightly over one year. At compound interest, this works out to interest earned—and unpaid—of over two billion dollars. Later, when the hostages were returned to the United States, the United States agreed to pay, in partial settlement, interest of $800 million to Iran. Clearly, there is no entitlement under customary international law to confiscate the interest on another nation's bank accounts. Yet, again, there was no condemnation of the American action by the international community, not even from nations that regard the inviolability of their own bank accounts abroad as something more important than life itself. There is only one explanation: the international community did not regard the American action as endangering the status of governmental bank accounts in foreign banks, but rather as *preserving* the entire system of entitlements. The American action was in retaliation for a blatant, historically unprecedented entitlement-violation by Iran. The United States acted to restore that entitlement (diplomatic immunity) by temporarily violating a different entitlement (Iran's property rights in its bank accounts). Significantly, the United States made no claim whatsoever to a general right to invade other nation's bank accounts. Instead, the United States described its invasion of Iran's bank accounts as a "freeze"—the word suggests that the freeze will be lifted as soon as the American diplomats are returned safely to the United States. More than that, the confiscation of some $1.2 billion in interest was generally perceived as a reasonable retaliation, if not punishment, for Iran's violation of the diplomatic-immunity entitlement.

The workings of international law are rarely as explicit as scholars might like them to be, but I believe we are entitled to infer from the reaction of the community of nations that they did not perceive a threat to the shared entitlement of preserving property rights in state-owned deposits in foreign banks as a result of the American action, but rather regarded the U.S. action as a temporary infringement of an Iranian entitlement for the limited purpose of enforcing the original entitlement of diplomatic immunity. I am not just speculating about the reaction of the international community. We have proof of the international reaction in the unanimous decision of the World Court that Iran had violated the diplomatic-immunity entitlement. The panel of judges represented states from all over the world, but not a single judge regarded Iran's action as legitimate. We can safely conclude that the international community accepted the legality of a strategy that violates an offending nation's entitlements in order to repudiate that nation's initial offense. In the Iran–United States case, the strategy worked well, for the American diplomatic personnel were all safely returned to the United States, and the United States lifted the freeze on Iranian assets. There was never any doubt that the U.S. froze the assets solely as an enforcement measure—to protect the international system of entitlements—and not as an act of aggression against Iran. Nor was there ever any doubt that Iran violated a basic entitlement when it held the American diplomats hostage. And when the whole incident was over, Iran did not make any claim that holding diplomats hostage was justified under international law. In short, the entire incident vindicated the notion of the enforcement mechanism that has evolved in international law.

If we need a label for this mechanism, we could call it "tit-for-a-different-tat." While the U.S.-Iranian example is dramatic, the strategy is employed on numerous occasions in the course of the complex interactions among states. The the tit-for-a-different-tat strategy makes sense in a legal system that has neither a central court of compulsory jurisdiction, nor a world legislature, nor a world police force. It depends most crucially on international recognition and acceptance of the basic distinction between initial action and enforcement action. If a nation initially violates another nation's entitlement, it has committed a wrongful act (what Kelsen calls a "delict"). But if the other nation retaliates by violating one of the violator's entitlements, then no wrongful act is committed. Rather, the retaliation itself is regarded as an enforcement action. It is not only perfectly legal under international law; without it, we might not have international law.

Some people might object that the notion of unilateral enforcement of international law, using a tit-for-a-different-tat strategy, indicates that international law is still a primitive or crude system of law. These people would seem to prefer a world government that enforced international law through a world executive, a world legislature, and a world court system. For my money, it's a cure far worse than the disease. A world government, at this stage in human history, could be stifling. There would be no shortage of bureaucrats at the United Nations willing and anxious to govern the world, but why should we turn over our rights and liberties to them?

I think the international enforcement system works tolerably well as it stands. The strategy of tit-for-a-different-tat seems to provide in most cases the right amount of enforcement. My fear about the strategy is not that it is ineffective, but rather that it could lead to an escalation of retaliation. Nation A commits a delict; nation B retaliates by depriving nation A of one of its entitlements; nation A counter-retaliates by depriving nation B of another of its entitlements; and so on, leading to general war. I have been unable to think of any logical reason why such runaway retaliation might not someday occur. Therefore, I think we have to stay on our guard. Clearly, multilateral enforcement of entitlement violations (through the Security Council enforcement system of the United Nations) is preferable to unilateral enforcement. We are seeing in recent years a far more activist Security Council. I would be satisfied so long as the United Nations confines itself to enforcement of existing international norms without trying to invent too many new norms itself (by becoming a super-legislature).

But the fact that runaway tit-for-a-different-tat entitlement-violation could occur in the future does not disable us from describing the reality of present international law. At the present time, I claim that customary international law is enforced primarily through the tit-for-a-different-tat strategy of entitlement violation. True, the international system could destroy itself through a runaway series of violations of entitlements. But unless and until that happens, the system continues to police itself by allowing unilateral enforcement of entitlements through the tit-for-tat, or more typically, tit-for-a-different-tat system.

On the whole it is an effective system—as effective for international law as is the enforcement of most laws in domestic systems via the state-sanctioned deprivation of one or more entitlements held by individual citizens or corporations. It would be impossible to understand why nations do or refrain from doing the things they do without understanding what entitlements are included in the bundle and how nations act to preserve their full complement of existing entitlements. In this sense, international law is a very realistic component of the picture that political scientists try to draw of how nations behave. The "serious students of law" who claim that international law isn't really "law" make the same mistake that some political scientists have made in the past in ignoring norms just to prove that they are being "scientific" in their "descriptions." A state cannot be described without reference to its entitlements, nor can its actions be fully understood without reference to the steps it takes to preserve those entitlements. In sum, this retaliatory entitlement-deprivation system constitutes the "physical sanction" that positivists require for a system of norms to be called a "legal" system.

Negative. John R. Bolton, "Is There Really 'Law' in International Affairs?" 10 Transnat'l Law. & Contemp. Problems 1 (2000).

To start, let us define in summary fashion what, at least in the United States, "law" is commonly understood to be. We understand "law" to be a system of commands, obligations and rules that regulate relations among individuals and associations, and the sources of legitimate coercive authority in society. These are the forces that can compel behavior and enforce compliance with rules.

For any system of law, there are two basic prerequisites for legitimacy (and hence compliance). *First*, it has to exist within a coherent structural framework—a constitution—that defines the government's authority, and by so doing, limits it, thus preventing arbitrary authority. The great scholar, Professor McIlwain, once said, "All constitutional government is by definition limited government."* It is critically important for a free person's understanding of law that there is an overarching structure within which the subsidiary aspects of the law develop. *Second*, the source of coercive authority—the "rule of law"—rests on popular sovereignty or public accountability through reasonably democratic popular controls over the creation, interpretation, and enforcement of laws, the three broad ways in which law develops. Any other definition of law is either incoherent or unacceptable to a free person. Of course, much of the world's law does not rest on popular sovereignty, even in many Western European countries commonly accepted as "democracies." In Chinese, for example, there is no distinction between the phrase "rule of law" and "rule by law," a distinction we see as fundamental for liberty purposes.

These admittedly somewhat abstract definitions and principles have very important practical implications. The first is that the sources of law are identifiable and authoritative. The second is that the mechanism for interpreting and resolving conflicts and disputes among parties under law is agreed upon. The third is that the source of law enforcement (including execution and compliance activities), as well as the methods and procedures for declaring and changing the law, is also agreed upon. This is true both in public and private law, in civil as well as criminal, and in law enforcement as well as the typical civil disputes that occupy much of our courts' time. These practical implications are all embodied in the United States Constitution and its system of government, exemplifying the kind of legal system acceptable to a free person. One need not argue that a proper structure of government *must* be like that of the United States, with three separate branches, but the Constitution is conceptually quite clear in defining the heads of authority for law creation, interpretation, and enforcement.

Among other problems with "international law," there are simply no agreed-upon sources. Recognizing this gaping hole, its advocates have written reams of attempted explanations, but even their best guesses are failures. For example, one way in which "international law" is said to develop is through treaties, the written, agreed-upon documents that nations sign and pledge to follow. Treaties are often analogized to contracts, agreements between people, businesses, or other kinds of associations. This analogy is fundamentally wrong. One of the simplest and best definitions of "contract" is from Restatement (Second) Con-

---

* Charles Howard Mcilwain, *Constitutionalism: Ancient and Modern* (1958), p. 21.

tracts, stating: "A contract is a promise or a set of promises for the breach of which the law gives a remedy...." This definition has two parts. The first part is "a promise," and the second is "for the breach of which the law gives a remedy." By "remedy" we mean that when one contracting party breaches his or her obligation, there is a judicial mechanism to either obtain damages for the breach of the promise or to get specific performance of that to which the parties had agreed. The Restatement's brief definition fully embodies the practical implications of real law described above. It is not just an abstract exchange whereby "I promise X and you promise Y." The promises take place within a system, where if one party breaches its promise, there is a defined way to get remedies. There is a process to decide which promises are legitimate and a procedure to enforce a court order that a party has breached a promise. The very concept of a contract, in other words, takes place within a coherent universe.

Compare this to a treaty. A treaty is an exchange of promises—period. It is a flat misunderstanding of reality to believe that there are enforcement mechanisms "out there" internationally that conform to the kind of legal system that exists in the United States. The U.S. Supreme Court long ago understood this critical difference, even if the dreamier supporters of international law could not.

A treaty is primarily a compact between independent nations. It depends for the enforcement of its provisions on the interest and the honor of the governments which are parties to it. If these fail, its infraction becomes the subject of international negotiations and reclamations, so far as the injured party chooses to seek redress, which may in the end be enforced by actual war.

This is not domestic law at work. Accordingly, there is no reason to consider treaties as "legally" binding internationally, and certainly not as "law" themselves.

It is at this point that advocates of international law usually deploy the "isolationist" broadsword, arguing that this view means the end of all treaties, international chaos, and a retreat into the "American cave." These are all overreactions. Simply because treaties are not "law" does not mean that states are not in some sense bound by them, or that states may dismiss or ignore treaty promises without consequence. Nor does it mean that failing to consider treaties as law unleashes anarchy upon the world. Consider three sentences about treaties:

> Sentence One: The United States is morally bound by its treaty obligations.
>
> Sentence Two: The United States is politically bound by its treaty obligations.
>
> Sentence Three: The United States is legally bound by its treaty obligations.

Now, two points that more fully explain the import of "de-legalizing" treaties that is manifested in the differences among these three sentences. First, these three sentences say three different things. Being morally bound is not the same as being politically bound, and being politically bound is not the same as being legally bound. Second, Sentences One and Two are true, while Sentence Three is false. There is no legal mechanism—no coherent structure—that exists today on a global level to enforce compliance with treaties, a fact international law advocates flatly ignore.

This is emphatically *not* to say that the United States should freely ignore its treaty obligations. Indeed, moral and political obligations in the real international world are often far more binding than "law." Take, for example, Article 5 of the NATO Treaty, the bedrock of foreign policy in the United States for fifty years, which provides explicitly "that an armed attack upon one or more [member] in Europe or North America shall be considered an attack against them all." Are we legally bound by Article 5? What if, during the Cold War, the signatories to the Warsaw Pact had attacked Germany, and the Chancellor had called the President of the United States and said: "We've got a problem here. The Soviets have attacked, and I am invoking Article 5 of the NATO Treaty?" Suppose then that the President had said: "Well, I have Article 5 here, and I don't read it to say that we're bound to come to your defense."

Would the Chancellor then have gone to court to obtain an injunction to force the United States to abide by Article 5? Of course not. Our word in that case is our political word and our moral word. It has nothing to do with legality. That is why, properly understood, the distinction between "legal" and other commitments implies not anarchy, but rather a truer, more realistic understanding of treaty obligations. Indeed, the precise "legal" obligation contained in Article 5 is surprisingly weak, providing only that each NATO member "will assist the Party or Parties so attacked by taking forthwith, individually and in concert with the other Parties, *such action as it deems necessary*, including the use of force, to restore and maintain the security of the North Atlantic area."

A second source of "international law" is the ways in which nations behave, the practices they engage in over the years, a source that evolves and becomes international law. This "state practice" is the basis of what is called "customary international law," which is said to be just as binding on nations as, for example, laws that have passed through the constitutional system of the United States. But this is plainly wrong. Practice is practice, and custom is custom; neither one is law. Customary international law changes under this definition when state practice changes, which led former Attorney General Bill Barr to opine: "Well, as I understand it, what you're saying is the only way to change international law is to break it." This telling remark shows the incoherence of treating "customary international law" as law.

Moreover, customary international law is always "out there" developing. In the debate over the International Criminal Court, Japanese

Ambassador Owada said, "We ought to leave open the possibility of expanding the jurisdiction of the International Criminal Court as new criminal offenses crystallize in the international system." Imagine citizens of the United States learning that their laws "crystallized" in Washington, rather than being enacted by both Houses of Congress. We would say unhesitatingly that we will not be governed by laws that "crystallize," but only by laws adopted through a defined constitutional process. Thus, with respect to treaties, one can at least argue that generally a president has to sign them, and the Senate has to give its advice and consent, so there is some semblance of formal consideration and decision.

This point is particularly important because of the campaign to incorporate customary international law into our federal law by judicial decision, an entirely separate battlefront where there is even less democratic involvement. The locus of this dispute recently has been the Alien Tort Statute, an obscure provision of the Judiciary Act of 1789, which provides that Federal District Courts have jurisdiction over certain suits by aliens for torts "committed in violation of the law of nations." A 1980 Federal appellate court decision essentially held that this statute opened U.S. courts to adjudicate claims based on "customary international law." A contrary opinion by Judge Robert H. Bork, writing in a divided panel of the District of Columbia Circuit, rejected that argument, holding that the Act may give the court jurisdiction, but it does not create a cause of action—that is, a substantive basis for judicial relief. The role of "customary international law," in areas well beyond the Alien Tort Statute, is now under intense debate in academic circles, and it has enormous implications. This is not simply a philosophical debate between "monism" and "dualism," but an intensely practical political struggle. If international law can, in effect, be incorporated into U.S. law by judicial decision, it is far easier and far less democratic than struggling to get Congress to adopt it by statute.

There is another important source of international law, which the academics refer to quite regularly: the writings of academics! This notion is pervasive in international law circles, especially among the academics who stand most to benefit from its uncritical acceptance, and reflects one of its most basic undemocratic aspects. There is no better response than William F. Buckley, Jr.'s famous statement that he would rather be governed by the first two thousand names in the Boston telephone directory than by the faculty of Harvard University.

In addition to the absence of legitimately authoritative sources of international law, there is no process to bind it to the political consent of the world's population. There are no international democratic institutions that provide legitimacy for any aspect of international law. There are also no definitive dispute resolution mechanisms, and there are certainly no agreed-upon enforcement, execution or compliance mechanisms. These are not just technical, mechanistic deficiencies that can be fixed by creating new institutions. Rather, these are conceptual and institutional flaws that show fundamentally why international law is not law. They highlight graphically the point that the analysis of international law is basically a liberty question. No free person should subject himself to an untried system of authority based so much on assumptions and so little on reality.

Advocates of "international law" acknowledge that these arguments are, indeed, accurate with respect to *domestic* law, but they say: "We are talking about *international* law, so, of course, none of that applies." This is their central mistake: the conceptual underpinnings for legitimate law, in both form and substance, must apply whether we deal with municipal, state, federal or international law. If they are absent, that law lacks legitimacy and, therefore, the binding force that is central to any acceptable definition of real law.

The lessons we should draw are clear: the way to deny the conclusions—the consequences of the growth of international law—is to deny the assumptions, and to argue that the underpinnings of international law rest on unacceptable premises for peoples who believe they are entitled to be free. This is why the relationship between international law, whatever it is, and the United States Constitution remains so central. Three possibilities exist in theory. First, international law is subordinate to the Constitution, a formulation that would make it essentially trivial for our purposes. Second, international law is equal to the Constitution, a formulation that would lead to chaos, because two such bodies of law cannot function as equivalents. Third, international law is superior to the Constitution; its requirements override the Constitution, and trump our constitutional arrangements.

If asked, "Does international law trump national constitutions?," most international lawyers would say, "Of course!" Most American citizens would emphatically disagree, however. We should be unashamed, unapologetic, uncompromising American constitutional hegemonists. International law is *not* superior to, and does not trump, the Constitution. The rest of the world may not like that approach, but abandoning it is the first step to abandoning the United States of America. International law is not law; it is a series of political and moral arrangements that stand or fall on their own merits, and anything else is simply theology and superstition masquerading as law.

An Exercise. Written by the editors for this Handbook.

The two articles you have just read differ sharply on the question of the enforceabilty of treaty obligations. In 1978 there was litigation between France and the United States before an international arbitral tribunal concerning rights under the Air Service Agreement to which the two countries were party. France had unilaterally terminated the practice by Pan Am of sending large jets from American airports to land first in London and then in Paris. France now required all passengers to disembark in London and then board smaller French planes if some of them wanted to go on to Paris.

When negotiations between the United States and France got nowhere, the United States retaliated by barring all French intercontinental jets from landing in Los Angeles.

The arbitral tribunal made four critical findings: (1) The initial French act violated the treaty. (2) The closure of Los Angeles to French intercontinental flights, if standing alone, would have violated the treaty. (3) Los Angeles was closed in retaliation to France's closure of Paris. (4) The Los Angeles closure inflicted somewhat greater economic damage upon France than the London closure inflicted upon the United States.

The ultimate question before the arbitral tribunal was whether the closure of Los Angeles was legal under international law. How would you decide this question? Why? You can compare your answer to that given by the tribunal by looking up *Case Concerning the Air Services Agreement of 23 March 1946, Arbitral Award of 9 December 1978,* 54 International Law Reports 304 (1979). Or you might read the article about the case by Lori Fisler Damrosch in 74 American Journal of International Law 785 (1980).

B. METHOD IN INTERNATIONAL LAW

Normal Science. Lassa Oppenheim, "The Science of International Law: Its Tasks and Method" 2 A.J.I.L. 313 (1908).

Having discussed the tasks of the science of international law, we can now turn our attention to its method. Now, whereas agreement with regard to the tasks is easily realized, there is no generally recognized method of the science of international law. The three schools of the Grotians, the Naturalists, and the Positivists are still in the field, and their methods are naturally different. The Grotians keep up the distinction of Grotius between the natural and the positive international law, the former comprising such rules of international law as are supposed to be based on the law of nature, the latter embracing such rules as are based on international custom and treaties. The Naturalists maintain that no positive law is possible for the regulation of the intercourse of the sovereign states, and that therefore all so-called international law is not real law, but only a part of the so-called law of nature. The Positivists recognize only a positive international law based on custom and treaties, and deny the very existence as well of a law of nature as of a natural international law. But besides these three schools there are to be mentioned the followers of Austin in England, who define international law as a part of the so-called positive morality; it is said to be "morality" because there can not be a law between sovereign states, yet it is "positive" morality because general opinion considers it binding.

All these schools are today represented by prominent men whose works have contributed to the progressive development of international law itself as well as of its science. To many it would therefore seem ridiculous to take part in the fray and to join one group and fight the others. As many roads lead to Rome, so many methods lead to good results. As long as a scholar joins at all the ranks of those who till the fields of the science of international law, why should he not be welcome, to whatever school he belongs? Let us judge him, so they say, not according to his method, but according to the fruits of his labor. Now, I quite agree that every worker is welcome, to whatever school he may belong, but it is nevertheless necessary to inquire into the question, Which method is the right one? For the right method secures the best results, and it is these we are aiming at. It is on account of the disagreement as regards the right method that we disagree so much as regards certain rules of international law. Scores of controversies in our science are merely due to the difference of method applied by the authors concerned. And how could it be otherwise? Do we not start from different standpoints? Do we not apply different standards of judgment? What greater contrast can there be than between him who preaches that no real law is possible between sovereign states, and him who asserts that there is such a law created by custom or set by conventions? How can two men come to the same results, if the one abstracts the rules of international law from the actual practice of the states, and the other from what he considers to be reasonable, just, and adequate? How can international law develop progressively if one man lays bare the gaps of the existing law and asks for their filling in through an agreement of the powers, whereas according to the opinion of the other man there are no such gaps, because the law of nature provides a complete system of rules of international law? How is it possible to offer a body of firm, distinct, and clear-cut rules of law, if rules of morality and of religion, if political aspirations and chimerical schemes for a better future, are constantly mixed up with what is really law?

Political Science. Steven R. Ratner and Anne–Marie Slaughter, "Introduction" to Symposium on Method in International Law 93 A.J.I.L. 291 (1999).

For Oppenheim, "method" was intimately associated with his view that international law was a science that had its own unique and rigorous approach to analyzing and solving questions—in the words of the *Oxford English Dictionary,* "a special form of procedure adopted in any branch of mental activity, whether for the purpose of teaching and exposition, or for that of investigation and inquiry." This scientific link between method and international law can be found in the thinking of other great scholars of an earlier era. Hans Kelsen spoke in his 1932 Hague lectures and his 1940–1941 Oliver Wendell Holmes lectures of the "technique of international law," which would fulfill the purposes of the law but which could not itself be understood or undertaken without an underlying theory. In a profoundly important attack on the positivist method in this *Journal* in 1940, Hans Morgenthau spoke of the need to "reëxamine the methodological assumptions with which the traditional science of international law starts" and to "reconcile the science of international law and its subject-matter." For Philip Allott, the methods employed by various international lawyers refer to the structure of their argumentation, in particular its logical discourse.

The scientific leanings of the earlier writers aside, most of these scholars seem to be speaking roughly of the same idea: the application of a conceptual apparatus or framework—a theory of international law—to the concrete problems faced in the international community.

To elucidate the theoretical underpinnings of contemporary scholarship through recourse to the methods employed by various theories, we decided upon seven methods for appraisal: legal positivism, the New Haven School, international legal process, critical legal studies, international law and international relations, feminist jurisprudence, and law and economics. In our view, they represent the major methods of international legal scholarship today. Our list does not include methods that may have been utilized by scholars in the past, or that dominated the scholarship of earlier eras—as the absence of Roman law, canon law, and socialist/Soviet law would indicate. It also excludes, owing to space constraints, other approaches that offer important insights, such as natural law, the comparative method and functionalism. Moreover, our identification of seven discrete methods does not preclude other useful ways of grouping international legal scholarship.

Positivism. Positivism summarizes a range of theories that focus upon describing the law as it is, backed up by effective sanctions, with reference to formal criteria, independently of moral or ethical considerations. For positivists, international law is no more or less than the rules to which states have agreed through treaties, custom, and perhaps other forms of consent. In the absence of such evidence of the will of states, positivists will assume that states remain at liberty to undertake whatever actions they please. Positivism also tends to view states as the only subjects of international law, thereby discounting the role of nonstate actors. It remains the lingua franca of most international lawyers, especially in continental Europe.

New Haven School (policy-oriented jurisprudence). Established by Harold Lasswell and Myres McDougal of Yale Law School beginning in the mid–1940s, the New Haven School eschews positivism's formal method of searching for rules as well as the concept of law as based on rules alone. It describes itself as a policy-oriented perspective, viewing international law as a process of decision making by which various actors in the world community clarify and implement their common interests in accordance with their expectations of appropriate processes and of effectiveness in controlling behavior. Perhaps the New Haven School's greatest contribution has been its emphasis on both what actors say and what they do.

International legal process. International legal process (ILP) refers to the approach first developed by Abram Chayes, Thomas Ehrlich and Andreas Lowenfeld at Harvard Law School in the 1960s. Building on the American legal process school, it has seen the key locus of inquiry of international law as the role of law in constraining decision makers and affecting the course of international affairs. Legal process theory has recently enjoyed a domestic revival, which seeks to underpin precepts about process with a set of normative values. Some ILP scholars are following suit.

Critical legal studies. Critical legal studies (CLS) scholars have sought to move beyond what constitutes law, or the relevance of law to policy, to focus on the contradictions, hypocrisies and failings of international legal discourse. The diverse group of scholars who often identify themselves as part of the "New Stream" have emphasized the importance of culture to legal development and offered a critical view of the progress of the law in its confrontations with state sovereignty. Like the deconstruction movement, which is the intellectual font of many of its ideas, critical legal studies has focused on the importance of language.

International law and international relations. IR/IL is a purposefully interdisciplinary approach that seeks to incorporate into international law the insights of international relations theory regarding the behavior of international actors. The most recent round of IR/IL scholarship seeks to draw on contemporary developments and strands in international relations theory, which is itself a relatively young discipline. The results are diverse, ranging from studies of compliance, to analyses of the stability and effectiveness of international institutions, to the ways that models of state conduct affect the content and subject of international rules.

Feminist jurisprudence. Feminist scholars of international law seek to examine how both legal norms and processes reflect the domination of men, and to reexamine and reform these norms and processes so as to take account of women. Feminist jurisprudence has devoted particular attention to the shortcomings in the international protection of women's rights, but it has also asserted deeper structural challenges to international law, criticizing the way law is made and applied as insufficiently attentive to the role of women. Feminist jurisprudence has also taken an active advocacy role.

Law and economics. In its domestic incarnation, which has proved highly significant and enduring, law and economics has both a descriptive component that seeks to explain existing rules as reflecting the most economically efficient outcome, and a normative component that evaluates proposed changes in the law and urges adoption of those that maximize wealth. Game theory and public choice theory are often considered part of law and economics. In the international area, it has begun to address commercial and environmental issues.

Although each of these methods has its own defining characteristics, it is equally apparent that each is a *living* method, employed by a diverse community of scholars who help ensure its continual evolution. If positivism is simplistically termed the most conservative of the methods, it is safe to say that the positivist method of today might well have been unrecognizable to a lawyer one hundred years ago; if critical legal studies is in some sense the most radical of the methods in the questions it poses about the nature of international law, it too has undergone transformations since its arrival in scholarly circles in the 1980s.

Several additional themes are worth considering by the reader. The first is the distinctiveness and independence of international law as a discipline for approaching questions of international relations—what David Kennedy calls "law's claim to special knowledge." More specifically, we need to ask whether international law has one method, one that presumably distinguishes it from other fields, as Oppenheim so confidently held in 1908, whether there are multiple methods, or whether, perhaps, there is no method unique to our field. The first view may seem antiquated, and indeed in contradiction to the very idea of a symposium considering seven distinct methods. But in appraising the six methods other than positivism, it is worth reflecting upon whether they are, in fact, legal methods, or interdisciplinary methods of the "law and (sociology, international relations, economics, postmodern literary theory)" variety: that is, do our nonpositivist authors seek to provide an alternative that can be recognized as a legal method, or a new method that combines legal and nonlegal aspects? Is it possible, indeed, that the use of analytic approaches from disciplines outside the law serves to rob these methods of any distinctive legal quality?

The contribution by the positivists, and indeed their critique of the other methods, suggests that they regard their method as offering such a distinctive—or, in the words of Hans Kelsen, "pure"—quality. Readers may find that some papers—the overtly interdisciplinary methods of IR/IL and law and economics—come close to accepting positivism's claim in this regard, but assert that their methods nonetheless offer critical intellectual tools for the sophisticated practitioner or scholar. Other papers—in particular, those of the New Haven School and international legal process—suggest that they accept the idea of a legal method but find positivism's version too confining for real-world lawyers involved in decision making. Still others from the more critical perspective—CLS and feminist jurisprudence—seem to find embedded in these very questions objectionable assumptions about the nature of law and hence a distinctively "legal" method.

In addition, lawyers often seek what we call rigor in legal analysis. Do these methods enlighten us as to what such rigor entails? Methods built on injecting the theoretical insights of outside disciplines, such as IR/IL and law and economics, the reader will note, claim to bring more rigor into the study of atrocities in internal conflicts by explicitly and systematically treating aspects of the behavior of international actors that other methods either ignore or treat only in an ad hoc manner. Policy-oriented jurisprudence also claims to have constructed a theoretical architecture that promises the practitioner or scholar a method to dissect and rigorously appraise numerous variables. But the critical approaches might label these as suffering from an incomplete or artificial rigor, one that does not delve deep enough to discover the biases of those applying them. This leads to the broader question of whether, as suggested by CLS, each method has its own unique view of what constitutes rigor: for each method that claims its sequence of intellectual operations or its core factors for analysis (ranging from economic efficiency to the gendered nature of law) enhance rigor, other methods will proclaim that reliance on those factors actually reduces it by bringing in extraneous, even diversionary, variables.

A second and related question concerns the usefulness of these various methods to the practicing lawyer (whether in private, governmental or nongovernmental circles), as opposed to the academic analyst. To what extent are each of the methods helpful or necessary tools for actual decision makers, as opposed to those who have the luxury, as it were, to reflect on more comprehensively, and dissect, a particular issue? The proponents of most of the methods will hasten to insist on their relevance—if not, indeed, indispensability—for the practitioner. But in what situations and arenas will and should practitioners use each method? Is one method better for the brief before the court, another for the internal memo (to a client or other decision maker), and still another for the lobbying document before the government or international organization? Some methods might be challenged by practitioners as substituting a focus on method for attention to substance. Is this a valid criticism?

A third major theme to consider for those who do not find themselves already attached to one particular method, and even for those who do, is how the methods relate to each other. Do they accept certain common premises? To what extent do they even apply the same lenses but simply use different terms for them? From one perspective, the brief introduction provided here already suggests that three pairs of the methods seem closely related: international law/international relations and law and economics (with their focus on rational behavior of actors); the New Haven School and international legal process (with their focus on the decision-making process itself); and critical legal studies and law and feminism (with their challenges to the identity of the decision makers and the logic of the process). But other linkages can be found, e.g., in the importance of unequal distribution of political power to the New Haven School, law and economics, and feminist jurisprudence. On the other hand, some of the methods seem to be speaking almost different languages from each other, with few shared assumptions about international law. The process that positivists see of states consenting to specific rules that determine the regime for accountability for civil war atrocities appears in many ways remote from the one that feminists see of men forcing through rules for their own benefit. Indeed, CLS challenges the notion of shared assumptions entirely, suggesting that they are merely the personal preferences of those employing the various methods.

This question of common features raises a second-order methodological question: namely, for the lawyer who is contemplating writing about a new subject—whether the legal issues associated with the space station, rights for indigenous peoples, or trends in the practice of recognition—is there some method by which she can decide which of the seven (or more) methods to employ? It may be enticing for the lawyer or scholar, seeing the insights offered by various methods, to pick and choose from each those aspects that sound most appealing. But such intellectual eclecticism may end up eating away at the core premises of each method, leaving a sort of bland gray instead. And again, the critical perspectives remind us of the need to ask whether a rational choice among the methods is even possible.

Fourth, and finally, what do the existing methods and the directions in which they take legal inquiry suggest about the future of the field? Each of the methods we consider here (with the possible exception of international law and international relations) originated in an approach to domestic law. This, of course, reinforces the conceptual connections between international law and domestic law. But the movement from the domestic to the international has not followed one trajectory; the differences between the two arenas make one model of transposition too facile. International legal process, for instance, has not incorporated certain normative components of the domestic legal process method. Feminism has taken into account numerous actors not involved in domestic feminist jurisprudential debates, e.g., international organizations. CLS emerged on the international scene within a decade of its arrival in domestic circles, while law and economics has taken many more years to make this move. Is there some mapping operation to understand or predict the receptivity of our field to innovations in domestic law, or is it a matter of ad hoc individual initiative by certain scholars?

Moreover, one can ask if the origin of most of these methods in the domestic paradigm means that international lawyers must await new sources of thinking within domestic law before bringing new insights and methods to international law. Perhaps, instead, international legal scholarship can build upon the differences between international law and domestic law to create new methods of inquiry—methods that might, in a reversal of fortune, trickle down (or over) to our domestic law colleagues instead of the other way around. For example, can concepts of legitimacy or justice now advocated as lodestars for decision making in international law form the basis for a new method of international law? (Such a method might inspire yet another take on the problem of accountability for civil war atrocities.)

But there may be limits here, too. The proliferation of new issues for consideration by international law does not in itself require new methods of international law, just methods sophisticated enough—or basic enough—to handle different subject areas. Critical legal studies, with its deconstructionist bent, may at times seem like the last method, if indeed its exponents are willing to regard it as a method. On the other hand, just as the predicted "end of history" has proved premature, so it may be that the end of new methods is not yet upon us. In that respect, some clarity in understanding the potentials and limitations of the principal methods currently employed may plant the seeds for new methodological projects that can invigorate our field.

Chapter 3

TREATIES AND CUSTOM IN INTERNATIONAL LAW

Editors' introduction: All the rules of international law are found either in treaties or in customary law. Treaties are directly binding on the states that have signed and ratified them. Customary law is binding on all states irrespective of consent or acquiescence. Treaties are "embedded" in customary law because it is the latter that provides for the bindingness of treaties and for their interpretation.

A. TREATY LAW

Interpretation. Ian Johnstone, "Treaty Interpretation: The Authority of Interpretive Communities" 12 Mich. J. Int'l L. 371 (1991).

The defining issue in both legal and literary interpretation can be characterized as follows: to what extent does the text have a determinate meaning, and to what extent is the reader free to interpret it as he or she chooses? This question is especially relevant to treaty interpretation where, more often than not, the contracting parties themselves have the final say about the meaning of particular provisions of the agreement in question (a phenomenon that can be labelled "auto-interpretation"). Because many international instruments do not provide for the submission of disputes to impartial tribunals, interpretation is a responsibility of domestic officials who are institutionally predisposed to interpretations preferred by their State and government.

Skepticism about the determinacy of meaning combined with the absence of an impartial interpreter can lead to the discomforting conclusion that treaty auto-interpretation is an unconstrained activity determined entirely by short-term national interests and power politics. In this article, I seek to counter that perception by positing the existence of a structure of constraints embedded in the process of treaty interpretation despite the absence of a disinterested interpreter. Interpretive authority, it will be argued, resides in neither the text nor the reader individually, but with the community of professionals engaged in the enterprise of treaty interpretation and implementation. This "interpretive community" is defined and constituted by a set of conventions and institutional practices that structure the interpretive process.

Of primary importance is the notion that treaties, unlike works of literature, embody a commitment to a distinctive process of interpretation. This commitment is rooted in the fact that a treaty is the product of the consensual activity of two or more States, and its terms embody the collective expectations and interests of the parties. Because the parties to the treaty comprise the collective norm-creating body, the competence of authoritative interpretation is vested in the composite organ they form rather than either of them individually. If the treaty does not provide for a dispute resolution procedure, then an authoritative interpretation can only result from a process that embodies this notion of the parties as a composite law-making entity in some other way. In entering into a treaty, a State binds itself not only to the terms of the instrument (however interpreted) but also a process of intersubjective interpretation: the interpretive task is to ascertain what the text means to the parties collectively rather than to each individually. The activities and perspectives of the interpretive communities associated with this enterprise render treaty auto-interpretation something other than the exercise of unilateral political will.

The interpretive process, then, must be understood as part of an ongoing relationship in which the parties generate, elaborate and refine shared understandings and expectations. McDougal, Lasswell and Miller describe the aim of interpretation as follows:

> It is to discover the shared expectations that the parties to the relevant communication succeeded in creating in each other. It would be an act of distortion on behalf of one party against another to ascertain and to give effect to his version of a supposed agreement if investigation shows that the expectations of this party were not matched by the expectations of the other.*

The authors were mainly concerned with articulating a theory of interpretation that international tribunals could adopt in interpreting treaties, and it must be refined in the context of auto-interpretation. The argument being presented in this article is that, in entering into a treaty, the parties assent not only to the terms of the agreement but also to a process of interpretation whose goal is an intersubjective understanding of the treaty terms. In Stanley Fish's terminology, the parties create an "interpretive community."**

The interpretive task is to "uncover together" the meaning of the treaty; while auto-interpretation is carried on by individual participants, the process is essentially interactive. Intersubjective interpretation is not simply a matter of finding the points agreement between the parties; it

---

* Myres McDougal, H. Lasswell, & J. Miller, The Interpretation of Agreements and World Public Order: Principles of Content and Procedure xvi (1967).

** Stanley Fish, Is There a Text in This Class? The Authority of Interpretive Communities (1980).

is to engage in a collectively meaningful activity, in an activity collectively understood.

The parties can be viewed as having implicitly agreed to a process of intersubjective interpretation because, while they expect disagreement over the meaning of terms, they do not expect every disagreement to signify a desire on the part of one or the other to revoke the treaty or terminate the relationship embodied in it. States comply with treaties primarily because they have an interest in reciprocal compliance by the other party or parties. Reciprocity is particularly important to security-related agreements because the parties' mutual interest in preserving them extends beyond the perceived advantages of the treaties themselves. Security relations in the nuclear age thrust every nation into a continuing relationship with every other nation, a relationship that outlives particular agreements.

Thus, decisionmakers in each State are conscious of the effects of their immediate actions on future relations. Arms control treaties and other security-related arrangements are important events in the overall relationship, but not the complete embodiment of it. It is precisely because they are situated within a broader relationship that such agreements exist and are complied with even in the absence of enforcement mechanisms.

In understanding how treaty auto-interpretation is constrained, two interpretive communities can be identified: the community interpreters directly responsible for the conclusion and implementation of a particular treaty, and a broader, international community consisting of all experts and officials engaged in the various professional activities associated with treaty practice. The conventions and institutional practices of both interpretive communities have constraining effect, although the contribution of the latter is derivative in that its authority can be traced to the implicit agreement between the parties to engage in intersubjective interpretation.

1. *The Narrow Interpretative Community.* The exercise of formulating, negotiating, ratifying, and implementing a treaty generates an interpretive community of individuals within each contracting party who share what Fish calls "assumed distinctions, categories of understanding, and stipulations of relevance and irrelevance."

That is, the process of producing and living under a treaty generates a community (not out of whole cloth but out of already existing communities with an elaborate web of relationships to the new community) of people and institutions associated with the treaty. These people are the officials within each State (from the leader down) who have or had responsibility for any of the various steps involved in producing the treaty.

The constraining effect of this narrow interpretive community is felt, in part, though the expectations and beliefs controlled by the agreement. In the period prior to the making of an agreement, some sort of relationship exists (or the agreement would not have been possible) that generates a body of knowledge shared by the parties. Officials within each State learn about the others' interests, values and assumptions, as well as their perspectives on the various components of the relationship. An agreement "crystallizes the learning of a particular period"* and the contacts made help spread common understandings about the precise terms of the agreement as well as its significance to the broader relationship. The agreement becomes a focal point around which expectations converge. Furthermore, by communicating and exchanging information the governments come to *know* their partners in the agreement and not merely *know about* them. The participants in the enterprise come to inhabit a common world—a world that does not simply come out of the shared beliefs and attitudes of it inhabitants but in fact generates those beliefs and attitudes through common participation.

Subjective interpretation is constrained, both in terms of interpretations that are actually proffered and those that become authoritative, not by external rules of interpretation but by the existence of a relatively unified interpretive community. When disputes over the meaning of the text do arise, members of the community operate within a common frame of reference as to how the dispute should be resolve. Furthermore, the members share a predisposition toward arriving at a mutually acceptable interpretation. Agreement is far from automotive, because many words (and the rules, principles, purposes and policies they convey) are ambiguous and manipulable, and the interests of the parties will remain, in some respects, divergent. But the criterion of mutual acceptability sets an outer limit on the extent to which the can be manipulated. The limit is not a rule of interpretation but a convention of the enterprise. The parties can argue with one another about the meaning of words, but the mere fact that they argue with one another (and not only within domestic constituencies) reflects their continuing commitment to the relationship. The debate is constrained because governments are impelled to justify their positions on grounds other than national self-interest. Otherwise their arguments would not be persuasive to others nor accepted by members of the relevant interpretive communities. The outer limit of an acceptable interpretation is not determined according to transcendent standards but according to the shared standards and expectations of the relevant community.

The process differs from negotiation in that the parties operate within an institutional and intellectual framework already in place, a framework they have implicitly agreed to respect. Failure to respect that framework represents something more serious than a decision not to agree on the specific terms of the relationship embodied in the treaty—it represents a breakdown of the relationship. Obviously, the constraint is not absolute, because, as indicated above, sovereign States can withdraw from the relationship if they perceive that it is in their interest to do so. But the constraint on interpretation does exist insofar as certain inter-

---

* Nye, Nuclear Learning and U.S.-Soviet Security Regimes, 41 Int'l Org. 371, 398 (1987).

pretive activities and positions will be regarded as inconsistent with the enterprise in which the text and interpreter are situated. States may be able to abrogate a treaty but, as long as the relationship embodied in the treaty continues to exist, the constraints of treaty practice (of being in a relationship) limit interpretive discretion.

The conventions of the enterprise operate within the interpretive community not only through expectations and beliefs, but also at the institutional level. For example, in addition to creating international obligations, a treaty acts as an internal directive guiding bureaucratic behavior. Bureaucracies are notoriously status quo oriented; caution rather than creativity and risk-taking characterizes bureaucratic behavior. Violation of an international agreement is not among the options that would typically be suggested by low-level officials when decisions are being made within bureaucracies. Furthermore, a treaty inhibits not only conduct that is clearly prohibited by its terms, but also activities falling within the doubtful zone. Low-level officials do not normally have an incentive to take responsibility for an action that may become the basis for a charge of treaty violation. Of course high-level officials are not inhibited in this way and the top leadership sets goals priorities and policies. However, subordinates influence policy by providing information which effectively defines the situation for superiors. The information provided by these low-level officials is a product of the climate of opinion that arose from process of negotiating and ratifying the treaty. This climate of opinion pervades the environment within which all political and bureaucratic actors must function. It is not easily overridden and thus the actors must, in some measure, either adapt to the climate of opinion or reject it with serious consequences. In this way, the interpretive community that crystallizes around a treaty perpetuates itself. The decision to break a treaty or withdraw from it will occur at the highest levels, but interpretation is shaped by the underlying bureaucratic and organizational structure of less-than-monolithic government.

2. *The Broader Interpretive Community.* Beyond the immediate interpretive community centered around the treaty itself, interpretation is constrained by an amorphous community of all those regarded as possessing the knowledge of an expert or professional in the relevant field. As Oscar Schachter explains, governments cannot escape legal appraisals of their conduct by other governments (expressed either individually or in collective bodies), political parties, international lawyers, non-governmental organizations and other organs of public opinion.

In the realm of military security, this community judgment is influenced by the opinions of governmental and non-governmental experts on international law, world politics and strategic affairs. The competency or expertise comes from training and immersion in some feature of the enterprise in which the experts are engaged. As participants in the field of practice, they have come to understand its purposes and conventions, learned not merely as a set of abstract rules but through the acquisition of know-how, a mastering of the discipline or technique. Having participated in the techniques and discourse of international law, treaty interpretation and/or the subject matter of the treaty, they have become competent in the field.

The outlying interpretive community represents the institutional mechanism closest to an impartial arbiter that the structure of treaty auto-interpretation provides. It constrains interpretation primarily because States have an interest in maintaining a reputation for good faith adherence to treaties. As Henkin states:

> Every nation's foreign policy depends substantially on its "credit"—on maintaining the expectation that it will live up to international mores and obligations. Considerations of "honor," "prestige," "leadership," "influence," "reputation," which figure prominently in governmental decisions, often weigh in favor of observing law. Nations generally desire a reputation for principled behavior, for propriety and respectability.

This interest combined with the implicit agreement between the parties to engage in intersubjective interpretation means the outlying interpretive community effectively checks and structures the interpretive activities of the parties. An interpretation put forward by an official agent does not acquire authoritative status by that fact alone. Rather, it works as a signal within an interpretive system or "mechanism for the endless negotiation of what will be authorized or nonauthorized."*

It is evaluated by the outlying community and judged in terms of its conformity with the conventions and purposes of the enterprise. In this way, the international interpretive community monitors the parties and provides indirect reassurance to each that the other or others will not engage in subjective interpretation. The influence of this community is felt directly in terms of explicit evaluations of the appropriateness of a particular interpretation and indirectly in the way States measure their own interpretations against anticipated judgment of the international community. Because all States have a stake in maintaining a reputation for good faith compliance with treaty commitments, they will hesitate before publicly announcing a construction likely to be branded as improper or far-fetched. Of course, they may elect to do so, but that only signifies that constraint is not absolute: it does not count as an argument against the existence of a constraint.

Now that the Cold War is over and international affairs, in all probability, will no longer be dominated by superpower conflict, a new era of collective security and international law may be upon us. Future disputes, more than in the recent past, will be disputes over the meaning of legal texts and legal norms. There will continue to be much room for argument, but the form the arguments take will be constrained by the distinctive purposes and practices of the legal enterprise. The existence

---

* Stanley Fish, Is There a Text in This Class? The Authority of Interpretive Communities 357 (1980).

of a legal text or norm is evidence of a commitment to the relationship embodied therein. The relationship represents, on one level, a set of shared understandings about the terms of the relationship. But the generalized character of words and the elusiveness of meaning indicate that the commitment is and must be something more than an agreement to abide by substantive rules of behavior. It is also a commitment to a process of constructing the meaning of the relationship together.

There are, however, limits to the influence of interpretive communities within the existing international legal system. Many if not most international legal disputes (like domestic legal disputes) turn on facts as opposed to law. Yet access to these facts is much more restricted than access to the legal materials. Thus, while members of a community can often be counted on to interpret a legal norm (written or unwritten) in common, such communities rarely exist when it comes to factual assessments. To the extent that the "facts" of international life are not self-evident, what actually happened is less important than what relevant legal authorities think (or say) happened. If the relevant authority is the interpretive community, as I have argued, then the facts that count are those upon which there is consensus among members of the community. While interpretive communities perform the task of authoritative interpretation admirably, their capacity to identify and evaluate relevant facts is much more restricted. The facts that surface in international disputes do so through an imperfect process, dominated by the selective revelations of national governments. Thus, perhaps the most important lesson for the international legal system to be learned from this examination of the role of interpretive communities is the need for new institutions and procedures, not for authoritative legal interpretation, but for fact-finding and fact-assessment.

Compliance. Frederic L. Kirgis, "North Korea's Withdrawal from the Nuclear Nonproliferation Treaty" ASIL Insights (January 2003), http://www.asil.org/insights/insigh96.htm.

On January 10, 2003, North Korea announced (a) that it was withdrawing from the Nuclear Nonproliferation Treaty (NPT), effective immediately, and (b) that its withdrawal from the NPT left it free from the binding force of its Safeguards Agreement with the International Atomic Energy Agency (IAEA).

North Korea became a party to the NPT in 1985 as a non-nuclear-weapon state. Article III of the NPT requires each non-nuclear-weapon state to accept safeguards in an agreement with the IAEA, in order to verify its compliance with its obligation under Article II to refrain from manufacturing or acquiring nuclear explosives. Article X, paragraph 1 of the NPT provides:

> Each party shall in exercising its national sovereignty have the right to withdraw from the Treaty if it decides that extraordinary events, related to the subject matter of this Treaty, have jeopardized the supreme interests of its country. It shall give notice of such with-

drawal to all other Parties to the Treaty and to the United Nations Security Council three months in advance. Such notice shall include a statement of the extraordinary events it regards as having jeopardized its supreme interests.

In 1992, North Korea entered into its Safeguards Agreement with the IAEA under Article III of the NPT. The Safeguards Agreement provides for measurements and observations of North Korean nuclear material and facilities by IAEA inspectors. Article 26 of the Safeguards Agreement provides, "This Agreement shall remain in force as long as the Democratic People's Republic of Korea is party to the Treaty [the NPT]." Consequently, if North Korea has validly withdrawn from the NPT pursuant to its January 2003 announcement, the Safeguards Agreement would no longer be in force. (North Korea's withdrawal from the IAEA, which occurred in 1994, did not amount to a withdrawal from the NPT and did not terminate the Safeguards Agreement.)

North Korea's stated reasons for withdrawing from the NPT were that the United States was threatening its security by its hostile policy toward North Korea. According to North Korea, the United States had singled it out as a target of a pre-emptive nuclear attack and had threatened it with a blockade and military punishment. The question regarding North Korea's right to withdraw from the NPT under Article X, above, is not whether North Korea's allegations regarding the United States' intent or policies are true in any objective sense. Instead, Article X allows each party to make its own decision as to whether extraordinary events, related to the subject matter of the NPT, have jeopardized its supreme interests. Arguably, customary international law would impose a good faith requirement on the party deciding that extraordinary events have jeopardized its supreme interests, but the NPT does not establish any mechanism for making a determination as to whether a party has acted in good faith.

If, as appears to be the case, North Korea relied solely on Article X of the NPT for its right of withdrawal (as distinguished from relying on the general law of treaties, which permits termination of treaty obligations under certain circumstances), it has failed to comply with the three-month notice requirement. Noncompliance with the notice requirement does not necessarily mean that the withdrawal from the NPT is invalid. The requirement is couched in terms of a promise to give three months' notice, rather than as a condition that would have to be met in order to make the withdrawal effective. It could be argued that the withdrawal becomes effective only after the elapse of three months, regardless of North Korea's intent to withdraw immediately, but even that is not certain. If the withdrawal is effective immediately, as North Korea has asserted, any state that can show harm from the failure to give three months' notice would be entitled, in theory, to some form of reparation from North Korea.

Even if the withdrawal is proper under the strict terms of Article X and is effective immediately, the United Nations Security Council could decide that the withdrawal, considered in conjunction with North Korea's stated intent to resume missile testing, to begin reprocessing spent fuel rods and to reactivate its nuclear facilities, and its expulsion of IAEA inspectors, amount to a threat to the peace. The Security Council could make that determination on its own initiative, or on a referral from the IAEA Board of Governors based on North Korea's noncompliance with its obligations under the Safeguards Agreement. Acting under Chapter VII of the U.N. Charter, the Security Council could impose mandatory economic, diplomatic or even military sanctions on North Korea. Any proposed resolution to impose such sanctions, however, would be subject to a possible veto by any of the permanent Security Council members (China, France, Russia, the United Kingdom and the United States).

Interim Treaty Obligations. Jan Klabbers, "How to Defeat a Treaty's Object and Purpose Pending Entry into Force: Toward Manifest Intent" 34 Vanderbilt J. Transnat'l L. 284 (2001).

Imagine this: State X is among the first to sign and ratify a convention against arbitrary detention. In the period of time between the ratification by State X and the entry into force of the convention, State X continues to detain a number of individuals arbitrarily. Does State X, in doing so, violate international law?

Or picture this: State Y signs a disarmament convention and plans to ratify it at the earliest possible date, but in the meantime State Y continues to procure the very armaments that the convention will ban when it enters into force. Is State Y violating international law?

Or consider this: State Z has ratified an extensive free trade agreement that, upon entry into force, will prohibit any new tariffs and similar charges and will be self-executing. A week or so before the agreement enters into force, State Z increases tariffs on products coming from one of its prospective partners, to the detriment of a producer operating from within that trading partner. Is State Z acting in violation of international law?

The three scenarios sketched above are more or less hypothetical, but not completely devoid of realism. The third scenario is, in fact, a simplified and stylized version of the facts that gave rise to the Opel Austria case, decided by the Court of First Instance of the European Community in early 1997.

The other examples also are not too far removed from real life occurrences. Angola endured a storm of criticism by continuing to use landmines after having signed the anti-landmine convention. India met with fierce opposition when it announced its intention to block the entry into force of the Comprehensive Nuclear Test Ban Treaty after lengthy negotiations but before it signed the convention. Some commentators analyzed the 1994 agreement facilitating the entry into force of the United Nations Convention on the Law of the Sea in terms of whether it violated the Convention itself prior to its entry into force. In addition, the conclusion of the Chemical Weapons Convention in 1993 spurred the Committee on Arms Control and Disarmament Law of the International Law Association to investigate whether or not obligations may exist for signatories to arms control agreements prior to their entries into force.

This recent discovery* of the interim obligation is not merely coincidental. Note that all of the above examples—a human rights convention, an arms control treaty, and a complex free trade agreement—are not strictly contractual in nature; instead, they aspire to create institutions and establish norms of general application. They are, to use the classic term, law-making treaties.

This suggests that there is something about law-making conventions which makes their effects desirable (if not their formal entry into force) without any delay. Indeed, it is awkward to argue that states have a right to lay landmines if they have signed, and perhaps have ratified, a treaty prohibiting such practices, simply because the calendar has not yet reached a certain date. Any suffering in the interim is suffering for formalities. Surely international law must have a rule preventing such situations, and many contend that this rule is the one embodied in Article 18 of the Vienna Convention on the Law of Treaties, widely known as the "interim obligation."

According to its very terms the interim obligation provision of Article 18 of the Vienna Convention cannot be invoked without more. Its success depends on whether behavior would defeat the object and purpose of the treaty concerned, and it is here that a paradox sets in. Instead of defeating the object and purpose of a law-making convention, any behavior irreconcilable with it, prior to its entry into force, actually serves to emphasize the desirability of its entry into force. The behavior, rather, strengthens the very point of the treaty.

Particularly with non-contractual, normative, multilateral arrangements, the interim obligation as laid down in Article 18 of the Vienna Convention does not provide much relief. The objective test it seemingly prescribes makes no sense in a normative context (as one can hardly defeat the object and purpose of generally desirable behavior), and inevitably lapses into a test of either subjective intent or legitimate expectations (or hypothetically, both), and those turn out to be of little use as soon as they need to be applied. Consequently, both judicial practice and post-Vienna Convention scholarship turn away from the letter of Article 18 and apply, while often ostensibly referring to legitimate expectations, really a simple but effective manifest intent test, which is the following: if behavior seems unwarranted and condemnable, it may be assumed to have been inspired by less than lofty motivations and ought to be condemned, regardless of whether anyone's legitimate expectations are really frustrated or can reasonably be said to have been frustrated, regardless of actual proof of bad faith.

---

* The scarce nature of references to the interim obligation in textbooks written after the conclusion of the 1969 Vienna Convention on the Law of Treaties suggests that the present situation marks a discovery, or perhaps a rediscovery.

Only such a conception can explain why the EC Court of First Instance could find the imposition of a tariff shortly before the entry into force of an agreement prohibiting them to constitute a violation of the interim obligation. Only such a conception can explain why authors can condemn the purchase or production of arms on the eve of a disarmament agreement or why states can be accused of violating international law by laying mines after having signed a convention not to do so. Conversely, only such a conception can explain why a Dutch tribunal could reject a plea for a family reunion despite the Dutch having already signed a convention which would probably support the plea or why the EC Court could ignore a plea that an effort to manage the modalities of accession to the EC would violate international law. In addition, only such a conception can explain why authors can persuasively conclude that to drastically change the terms of a large convention on the law of the sea before its entry into force is nonetheless not in violation of the interim obligation.

As traditionally conceived, the interim obligation as laid down in Article 18 of the Vienna Convention on the Law of Treaties was, in effect, meant to serve in limited circumstances only and can only provide a meaningful service in the limited confines of contractual situations. Where, by contrast, international agreements are concluded to further the community interest, Article 18 as drafted and conceived can only disappoint.

Instead of simply discarding the idea of the interim obligation as unworkable, or positing that some treaties are qualitatively different so as to warrant that they effectively enter into force upon signature even if the text itself prescribes ratification, the more sensible approach is to help the interim obligation adapt to circumstances that were never considered during the drafting stage. Such relatively painless adaptation pays homage to the vitality and flexibility of international law, and the law of treaties in particular. On the relatively few occasions where Article 18 arguments have been made in recent decades (be it by courts or by authors), they have invariably involved a test different from anything contemplated by the ILC or self-evident under the terms of Article 18 itself. Such applications of the interim obligation are best explained with the help of a "manifest intent test," which is useful shorthand for saying that where behavior pending entry into force of an agreement is generally held to be morally obnoxious in light of what the agreement itself represents, then it violates the interim obligation. Such an approach has the dual benefit of allowing the law to remain flexible while remaining faithful to some of our dearest moral convictions, which is exactly what these situations require.

Rebus Sic Stantibus. Hans Kelsen, *Principles of International Law* (1952), excerpt.

According to a widespread opinion, a treaty ceases to be valid as the effect of a vital change of circumstances; or, as this principle is usually formulated, according to the clausula rebus sic stantibus ("Clause concerning vital change of circumstances"). In order to justify the principle that a contracting party to a treaty can withdraw unilaterally from the treaty or, what amounts to the same, declare that it considers itself no longer bound by the treaty if the circumstances under which it has concluded the treaty or adhered to it have essentially changed, some writers maintain that if the change of circumstances is so essential that compliance with the treaty could impair the very existence of the state, the latter cannot be considered as bound by the treaty. Its fundamental right to existence is stronger than its obligation under the rule pacta sunt sevanda. They sometimes refer to the fact that the principle in question is recognized by many national legal orders which permit a person to cancel a contract for the reason that the circumstances under which it has been concluded have essentially changed.

But there exists an important difference between the clausula rebus sic stantibus as part of national law and the same principle as part of international law. Under national law an objective and impartial authority is established to decide the questions as to whether a vital change of circumstances has taken place, whereas under general international law the parties to the treaty are themselves competent to decide this question. The most serious argument against the doctrine that, according to a rule of international law, a treaty loses it validity when the circumstances under which it had been concluded have essentially changed, is this: that it is the function of the law in general and treaties in particular to stabilize the legal relations between states in the stream of changing circumstances. If circumstances did not change, the binding force conferred upon treaties by the law would be almost superfluous. The clausula rebus sic stantibus is in opposition to one of the most important purposes of the international legal order, its purpose of stabilizing international relations.

As a matter of fact, it is hardly possible to prove that the clausula is part of positive international law. When in 1870 Russia tried to withdraw unilaterally from the Treaty of Paris of 1856, which imposed upon Russia the obligation not to maintain a fleet in the Black Sea, the parties to the Treaty of Paris in a conference held at London in 1871 adopted the following declaration: "It is an essential principle of international law that no power can free itself from obligations imposed upon it by a treaty or modify its terms, except with the consent of the contracting parties by means of an amicable agreement." This is an open rejection of the clausula rebus sic stantibus. The relatively few cases in which states have referred to essential change of circumstances to justify their non-compliance with treaty obligations may be interpreted simply as violations of international law rather than as evidence of the clausula rebus sic stantibus as a rule of positive international law.

Treaty Withdrawal. The White House, "Remarks by the President on National Missile Defense" 13 December 2001.

Today, I have given formal notice to Russia, in accordance with the treaty, that the United States of America is withdrawing from this almost 30 year old treaty. I have concluded the ABM treaty hinders our government's ability to develop ways to protect our people from future terrorist or rogue state missile attacks.

The 1972 ABM treaty was signed by the United States and the Soviet Union at a much different time, in a vastly different world. One of the signatories, the Soviet Union, no longer exists. And neither does the hostility that once led both our countries to keep thousands of nuclear weapons on hair-trigger alert, pointed at each other. The grim theory was that neither side would launch a nuclear attack because it knew the other would respond, thereby destroying both.

Today, as the events of September the 11th made all too clear, the greatest threats to both our countries come not from each other, or other big powers in the world, but from terrorists who strike without warning, or rogue states who seek weapons of mass destruction.

We know that the terrorists, and some of those who support them, seek the ability to deliver death and destruction to our doorstep via missile. And we must have the freedom and the flexibility to develop effective defenses against those attacks. Defending the American people is my highest priority as Commander in Chief, and I cannot and will not allow the United States to remain in a treaty that prevents us from developing effective defenses.

Consequences. Rachel Brewster, "The Domestic Origins of International Agreements" 44 Va. J. Int'l L. 501 (2004).

Governments can withdraw from international agreements if policymakers wish to change a policy but not violate any international agreements. While this solution may appear to lower the costs of changing domestic policies embedded in treaties, it is not clear that this strategy will be less costly in many circumstances. First, the government would need to withdraw from the entire treaty (unless there was a clause specifically permitting withdrawal from one section of the agreement) and would lose all of the benefits of the agreement. Because treaties are often agreements on multiple issues, legislators cannot simply change just one aspect of the agreement—as they could if the policy was established as a statute.

Moreover, treaties are not necessarily discrete instruments. The existence of one treaty may be important for the maintenance of other international agreements. Thus when considering termination, a government will have to consider whether withdrawal from one treaty will prompt other states to withdraw from other treaties. This linkage between treaties can be formal or informal. Some treaty arrangements make acceptance of several agreements mandatory. For instance, parties to the WTO must accept the minimum intellectual property standards under the Trade Related Intellectual Property Rights Agreement and cannot terminate that agreement and still retain the other WTO trade benefits. In other areas, such as arms control, treaties are only politically related: The termination of one agreement may lead other governments to consider terminating other agreements.

Reservations. Catherine Logan Piper, "Reservations to Multilateral Treaties: The Goal of Universality" 71 Iowa L. Rev. 295 (1985).

The three major classifications of treaty-qualifying unilateral statements are reservations, understandings, and declarations. A reservation is a formal declaration made by a state when it joins a treaty, a declaration that acts to limit or modify the effect of the treaty in application to the reserving state. A reservation is external to the text of the treaty and is an attempt to alter the negotiated package. Because reservations are made outside of the treaty negotiations, their amendment to the multilateral treaty may conflict with the original text of the treaty. The ultimate effect of the reservation will depend on the practice or rule of reservations applied and the existence or nonexistence of special provisions within the treaty governing inclusion and effect of reservations.

The term "understanding" is used to designate a statement not intended to alter or limit the effect of the treaty, but rather to set forth a state's interpretation or explanation of a treaty provision. In practice, understandings are sometimes used to provide a memorandum of the nation's interpretation at the time of signing in case of future judicial or arbitral proceedings.

A declaration is a unilateral statement of policy or opinion that, like an understanding, is not intended to alter or limit any provision of the treaty. It is considered to have the least effect on the original treaty text and is used primarily to articulate a signatory's purpose, position, or expectation, concerning the treaty in question.

The use of the labels "reservation," "understanding," and "declaration" have created much confusion on both the international level and the domestic level. The problem arises because the label attached is not conclusive as to the substantive effect the statement has on the treaty. This is especially evident when dealing with understandings. A state may condition acceptance of a treaty on a specific interpretation, which may later be found contrary to the plain language of the treaty or the intended meaning of other parties. As such, the understanding in effect alters or modifies the original treaty and amounts to a reservation. If a state were allowed to determine conclusively the treatment of a unilateral statement by attaching a label, the statement could alter the multilateral treaty and negate the application of reservation law. It is necessary, therefore, to distinguish qualifying statements by comparing the substance or contents of the statement with the original text of the treaty. If the qualifying statement in application alters the legal effect of the treaty, the statement should be considered a reservation and be governed by the applicable reservation law.

Flexible Approach to Reservations. Henry J. Bourguignon, "The Belios Case: New Light on Reservations to Multilateral Treaties" 29 Va. J. Int'l L. 347 (1989).

In 1950, when the European Convention on Human Rights was drafted and ratified, European authors generally adopted a contract view of treaties. Any reservation made by a State at the time of its ratification or accession to a multilateral treaty, therefore, amounted to a counter-offer rather than an acceptance. Ratifications with reservations, according to this approach, required the unanimous consent of all the other parties. The counter-offer had to be accepted. That is, all the parties had to assent to the reservation or else the ratification or accession of the reserving State amounted to a nullity. One State party accordingly could object to the reservation and prevent the reserving State from becoming a party to the treaty. This rule of unanimous consent meticulously preserved the integrity of the treaty text, but at the price of discouraging its wider application.

In the next year, 1951, the International Court of Justice held that the unanimous consent rule had not achieved the status of a rule of international law. In response to a request from the United Nations General Assembly, the Court issued an advisory opinion on the law of reservations as it applied to the Convention on the Prevention and Punishment of Genocide.

The Court's majority framed the principal issue as

> whether a contracting State which has made a reservation can, while still maintaining it, be regarded as being a party to the Convention, when there is a divergence of views between the contracting parties concerning this reservation, some accepting the reservation, others refusing to accept it.

The Court acknowledged the general principles that a State cannot be bound by a treaty without its consent, and likewise that no reservation can be effective against it without its agreement. It also recognized the contractual nature of multilateral conventions, which the parties cannot frustrate by unilateral measures. Notwithstanding these general principles, the Court observed that the universal and humanitarian character of the Genocide Convention merited a more flexible application.

The Court noted that the desire for a wide degree of participation in multilateral conventions had led to a more liberal resort to reservations, even to the point of regarding as parties to conventions States whose reservations had been objected to by other parties. Whether these flexible principles applied to a given convention depended on that convention's purpose and provisions. According to the Court, the Genocide Convention condemned crimes against humanity and embraced principles binding on States even absent any conventional obligations. The Convention also called for universal cooperation in combating genocide. Thus it justified a more flexible approach to reservations to the treaty. Especially in the case of such multilateral humanitarian conventions, the Court wrote, the contracting States have only a single common interest, and "cannot speak of individual advantages or disadvantages to States, or of the maintenance of perfect contractual balance between rights and duties." The exclusion of one or more States from the Convention because of objections to their reservations would restrict the scope of its application and detract from its moral authority.

The Court therefore constructed a new test for determining when a reservation to a humanitarian treaty bars the reserving State from participation in the treaty:

> It follows that it is the compatibility of a reservation with the object and purpose of the Convention that must furnish the criterion for the attitude of a State in making the reservation on accession as well as for the appraisal by a State in objecting to the reservation.

Thus, at least in the case of multilateral humanitarian conventions such as the Genocide Convention (or the European Convention), a reserving party remains a party so long as its reservation, even if objected to by some of the other parties, is compatible with the convention's object and purpose. The appraisal of a reservation and the effect of objections to it, then, would depend not on a general rule but on the circumstances of a particular case. The Court indicated that States should appraise the validity of reservations by the compatibility criterion. If a State did object, it would not be bound by the reservation, but under the flexible principles its objection would affect only the relationship between the reserving and objecting States, and would not exclude the reserving State from the convention. Multilateral treaties therefore took on the appearance of a matrix of slightly varying bilateral treaties.

In the decade and a half following the Genocide Convention case, the International Law Commission struggled with the problem of reservations. Over the course of the debates, the more flexible system of reservations suggested by the Genocide Convention opinion and followed in inter-American practice was eventually accepted by the Commission. Ultimately in 1969 this more flexible system became the core of the clauses on reservations in the Vienna Convention on the Law of Treaties.

The Vienna Convention sets forth as a general rule the right of States to make reservations to treaties, except in three circumstances:

> (a) the reservation is prohibited by the treaty;
>
> (b) the treaty provides that only specified reservations, which do not include the reservation in question, may be made; or
>
> (c) in cases not falling under sub-paragraphs (a) and (b), the reservation is incompatible with the object and purpose of the treaty.

By this last condition the Vienna Convention thus adopted the compatibility test set forth in the Genocide Convention opinion. The International Court in that case had limited the test to multilateral humanitarian conventions, but the Vienna Convention adopted it was the test for treaties in general.

With regard to the acceptance of and objection to reservations, the Convention constructs a more elaborate framework. Generally, acceptance of a reservation by another contracting State constitutes the reserving State as a party to the treaty in relation to that other State; acceptance is considered tacit if no objection is raised within twelve months. The reservation modifies the relevant provisions of the treaty for both the reserving and accepting State with regard to each other; it does not modify the treaty among the other parties.

B. CRITICISMS OF CURRENT TREATY PRACTICE

Is U.S. Treaty Ratification a Charade? Kenneth Roth, "The Charade of US Ratification of International Human Rights Treaties" 1 Chi. J. Int'l. L. 1 (2000).

It is sadly academic to ask whether international human rights law should trump US domestic law. That is because, on the few occasions when the US government has ratified a human rights treaty, it has done so in a way designed to preclude the treaty from having any domestic effect. Washington pretends to join the international human rights system, but it refuses to permit this system to improve the rights of US citizens.

The US government's approach to the ratification of international human rights treaties is unique. Once the government signs a treaty, the pact is sent to Justice Department lawyers who comb through it looking for any requirement that in their view might be more protective of US citizens' rights than pre-existing US law. In each case, a reservation, declaration, or understanding is drafted to negate the additional rights protection. These qualifications are then submitted to the Senate as part of the ratification package.*

For example, Article 6(5) of the International Covenant on Civil and Political Rights (ICCPR) prohibits the imposition of the death penalty "for crimes committed by persons below eighteen years of age." To preserve the power to execute such juvenile offenders, the US government insisted on a reservation effectively negating this provision.** In taking this extraordinary step, the United States ensured its place with the mere handful of governments worldwide that persist in the barbaric practice of executing offenders who were children when they committed

---

* This effort should be distinguished from the US government's parallel, legitimate effort to ensure that the ratification process enhances US citizens' rights by identifying and entering reservations to any treaty provision that might detract from pre-existing rights. For example, Article 20 of the International Covenant on Civil and Political Rights requires prohibition of "[a]ny propaganda for war." The US ratification of the ICCPR appropriately contains a reservation rejecting any requirement that speech be restricted in a manner that violates the free speech provisions of the First Amendment.

** The reservation reads: "The United States reserves the right, subject to its constitutional constraints, to impose capital punishment on any person (other than a pregnant woman) duly convicted under existing or future laws permitting the imposition of capital punishment, including such punishment for crimes committed by persons below eighteen years of age." US Reservations, Declarations, and Understandings, International Covenant on Civil and Political Rights, 102d Congress, 2d Sess in 138 Cong Rec S 4781 (Apr 2, 1992).

their crimes—such paragons of human rights virtue as Iran, Nigeria, Pakistan, Saudi Arabia and Yemen. Indeed, this US reservation was particularly egregious because it concerned a rights—the right to life—from which the ICCPR precludes derogation.

Similarly, the US government entered a reservation limiting the conduct prohibited by the Convention Against Torture and Other Cruel, Inhuman or Degrading Treatment or Punishment ("Torture Convention"). The problem, from the government's perspective, was the Article 16 of the convention precludes not only "cruel and unusual punishments"—the prohibition contained in the Eighth Amendment of the US Constitution—but also "degrading treatment." To avoid any possibility of this provision being interpreted to impose a higher official standard of conduct, the US government adopted a reservation stating that the Torture Convention prohibits no more than the "cruel and unusual punishment" provisions of the US Constitution.

After this exercise of stripping human rights treaties of any protections that might add to US law, the government takes out a sort of insurance policy against the possibility that the Justice Department lawyers might have made a mistake. To ensure that some new hidden right is not lurking in parts of the treaty for which no reservation, declaration or understanding was entered, the US government first declares that the treaty is "not self-executing," meaning that it has no force of law without so-called implementing legislation. This step is not necessarily objectionable in itself, since it ensures that new rights are endorsed by both houses of Congress through the traditional legislative process, rather than through the unicameral ratification process, which requires the consent of only the Senate. But then, the government announces that implementing legislation is unnecessary because, according to the Justice Department lawyers, all the rights for which reservations, declarations or understandings were not registered are already protected by US law.

The result is that US citizens are left with no capacity to invoke the treaty in the US courts. The non-self-executing declaration precludes stating a cause of action under the treaty, and the lack of implementing legislation means that there is no alternative route to assert a claim.

Reservations and Human Rights. Madeline Morris, "A Few Reservations About Reservations" 1 Chi. J. Int'l L. 341 (2000).

The flexible reservations regime, with its object-and-purpose test, is designed to maximize treaty participation by states with different political, cultural, and economic circumstances while, at the same time, retaining the integrity of the treaties sufficiently for them to be meaningful and effective. Looking at the relationship of the United States and of other states to the International Covenant on Civil and Political Rights (ICCPR) . . . , we will find that different types of flexibility will be required for different reasons if we are to have the broadest possible meaningful participation in the treaty.

In examining the relationship of the United States to the ICCPR, one may begin by observing that the law of the United States is so largely consistent with the norms embodied in the ICCPR that major changes in US law would not be expected to come about in response to the treaty. The major precepts of human rights law embodied in the ICCPR (such as equality before the law; freedoms of belief, expression, and association; rights to privacy and the like) are already essential features of US constitutional law. The features of the ICCPR that the United States has not adopted (such as the prohibition of execution of juveniles or the prohibition of "hate speech") concern matters that have been considered and rejected in legitimate domestic lawmaking processes. These "omitted rights" are, indeed, matters about which reasonable persons, apparently, may disagree. It is not clear why such matters should be viewed as outside the realm of regular political decision-making. If a functioning democratic process produces a decision not to undertake a particular human rights treaty obligation, then it is hard to see what more there is to say about it—other than to seek further change, if it is desired, through the political process.

In the United States, democratic processes have thus far precluded adherence to some aspects of the ICCPR and some other human rights treaty provisions. Other states may confront other circumstances that preclude their undertaking or fulfilling some provisions of the ICCPR and other human rights treaties.

For instance, states that are emerging from violent conflicts involving widespread war crimes or crimes against humanity may need to place reservations on the human rights treaties to which they accede and, equally likely, may confront serious dilemmas in attempting to implement even rather major precepts of the human rights treaties to which they are already parties. The relevant treaties may arguably entail obligations to prosecute perpetrators of genocide, war crimes, or crimes against humanity. But such states (particularly new or transitional regimes) may be unable to conduct such prosecutions without the risk of civil war or something closely resembling it. These states also may have problems providing adequate due process at trial if they do conduct prosecutions and may have problems providing adequate conditions of incarceration for such sentences as may be imposed. The options available to states under these circumstances will include formal or de facto amnesties, prosecutions that fall below international human rights standards, or some combination of the two. Any such choices may run afoul of some provisions of human rights treaties to which the state is a party or would like to become a party.

In such post-conflict situations, full adherence to and compliance with all human rights treaty provisions may be precluded as a result of internally disrupted governmental systems. By contrast, in the United States (and some other states), full adherence to all human rights treaty provisions may be precluded precisely as a result of internally functioning governmental systems. For very different reasons in the two sorts of cases, compliance with the full set of human rights norms proposed in the ICCPR will not be forthcoming. There is also, no doubt, a third sort of case, in which adherence to or compliance with human rights obligations—even the very core human rights obligations—is not forthcoming because of internally nefarious governmental systems.

The crucial question is: What response would best serve the ultimate goals of human rights, given this array of reasons for less than full conformity with human rights treaties? It may be unwise to focus energies on pressing for full conformity in countries where the core human rights are legally protected but adherence to certain provisions is not forthcoming because of a reasoned choice that has emerged from a functioning democratic process. Similarly, as long as the core precepts are respected, it may not be wise to focus energies on pressing for full conformity with human rights treaties where conformity is not forthcoming because the governmental system has collapsed or is confronted with circumstances that prevent full conformity. A wiser strategy may be to reserve the focus of condemnation for regimes that violate the core precepts of human rights or fail to fulfill the human rights obligations that they have undertaken when they have the capacity to do so.

The best strategy for affording the greatest protection for human rights may thus be to focus on attaining compliance on the core issues while providing appropriate flexibility—a "margin of appreciation," as the Europeans call it—on issues as they move further from the core precepts. What that flexibility or margin of appreciation will entail will depend upon the specifics of the national context and the proximity of the issues at stake to the core human rights requirements. In some countries, applying this sort of approach may mean, for instance, accepting some forms of amnesty or other such concessions in post-conflict situations. In the United States, it may mean accepting less than wholesale incorporation of human rights treaties like the ICCPR if that is what emerges from the political process.

How to evaluate the compatibility of reservations with the object and purpose of the ICCPR is a complex question. The rather modest point of the present essay is that the compatibility determination should be made in a manner consistent with a flexible strategy that fosters incremental progress through allowing for variation. The flexible reservations regime was designed to foster the acceptance, and hence the effectiveness, of treaties that foster human rights. We should not undermine that advance by interpreting the object-and-purpose test in such a way as to exclude most of the reservations that would be doing the work in garnering support and participation in the treaties.

Reservations and State Practice. Ryan Goodman, "Human Rights Treaties, Invalid Reservations, and State Consent" 96 A.J.I.L. 531 (2002).

In consenting to multilateral human rights treaties, states generally try to accomplish two goals: (1) to promote human rights standards (whether domestically or internationally or both); and (2) to minimize the treaty's infringement on aspects of domestic sovereignty that the state does not want to relinquish. Reservations are devices for meeting both goals. By submitting a reservation as a condition of ratification, a state can become a party to a multilateral treaty while limiting aspects of the agreement that contravene domestic interests the state seeks to protect.

On its face, this description simply reiterates the standard account that reservations are essential to obtaining the universal ratification of treaties. That is, without the ability to submit a reservation, many states would be unwilling to assent to all terms of a particular treaty and thus would never submit to ratification. The politics of treaty relations, however, adds a complication to this account. For fairly straightforward reasons, a state may include more reservations than required to obtain its consent. Whether counting on other states not to object to its reservations or discounting the cost of such objections, a state may include supererogatory conditions in its package of reservations. Although some reservations are essential—integral to the state's consent to the treaty—others may be described as what Judge Armand–Ugon, in a related context, called "an accessory stipulation."

In various multilateral agreements, especially those without a juridical supervisory organ, states may incur little cost for submitting accessory reservations. Under the Vienna Convention, state R generally suffers only bilateral costs if another state objects to its reservation. That is, the effect of state O's objection to state R's reservation is either (1) that the treaty terms to which the reservation relates do not apply between the two states, or (2) that the treaty as a whole does not enter into force between the two states. Primarily owing to diplomatic sensitivities, states avoid choosing the second option, if they are politically willing to enter an objection at all. As for the first option, because the rule of reciprocity produces the exact same result as the reservation, state R loses nothing if state O selects this alternative. States consequently have little incentive to avoid submitting accessory reservations.

The administrative costs of monitoring and reviewing other states' reservations make states "sluggish in their reaction to reservations.... It is a fact of international life."* This feature of treaty practice is even more pronounced in the area of human rights. Human rights treaties do not involve the kind of reciprocal duties between states that directly affect one another's domestic interests. Admittedly, some states, especially leading military powers, may consider grave human rights violations in other countries a threat to their own security interests, and some states may perceive the promotion of universal human rights standards as a constitutive part of their country's political identity. Still, neither of these interests is as direct, or affects domestic constituencies as immediately, as the reciprocal duties imposed in other multilateral contexts such as trade and arms control. A state may find another state's reservations objectionable, or even violative of the basic understanding

---

* Ian Sinclair, *The Vienna Convention on the Law of Treaties* 63 (2d Rev. Ed. 1984).

of the treaty, but unless the former's own domestic interests are directly implicated, monitoring, scrutinizing, and reacting to other states' reservations are simply not priorities.

The political context of human rights agreements is thus conducive to the submission, if not piling on, of accessory reservations. The package of reservations a state submits reflects the ideal relationship it wishes to have in relation to the treaty, not the essential one it requires so as to be bound. Consequently, a severance determination must distinguish between essential and accessory reservations, weighing the dual goals of treaty ratification in that calculation. By taking these factors and the various modalities of state practice into account, we can assess which reservations regime best protects state consent.

C. CUSTOMARY LAW

A Definition. "Custom," from *Akehurst's Modern Introduction to International Law* (7th ed.), Peter Malanczuk, editor (1997), excerpt.

The second source of international law listed in the Statute of the International Court of Justice is "international custom, as evidence of a general practice accepted as law." As confirmed by the ICJ in the *Nicaragua* case, custom in constituted by two elements, the objective one of "a general practice," and the subjective on "accepted as law," the so-called *opinion juris*. In the *Continental Shelf (Libya v. Malta)* case, the Court stated that the substance of customary international law must be "looked for primarily in the actual practice and *opinion juris* of States." The definition has given rise to some vexed theoretical questions, such as: How is it possible to make law by practice? And how can something be accepted as law before it has actually developed into law?

An Evaluation. Anthony D'Amato, "Why Do We Need Customary Law?" Written for this Handbook.

Many people feel a need to take the uncertainty out of international law. Let us for a moment suppose that, for every international dispute, there were a treaty provision exactly on point. Could we then say that all of international law has at last been written down, in a form that is ascertainable, retrievable, and definitive?

The answer—assuming the question makes sense—is a grudging "maybe." The written words that are presumably on point would still be subject to interpretation. That interpretation would take place against a context of underlying law. That underlying law would either be textual (i.e., other treaty provisions) or customary (unwritten law) or both—and part of the dispute would be, what law should be referred to in order to settle disputes over interpretation? But even if the treaty provision seems transparently clear, the disputing parties would still have to resort to an underlying customary law regarding the bindingness of the treaties, since treaties cannot provide for their own bindingness—it takes something outside the treaty to say that the treaty itself is binding. And along with the question of bindingness is the question whether events subsequent to the entering into force of the treaty somehow change or modify the treaty provisions. Or to put this point more dramatically, a minute after a treaty is signed, its provisions may seem to be clear; but fifty years after it is signed, things in the real world will have changed enough so that doubt is cast upon the continuing application of the old words of the treaty or whether those words should be reinterpreted in light of history. Moreover, subsequent events could even change the treaty provisions under what in international law is known as clausula rebus sic stantibus—the customary law of changed conditions.

The foregoing considerations are all on the assumption that the question makes sense. But does it really make sense to think that treaties can be so fine-meshed that they take into account all future disputes and provide for the unambiguous resolution of all of those future disputes? Consider the best statutory schemes in the most legally advanced countries: no matter what the statute says, the legislature meets more or less continuously and revises the statutes that seem to get out of touch with events. Moreover, a judicial system provides a continuous interpretation of the statutes, providing a gloss of the meaning of the fine-meshed statutory provisions. Is it not folly to expect that, in the international system, a set of treaties can provide for the resolution of all future disputes in the absence of legislatures and courts?

Well, why not have a Treaty Revision Commission in constant session, so as to keep updating the provisions in treaties? Alas, the Treaty Revision Commission usually will not know that it has a problem with a particular treaty until a dispute arises. But as soon as a dispute arises, then the parties will want to have their dispute settled on the basis of the existing treaty language, and not on the basis of new language proposed by the Commission.

But the most important objection to the idea of the assumption that we can have a fine-meshed system of international treaties capable of resolving every dispute is precisely that nearly all disputes that could be settled by resort to a clear treaty provision simply do not become disputes at all! Disputes tend to arise when a treaty provision does *not* cover the dispute, or when its coverage is ambiguous or otherwise contestable. But you might object, taking a cue from Jeremy Bentham's (never-realized) wish, that the more fine-meshed the treaty system, the fewer disputes—or at least, the fewer important disputes—will tend to arise. Alas, this wish is not realizable, at least if a long demonstration I made in 1983 of the concept is sound (and so far, no one has contested it).* I believe I was successful in showing at that time that real-world variety outpaces any conceivable attempt by legislators to subsume it under fine-meshed legislation. That real-world variety results in a race between events and statutes, each trying to catch up with the latter, a process that if left to itself results in grotesque statutory schemes such as the present Internal Revenue Code and its accompanying Regulations.

* See Anthony D'Amato, Legal Uncertainty, 71 Calif. L. Rev. 1, 4–8 (1983).

The most that a detailed statute can do is substitute statutory language for what otherwise would be resort to the underlying common law—in effect, making a change in the material the judge must read (code provisions instead of judicial decisions), but without materially affecting one's ability to order one's affairs or predict the outcome of future disputes. Indeed, the civil law tradition of Continental European countries is a large exemplary demonstration of this thesis. European law is no more predictable or certain than the law in common-law countries, despite the presence in the European systems of what appear to be detailed, fine-meshed codes.

Thus, there is no getting away from customary international law even as treaties become more refined and comprehensive. For the ultimate power of customary international law is that it binds all states irrespective of their consent to specific rules. Thus it constitutes a default law—a law that applies to every dispute whenever a more specific treaty provision does not (for whatever reason of interpretation or clausula rebus sic stantibus) provide a sufficiently clear text to settle the dispute. There is no source of international law other than customary law that provides this kind of comprehensive default rules.

In the next section, W. Michael Reisman focuses on "incidents" as providing the basic precedents that incorporate and develop international customary norms. I wholly endorse Professor Reisman's arguments insofar as they apply to what has traditionally been called the "practice" component of international customary law. As I have advised law review editors on many occasions, the "case note" in international law should really be the "incident note." For what forms the real basis for general international law applicable to all states—that is, for customary international law—is not the occasional judicial decision but rather the typical "incident" that embodies the states' own *resolution of international claim-conflicts*. The real-world "incident" is the full equivalent of a binding judicial decision in domestic law; it embodies the pragmatic resolution of a conflict in the international system by the state actors who are most concerned with the particular incident in question, and hence it has precedential value in customary law.* Even its value is pragmatic, for as Professor Reisman argues, the kinds of results states have previously achieved in resolving their conflicts of claims have profound instructional value for resolving the present situation. "Law" in this instructional sense is an application of the trite saying, "there's no use re-inventing the wheel." But it is even more than that. Once the wheel is invented, new technology takes the invention of the wheel into account, so that, in another common saying, "there's no going back." Similarly, in international law, when the ribbons are tied on one "incident," future incidents will never be quite the same. Future incidents

---

* I also add, on these occasions, that researching an international incident is a lot more fun, and a lot more creative, than the rather sterile job of parsing a given judicial decision. The result is that an analysis of an international law "incident" will have a lasting value for practitioners and scholars, in contrast to the typical "case note" that is hardly ever read.

will be played out in light of the former incident. Thus there are two reasons for counting "incidents" as formative of customary international law: that they point the way to a resolution that has already "worked" in the past, and that their very position in the history of the development of international customary law has restructured all future reasonable expectations in light of the way they were in fact resolved.

The argument I made previously, that customary international law applies to states irrespective of their consent, follows from treating international "incidents" the same way domestic law treats precedents. If you have a domestic-law case, the court will cite prior cases *in which you played absolutely no part*. This prior law was created without your consent, and now it is binding upon you. What has happened is that you have not consented to the rules of law as they were developed in prior cases; instead you have consented to the *process* of common-law development of legal rules. Similarly, states do not consent to the specific rules of customary law, but only to the "metarule" of customary law formation. There are many proofs of this proposition. For example, customary rules immediately bind new states who come into existence in the international system, yet no state coming into existence has ever, in the history of international law, announced its non-consent to some of the norms of international law. No new state has ever felt entitled to "pick and choose" among the existing norms of custom. Indeed, new states find it to their immense advantage to accept all the rules of the system, because among those rules are basic rules that guarantee to the new state the things it wants most of all—secure borders and acceptance as an equal into the international community. To attempt to pick and choose from among the existing norms of international law would be to risk being declared a non-state or an outlaw state, and no new state has ever wished to be placed in such a position.

Custom, treaty interpretation, general principles of international law—all are metarules. They are rules about rules. But these metarules were not handed down on a stone tablet from a mountaintop. They are not written in granite.* Just like the regular rules, the metarules have also arisen out of the practice of states. They are inferred from the way that states deal with the regular rules.

So, what then is custom? I believe that there is a determinate answer to this question, but it is not one that is reducible to a sentence or a sound byte. Rather, the ascertainment of a customary rule of international law requires a certain amount of professional training. The bad news is that there are no short cuts, but that's also the good news. You have to develop an expertise, but once you develop it, you will have it and and can put it to professional use. It will give you an advantage, but it's the right kind of advantage—one that is attained not by money or social class or privilege but by personal effort.

---

* And if I were saying this in the classroom, I would find it impossible to resist adding one of my terrible puns—"Nor should they be taken for granite."

The training I'm talking about would consist of three tasks. First, one should undertake an unhurried perusal of the nature of customary law as it has developed down to the present day, determining for oneself the context in which questions of custom arise and the questions arising from that context that we should ask of any coherent theory of custom. Second, one should engage in some practice, which can take the form of a research paper or a brief that argues for or against an alleged rule of custom—one that involves doing the library work and the thinking that is needed to prove one's case. Third, one should think through the connections between the first and second tasks, calibrating the conclusions in the first task against the conclusions reached in the second task. We should engage in what the philosopher Nelson Goodman called the "delicate process of making mutual adjustments between rules and accepted inferences."

Incidents. W. Michael Reisman, "International Incidents: Introduction to a New Genre in the Study of International Law" 10 Yale J. Int'l L. 1 (1984).

Students of international law, like their domestic counterparts, frequently tend to define decisions in terms of the institutions rendering them. In the domestic law systems of Western Europe and North America, courts, for historical reasons, have been deemed to be the authoritative appliers of the law. Hence legal decisions are defined essentially as the handicraft of those courts. Insofar as there is a congruence between actual political power in the community and the authority of courts, that focus can provide a cogent indicator of decisions. In fact, such a congruence is rarely perfect, and the identification of judgments as decisions in a larger sense frequently leads to the distortions characteristic of much academic law.

Indeed, even in effectively organized legal systems, which are characterized by a general convergence of authority and control, key parts of "book law" may fail to approximate the actual normative expectations of elites. This may occur for two major reasons, inherent in the very character of law: discrepancies between myth system and operational code and the differential rates of decay of text and context. People who seek legal advice plainly require it with regard to both the myth system and the operational code: myth system because it is applied in part by some control institutions, operational code because it is applied by others. Myth system is readily retrievable through conventional research in the formal repositories of law. Operational code, in contrast, must be sought in elite behavior.

Even if there is little divergence between myth system and operational code, the differing rate of decay of text and context may limit the usefulness of formal sources of law. The proverbial decrees of the Medes and the Persians still exist; the context in which they were created and in which they had legal relevance is gone. Whether a particular exercise of lawmaking seeks to stabilize or change a situation, if it is concerned not with ornamenting myth but with doing what it says it is doing, there must be a minimum congruence between the socio-political context prevailing at the time and the socio-political presumptions of the legislation. Once legislation is expressed in relatively enduring textual form, however, its rate of decay is minimal, while the rate of decay of the environing socio-political situation will always be greater and may, indeed, be extremely rapid.

Where fidelity to text acquires in itself a symbolic political value, texts whose literal congruence with the socio-political situation is less than when they were created may misguide those who would rely on them. At the very least, those who would rely on them may need a validation technique for determining their degree of accuracy. Courts may serve this purpose, but if they themselves and the ambit of their jurisdiction are creatures of legislation, a functional and non-institutional test is required.

In the international arena, the law is applied, for the most part, through a variety of informal channels, and rarely benefits from formal appraisal by a court or tribunal. The International Court, with its usual load of two or three cases per year, and public international arbitral tribunals, with scarcely more than that, can hardly be deemed to represent international decision.

Despite the relative inactivity of these institutions, many international scholars continue to view them as the virtual apotheosis and most authoritative expression of international law. The deference given ad hoc arbitral tribunals is symptomatic of this general problem and sometimes takes the most extraordinary form. A tribunal established by one party, in the absence of the other, and composed of a single person, let us say a professor of international law, is treated by other scholars as an authoritative oracle of international law. At the same time, commentators who defer to such an award will insist that a contrary General Assembly vote, supported by virtually every member state, is not indicative of international law but is only a "recommendation."

There are, to be sure, certain methodological advantages in using the international case as an epistemic unit. Part of the attraction lies in its relative simplicity, economy, and availability. Once there is fundamental agreement among scholars that the case is an epistemic unit, there need be no detailed investigation of factual material outside of the case, for the case carries its own authoritative factual statement. Alternative methods of research could require extensive field work or culling through thousands of pages of documents of uneven probative value, in order to determine what the decision actually was. A case presents that decision in a neat "bite-sized" and easily digestible package, creating in the process an illusion of consensus about the underlying events that probably does not exist.

"Stipulating" the facts permits students of this epistemic unit to get on with discussions of the law, freed from complicating political issues. For those who confuse clerical tidiness with scientific method, there is the ecstasy of imagining that the case method is "scientific," an enthusiasm apparently animating many of the consumers of Langdell's work. And of course, there is the latent drive among all who have been given professional legal training to view things in terms of courts. Outside of the United States, admiration for the stability and achievements of the American political-legal system leads many scholars to seek to adopt the American legal style, as if the method of observation can bring about qualitative changes in the things observed.

Yielding to these attractions, contemporary international legal science has adopted a decisional unit that is convenient for scholars but ill-tooled for the subject matter. It is reminiscent of the familiar story of a man, out walking one night on a street in Vienna, who happens on another well-dressed and plainly sober citizen who is crawling about on all fours in the light cast by a street lamp. Naturally, the first fellow stops to find out if there is something wrong. When the man on the ground explains that he has lost his watch, the passerby offers to help him find it and asks exactly where it fell. "Back there," the man on the ground motions, pointing into the darkness on the other side of the street. "Then why aren't you looking there?" the first fellow asks in exasperation. "Because," the man on the ground explains as if it were perfectly obvious, "it's dark over there and I can't see. But here it's light."

The transposition of the case unit to the international arena has permitted international lawyers to dwell in a comforting pool of light. Yet much of the resulting international legal description is patently out of step with elite expectations. The discrepancy is so painfully obvious that, outside the small circle of international lawyers, it brings discredit upon the very notion of international law. An alternative that would take account of the limited cogency in the international arena of the case as an epistemic unit would develop an additional unit which might be referred to generically as the "incident." I define an "incident" as an overt conflict between two or more actors in the international system. It must be perceived as such by other key actors and resolved in some nonjudicial fashion. Finally, and of critical importance, its resolution must provide some indications of what elites in a variety of effective processes consider to be acceptable behavior. Though the incident is "resolved" in a factual if not authoritative sense, without the judicial imprimatur which routinely indicates law in domestic settings, the incident may often be a more reliable indicator of international law than are codes or case law.* Among the formidable challenges posed by this

---

* Note that the inquiry being proposed here is quite different from the routine examination of "practice" in international law. That inquiry seeks to establish the existence of a bilateral or general norm or custom, by examining, ostensibly, a broad pattern of practice of states. There are many intellectual difficulties with the inquiry into practice. Neither the volume nor the degree of uniformity of practice required has ever been stated with precision. Moreover, examinations of practice do not control for the variable of power. They do not seek to identify who, among a large cast of characters, is effective. The incident, in contrast, is not based on a large volume or flow of supposedly "uniform" events, but instead takes a single critical event as a prism through which the reactions of elites to particular behavior may be examined and assessed as an indication of their views of law.

proposal is the development of criteria by which incidents are to be selected. Napoleon's remark that history is a collection of lies we all agree upon has an especially wicked relevance when we consider as a source of history the recital of the facts contained in judicial opinions. The statement of "relevant" facts determined by a court would rarely satisfy a historian; indeed, what the court leaves out is often of most interest to the student of politics and history. Consider a few examples.

The Schooner Exchange judgment of Chief Justice Marshall is usually cited as the cornerstone for the doctrine that the public acts of foreign governments will not be reviewed by the courts of another state even if the effects of the act are felt in that other state. Somehow the judgment never states the extraordinary fact that the case was being decided against the background of the War of 1812, in which the British had set fire to Washington. France, the real defendant, was the only ally of the United States. It seems most unlikely under these circumstances that any United States court would have risked imperiling that relationship.

In the Corfu Channel Case (United Kingdom v. Albania), the International Court somehow never mentions the fact that the Greek Civil War was under way, that the United Kingdom was a major supporter of the Royalist cause, and that Albania, as a proxy for another superpower, was supporting the Communist insurgency. The presence of the British ships in the Straits of Corfu unquestionably constituted a manifest military communication to the Albanians and others about the limits of British tolerance, the susceptibility of Albania to coastal attacks, and the capacity of the British fleet to project its force into that arena.

The point need not be belabored. What these cases demonstrate is that there is no authoritative institution to decree or stipulate that the facts which have been assembled in judgments meet the standards of historical accuracy.

Indeed, legal science is often impatient to finish with "the facts" and to get on with "the law." First instance factual determinations are only rarely reviewed. Subsequent instances simplify the facts even further. In American legal education, the tendency of first-year students to seek to learn more about the facts of the case is often characterized as a frivolous interest; students are urged to get on with the legal analysis.

There are some cogent reasons for this cultivated astigmatism. Every science develops its own specialized lens in order to focus more sharply and intensively on that aspect of life of interest to it. The particular focus of legal science distinguishes it from history and sociology and does, indeed, permit it to concentrate more effectively on the normative or policy dimensions of problems. But sometimes, sticky political problems or issues can be concealed under a bare factual statement and the infinitely obscurantist potentialities of legal language. These selective abbreviations, whatever their intra-disciplinary justification, inevitably produce a legal version of the facts which historians and political advisers often see as, at best, thin and brittle, and, at worst, caricatures of what actually transpired. Since a fuller and more accurate understanding of the facts is indispensable to ascertaining what was actually decided, the versions of the facts often presented by judges may undermine the effectiveness of the predictive function of case law.

The sporadic fashion in which the facts become available in incidents presents a special problem. Many facts are concealed for years or even generations. The attack on Pearl Harbor, for example, could not be described with any accuracy until the archives in all the relevant capitals were at last made accessible to historians. It took a generation for scholars to provide a comprehensive picture that could demonstrate the incorrectness of many of their initial conclusions about the incident. Similarly, the extent of U.S. involvement in the overthrow of the Mossadegh government in Iran and the reinstallation of the Pahlavi dynasty in 1953 was not established until years later.

This is not a problem unique to incidents. In some cases, national courts refuse to exercise jurisdiction because information indispensable to judgment cannot be secured. In international law, judgments of the ICJ may be reopened and revised on the basis of new facts or new information (Article 61 of the Court's Statute). If anything, the problem is considerably less severe in the study of incidents. The student of incidents, it will be recalled, is not involved in judging the lawfulness of the behavior of actors in the incident concerned, but rather evaluates the reactions of other relevant actors and, through those reactions, the subjective conceptions of right and/or tolerable behavior entertained by those other actors. Hence what is important in this exercise is not so much what happened as what effective elites think happened and how they react.

A related practical difficulty in constructing the genre of incidents is the question of boundaries: where does a particular incident begin and where does it end? A case presupposes a consensus that critical events begin and end at some point. An incident is not bounded with such precision. Because of this, there is some question as to when it ends, if at all. Territorial losses, for example, may be viewed by the party securing acquisition as completed incidents, with title consolidated by adverse possession. But the losing party may continue to view the lost territories as its own and dream and plan for their repatriation. Hence the two parties to an incident may have diametrically opposite conceptions of when the incident ended. It is the observer of the incident who must, in effect, establish boundaries in time. Those boundaries are determined primarily by the norms the observer chooses to examine.

In conclusion, an incident genre whose practitioners continue to update and correct the expression of the code of international law is required. If it is established and adopted (and adapted) by a number of other scholars, it can ultimately yield an abundant literature of international appraisal, richer than the limited number of cases decided by courts, more representative of actual decision trends, more indicative of the political context in which decisions are taken and implemented and, most importantly, more accurate in expressing international normative expectations.

Custom and Force. Anthony Clark Arend, "International Law and the Preemptive Use of Military Force" The Washington Quarterly 89 (2003).

As international law relating to the recourse to force developed over the centuries and culminated in the UN Charter, the main purpose of the law was to address conventional threats posed by conventional actors: states. Both weapons of mass destruction (WMD) and terrorism pose threats unanticipated by traditional international law. When the charter was adopted in 1945, its framers sought to prevent the types of conflict that had precipitated World War II—circumstances in which regular armies engaged in clear, overt acts of aggression against other states. As a consequence, Article 2(4) prohibits the threat and use of force by states against states, and Article 51 acknowledges a state's inherent right of self-defense if an armed attack occurs. Even if UN Charter provisions are understood in light of customary international law allowing anticipatory self-defense, the charter's focus is still on states using force the conventional way.

Neither WMD nor terrorist actors were envisioned in this framework. The three main WMD types—chemical, biological, and nuclear—could not have seriously been on the mind of the delegates while they were drafting the UN Charter. Even though chemical weapons had been used during World War I, they had not proven to be particularly militarily useful and, in any case, were not used in any significant way as an instrument of war in World War II. The very idea of nuclear weapons was a carefully guarded secret until August 1945 and thus could not have figured into the deliberations on the charter in the spring of 1945. Indeed, as John Foster Dulles would later observe, the UN Charter was a "pre-atomic" document. Terrorism, although certainly not a recent phenomenon, was not addressed in traditional international law relating to the recourse to force. Prior to the twentieth century, customary international law dealt with state actors. Even major multilateral treaties that related to use-of-force issues, such as the League of Nations Covenant, the Kellogg–Briand Pact of 1928, as well as the UN Charter, addressed their provisions only to states.

It is precisely in this lacuna in international law that the problem lies. WMD and terrorism can strike at states in ways that customary international law did not address. Underlying international law dealing with the recourse to force is the principle that states have a right to use force to defend themselves effectively. When conventional troops prepare to commit an act of aggression, the basic criteria of *Caroline** would

---

* [Emerging from a 1837 incident, the criteria oblige a state asserting self-defense to demonstrate its "necessity ... as instant, overwhelming, and leaving no choice of means, and no moment for deliberation."—Eds.]

seem to make sense. The soon-to-be aggressor would be taking enough overt actions, and the attack itself would require mobilization, which would give the victim enough lead time.

Both WMD and terrorism, however, are different. It can be very difficult to determine whether a state possesses WMD, and by the time its use is imminent, it could be extremely difficult for a state to mount an effective defense. Similarly, terrorists use tactics that may make it all but impossible to detect an action until it is well underway or even finished. As a consequence, it could be argued that it would make more sense to target known WMD facilities or known terrorist camps or training areas long in advance of an imminent attack if the goal is to preserve the state's right to effective self-defense.

From a legal perspective, there is great difficulty with this relaxation of the Caroline criterion of necessity. Where does one draw the line? If imminence is no longer going to be a prerequisite for preemptive force, what is? With respect to WMD, would it be simple possession of such weapons? Such an approach is especially problematic. Given the current realities in the international system, India would be able to use force against Pakistan, and vice versa. Many states could target the United States, Great Britain, France, China, and Russia.

What about hostile intent as a criterion? Perhaps it could be argued that, if the state that possessed these weapons had hostile intent toward other states, this would justify preemption. But, a hostile-intent approach could be even more permissive. It could be claimed that preemptive force would be justified if a state were in the early stages of developing a nuclear weapons program—long before actual possession. In a sense, Israel was making this kind of claim when it struck the Osirak reactor in 1981, but this extremely permissive approach was clearly rejected by the Security Council.

What would be the standard for terrorism? If there is a group such as Al Qaeda that has been committing a series of attacks against the United States, preemption is not really at issue. Rather, the United States and its allies are simply engaging in standard self-defense against an ongoing, armed attack. The problem would present itself if there were a group that had not yet committed an action but seemed likely to act at some point in the future. Short of an imminent attack, when would a state lawfully be able to preempt that group?

So, here is the difficulty. Although it is true that contemporary international law dealing with the recourse to force in self-defense does not adequately address the problem of WMD and terrorism, no clear legal standard has yet emerged to determine when preemptive force would be permissible in such cases. Some scholars have suggested standards, but it does not seem that either treaty law or custom has yet to endorse one.

Custom and Torture. A. Mark Weisburd, "Customary International Law and Torture: The Case of India" 2 Chi. J. Int'l L. 81 (2001).

The most recent report of the current Special Rapporteur on Torture for the Commission on Human Rights includes the following paragraph relating to India:

> By letter dated 19 November 1999, the Special Rapporteur advised the Government that he had received information alleging routine torture in detention facilities throughout the country. The police and jailers allegedly torture or ill-treat new prisoners to obtain money and personal articles. Police are reported to torture detainees frequently during custodial detention.

Similarly, the US Department of State in February, 2000, reported regarding India as follows:

> The law prohibits torture, and confessions extracted by force are generally inadmissible in court; however, torture is common throughout the country, and authorities often use torture during interrogations. In other instances, they torture detainees to extort money and sometimes as summary punishment...
>
> The UN Special Rapporteur on Torture noted in 1997 that methods of torture included beatings, rape, crushing the leg muscles with a wooden roller, burning with heated objects, and electric shocks. Because many alleged torture victims die in custody, and others are afraid to speak out, there are few firsthand accounts, although marks of torture often have been found on the bodies of deceased detainees. The UN Special Rapporteurs on Torture and on Extrajudicial Killings renewed their requests to visit during the year, but the Government did not permit them to do so.
>
> The prevalence of torture by police in detention facilities throughout the country is borne out by the number of cases of deaths in police custody... Although police officers are subject to prosecution for such offenses under Section 302 of the Penal Code, the Government often fails to hold them accountable.

The overall picture for India with regard to torture is not good. Although its internal law has been interpreted as forbidding torture—and in fact contains provisions aimed at preventing it—these provisions are not enforced, and their effect is lessened by the operation of other enactments. In fact, police torture is common.

In evaluating the international legal standing of a practice, it is of course not enough to determine the behavior of one state. The reaction of other states to that behavior is at least as important. However, in the case of torture in India, other states appear to take little public interest in the matter, other than with respect to some incidents in connection with separatist violence. From 1990 on, no mention is made in any of the volumes of *The Australian Year Book of International Law*, *The British Year Book of International Law*, *The Canadian Yearbook of International Law*, or *The South African Yearbook of International Law* regarding

India's record of torture, even though each of these publications provides considerable detail regarding the actions take by governments of each of these states as those actions bear on questions of international law.

The attitude of the United States toward torture in India is not easily characterized. In recent years the United States has not seriously criticized India's apparent indifference to the routine use of torture by its law enforcement officers. Public statements by US officials stress the democratic character of Indian political system, and simply do not address the human rights violations committed by the police in India.

The foregoing account makes clear 1) that Indian police officers regularly torture persons in their custody; 2) that this behavior, though contrary to Indian law and condemned by Indian courts, seems to be tolerated by leading government officials (or in any case the suppression of this behavior is not treated as a matter of high priority); 3) that at least in the past India has denied the applicability of customary international law to the behavior of its officials; and 4) that other states, though calling attention to India's behavior, have apparently made no public protest regarding this endemic torture, but rather have focused on the admittedly democratic character of the Indian government. What is the impact of these observations on any putative rule of international law forbidding official torture?

Preliminarily, it is clear that there can be any doubt as to the answer to this question only as regards customary international law. To the extent that India's treaty obligations preclude official torture, its record in this area demonstrates that it has violated those obligations. Most obviously, India is in almost continuous violation of Article 7 of the International Covenant on Civil and Political Rights. Indeed, its behavior in this regard has drawn the attention of the expert body that reviews the reports required by that Covenant.

But what impact does India's behavior have on customary international law? How does it affect arguments that torture is contrary to the international legal obligations of states not parties to any treaty forbidding torture?

One answer to this question would start with the assumption that customary international law is created by states' behavior. More specifically, this approach would inquire whether agents of any significant number of states regularly used torture in such a way that their political superiors could be presumed to be aware of the practice. If a given state could be said at least to acquiesce in the use of torture by its servants, it would also be relevant to know how other states reacted to that situation. On this view, behavior in which large numbers of states engaged and which evoked no significant reaction from other states could not be said to violate customary law. Necessarily therefore, any putative prohibition on the behavior could not be of *jus cogens* status. The sorts of evidence of customary international law on which the Special Rapporteur and the American Law Institute relied would not be irrelevant—they could usefully illuminate ambiguous cases—but such evidence would not control in the face of proof of actual practice at variance with the thrust of non-binding resolutions, International Law Commission drafts, and so on.

If this approach were followed, India's practice would seem to make it very difficult to argue that official torture violates customary international—the government of a country comprising approximately one-sixth of the population of world tolerates widespread and widely-reported torture by its police. This situation, moreover, has generated little international criticism of the state in question, and no international sanctions. Further, Indian use of torture is not new, but has taken place throughout the period during which many claimed that a prohibition against torture was becoming part of customary international law.

In short, there is good reason to doubt that international law can be unaffected by an important state's refusal both to conform its behavior to a putative rule of law or to accept that international law could properly bind it regarding the matter. Equally, it is doubtful that a rule, the violation of which by one state in concrete cases is simply ignored by other states, could fairly be described as a "rule" of customary law. India's tolerance of official torture and other states' indifference to the practice thus combine to severely weaken any argument that torture is a violation of customary international law.

A Brief Reply. Anthony D'Amato, "Custom and Treaty: A Response to Professor Weisburd," 21 Vanderbilt Journal International Law 459 (1988).

Nearly all international scholars agree that official torture is prohibited by international law. Yet Professor Mark Weisburd does us a service in forcing us to rethink the conventional wisdom.

He writes that torture in Indian prisons "seems to be tolerated by leading government officials." But he admits that "the practice is contrary to Indian law and condemned by Indian courts." Is he claiming that the judges on Indian courts are *not* government officials? Moreover, why does he suggest that a practice that "seems to be tolerated" by some officials is worthy of more consideration than that same practice being "condemned" by other officials?

Professor Weisburd and I have debated this question before. I now quote portions of my article that was published in 1988 and cited above:

Governments do not admit torturing people; they invariably deny that it happens. Nor do they proclaim that any torture within their territory is legally permissible. And they certainly do not raise it to the level of a legal principle that would make torture legal for all states under international law.

The opposite of this was true of medieval state practice. Governments then openly engaged in torture. So did the Church and the medical profession. Governments said publicly that torture brought out the truth. The Inquisitors added that if the tortured person was innocent he was being done a favor by being sent directly to heaven, while if he was guilty he was simply getting a preview of hell. Even doctors engaged in tortuous medical treatment with red-hot instruments, which was widely believed to cleanse the soul and cast out devils (who presumably could not stand the heat). If this were 1488 instead of 1988, I would have to concede to Professor Weisburd that state practice had given rise to a customary international rule allowing torture.

I believe that the torture that occurs in prisons in many countries today is done surreptitiously and without a claim of right or legality. States hide it, cover it up, and minimize it. These are indicia of violations of law and not assertions of legality.

Chapter 4

THE IDENTITY AND ROLE OF THE STATE

Editors' introduction: Even as the effectiveness of state sovereignty is debated in today's globalized world, states remain the primary authors of international law. Consequently, the rules that define statehood and lay out the broad rights and responsibilities of states are written to enhance the stability of the international system. While reviewing the chapter, the reader might consider the stabilizing function of those rules and the ways they serve to safeguard the integrity of the state system. We return to contemporary challenges to the state system, such as economic globalization, in later chapters.

A. PERSONALITY

Classic Conception. Lassa Oppenheim, *International Law: A Treatise* (2nd ed., 1912), pp. 107–15.*

The conception of International Persons is derived from the conception of the Law of Nations. As this law is the body of rules which the civilized States consider legally binding in their intercourse, every State which belongs to the civilized States, and is, therefore, a member of the Family of Nations, is an International Person. Sovereign States exclusively are International Persons—i.e. subjects of International Law.

In contradistinction to Sovereign States which are real, there are also apparent, but not real, International Persons—namely, Confederations of States, insurgents recognized as a belligerent Power in a civil war, and the Holy See. All these are not real subjects of International Law, but in some points are treated as though they were International Persons, without thereby becoming members of the Family of Nations.

It must be specially mentioned that the character of a subject of the Law of Nations and of an International Person can be attributed neither to monarchs, diplomatic envoys, private individuals, or churches, nor to

---

* [Oppenheim's book is generally acknowledged as the most influential treatise on international law in the twentieth century.—Eds.]

chartered companies, nations, or races after the loss of their State (as, for instance, the Jews or the Poles), and organized wandering tribes.

A State proper—in contradistinction to so-called Colonial States—is in existence when a people is settled in a country under its own Sovereign Government. The conditions which must obtain for the existence of a State are therefore four:

> There must, first, be a people. A people is an aggregate of individuals of both sexes who live together as a community in spite of the fact that they may belong to different races or creeds, or be of different color.
>
> There must, secondly, be a country in which the people has settled down. A wandering people, such as the Jews were whilst in the desert for forty years before their conquest of the Holy Land, is not a State. But it matters not whether the country is small or large; it may consist, as with City States, of one town only.
>
> There must, thirdly, be a Government—that is, one or more persons who are the representatives of the people and rule according to the law of the land. An anarchistic community is not a State.
>
> There must, fourthly and lastly, be a Sovereign Government. Sovereignty is supreme authority, an authority which is independent of any other earthly authority. Sovereignty in the strict and narrowest sense of the term includes, therefore, independence all round, within and without the borders of the country.

The term Sovereignty was introduced into political science by Bodin in his celebrated work, "De la republique," which appeared in 1577. Before Bodin, at the end of the Middle Ages, the word sovereign was used in France for an authority, political or other, which had no other authority above itself. Thus the highest courts were called Cours Souverains. Bodin, however, gave quite a new meaning to the old conception. Being under the influence and in favor of the policy of centralization initiated by Louis XI of France (1461–1483), the founder of French absolutism, he defined sovereignty as "the absolute and perpetual power within a State." Such power is the supreme power within a State without any restriction whatever except the Commandments of God and the Law of Nature. No constitution can limit sovereignty, which is an attribute of the king in a monarchy and of the people in a democracy. A Sovereign is above positive law. A contract only is binding upon the Sovereign, because the Law of Nature commands that a contract shall be binding.

The conception of sovereignty thus introduced was at once accepted by writers on politics of the sixteenth century, but the majority of these writers taught that sovereignty could be restricted by a constitution and by positive law. Thus at once a somewhat weaker conception of sovereignty than that of Bodin made its appearance. On the other hand, in the seventeenth century, Hobbes went even beyond Bodin, maintaining that a Sovereign was not bound by anything and had a right over everything, even over religion. Whereas a good many publicists followed

Hobbes, others, especially Pufendorf, denied, in contradistinction to Hobbes, that sovereignty includes omnipotence. According to Pufendorf, sovereignty is the supreme power in a State, but not absolute power, and sovereignty may well be Constitutionally restricted. Yet in spite of all the differences in defining sovereignty, all authors of the sixteenth and seventeenth centuries agree that sovereignty is indivisible and contains the centralization of all power in the hands of the Sovereign, whether a monarch or the people itself in a republic.

Normative Critique. Virginia Black, "A Normative Critique of State Personality," from *Why Nations Find it Hard to be Good to Each Other*, 4 *Vera Lex* 7 (1983–84).

Hugo Grotius held to a doctrine sometimes called "parallelism." Since individual persons can be virtuous and just, reasonable, dutiful and sociable, keep contracts and obey laws, then corporate organizations like the state can also be virtuous, reasonable and just, can be sociable, obey laws, conform to the same duties as individuals, etc. It seems that Grotius thought such analogous predication an exemplary condition for international peace. As civil law regards and regulates the rights and interests of persons, so should international law regard and regulate the rights and interests of nations. This doctrine of transferable virtue, transferring "up" to a complex organ from a less complex organ—from persons' interactions to nations' interactions—may find its philosophic origin in Plato who thought justice in the state was the same as justice in the person, only on a grander scale.

But justice within the state cannot be the same as justice among states. There is a natural law that serious wrong should be redressed. A person goes to court. Where does a nation go when it believes it has suffered serious wrong? Perhaps it wages a just war. Is a just war, by any stretch of imagination, to be compared to a day in court?

I think that the non-transferability of personal action to state action lies in certain assumptions and inferences. Predictions in the premises harbor implicit ideas about the state; these ideas are non-referring and imprecise and so they are incorrectly applied. In short, we carry around a false understanding of what nations are, what are their sustaining attributes, and how upon the basis of these attributes nations are necessitated to "act" in the world.

Perhaps out of man's desire for permanence, he grants the state a monopoly of power to maintain and defend itself; as a consequence the state's necessary and sufficient function is to coerce. The state must therefore regard in a lesser light all other impositions except as they sustain or augment this condition of power. The state is like no other conglomerate. Born out of the human passion for unity and the fear of attack, it is sui generis.

Why are personal virtues and the good actions that they entail not readily transferable to "virtuous actions" among states? Why do the principled, prudent or kindly acts of persons not readily find a similar moral intelligence in nations vis-a-vis their interactions? Treaties are broken. Promised assistance is withdrawn. Barriers to trade are erected. The civil law that regulates the peace within brings no peace without, for civil law, by definition, is non-extendible. Jural decisions that resolve domestic conflict fail utterly to resolve international conflict. No court would even try to adjudicate a vital conflict between states of unequal powers with any prospect of enforcement. A summons to "appear in court" is too foolish to think about. What, then, is the difference between person and nations?

(1) Individuals have one mind: they show unity of consciousness, will, purpose. This imparts meaning and stability to their beliefs so that, acting in light of this meaning, they know when their purposes are effected. Since individuals discern and evaluate situations uniquely, they may assess or try to alter results with good success. Hence they can discriminatingly reject or re-adapt means and methods while formulating their own time frames for calling gains or losses or for shifting "costs" from one preference to another.

(2) When singleness of mind stands behind individuals' values and the meanings persons place on things, effective motivation results. This coincidence of thought, value, drive and action, we call personal freedom. Measuring and using their own resources, persons' discrete perceptions, energies, intentions, and memories can move their will consistently toward a desired end. Successful action, in turn, reinforces useful habituation.

(3) Persons enjoy sentience, empathy, appetitus socialis to shape and forward their motivations toward avoiding the injury of others, and toward benefiting them as well. "Here," said David Hume, "is the difference between kingdoms and individuals. Human nature cannot by any means subsist without the association of individuals. But nations can subsist without intercourse." Nations lack these affectional wellsprings of moral action, and so they have little incentive—nor do they need—to be good to each other. In the long and short run, it is often not clear to them what they gain by it. Officials can break promises, lie, or even innocently falsify, because personal accountability and shame do not exist with states. Only moral persons enjoy a conscience.

(4) Importantly, individuals are shaped by social influence. Social norms and moral and religious teachings educate them. Law guides them. Enforcements restrain them. When these influences exert themselves upon persons' unitary mind and feeling, the product can, in rough measure, be known. Because persons, being free, can respond intelligently in light of these influences in a kind of self-creating spiral, they themselves can use, evaluate, modify, or even disregard the effects upon them of social influences. Reciprocal adaptation results between individuals and the social environment. Since regular reciprocal adaptation reinforces customs, regularities, and rules, interpersonal expectations become habituated. This makes for civil order. Under these conditions of

internal accord, personal virtue develops and the moral actions of individuals can emerge.

Nations enjoy none of these qualities and relations of social intelligence—neither personal freedom, meaning, nor motivation. Unlike individuals, nations lack a natural unity of mind, feeling, and continuity of will. They suffer no pain. They have no incentive to develop virtue. Education, critical thinking, parental modeling, moral or religious suasion—none of these non-responding sensors influences the state toward intelligent habits of action. Law does not dependably deter the state. Enforcements by other nations leave the state not constrained but afraid. How, then, can the state "know" when it has acted wisely or well? If except by fictional extension there is no such thing as a "national will," then the moral and motivational similarities presumed to exist between nations and persons when, say, both are thought to be just or to engage in just interactions, are a vague illusion.

How, then, can we expect association between nations to parallel the delicate adjustments which free persons arrange among themselves, or to submit to universal principles of common good that benefit all nations fairly? The disanalogy is outstanding.

Not all "national acts" are, however, inconceivable. Prisoners can be exchanged between nations. Trade boycotts can work and tariffs can be laid down or lifted by negotiation. States can award money remuneration for damage to the property of another. The judgment of a world court may be listened to if facilitating opinions are in place, if no nation's vital interests are wronged, and if participating parties see gain to themselves. Free trade exchanges work wonderfully between nations, but of course these are the actions of persons and their associations left unfettered by the state.

Let us be clear, though, that in repudiating moral parallelism we are not falling into Hobbes' idea of the state an absolute and aggressive sovereign power. The state must always be under law. In defining persons as fearful, selfish, artificial person, Hobbes commits the same error of personalization. The difference between Hobbes and Grotius lies in their view of human nature which is then analogized upon how states act, or should act, toward one another.

We can think of a world society, however, if we mean by this that other peoples, no matter from what nation, deserve our aid and friendship, respect and non-violation by individuals differs in every way from the idea of a world of their rights and interests. Moral universalism realized wide legislative sovereign with enforcement powers or from the notion that the parameters of interstate relations are fashioned upon the parameters of the natural moral inclinations or sociability of man.

B. NATIONALITY

Statelessness. Paul Weis, *Nationality and Statelessness in International Law* (1979), excerpt.

International law confers, in general, rights and obligations on States. International law does not, therefore, directly confer nationality on or withdraw it from individuals. It follows, however, from the rights and duties of States that they are bound by international law to behave in a certain manner when regulating questions of nationality. From the general rules of international law governing the relations between States, a few rules can be derived which limit the freedom of States to confer or withdraw their nationality. While questions of nationality are normally determined by municipal law, this legislative competence of States does not amount to omnipotence. The rules of customary international law relating to nationality are mainly indirect rules, derived from the rules governing the relations between States, particularly from those relating to State jurisdiction; one can, therefore, speak only of a so-called international law of nationality. These rules are mainly negative rules, restricting the freedom of States to confer or withdraw nationality.

There are no rules of customary international law which impose a duty on States to confer their nationality on certain individuals at birth. In so far as rules of international law relating to acquisition of nationality exist, they concern acquisition subsequent to birth, that is, by naturalization in the wider sense. There is no rule of international law which restricts the right of States to grant naturalization in the narrower sense, that is, the conferment of nationality by a formal act to persons residing in its territory, on application, or which stipulates a prior period of residence. The naturalization of persons residing abroad requires, however, recognition by the State of residence in order to have legal effect there. The conditions for naturalization are determined by municipal law. International law, while requiring the existence of personal ties, a social fact of attachment, between naturalizing State and the individual, does not lay down any rules defining the nature of these ties; this is a matter for municipal law.

It is, however, an accepted rule of international law that naturalization of foreign nationals must be based on a voluntary act of the individual. Conferment of nationality by operation of law, without any specific voluntary act on the part of the individual, has therefore to be considered only as an offer of naturalization requiring acceptance; such acceptance may be explicit or implicit. Whether any particular act of the individual is considered as tacit acceptance depends on whether it is recognized as such by the practice of States: it depends on the development of international law. The reason for the rule that naturalization may not be conferred on foreigners against the will of the individual is that such naturalization results in an infringement of the right of protection of the previous State of nationality. It follows, therefore, that the compulsory naturalization of stateless persons is not inconsistent with international law.

The right of States to withdraw their nationality from individuals is, on the whole, not limited by international law. Deprivation of nationality, even mass denationalization, is not prohibited by international law, with the possible exception of the prohibition of discriminatory denationalization. There is no rule of international law in its present state of development which requires a state to admit former nationals to its territory, although a State may be bound to admit a denationalized person in those exceptional cases where deprivation of nationality has been resorted to in order to deprive the State of residence of the possibility of expulsion—as it would, in this case, infringe the right to expel aliens inherent in territorial jurisdiction.

Whether acquisition of another nationality by a national entails the loss of his existing nationality depends on the municipal law of the State concerned. Nationality is no longer considered as inalienable. According to the laws of many countries, release from nationality upon acquisition of another nationality requires special authorization (expatriation permits); but it may be concluded from consistent treaty practice and from the administrative practice of most States that such authorization must not be withheld without valid reasons where the acquisition of foreign nationality has taken place voluntarily, in a manner consistent with international law and in good faith. If authorization is refused in violation of this rule, the person concerned retains his nationality according to municipal law but such nationality need not be recognized by other States and will be disregarded by international tribunals: in other words, it will be denied extraterritorial effect.

The relative freedom of States in the field of nationality law leads to what are usually called conflicts of nationality laws: statelessness and plural nationality. Statelessness is not prohibited by international law and its reduction or elimination can, therefore, only be effected by treaty. Similarly, international law cannot prevent plural nationality, but any nationality held by an individual under municipal law which is inconsistent with international law will be disregarded in international law. In this sense one may speak of rules of international law for the solution of conflicts of nationality laws. Thus, for example, the nationality retained by a naturalized person owing to refusal of an expatriation permit without valid reason, or the nationality of the predecessor State retained by an individual who has become a national of the successor State under its law, consistent with international law, in consequence of transfer of territory based on a valid title, are irrelevant in international law; they do not have to be recognized by other States or by international tribunals.

Apart from the few rules of international law for the solution of conflicts of nationality laws, international law contains only rules for the solution of difficulties arising from plural nationality, for example:

(1) Each of the States whose nationality a person possesses may regard him as a national.

(2) The principle of equality, i.e., that protection may not be afforded by the State of nationality against a State whose nationality the person also possesses, has been embodied in the Hague Convention of 1930 and was considered as well established some time ago. It still reflects the normal practice of States but lately international tribunals have applied the principle of effective or active nationality, the so-called "link concept," i.e., they considered the nationality of

the State with which the claimant is more closely connected as determining for the admissibility of the claim.

(3) Different tests are applied as to the nationality which is to be ascribed to plural nationals in a third State, or by an international tribunal in cases where the person on whose behalf the claim is made also holds a nationality other than that of the States between which the tribunal is called upon to adjudicate.

Recently, particularly since the decision of the World Court in the Nottebohm Case, the test of effective nationality has gained ground. It plays an important role when the question of nationality is relevant for the purpose of municipal law of a third State or for purposes of international law.

It is difficult to speak of rules of international law as to evidence of nationality because such rules, if any, have been developed by international tribunals acting on the basis of specific arbitral agreements and because before such tribunals the question of nationality is a question of law rather than one of fact. The principle that international tribunals are not bound by municipal rules of evidence seems, however, to be generally accepted.

It follows from the nature of the question of nationality before international tribunals that they may disregard a nationality possessed according to municipal law, even though conclusively proved, if the municipal law is inconsistent with international law or if the nationality has, in the determination of the tribunal, been acquired by fraud, misrepresentation or concealment of material facts.

While nationality is still the primary link between the individual and international law, it is no longer the only link. There is an increasing tendency to provide the rights of individuals—apart from their international protection by the State of nationality and even in relation to the State of nationality—with the safeguards of international law by the conclusion of plurilateral or multilateral treaties for the protection of human rights. There is, moreover, an increasing tendency to regulate, by the conclusion of multilateral agreements relating to the status of refugees and stateless persons, the status of persons devoid of diplomatic protection, in international law. Such tendencies may to a certain extent reduce the importance of nationality in the international sphere; it is nonetheless an essential legal attribute of human personality.

Women's Equality and Nationality. Karen Knop and Christine Chinkin, "Remembering Chrystal Macmillan: Women's Equality and Nationality in International Law" 22 Mich. J. Int'l L. 523 (2001).

Each state determines under its own law who are its nationals. In the Nottebohm case, the International Court of Justice stated that "international law leaves it to each State to lay down the rules governing the grant of its own nationality." A state's discretion is limited by customary international law and jus cogens, and is also limited where the state has entered into human rights treaties, whereby it binds itself under international law to provide particular safeguards under its domestic law.*

In international law, nationality secures rights for the individual by associating her with a state. Traditionally the subjects of international law are states; individuals are not subjects of international law. By associating individual with state, nationality makes one state's interference with the national of another a violation of the other state's sovereignty. Nationality thereby provides the state of nationality with the standing to make a diplomatic claim with respect to the harms constituting violations of international law caused to that individual. When a state attempts to raise such a claim, however, its grant of nationality and hence its standing may be challenged on the ground that the individual has no genuine link to the state.

It is important not to overestimate the effectiveness of the diplomatic protection function of nationality. As with any discussion of nationality, there is the risk of implying that every individual is either the national of some state (and therefore enjoys the rights and benefits of nationality) or stateless (and therefore does not). But there are individuals who are simply without status altogether. An example is the hill-tribe women who belong to one of the cultural groups that live in northern Thailand or along western border uplands and that have distinct cultural identities and languages. Many of these groups have moved into Thailand at different times over the twentieth century, and the nationality of some continues to be unclear.

Even if an individual has a nationality, she is not always able to document it. This has been a problem for, among others, Polish women who are part of the recent wave of women trafficked from Central and Eastern Europe into Western Europe to work in the sex trade. For these women, nationality is not a means to diplomatic protection because often their passports have been taken away by a pimp or brothel owner, and they cannot prove their nationality. Similar problems are encountered by women in the "maid trade": the temporary legal migration of unaccompanied women from less developed Asian states to Western Asia (the Middle East) or to prosperous East Asian states (for example, Singapore) to take positions as live-in domestic servants. Where their passports are seized by their employers, they may have difficulty getting help should they be exploited or abused, or returning home should they decide to do so. With respect to trafficking, article 8 of the Protocol to Prevent, Suppress and Punish Trafficking in Persons, Especially Women and Children, which supplements the new United Nations Convention Against Transnational Organized Crime, anticipates that victims may not have proper documentation and provides for the issuing of travel documents or whatever other authorization may be necessary to enable the person to return to her state of nationality or permanent residence.

---

* It has been argued, for example, that the deprivation by the South African government of the nationality of Africans in the so-called independent Bantustans (Transkei, Bophuthatswana, Venda and Ciskei) during the apartheid era violated the prohibition on denationalization on the grounds of race. See John Dugard, *International Law: A South African Perspective* 451 (2d ed. 2000).

In any event, a state is not obliged to provide diplomatic protection to its nationals. Saskia Sassen's analysis of the feminization of survival in the global economy indicates why a state is not necessarily disposed to help its female nationals abroad:

> The last decade has seen a growing presence of women in a variety of cross-border circuits that have become a source for livelihood, profit-making, and the accrual of foreign currency... They include the illegal trafficking in people for the sex industry and for various types of formal and informal labor markets. They also include cross-border migrations, both documented and not, which have provided an important source of convertible currency for governments in home countries. The formation and strengthening of these circuits is largely a consequence of broader structural conditions. Among the key actors emerging in these particular circuits are the women themselves in search of work, but also, and increasingly so, illegal traffickers and contractors as well as the governments of home countries.

In a Bangladesh case, however, the father of a girl abducted by child traffickers argued successfully that the government's failure to assist in repatriating her violated the constitutional provisions on equal protection and protection of law generally.

Finally, a state traditionally could not make a diplomatic claim on behalf of its national against another state if its national was also a national of that other state, although there have been cases more recently where the state of effective nationality was allowed to bring a claim. Until recently, the United Kingdom took the traditional position in the case of British–Asian women who alleged that they were forced into marriage* while visiting the Asian country of their ancestry. The United Kingdom assisted these women in various ways, but refused to intervene officially in any dispute because the women were dual nationals who were in the state of their second nationality. In response to a report on forced marriage by a government working group, however, the British Foreign and Commonwealth Office and Home Office have outlined a new position on diplomatic assistance in such cases. Their joint Action Plan, produced in 2000, states that the United Kingdom will assume a right of consular protection for its dual nationals until proven otherwise, will explore and test the right of consular protection for dual nationals not habitually resident in-country, and, where dual nationality is an impediment, will treat the problem as a human rights issue.

C. STATE JURISDICTION

Civil Jurisdiction. Michael Akehurst, "Jurisdiction in International Law" 46 British Year Book of International Law 1 (1972–73), excerpt.

A State which denies foreigners access to its courts may be guilty of denial of justice. Conversely, a State's jurisdiction is limited by rules

---

* Forced marriages should be distinguished from arranged marriages. Forced marriages involve coercion, whereas arranged marriages may be consented to by both parties.

about sovereign, diplomatic and other immunities. But, apart from that, are there any rules of public international law which limit the jurisdiction of a State's courts in civil trials?

1. *The Defendant is Temporarily Present.* At common law the court of a State acquired jurisdiction in personam if (and only if) a writ was served on the defendant while he was in the State concerned. Although other bases of jurisdiction have been added by statute, this remains the main basis of jurisdiction in common law countries. What is remarkable is that the court's jurisdiction is not affected by the brevity of the defendant's stay in the country concerned; in theory a visit lasting a few seconds would be sufficient. It is true that an English court can halt proceedings when this is necessary to prevent injustice to the defendant; but the fact that a writ has been served on a foreigner temporarily present in England is not necessarily regarded as a source of injustice.

Service on someone who is present for only a few hours has been held to be sufficient to give jurisdiction in the United States, and the courts have made it clear that this rule applies when the party is in the State, however transiently. In one case the defendant was served with process on board an aircraft flying over Arkansas, and this was held to give jurisdiction to the District Court in Arkansas. Recently, however, United States courts have often dismissed such cases on the grounds of forum non conveniens.

In continental countries service of process is often required to give the defendant notice of proceedings, but it does not create jurisdiction; jurisdiction must exist already before a writ can be served (the most common basis of jurisdiction being the habitual residence of the defendant). The practice followed by common law countries is virtually unknown in other countries, and a judgment given by a court which based its jurisdiction solely on the temporary presence of the defendant would almost certainly be refused recognition outside the common law world. However, no State appears to have protested that such jurisdiction is contrary to international law, even though it is obvious that the practice followed in common law countries enables a State to exercise jurisdiction over cases and parties having no real connection with that State.

2. *The Defendant Has Assets Within the State.* A number of countries claim jurisdiction whenever the defendant has assets within the State concerned. In some States (the Netherlands, South Africa, many states in the United States), jurisdiction is limited to the value of the assets; in other States (Austria, Belgium, Denmark, Germany, Scotland, Sweden, Japan, palis of Switzerland), it is not so limited. As a result, a tourist who left his slippers behind in a hotel bedroom might find the local court claiming jurisdiction over all sorts of unrelated claims against him, running into millions of pounds. It is obvious that this rule enables a State to exercise jurisdiction over cases and parties having no real connection with that State, but no State seems to have protested that such jurisdiction is contrary to international law.

3. *Nationality or residence of the plaintiff.* Article 14 of the French Civil Code gives French courts jurisdiction if the plaintiff has French nationality. A similar rule existed in medieval Belgium, in the Netherlands until 1940 and in Greece until 1946. At the present day such rules exist in Haiti, Luxembourg, Quebec and Romania. Courts in Portugal and the Netherlands claim jurisdiction on the grounds of the plaintiff's domicile.

Judgments given on the basis of such provisions are unlikely to be recognized in other countries. In 1883 an Italian court held that Article 14 of the French Civil Code was contrary to the law of nations, but Italian courts usually hold that it is merely contrary to Italian public policy, as a reason for not recognizing such French judgments. There is no record of diplomatic protests concerning such grounds of jurisdiction.

Such jurisdiction may be unusual in proceedings in personam, but in the case of matrimonial proceedings it is normal. The traditional rule, not only in England but also throughout western Europe, was that jurisdiction was vested in the court of the husband's domicile. This meant that, after the husband and wife had separated, the husband might acquire a new domicile in a country where his wife had never set foot and institute proceedings there against his wife. The tendency of modern legislation is to extend this privilege to the wife, instead of insisting that proceedings must be brought in the court of the defendant's domicile. At the present day the plaintiff's domicile or residence is a basis of jurisdiction in the majority of countries. Jurisdiction is claimed on the basis of the plaintiff's nationality in a number of Eastern European countries, including Greece and Yugoslavia; nationality of either spouse is a ground for recognition under English law.

4. *Title to foreign land.* It has sometimes been suggested that it would be contrary to international law for a municipal court to decide title to foreign land. But courts in Austria, Germany and Italy have done precisely this, without provoking diplomatic protests. English courts refrain from exercising such jurisdiction, probably because they realize the futility of giving judgment which cannot be enforced against the wishes of the local State, but they circumvent this rule by means of the equitable jurisdiction in personam. (French courts have also sometimes dealt indirectly with title to foreign land by exercising jurisdiction in personam.)

The idea that international law prohibits a municipal court from deciding title to foreign land probably arises from confusing ownership of land with sovereignty over territory. The fallacy in this reasoning is too obvious to require demonstration.

5. *Jurisdiction based on subject-matter.* One might imagine that it would be perfectly reasonable for a State to exercise jurisdiction over a case if the subject-matter of the case had a close connection with that State; if a State's courts can try crimes committed on the State's territory, why should they not try torts and breaches of contract committed on the State's territory? But Joseph Story argued, early in the

nineteenth century, that jurisdiction in personam must be based on the physical presence of the defendant within the State's territory when proceedings are started. A number of English and American judgments have held that the subject-matter of a case was, by itself, insufficient to confer jurisdiction in personam, and in the Daylight case the United States Government argued that public international law prevented Mexico's hearing a case involving an absent United States citizen whose ship had collided with a Mexican Government ship off the coast of Mexico.*

Story's attitude clearly does not represent modern international law, because at the present day a very large number of States claim jurisdiction founded on the subject matter of cases (e.g., torts committed on the territory of the State concerned, contracts governed by its law, etc.). Moreover, there are obvious advantages in attributing jurisdiction to the State where the facts occurred, and whose law has the closest connection with those facts.

Criminal Jurisdiction. Michael Akehurst, "Jurisdiction in International Law" 46 British Year Book of International Law 1 (1972–73), excerpt.

1. *Territorial.* One of the main functions of a State is to maintain order within its own territory, so it is not surprising that the territorial principle is the most frequently invoked ground for criminal jurisdiction; even in continental countries, which also rely on the nationality principle to a far greater extent than common law countries, prosecutions based on the territorial principle far outnumber prosecutions based on the nationality principle.

It often happens that a crime is committed partly in one country and partly in another; the example always given in textbooks is firing a gun across a frontier. At the turn of the century some writers argued in favor of conferring jurisdiction on the State where the crime was initiated, others argued in favor of conferring jurisdiction on the State where the crime was completed. But the arguments were so evenly matched that it was eventually realized that there was no logical reason for preferring the claims of one State over the claims of the other; and the only alternative to granting jurisdiction to neither State (which would have led to intolerable results) was to grant jurisdiction to both States. In some cases jurisdiction may be shared by more than two States, e.g., if X writes a fraudulent letter from State A to Y in State B, and Y, relying on the letter, sends money to X in State C.

Logically a State should be able to claim jurisdiction only if the offense has been committed, in part or in whole, in its territory; it must

---

* Foreign Relations of the U.S. (1884), p. 359. The United States was trying to present a claim on the international plane on behalf of the shipowner, and Mexico was arguing that he ought to exhaust local remedies in Mexico first. If the Mexican contention had prevailed, the United States shipowner would have appeared in the Mexican court as plaintiff, and not (as the United States argument appears to suggest) as defendant—which only confirms the total illogicality of the attitude adopted by the United States government.

prove that a constituent element of the offense occurred in its territory. Sometimes this rule has been stretched by using the device of the continuing offense. A thief who steals goods in State A and brings them to State B is regarded as having committed theft in B as well as in A, because theft is a continuing offense. Similarly a couple who commit bigamy in A and subsequently cohabit in B can be prosecuted in B as well as in A, because bigamy is deemed to be a continuing offense as long as the parties bigamously cohabit. This is clearly a legal fiction and goes against the logic of the law, but it is relatively harmless.

Some States, however, go considerably further, and claim jurisdiction over offenses committed abroad which merely produce effects on their territory, even though those effects were not a constituent element of the crime. Moreover, a man can be convicted of a crime in the State where the effects of his act are felt, even though his act was not a crime in the State where it occurred.

Once we abandon the "constituent elements" approach in favor of the "effects" approach, we embark on a slippery slope which leads away from the territorial principle towards universal jurisdiction. If, for instance, a man commits arson against a factory and the company owning the factory becomes insolvent as a result, the effects may be felt all over the world—losses may be suffered by the company's suppliers, customers and creditors. Clearly the line must be drawn somewhere. But where?

It is submitted that jurisdiction can be claimed only by the State where the primary effect is felt. In order to determine whether the effects are primary or secondary, it is necessary to take two factors into account: (1) Are the effects felt in one State more direct than the effects felt in other States? (2) Are the effects felt in one State more substantial than the effects felt in other States? This test fits the decided cases, in the sense that jurisdiction has been claimed in practice only by States where the primary effects of an act have been felt. This test enables jurisdiction to be exercised by one or two States which have a legitimate interest in exercising jurisdiction, but it prevents the exercise of jurisdiction by States with no legitimate interest. The requirement of directness would, for instance, prevent jurisdiction being based on the economic effects of a crime on the victim's creditors, dependents or employees. The requirement that effects must be substantial would, for instance, prevent jurisdiction being exercised over a radio station by every State where the broadcast was heard; jurisdiction could be exercised only by the State where the majority of the listeners lived.

In borderline cases it may be relevant to take the accused's intentions and motives into account. Thus, in the case of broadcasting, it would be legitimate to examine whether the broadcast was aimed at the country claiming jurisdiction. Similarly, if a man built a high building near the frontier of one State which interfered with access by aircraft to an airport on the other side of the frontier, it would be reasonable to suggest that the State in which the airport was situated would have jurisdiction only if the builder's motive was to obstruct the aircraft. But, apart from such borderline cases, intentions and motives are irrelevant; many crimes, after all, do not require mens rea. Thus in the Lotus case Turkey was allowed to assume jurisdiction under the objective territorial principle over a crime of inadvertence.

It is submitted that the "primary effects" approach provides a better means of keeping the jurisdiction of States within reasonable bounds than the "constituent elements" approach does. Take the example of broadcasting. The constituent elements of broadcasting a defamatory or seditious statement include, in most legal systems, the reception of the statement by a third person. Under the "constituent elements" approach, jurisdiction could be claimed by any State where the statement was heard, which would produce absurd results. (One could take other examples besides broadcasting, e.g., polluting the atmosphere.) Moreover, if a State wishes to punish someone for causing certain effects, it can evade the restrictions imposed by the "constituent elements" approach by creating a new offense, the constituent elements of which include the effects in question. Suppose A kills B in State X, leaving B's widow in State Y destitute. Y cannot try A for murder, but it could create a new offense of causing the destitution of widows by killing their husbands, and try A for that. This would be lawful under the "constituent elements" approach, because one of the constituent elements of the new offense (the destitution of the widow) has occurred in State Y. But it would not be lawful under the "primary effects" approach, because the destitution of B's widow is only an indirect and relatively non-substantial effect of A's act.

Finally, a few words should be said about liability for omissions. If a man undertakes by contract to do something in a particular State, he can be punished for breaking his contract; if he acquires property in a particular State, he can be punished for not paying taxes on it; by marrying a wife he undertakes to support her and can therefore be punished for not supporting her by the State where she resides. But these examples have one thing in common—a voluntary undertaking (making a contract, acquiring property, marrying). In the absence of such an undertaking, it is submitted that a positive duty to act can be imposed only by the State where an individual is present or carrying on business at the time when action is called for—otherwise jurisdiction over omissions, far from being based on the territorial principle, would in practice be based on the universality principle, because an omission cannot be localized and occurs everywhere simultaneously.

2. *Nationality.* A State has jurisdiction over crimes committed by its nationals abroad. Some States require proof that the act is also criminal under the lex loci, or restrict jurisdiction to serious crimes or cases where the injured party or his government requests prosecution (e.g., France, Turkey); others do not (e.g., India, South Korea, Austria, Poland, U.S.S.R.). It would seem that such restrictions are not required by international law; a State has an unlimited right to base jurisdiction on the nationality of the accused. It should be noted, however, that the nationality of each accused must be considered separately; jurisdiction

over an accused national does not carry with it jurisdiction over his alien accomplices.

Common law countries claim jurisdiction on this ground over a comparatively small number of offenses, but they have not objected to the wider claims made by continental countries; on the contrary, the United States has (by providing evidence, etc.) aided Greece and Italy to prosecute their nationals for crimes committed in the United States.

Sometimes jurisdiction is based on some other personal link between the accused and the State claiming jurisdiction. For instance, Denmark, Iceland, Liberia, Norway, and Sweden claim jurisdiction over crimes committed abroad by their permanent residents. In a few cases the United Kingdom has also based jurisdiction on residence. States often claim extraterritorial jurisdiction over members of their armed forces and (in connection with crimes committed in the course of their duties) over their civilian officials. The United States and the United Kingdom also claim jurisdiction over crimes committed on foreign territory by members of the crews of their merchant vessels.

3. *Protective.* During the nineteenth century, continental countries began to claim jurisdiction over acts committed by aliens abroad which threatened the State. The principle is well established, but the range of acts covered by the principle is not free from controversy. The Harvard Research Draft Convention speaks of crimes against the security, territorial integrity or political independence of the State, and the counterfeiting of the seals, currency, instruments of credit, stamps, passports or public documents issued by the State. The exercise of jurisdiction over these offenses is unobjectionable, but some States make wider claims to jurisdiction. Article 13 of the Ethiopian Penal Law of 1957 speaks, inter alia, of offenses against the servants or essential interests of the State. The Hungarian Penal Code spoke of offenses against "a fundamental interest relating to the democratic, political and economic order of the Hungarian People's Republic." Laws drafted as widely as this are obviously open to abuse.

The decided cases also reveal examples of abuse. A Jewish alien who had sexual intercourse with a German girl in Czechoslovakia was convicted by a German court under the protective principle, because his act threatened the racial purity of the German nation. Now that such racial ideologies are discredited, this case is unlikely to constitute a precedent for the future. But the cold war has produced other abuses of the protective principle; an American was convicted in Czechoslovakia for doing research work for Radio Free Europe in West Germany, and foreign companies which buy United States goods and undertake not to re-export them to Communist countries can be prosecuted in the United States if they break that undertaking. French and Belgian courts convicted aliens who aided Germany abroad during both world wars; such decisions are defensible in cases where the accused persons were nationals of allied powers, but not in cases where nationals of neutral countries were convicted for acts done in their own countries.

In addition, the protective principle needs to be limited in the same way as the "effects" doctrine—a State can claim jurisdiction only if the primary effect of the accused's action was to threaten that State. If this were not so, a State would be able to punish the editors of all the newspapers in the world for criticizing its government.

4. *Universality*. For centuries there has been universal jurisdiction to try pirates. War crimes are often mentioned as another example of universal jurisdiction, but until recently universal jurisdiction to try war crimes was a matter of controversy. Courts trying war crimes often used to think that war crimes were subject to the same jurisdictional rules as ordinary crimes; even after the Second World War the Netherlands' courts held that international law authorized a State to try war crimes only if they were committed in its territory, against its nationals or against its national interests. However, in other war crimes trials which resulted from the Second World War, the courts of one allied national frequently tried war crimes committed on foreign territory by foreign nationals against the nationals of other allied nations, or even against the nationals of enemy States themselves. Several commentators explained this by saying that States have a universal jurisdiction to try war crimes, and Israeli comis relied heavily on the universality principle in the Eichmann case.

5. *Passive Personality*. A number of States claim jurisdiction over crimes committed by foreigners in foreign countries if the victim of the crime was one of their own nationals. This "passive personality principle" has always been regarded as totally unacceptable in English-speaking countries. Some writers from English-speaking countries erroneously imagine that the criminal law of all countries was originally based on the territorial principle, and that other bases of jurisdiction are recent (and usually questionable) innovations.

The English-speaking countries are not alone in regarding such jurisdiction as contrary to international law. France is of the same opinion, which was shared by individual judges in the Lotus case and by the arbitrator in the Costa Rica Packet case. It is also significant that many countries believe that international law prohibits a State from trying crimes committed by foreigners on foreign ships within its ports, unless the crime disturbs the peace of the port, which suggests a fortiori that a State cannot try crimes committed by foreigners on foreign territory (unless perhaps the effects of the crime are felt in the State claiming jurisdiction).

In a situation like this, where different States have different ideas about the content of the relevant rules of international law, there are two possible solutions. One is to fall back on the Soviet idea of custom as an implied agreement and to say that there are different rules of customary law in force between different groups of States. The other solution is to try to find some common ground between the two groups of States; and this common ground may be easier to find if we examine the reasons why some States oppose the universality and passive personality principles and why others support them.

One suspects that the unstated reason for the attitude adopted by the United States, United Kingdom and French Governments is that they fear that in some other countries courts are biased and punishments inhuman. However, there are others rules of international law which guarantee a minimum international standard for the treatment of aliens, so one cannot invoke the possibility of jurisdiction being abused as a reason for denying jurisdiction altogether. A stronger argument is contained in Brierly's famous statement: "The suggestion that every individual is or may be subject to the laws of every State at all times and in all places is intolerable." But surely it is intolerable only if the laws vary from place to place; if they are the same in all countries the individual suffers little hardship.

Supporters of the universality and passive personality principles argue that States should work together for the punishment of crime and that the presence within a State of an unpunished criminal is socially dangerous. But these arguments (particularly the first) presuppose that the act in question is a crime in all countries (or at least in the State where it was committed as well in the State claiming jurisdiction).

One solution would be for the State claiming jurisdiction to try the accused under the law of the State where the crime was committed. No State has applied this solution in modern times, but a number of States, while applying their own law, do require proof that the act in question was a crime under the law of the State where the act was performed. It is necessary to add a number of corollaries, to make sure that the accused is in the same position as he would have been if he had been tried in the State where the crime was committed. Thus periods of limitation laid down by the lex loci should be respected, and the penalty imposed should not be greater than the penalty imposed by the lex loci. The accused should also be able to plead, as a bar to prosecution, the fact that he has already been tried in the State where the crime was committed.

Nationality and Jurisdiction. Zsuzsanna Deen–Racsmany, "The Nationality of the Offender and the Jurisdiction of the International Criminal Court" 95 A.J.I.L. 606 (2001).

According to the nationality principle, states may exercise jurisdiction over offenses committed by their nationals abroad. Whereas civil-law systems apply the principle frequently and without distinctions, common-law jurisdictions tend to confine it to serious offenses or to impose a double criminality requirement. Even though it is not applied uniformly, the nationality of the accused is clearly a universally accepted basis for extraterritorial jurisdiction in relation to the crimes covered by the International Criminal Court (ICC) Statute.

While the principle is most frequently justified on grounds of the allegiance owed by a person to his state of nationality and state sovereignty, a more pragmatic reason is that many countries—mainly those with a civil-law tradition—generally do not extradite their own nationals. Jurisdiction over crimes committed by nationals abroad is necessary to prevent such crimes and criminals from escaping prosecution.

The application of the nationality principle is usually straightforward. Nonetheless, complications may arise regarding criminal jurisdiction over, say, multiple nationals. Although commentators have recognized some of the problems related to dual nationality and criminal jurisdiction, these problems have not been studied in detail.

In proceedings before the ICC, absent a jurisdictional ground other than active personality, a multiple national accused could claim that since one of the states of which he is a national—whether or not the state of his dominant nationality*—has not accepted its jurisdiction, the court is not competent to deal with the case. This argument could be made under Article 19(2) of the Rome Statute, which provides that "challenges to the jurisdiction of the Court may be made by: (a) An accused or a person for whom a warrant of arrest or a summons to appear has been issued under article 58." Similarly, a "State from which acceptance of jurisdiction is required under article 12" could raise such objections.

The pretrial chamber would have to decide on such challenges as a preliminary jurisdictional issue. As part of this decision, the chamber would need to determine whether each state of the accused's nationality must have accepted its jurisdiction. It might even be required to examine whether the objecting state can validly consider the suspect as its national and whether it is the state of his dominant nationality. Although the ICC would have the power to decide on questions relating to its own jurisdiction, these issues should preferably be examined and, if possible, settled before the court is established.

D. STATE SUCCESSION

Creation of States. James Crawford, from *The Creation of States in International Law* (1979), excerpt.

1. *International legal personality*. The term "international legal personality" has been defined as "the capacity to be bearer of rights and duties under international law."** The term "capacity" in this context is perhaps unfortunate: any person or aggregate of persons presumably has capacity to be given rights and duties by States. The question is not "capacity" but the extent to which the entity in question actually has such rights and duties. To say that a particular entity is an international

---

* Dominant nationality can be defined as the nationality of the state with which the person has the strongest factual ties. In international arbitrations it was frequently a contentious issue whether the tribunal or commission had jurisdiction over dual nationals. While they tended to assume jurisdiction irrespective of the claimant's dominant nationality where the other nationality was not that of the defendant state.

** Georg Schwarzenberger, *A Manual of International Law* 53 (6th ed. 1976).

legal person is to say only that the entity is in fact accorded particular rights, or subjected to particular duties, under international law.

2. *Sovereignty.* The term "sovereignty" has a long and troubled history, and a variety of meanings. In its most common modern usage, sovereignty is the term for the totality of international rights and duties recognized by international law as residing in an independent territorial unit—the State. It is not itself a right nor is it a criterion for statehood. It is a somewhat unhelpful, but firmly established, description of statehood, a brief term for the State's attribute of more-or-less plenary competence. No further legal consequences attach to sovereignty than attach to statehood itself.

3. *State and Government.* The distinction between State and Government has received little attention, although it is a problem of considerable intrinsic difficulty. One of the prerequisites for statehood is the existence of an effective government; the main, indeed, for most purposes the only, organ by which the State acts in international relations is its (central) government. There would thus seem to be a close relation between the two concepts. According to O'Connell: "Until the middle of the nineteenth century, both types of change [change of State and change of government] were assimilated; and the problems they raised were uniformly solved. With the abstraction of the concept of sovereignty, however, a conceptual chasm was opened between change of sovereignty and change of government."* This post-Hegelian development O'Connell criticizes as "dogmatic" and "arbitrary." In the context of succession to obligations—that is, in the context of the legal effects of changes in State or government—it is more useful and more cogent in his view to pay regard not to any such distinction but to the real changes or continuities in political, social and administrative structure. He thus advocates, in effect, a return to the eighteenth-century position of practical assimilation of changes of State and government.

It can readily be admitted that some changes of government have greater and more traumatic effects than many changes of State personality. Nonetheless it seems a fair assumption that changes in State personality are more likely to be of greater social and structural importance than changes in government. In any case international law does distinguish between change of State personality and change of government. Thus, prima facie, the State continues to exist, with concomitant rights and obligations, despite revolutionary changes in government, or despite a period in which there is no, or no effective, government. Belligerent occupation, it is established, does not affect the continuity of the State, even where there exists no government claiming to represent the occupied State. The legal position of governments-in-exile is thus dependent on the distinction between government and State. The con-

---

* I D.P. O'Connell, *State Succession in Municipal Law and International Law* 5–6 (1967).

cept of representation of States in international organizations also depends upon the distinction.

Moreover, in the context of State succession, it is important to note that, in arguing for a closer identification of State and Government, O'Connell is seeking to maximize the extent to which treaty obligations and the like are legally transmitted from one State to its successor. However, the law of State succession has developed otherwise: it is now generally accepted that successor States, in particular newly independent States, have substantial freedom as to the succession of treaty rights and obligations. To obliterate the distinction between "change of State" and "change of government" would now only decrease the stability of legal relations between governments, and would thus have precisely the opposite effect from that for which O'Connell was arguing.

4. *State Personality and State Succession.* There is then a clear distinction in principle between the legal personality of the State, and the government for the time being of the State. This serves to distinguish in turn the field of State personality (which includes the topics of identity and continuity of States) and that of State succession. State succession depends upon the conclusion reached as to State personality. However, in some areas, the principles and policy considerations involved are the same. In particular the problem of State succession in the case of devolving territories (for example, the British Dominions) is in part a matter of succession and in part a matter of personality. Nonetheless the two areas remain formally distinct.

State Continuity. James Crawford, *The Creation of States in International Law* (1979), excerpt.

There is a fundamental distinction between cases where the "same" State can be said to continue to exist, despite changes of government, territory, or population, and cases where one State can be said to have replaced another with respect to certain territory. The law of State succession depends on this distinction, and it must therefore, presumably, be possible to distinguish cases of continuity from cases of succession. Nonetheless in many situations in practice the distinction is arbitrary, and it may depend in particular cases not on the substance of a particular transaction but on the way in which that transaction was carried out. The notion of "continuity" has thus been criticized as misleading and over-general. Yet in practice, claims to "continuity" are made and recognized.

Certainly, it is one thing to determine that entity A is a State at a particular time, and another to determine that entity A1, at some other time, is the "same" State, for relevant purposes. However, allowing greater latitude to recognition and the views of the actors concerned, one would have thought that reasonable solutions to problems of identity could have been found by reference to the basic criteria of statehood as affecting the entities at the relevant times. A different approach has been adopted in Marek's leading study;* there, identity is defined by reference to the legal obligations of the State in question, rather than by application of the criteria for statehood. Thus Marek defines "the identity of a State" as the identity of its international rights and obligations, before and after the event which called that identity in question, and solely on the basis of the customary norm pacta sunt servanda. Where a State is identical in the sense defined, it is by definition continuous as between the two occasions referred to. State continuity is merely "the dynamic predicate of State identity." It is therefore impossible, in Marek's view, that a State should finally disappear, and then reappear as the "same" State: the extinction of a State puts an end to any possible identity of continuity.

To the view that State identity means identity of legal rights and obligations, several objections may be proposed. In the first place, the existence of a State might seem to be separate from the legal relations of that State, and certainly from its conventional legal relations. This is not to say that the State is some meta-legal "thing": qua legal person it is, in a sense, merely the sum of its rights, duties, and notably, powers and immunities. But the assertion that the customary rights, etc. of entity A are the "same" as those of entity A1, two weeks or two years later, may not be self-evident and is certainly not self-explanatory. To say that a particular entity is the "same" in this context (given that other entities may have equal rights) is merely to say that the relevant rights exist with respect to, or are attributed to, the same State—that is, the same, or substantially the same, territorial governmental entity. Particular rights, duties and powers, in terms of the creation of States, are not criteria for, but rather the consequences of, statehood.

It therefore seems sensible to make continuity, identity, and extinction depend on variants of these basic criteria; that is, primarily, territory, population, and independent government, and, as subsidiary criteria (but criteria which may be particularly important in doubtful or marginal cases), permanence and recognition.

Problems do however arise where the constitutive elements of statehood undergo substantial change. The following rules are established under customary international law.

    1. *Territorial changes.* It is established that acquisition or loss of territory does not per se affect the continuity of the State. This may be so even where the territory acquired or lost is substantially greater in area than the original or remaining State territory. The presumption of continuity is particularly strong where the constitutional system of the State prior to acquisition or loss continues in force.

    The presumption of continuity despite territorial change is somewhat dramatically illustrated by the case of "imperial" States.

---

* K. Marek, Identity and Continuity of States in Public International Law 68–76 (1954).

The United Kingdom remains the same State despite the loss since 1920 of a massive Empire: indeed its continuity has never been questioned. Turkey was also regarded as a continuation of the Ottoman Empire. The cases of Austria and Hungary are more doubtful.*

2. *Changes in population.* Changes in population are of course concomitants of territorial changes (in the absence of a transfer of population), and the same considerations apply.

3. *Changes in government.* It has long been established that, in the case of an internal revolution, merely altering the municipal constitution and form of government, the State remains the same; it neither loses any of its rights, nor is discharged from any of its obligations. Despite the question-begging nature of this and other formulations, the rule that revolution prima facie does not affect the continuity of the State in which it occurs has been consistently applied to the innumerable revolutions, coups d'etat and the like in the nineteenth and twentieth centuries. After some hesitation, it was for example established that the Soviet Union was a continuation of Imperial Russia. A fortiori, continuity is not affected by alterations in a municipal constitution according to its own amendment provisions; or by a change in the name of the State; or by non-recognition of the revolutionary government of a State. Although it is sometimes argued that "socialist revolutions," which result in a changed class-structure of the State, bring about a fundamental discontinuity in relations, it is not at all clear whether this claim is directed to the notion of legal continuity of the State, or is a claim to a more liberal regime of succession. Neither the Soviet Union or the People's Republic of China have asserted such discontinuity; problems of succession of governments in the two cases have tended to be worked out on an ad hoc basis.

4. *Changes in international status.* It is established in practice that, for example, international protectorates or protected States continue the legal personality of the preprotectorate State. Where there are substantial changes in the entity concerned, continuity may depend upon recognition (as in the case of India after 1947). The predominant view was that Austria and Hungary after 1918 continued the legal personality of the two States of the Dual Monarchy. Where the change in status is a result of external imposition (in particular of a puppet entity), continuity is not to be presumed, since, in the absence of general recognition, such an entity lacks any international status other than as agent of the belligerent.

* The Treaties of Saint–Germain and Trianon assumed continuity of Austria and Hungary with the two kingdoms of the Dual Monarchy. Marek, at 199–236, denies that either Austria or Hungary before 1918 possessed separate international status, and thus denies the possibility of continuity.

5. *Belligerent occupation.* It is well established that belligerent occupation does not affect the continuity of the State: as a result, governments-in-exile have frequently been recognized as governments of an enemy-occupied State. The continuity of a State under belligerent occupation remains until the peace settlement, or, probably, until the point when all effective organized resistance to the invader has ceased.

6. *Continuity and illegal annexation.* State practice in the period since 1930 has established, not without some uncertainty, the proposition that annexation of the territory of a State as a result of the illegal use of force does not effect the extinction of the State. The various States (Ethiopia, Austria, Czechoslovakia, Poland, and Albania) effectively submerged by external illegal force in the period 1935–40 were reconstituted by the Allies during, or at the termination of, hostilities. The view was on the whole taken that the legal existence of these States was preserved from extinction.

7. *Identity without continuity.* The case of Syria demonstrates the possibility that a State which has for a time been extinguished may be reestablished on the same or substantially the same territory and be regarded as for relevant purposes the same entity as before extinction. Syria's United Nations membership apparently revived upon its secession from the United Arab Republic in 1961, without the need for readmission. The South African Republic also seems to have been regarded as the same State before and after a period of extinction (1877–81). However, where state existence is terminated either by consent of the entities concerned (as with the United Arab Republic) or validly in accordance with international law at the time (as with the South African Republic), any subsequent assertion of "identity" takes on decidedly fictional overtones. This is especially so where (as with Poland from 1795 to 1918) the period of extinction lasts for more than a few years.

8. *Extinction.* Effective submersion or disappearance of separate State organs in those of another State, over any considerable period of time, will result in the extinction of the State, so long at least as no substantial international illegality is involved. This is particularly so where the previous State organs voluntarily relinquished separate identity, for example in the case of the union of two States. More difficult is the case of annexation of the entire territory of a State by external force—a situation which occurred with some frequency in the period 1935–40. As we have seen, the international community did not regard those annexations as cases of extinction. The difficulty remains: how long could it be said that the legal identity of the State was preserved, despite its lack of effective control, in face of effective but illegal annexation? Post–1945 practice has been of little assistance in determining this issue, since illegal invasion of a State for the purpose of its annexation has

not occurred with any frequency.* The most significant case, that of the Baltic States, sheds little light on the problem. Marek seems to regard that case as one of extinction: "the final loss of independence, either by way of a legal settlement or by way of a total obliteration of the entire international delimitation of the State." If, on the other hand, it is concluded that continued recognition of Latvia, Lithuania, and Estonia signifies their continued existence as States, then it may be that the rule protecting State personality against illegal annexation has achieved relatively peremptory, permanent force. The absence of more recent and explicit State practice is hardly regrettable; it would seem to preclude any more conclusive assessment of the effect of continued effective but illegal annexation upon statehood.

Economic Succession. Paul Williams and Jennifer Harris, "State Succession to Debts and Assets: The Modern Law and Policy" 42 Harv. Int'l L.J. 355 (2001).

On the whole, international law has played a constructive role in facilitating cooperative state break-up where the successor states share a desire to dissolve the predecessor state. In the case of a non-consensual break-up, international law has been fairly ineffective beyond providing principles from which the unjustly treated successor states could argue. Similarly, creditor states have been less obliged to follow the principles of international law, whereas successor states generally have been held to those principles by the creditor states or other successor states.

International law has played an effective role in further preserving the rights of creditor states and in countenancing reasonable agreements reached by the successor states. In all of the recent cases of state succession, the creditor states relied upon the international law of *pacta sunt servanda* and the 1983 Vienna Convention to require that the successor states were bound by the debt of the predecessor state and to dictate or consent to an allocation of that debt. This reliance on international law naturally was coupled with a clear warning that if the successor states wished to participate in the financial community, they would have to agree to service their allocation of debt. In the case of the former Czechoslovakia, the creditor states also successfully relied upon international law to sanction the agreement of the successor states to allocate the debt on a two-to-one basis.

Although international law provided for the link between the allocation of the debts and assets of the predecessor state, this link was only established in the cases of the former Soviet Union and Czechoslovakia upon the initiative and for the benefit of the successor states. With respect to the former Soviet Union, the creditor states ignored this link

---

* [Indeed, the attempted annexation of Kuwait by Iraq in 1991 seemed amazingly anachronistic to everyone (except Saddam Hussein). Of course, the international community found his attempt intolerable, and multilateral force was used to drive the Iraqi army our of Kuwait and to impose sanctions upon Iraq for its illegal aggression.—Eds.]

and pursued their own interest in joint and several liability. In the case of the former Yugoslavia, the successor states were unable to establish a link between the allocation of debts and assets among themselves, and the creditor states showed no interest in establishing such a link. The lack of interest on the part of creditor states in establishing a link between the allocation of debts and assets was short-sighted. If such a link were created, successor states would be more willing and able to service their share of the debt. Not only would the successor states see the allocation as just and fair, but they would be able to use or convert their assets in order to generate income to pay the debt.

Similarly, although international law provides for an equitable allocation of debts and assets, it has not been able to force or dictate an allocation by the successor states in non-consensual break-ups, nor has it been able to persuade third-party states to become involved in allocating or preserving the assets for future allocation. Creditor states, in fact, have relied upon the lack of an obligation in international law to preserve or allocate the assets of the predecessor state as justification for their inaction. In the absence of an effective utilization of international law to preserve or allocate the assets of a predecessor state, it appears that the old axiom that possession is nine-tenths of the law takes precedence. Although international law has not been effectively used to ensure that those states seizing the assets of the predecessor state are entitled to retain those assets, caution should be exercised in future dissolutions such that international law is not used for such purpose.

International law has been useful in consensual break-ups for providing guidance as to how to allocate debts and assets. With respect to debts, it does appear that whether or not the break-up is consensual, the creditor states will invoke the principles of equitable allocation and consent of creditors to ensure that the debt is fully allocated in a manner likely to ensure that it is properly serviced. Interestingly, the expansion of international law with respect to the definition of an equitable allocation occurred at the initiative of the successor states themselves and absent any meaningful assistance from the legal experts of the Committee of Legal Advisors on Public International Law or the EC Arbitration Commission.

The enhanced application of the role of international law with respect to succession to the debts and assets of predecessor states would benefit from: (1) a requirement to consider the allocation of assets when assigning liability for debts; (2) a detailed definition of an equitable allocation, with criteria such as proportion of population and economic indicators as employed in the cases of the former Soviet Union and former Czechoslovakia; (3) a greater willingness and ability of international legal bodies to articulate and apply the principles of international law and to reject expedited and vague conclusions; and (4) the rejection of inequitable principles such as joint and several liability for all successor states regardless of their share of the assets or actual ability to repay the entire debt of the predecessor state.

The reasonable and relatively fair application of the principles of international law, as well as their significant evolution and refinement, in the break-ups of the Soviet Union, Yugoslavia, and Czechoslovakia demonstrates the utility of relying on international law to structure a resolution of the many questions relating to state succession to debts and assets. With the modifications suggested above, the modern law and policy of state succession to debts and assets may be relied on to aid in the resolution of highly contentious disputes arising from the future break-ups of states, and may thus enable successor states, international mediators, and other interested third parties to resolve more readily many of the other political and legal issues that arise when a state breaks up.

Succession and State Identity. Matthew Craven, "The Problem of State Succession and the Identity of States under International Law" 9 Euro. J. Int'l L. 1 142 (1998).

Even if the elimination of "personality" or "identity" from the law of state succession cannot be supported, there does remain, nevertheless, a need to re-evaluate such concepts in light of their apparent indeterminacy. Indeed, it is considered that at this point legal doctrine has been fundamentally misleading. The initial assumption of most writers has been that the matter of identity is primarily one analogous to that of statehood or personality. As Kunz remarked, "[t]he problem of identity of states is not the antithesis of the problem of state succession but of the problem of the extinction of States."* The result is that it is common to find pronouncements to the effect that international law has no real understanding of when a state ceases to exist. The point being made is not so much that the existence of the state is merely a presupposition of the law, an argument associated with early voluntarists, but rather that the conditions for the extinction of the state are particular, and more complex.

When examined closely, however, this argument becomes difficult to comprehend. Assuming that international law does possess certain criteria that condition the "existence" of the state, or at least its participation in the legal community, then logically those criteria should also apply as regards its "legal demise." Thus, the general criteria for statehood (which for purposes of argument are taken to be government, territory, population and independence) should presumably govern not merely the legal "creation" of states, but also their "extinction." So, where the territory of a state becomes submerged by the sea, or where the population of a state evacuates en masse to other territories, or where it falls into a state of extended anarchy, it should be possible to conclude that the state has ceased to exist.**

* J. Kunz, *The Changing Law of Nations* (1964), at 288. Kunz is right that the problem of identity is not the antithesis of the problem of succession. However, even in cases of continuity, issues of succession might arise.

** Independence is more difficult insofar as it is a relational concept. Loss of independence assumes a certain identity of the subject, which cannot easily be presumed in the case of corporate entities.

What has to be understood, however, is that the traditional criteria for statehood are both abstract and exclusionary. They are abstract in the sense that they do not require the possession of a particular territorial locus, the maintenance of a particular composition of population or, indeed, a particular form of government. Thus, it is commonly accepted that the continuity of the state is not affected by changes in government (even revolutionary changes) nor by the cession of territory. The requirements of statehood are also exclusionary in the sense that they operate as threshold evaluations primarily intended to exclude from international discourse those entities that are not, for example, fully independent. That they are not operated so clearly in the context of putative extinction is primarily a result of the fact that states are not in the habit of withdrawing recognition from entities once established. This, in turn, is primarily due to the fact that states are not willing to jeopardize legal relations with an entity where there is clearly no successor state. Thus, it is not surprising that states did not withdraw recognition from the state of Somalia during the period of disrule, nor from Albania despite the apparent total absence of government. The fact that there may be a presumption of continuity in such circumstances, however, does not detract from the point that the essential conditions for extinction are logically the same as those for the recognition of new states.

Perhaps this point may be best illustrated with respect to the dismemberment of Yugoslavia. In that case, the disengagement from the federation of Slovenia, Croatia, Bosnia–Herzegovina and Macedonia, left in place the remaining republics of Serbia and Montenegro. The approach of the Badinter Commission, and also apparently the UN, was to argue that the SFRY had ceased to exist as a state in virtue of the fact of dismemberment. But to accept that would be to say that Yugoslavia had ceased to exist as a state, despite the fact that it continued to possess, in the form of the FRY, all the material requirements for existence. The truth is that at no stage did the FRY lose, in its entirety, independence, territory, population or government: it continued to possess all these attributes, albeit in a reduced form. It is also interesting to note, in that regard, that no states actually withdrew recognition from Yugoslavia, or subsequently the FRY, at any stage.

What this suggests is that a distinction needs to be drawn between transformations that result in the extinction of the state, strictly understood, and those that result merely in a change in identity. In the case of Yugoslavia, what is at issue is not so much whether the FRY is a state, but whether it is the same as, or different from, the SFRY. The point of difference may be described as follows: whereas the concepts of statehood and personality proceed on the understanding that states have certain attributes or qualities in common and that they are thereby attributed with, or inherently enjoy, certain competencies under international law, the concept of identity, by contrast, is predicated upon a notion of difference. "Identity" assumes that individual states, whilst being members of a particular class of social or legal entities, also possess certain distinguishing features that differentiate one from another. Identity, therefore, presumes personality but is concerned with what is personal or exceptional in the nature of the subject. This can never be provided by reference to the traditional requirements of statehood.

Chapter 5

HUMAN RIGHTS

Editors' Introduction: The *concept* of universal human rights, or rights that belong to all individuals everywhere simply because they are human, is widely accepted today by states and citizens alike. Yet the *practice* of universal rights continues to be subject to uneven government application and contentious scholarly debate. The effect is that, while human rights principles are being globalized, the relevance of international human rights law is dependent on the particular realities and interpretations within each state. What role can international law play in harmonizing distinct cultural norms and so-called universal rights? Can the law be used to undercut longstanding systems of inequality or even bring reluctant states into compliance? The evolving human rights consciousness, embodied by the authors below, should take this debate in promising new directions.

A. INDIVIDUAL RIGHTS

Human Rights Consciousness. Douglass Cassel, "Does International Human Rights Law Make a Difference?" 2 Chi. J. Int'l L. 121 (2001).

As one strand in the rope that pulls rights forward, the value of international human rights law depends mainly on its interaction with the other strands. The central strand in the rope is the global growth in *human rights consciousness*. This in turn interweaves the concept of *rights,* as entitlements of individuals or groups on which claims or demands may be based, together with the notion that some rights are so fundamental they are inherent birthrights of all human beings, regardless of nationality or culture.

Other strands of the rope include non governmental human rights organizations, whose numbers, activities, and sophistication in international human rights law norms and institutions have grown dramatically at both national and international levels and rapidly evolving communications and transportation technology that makes possible far more effective transnational organizing by these human rights groups than was possible only two decades ago. Both communications and faster and lower cost transportation technology, by making possible frequent, well attended international conferences, have contributed to the growth of another strand in the rights revolution, transnational issue networks, energized by "epistemic communities" of like-minded rights advocates in nongovernmental groups, sympathetic governments, academia, and the media, who work together across national and professional boundaries to promote shared values and agendas.

Some remaining strands include domestic constitutions and laws, which increasingly incorporate international norms, national human rights institutions, established in dozens of countries in the last fifteen years, spreading democratization, and gradually extended rule of law. This list is not all-inclusive but merely points out some of the strands comprising this "rope." The purpose here is to recognize how international human rights law interweaves with these other strands, all growing both independently and in their relations with each other, to create an ever stronger rope that pulls international human rights forward. Other strands in the rope include the growing levels of affluence and education in most parts of the world, expansion in the number and reach of nonbinding international norms, and, of course, the explosive growth of international human rights law itself.

Does the necessity to bring in other factors suggest that international law, by itself, counts for little? For that matter, with all these other rights-protecting processes, who needs international law?

What such questions overlook is that all the foregoing processes of rights protection—including international human rights law—are interrelated and, over time, growing stronger. All the others are strengthened by international human rights law, which in turn is strengthened by each of them. Human rights groups, for example, make constant use of international human rights law in their organizing. National human rights ombudsmen regularly appeal to international norms in opposing local efforts to legislate lower standards. Constitutional courts increasingly look to international treaties and the jurisprudence of international courts in interpreting national constitutional rights.

In this process of mutual reinforcement, international law plays several distinctive roles:

(A) *Provides a common language.* Rights groups in Thailand and Chile, New York and Johannesburg can invoke the same set of rights expressed in the same language, interpreted by the same UN human rights bodies. In theory, this function could be played by nonlegal instruments. Indeed, at the outset of the modern rights revolution, it was played by the Universal Declaration, that instrument arguably evolved into customary international law. This function, then, is a by-product rather than a necessarily unique function of international human rights law. Nonetheless, in practice, the instruments of international law supply most of the vocabulary for transnational rights discourse.

(B) *Reinforces the universality of human rights.* Three quarters or more of all governments accept the main international human rights treaties: the International Covenant on Civil and Political Rights; UN treaties on rights of women and children and against racial discrimination; basic ILO treaties on labor rights; and the Geneva Conventions and Protocols on international humanitarian law. The numbers grow every year. Such broad participation in formally binding international instruments reinforces the claim that human rights are universal. This, in turn, strengthens their claim to being fundamental and hardens their currency in domestic and international political debate.

(C) *Legitimizes claims of rights.* Because international human rights treaties are adopted by governments, usually after prolonged and contested negotiations and followed in many countries by lengthy processes of ratification, they confer legitimacy on claims of rights, especially when those claims are asserted (as they usually are) against governments. Human rights groups can (and regularly do) say to governments: "It is not *we* who say that torture is illegal and must be investigated and punished; it is you who so declare, as parties to the Convention Against Torture."

(D) *Signals the perceived will of the international community.* Because of broad participation by governments, via formally serious processes of negotiations and ratifications, international human rights treaties are often perceived as expressing the will of the international community. While that perception may matter little in a powerful country such as the United States, it often carries considerable weight in smaller and weaker countries—which is to say, most of the world's nations.

During peace negotiations in Guatemala in the mid–1990s, for example, the military pressed for a blanket amnesty for its wartime violations of human rights. Human rights groups had few cards to play in opposition, other than the argument that under international law, amnesties could not be conferred for certain crimes against humanity. In need of international approval and financial support for post-war recovery programs, the government ultimately agreed to leave such crimes out of the amnesty. The perception that violating international law would flout the will of the international community—or at least that it could be so characterized by opponents—was a major factor in this decision. Only crimes whose prosecution is arguably required by international *law* were exempted. Those for which amnesty would merely offend international sensibilities were not exempted.

Perceived international will also plays a role in the tendency of newly democratic regimes to ratify human rights treaties and accept international enforcement mechanisms, as a kind of insurance policy against the return of authoritarian rule. Most recently, no sooner did Peru oust the regime of President Alberto Fujimori, who had purported to withdraw the country from the contentious jurisdiction of the Inter-American Court of Human Rights, than the new government promptly rejoined the Court.

(E) *Provides juridical precision.* Especially when international human rights law is put in treaty form, by which governments expect to be bound, negotiators strive to give it a degree of juridical precision generally lacking in political declarations and philosophical pronouncements. The room for debate as to its meaning—and hence pretense for evasion, or grounds for needless disagreement—is narrowed.

(F) *Creates increased expectations of compliance.* Because international human rights law is expressed as law, it generates increased expectations of compliance. This gives human rights claimants stronger ground to demand compliance, and narrows the defenses available to violators: they may deny that violations were committed, but they cannot easily deny their obligation to respect the relevant norm. A government may well have accepted an international obligation with no intention to comply, but this is a difficult thing to admit publicly. The government may find itself trapped by its own hypocrisy.

(G) *Encourages domestic judicial enforcement.* International human rights law, especially in treaty form, is susceptible to domestic judicial enforcement, whereas nonlegal instruments generally are not. Many constitutions, for example, expressly incorporate treaties into domestic law, and some accord special, higher domestic legal status to human rights treaties.

(H) *Encourages enforcement by international courts or agencies.* Because international human rights law is couched as law, it also lends itself to potential enforcement by international courts or agencies—a trend growing in practice. Outside Europe such enforcement is rare and even more rarely effective. Still, the mere threat or perception (even mistaken) of its potential gives human rights groups added leverage. Indeed, the very *uncertainty* of enforcement makes governments nervous. The uncertainty is aggravated by the trend toward increasing enforcement in new and unexpected ways—witness the surprise arrest of Chile's General Pinochet on a Spanish arrest warrant in London, or credit denials by the World Bank on human rights grounds, after decades of contending that the Bank could not consider human rights. Risk averse diplomats and bureaucrats often treat slaps on the wrist, administered by toothless international human rights bodies, as if they were matters to be taken seriously, precisely because they never know when such seemingly empty words may come back to haunt them.

(I) *Creates additional stigma.* International human rights law, especially international criminal law norms such as those proscribing crimes against humanity, adds to the moral sting and shame of violation. Granted, atrocities generate broad condemnation on moral grounds alone. Even so, in many cultures—including the culture of international diplomacy—criminal conduct carries its own, additional stigma, undermining the capacity of violators to defend their conduct, while enhancing the force of condemnations.

(J) Avoids moral relativism. State violence does not always provoke moral outrage. Populations victimized by opposing ethnic or rebel groups may tolerate, if not applaud, brutal retaliation. Yet in such situations international law, written for universal application, can keep its bearing. Even while few Peruvians, for example, protested the prison massacre of rebellious Shining Path guerrillas, the Inter American Court of Human Rights ruled against Peru's resort to excessive force. Similarly, after the Knesset failed to stop torture of Palestinian security suspects, the Israeli Supreme Court finally ended the practice. And while few Israelis today protest their government's selective assassinations of security suspects, Amnesty International rightly denounces these violations of international law. Where moral clarity may be lost in the passions of the moment, international law can not only condemn, but also teach, helping morality to regain its compass.

To some degree, as noted, these attributes of international law are not necessarily unique. Precision might be demanded, for example, even in a political declaration. But in practice this unique combination of attributes—commonality of terms, near universality of formal acceptance, legitimacy of adoption, perceived reflection of international will, relative normative precision, increased expectations of compliance, susceptibility to domestic legal enforcement, potential and uncertainty of international enforcement, the additional stigma of violation, and moral clarity—enables international human rights law to make a distinctive contribution in support of growing human rights consciousness, organizing, and national legal and institutional development.

Each of the other strands, in turn, reinforces the reach and credibility of international human rights law. Public human rights consciousness gives international human rights law more teeth, by imposing a cost on most governments—again excepting the most powerful—of openly violating or being credibly accused of violating international human rights law. Nongovernmental organizations are often the main users of enforcement procedures and the main lobbyists for stronger treaties and enforcement procedures. National human rights ombudsmen and courts, too, give international law greater currency and credibility by invoking it.

Reinforced by these interactions, international human rights law is then even better positioned to contribute legitimizing force to these other institutions. In other words, the interactions among strands in the rope are mutually reinforcing. The full impact of international human rights law is not limited to its initial, indirect impact on rights protection, through its strengthening of other strands in the rope, but also includes a secondary impact, made possible by the reinforcement it receives from the other strands.

Quantifying the ultimate benefit for rights protection of all these interacting processes, or even demonstrating a clear qualitative impact, would require an enormously sophisticated methodology, coupled with a herculean effort to gather a range of data, much of which may not exist or may not be reliable. Perhaps some day such an ambitious research agenda will be attempted. In the meantime, judgment, based on experience, and tested for plausibility against the leading international relations-international law theories, is the best guide for policy.

One way to detect the distinctive, indirect role of international law is to assume its absence. Without international human rights law—with only national laws or international philosophical declarations—could we count on a comparable degree of universality, legitimacy and precision in human rights norms, and of stigma and risk of potential sanction for violations? One would be hard pressed to make that case.

A Nobel Laureate Speaks. Excerpt from Shirin Ebadi's Nobel lecture, 10 December 2003.

Today coincides with the 55th anniversary of the adoption of the Universal Declaration of Human Rights, a declaration which begins with the recognition of the inherent dignity and the equal and inalienable rights of all members of the human family, as the guarantor of freedom, justice and peace. And it promises a world in which human beings shall enjoy freedom of expression and opinion, and be safeguarded and protected against fear and poverty.

Unfortunately, however, this year's report by the United Nations Development Programme (UNDP), as in the previous years, spells out the rise of a disaster which distances mankind from the idealistic world of the authors of the Universal Declaration of Human Rights. In 2002, almost 1.2 billion human beings lived in glaring poverty, earning less than one dollar a day. Over 50 countries were caught up in war or natural disasters. AIDS has so far claimed the lives of 22 million individuals, and turned 13 million children into orphans.

At the same time, in the past two years, some states have violated the universal principles and laws of human rights by using the catastrophe of 11 September and the war on international terrorism as a pretext. The United Nations General Assembly Resolution 57/219, of 18 December 2002, the United Nations Security Council Resolution 1456, of 20 January 2003, and the United Nations Commission on Human Rights Resolution 2003/68, of 25 April 2003, set out and underline that all states must ensure that any measures taken to combat terrorism must comply with all their obligations under international law, in particular international human rights and humanitarian law. However, regulations restricting human rights and basic freedoms, special bodies and extraordinary courts, which make fair adjudication difficult and at times impossible, have been justified and given legitimacy under the cloak of the war on terrorism.

The concerns of human rights' advocates increase when they observe that international human rights laws are breached not only by their recognized opponents under the pretext of cultural relativity, but that these principles are also violated in Western democracies, in other words countries which were themselves among the initial codifiers of the United Nations Charter and the Universal Declaration of Human Rights. It is in this framework that, for months, hundreds of individuals who were arrested in the course of military conflicts have been imprisoned in Guantánamo, without the benefit of the rights stipulated under the international Geneva conventions, the Universal Declaration of Human Rights and the [United Nations] International Covenant on Civil and Political Rights.

Moreover, a question which millions of citizens in the international civil society have been asking themselves for the past few years, particularly in recent months, and continue to ask, is this: why is it that some decisions and resolutions of the UN Security Council are binding, while some other resolutions of the Council have no binding force? Why is it that in the past 35 years, dozens of UN resolutions concerning the occupation of the Palestinian territories by the state of Israel have not been implemented promptly, yet, in the past 12 years, the state and people of Iraq, once on the recommendation of the Security Council, and the second time, in spite of UN Security Council opposition, were subjected to attack, military assault, economic sanctions, and, ultimately, military occupation?

Allow me to say a little about my country, region, culture and faith.

I am an Iranian. A descendent of Cyrus The Great. The very emperor who proclaimed at the pinnacle of power 2500 years ago that he would not reign over the people if they did not wish it. And he promised not to force any person to change his religion and faith and guaranteed freedom for all. The Charter of Cyrus The Great is one of the most important documents that should be studied in the history of human rights.

I am a Muslim. In the Koran the Prophet of Islam has been cited as saying: "Thou shalt believe in thine faith and I in my religion." That same divine book sees the mission of all prophets as that of inviting all human beings to uphold justice. Since the advent of Islam, too, Iran's civilization and culture has become imbued and infused with humanitarianism, respect for the life, belief and faith of others, propagation of tolerance and compromise and avoidance of violence, bloodshed and war. The luminaries of Iranian literature, in particular our Gnostic literature, from Hafiz, Mowlavi and Attar to Saadi, Sanaei, Naser Khosrow and Nezami, are emissaries of this humanitarian culture. Their message manifests itself in this poem by Saadi:

> The sons of Adam are limbs of one another Having been created of one essence. When the calamity of time afflicts one limb The other limbs cannot remain at rest.

The people of Iran have been battling against consecutive conflicts between tradition and modernity for over 100 years. By resorting to ancient traditions, some have tried and are trying to see the world through the eyes of their predecessors and to deal with the problems and difficulties of the existing world by virtue of the values of the ancients. But, many others, while respecting their historical and cultural past and their religion and faith, seek to go forth in step with world developments and not lag behind the caravan of civilization, development and progress. The people of Iran, particularly in the recent years, have shown that they deem participation in public affairs to be their right, and that they want to be masters of their own destiny.

This conflict is observed not merely in Iran, but also in many Muslim states. Some Muslims, under the pretext that democracy and human rights are not compatible with Islamic teachings and the traditional structure of Islamic societies, have justified despotic governments, and continue to do so. In fact, it is not so easy to rule over a people who are aware of their rights, using traditional, patriarchal and paternalistic methods.

Islam is a religion whose first sermon to the Prophet begins with the word "Recite!" The Koran swears by the pen and what it writes. Such a sermon and message cannot be in conflict with awareness, knowledge, wisdom, freedom of opinion and expression and cultural pluralism.

The discriminatory plight of women in Islamic states, too, whether in the sphere of civil law or in the realm of social, political and cultural justice, has its roots in the patriarchal and male-dominated culture prevailing in these societies, not in Islam. This culture does not tolerate freedom and democracy, just as it does not believe in the equal rights of men and women, and the liberation of women from male domination (fathers, husbands, brothers ...), because it would threaten the historical and traditional position of the rulers and guardians of that culture.

One has to say to those who have mooted the idea of a clash of civilizations, or prescribed war and military intervention for this region, and resorted to social, cultural, economic and political sluggishness of the South in a bid to justify their actions and opinions, that if you consider international human rights laws, including the nations' right to determine their own destinies, to be universal, and if you believe in the priority and superiority of parliamentary democracy over other political systems, then you cannot think only of your own security and comfort, selfishly and contemptuously. A quest for new means and ideas to enable the countries of the South, too, to enjoy human rights and democracy, while maintaining their political independence and territorial integrity of their respective countries, must be given top priority by the United Nations in respect of future developments and international relations.

The decision by the Nobel Peace Committee to award the 2003 prize to me, as the first Iranian and the first woman from a Muslim country, inspires me and millions of Iranians and nationals of Islamic states with the hope that our efforts, endeavours and struggles toward the realization of human rights and the establishment of democracy in our respective countries enjoy the support, backing and solidarity of international civil society. This prize belongs to the people of Iran. It belongs to the people of the Islamic states, and the people of the South for establishing human rights and democracy.

In the introduction to my speech, I spoke of human rights as a guarantor of freedom, justice and peace. If human rights fail to be manifested in codified laws or put into effect by states, then, as rendered in the preamble of the Universal Declaration of Human Rights, human beings will be left with no choice other than staging a "rebellion against tyranny and oppression." A human being divested of all dignity, a human being deprived of human rights, a human being gripped by starvation, a human being beaten by famine, war and illness, a humiliated human being and a plundered human being is not in any position or state to recover the rights he or she has lost.

If the 21st century wishes to free itself from the cycle of violence, acts of terror and war, and avoid repetition of the experience of the 20th century—that most disaster-ridden century of humankind—there is no other way except by understanding and putting into practice every human right for all mankind, irrespective of race, gender, faith, nationality or social status.

Universal Human Rights? Jiangyu Wang, "China and the Universal Human Rights Standards" 29 Syracuse J. Int'l L. & Com. 135 (2001).

To defend its human rights record and counterattack its critics, China mounted a number of arguments and employed some established theories of international law, embodied in its human rights White Papers and official statements. In China's White Papers and other official statements regarding human rights, the Chinese government put forward the following arguments as its defenses: critics are using a double standard because China drew condemnation while other countries in which violations were in some sense worse did not draw condemnation; prosperous Westerners insisted on immediate implementation of modern standards in a developing China; the West itself has committed human rights violations at least as deplorable as those it was criticizing; China has achieved great improvement in human rights while China's record was essentially no poorer than that of western countries. Among its defenses China also proclaimed the following theory:

> It is the Chinese government's firm position to put "people's rights to subsistence and development" over any other aspects of human rights.

This policy has been reiterated by official spokespersons and repeated in nearly every human rights White Paper. In the 1991 paper Human Rights in China, this policy was elaborated as follows:

> It is a simple truth that, for any country or nation, the right to subsistence is the most important of all human rights, without which the other rights are out of the question. The Universal

Declaration of Human Rights affirms that everyone has the right to life, liberty and the security of person. In old China, aggression by imperialism and oppression by feudalism and bureaucratic-capitalism deprived the people of all guarantee for their lives, and an uncountable number of them perished in war and famine. To solve their human rights problems, the first thing for the Chinese people to do is, for historical reasons, to secure the right to subsistence.

The same theory was reaffirmed in 50 Years of Progress in China's Human Rights; it states: "The Chinese government has always put the people's rights to subsistence and development first, focused on economic construction, and made efforts to develop social productivity." Numerous statistics were presented in the papers as evidence of "great improvements" in Chinese social and economic rights. For example, it was stated that from 1952 to 1998, China's industrial added value increased by 159 times, with an average annual growth rate of 11.6%. Also, "the livelihoods of both urban and rural people have leaped several stages in succession, and the consumption level has improved remarkably." Furthermore, in the past twenty years, while the poverty-stricken population throughout the world has risen each year, China has helped 200 million people rise above the poverty line. China continues to enhance its citizens' social rights, security and health systems by decreasing working time requirements and by focusing on cultural and educational guarantees.

China not only asserts social and economic rights domestically, but also proclaims those rights in the international forum. In 1997, the Chinese alternate representative spoke before the United Nations Human Rights Commission:

> The commission has not been able to give full play to its due role in facilitating the realization of economic, social and cultural rights and these rights have long been neglected in the commission. The Chinese delegation maintains that the full realization of the economic, social and cultural rights and the right to development is the urgent task with practical significance for the developing countries.

For a number of reasons, the concept of state sovereignty was at the core of China's concerns in its involvement in all issues of international law. At the early stage of the People's Republic, China asserted the supremacy of state sovereignty in order to prevent the Soviet Union from interfering with its internal affairs on the pretext of keeping in contact with part of the "socialist family." Later, China was also concerned with Western intervention in its internal affairs under the pretext of human rights. This position began to loosen upon the implementation of the "Reform And Open Door" policy in 1979. In their international law textbook, editors Wang Tieya and Wei Min, two well-respected legal scholars in China, listed as international obligations the preservation of the right to self-determination, the prevention of discrimination, the prevention and punishment of genocide, the prohibition against slavery and similar systems and customs, and the prevention and punishment of terrorism. This book also noted that "necessary measures taken by all states and international organization to suppress these behaviors were consistent with generally recognized principles of international law and should not be considered as intervening in the internal affairs of a state."

But after the Tiananmen Square event, this more liberal interpretation reverted back, in official policy, to the collective rights and nearly absolute state sovereignty doctrine. China continued to maintain that the international community had a legitimate role to play in upholding the protection of those collective human rights, but not in supporting individual rights. In the 1991 human rights White Paper, the Chinese government stated:

> China is firmly opposed to any country making use of the issue of human rights to sell its own values, ideology, political standards and mode of development, and to any country interfering in the internal affairs of other countries on the pretext of human rights, the internal affairs of developing countries in particular, and so hurting the sovereignty and dignity of many developing countries. China has always maintained that human rights are essentially matters within the domestic jurisdiction of a country. Respect for each country's sovereignty and non-interference in internal affairs are universally recognized principles of international law, which are applicable to all fields of international relations, and of course applicable to the field of human rights as well.

Meanwhile, in the same White Paper, China left a little room for the international aspect of human rights protection:

> The international community should interfere with and stop acts that endanger world peace and security, such as gross human rights violations caused by colonialism, racism, foreign aggression and occupation, as well as apartheid, racial discrimination, genocide, slave trade and serious violation of human rights by international terrorist organizations.

In line with its proposition of establishing a multi-polar world after the Cold War, Chinese officials have repeatedly argued that cultural standards differ in terms of human rights protection. No culture's concept of human rights has greater claim to be accepted than any others. Therefore, foreigners have no moral right to judge China's view of human rights over another country's view. Rather than placing universality of human rights over any particular cultural value, consideration should be given to the differing views on human rights held by countries with different political, economic and social systems, as well as different historical, religious and cultural backgrounds. International human rights activities should be carried on in the spirit of seeking common ground while reserving differences, mutual respect, and the promotion of understanding and cooperation.

Applying the above analysis to China's case, one could conclude that all three approaches fall short of serving as weapons against the basic universal human rights standards. In the Chinese society, some, but by no means all, essential traditional elements have been retained. China has incorporated into its system an ample amount of new elements from the outside world since the late Qing dynasty. Marxist–Leninist theory once dominated the society after 1949, but has been almost abandoned in real life in the most recent decades. Now Western social values seem to occupy many fields of Chinese life. In essence, the traditional society in which principles of social justice are based not on rights but on status and intermixing of privilege and responsibility have been under endless changes and amendments. Throughout history, Chinese society has had many instances of successfully absorbing outside cultural factors into its body (a most striking example of this cultural adoption is Buddhism, which was imported from India and ultimately became one of China's major religions). Thus, in this sense, it is very possible that China will continue to incrementally absorb outside practices by incorporating basic universal human rights standards into its culture and politics. Also, what is left of traditional Chinese values does not present a huge or troublesome obstacle to China's acceptance of basic human rights.*

B. CULTURAL RIGHTS

Cultural Values. Robert D. Sloane, "Outrelativizing Relativism: A Liberal Defense of the Universality of International Human Rights" 34 Vand. J. Transn'l L. 527 (2001).

In the era of the nation-state, rarely, if ever, do territorial boundaries embrace a single cultural tradition. A "cultural" rejection of universal human rights law may therefore reflect, not universal cultural norms, but particular perceptions, understandings, and interpretations of these norms.

Which interpretations tend to be at war with the prerogatives of universal human rights? This question invites a more cynical rejoinder to crude cultural relativism. Scholars and human rights activists alike observe that frequently it is not cultural values that inhibit societies from realizing a legal order that respects universal human rights; it is the self-serving manipulation of these values by elites. Authoritarian leaders often invoke cultural relativism to cloak the characteristic abuses of totalitarian rule:

> Arguments of cultural relativism regularly involve urban elites eloquently praising the glories of village life—a life that they or their parents struggled hard to escape. Government officials denounce the corrosive individualism of Western values while they line their

---

* As pointed out by some scholars, the concept of human rights in traditional China included both political freedoms, meaning individual freedoms and protection from unrestrained rulers, and economic rights, which were identified with the material welfare of the people. Illustrative teachings such as "wen zhu yi fu zhou ye, wei wen shi jun ye," (I just heard King Wu's killing of an evil person Zhou, but I never hear his regicide) indicate that subjects have a right to rise to overthrow a tyrant. Other teachings such as "cang lin shi er zhi li jie," (if you want people to obey law and rules, you must warrant their welfare) indicate that material welfare is people's primary need.

pockets with the proceeds of massive corruption. Leaders sing the praises of traditional communities while they wield arbitrary power antithetical to traditional values, pursue development policies, systematically undermine traditional communities, and replace traditional leaders with corrupt cronies and party hacks.*

U.N. Secretary–General Kofi Annan echoed this same conclusion in a recent statement at the Aspen Institute: "It is never the people who complain of human rights as a Western or Northern imposition. It is too often their leaders who do so. You do not need to explain the meaning of human rights to an Asian mother or an African father whose son or daughter has been tortured or killed. They understand it—tragically—far better than we ever will." Yet the use of culture to justify human rights violations need not be self-consciously cynical. At times, societal elites, such as the Brahmin caste in traditional Hindu society, rely subconsciously upon deeply ingrained cultural beliefs to legitimize their self-assessment of practices that offend human rights norms.

Finally, to the extent that states advance crude relativist objections to universal human rights, we should bear in mind that these arguments assume unjustifiably an identity between government objectives and cultural values. Human rights abuses, as noted above, imply official complicity. When they are not perpetrated directly by governmental, quasi-governmental, or paramilitary groups, human rights abuses nonetheless enjoy either official sanction or, at the very least, tolerance. Absent some form of official complicity, the abuse perhaps constitutes a crime but not, strictly speaking, a human rights violation. Thus, if crude relativism provides a respectable reason to abrogate international human rights, it must be true that a state's objectives may be identified legitimately with the cultural values invoked to defend the practice at issue. But the community and State are different institutions and to some extent in a contrary juxtaposition.

Not surprisingly, where many egregious patterns of human rights violations occur, it strains credulity to make this simple identification. In fact, when human rights abuses occur on a massive and systematic scale, it is frequently because the state, or, more commonly, one cultural or national elite that seizes control of the state, seeks to suppress or destroy certain other cultural, ethnic, or political groups within its territory. The war in the former Yugoslavia is a case in point. Likewise, in the Rwandan genocide of 1994, it was not culture per se, but a political elite's manipulation and exacerbation of preexisting socio-cultural divisions within Rwandan society that caused the systematic slaughter of Tutsi. Again, in the People's Republic of China of the 1960s and 1970s, nothing about Chinese—still less "Asian"—values sanctioned the massive destruction and terror of the Cultural Revolution. Indeed, ironically, this human rights catastrophe involved an attempt to eradicate traditional Chinese cultural values in the service of a state ideology that, far from being shared by its citizenry, grew out of the radical ideas of a long-

---

* Jack Donnelly, *Human Rights in Theory & Practice* (1989), excerpt.

dead social critique of nineteenth-century industrial Europe. In short, particularly in states that lack democratic institutions, the crude cultural relativist's identification of the state—and its objectives—with the cultural values of its people remains dubious.

Islamic Human Rights? Ann Elizabeth Mayer, *Islam and Human Rights: Tradition and Politics*, 3rd ed. (1999), excerpt.

Most current theorists of Islamic human rights persist in talking exclusively in terms of an idealized vision of Islamic social harmony, even though the evidence of centuries as well as the acts of current governments have manifestly demonstrated that this vision is unrealistic. Because of their otherworldly, idealistic focus, it is not surprising that the authors of Islamic human rights schemes produce rights provisions that seem grossly inadequate by the standards of international human rights and that fail to call for human rights protections that could address actual human rights problems.

Examples of the inadequate rights formulations show frivolous notions of entitlements. Some inadequate formulations seem to have resulted from an author gleaning from the Islamic sources the idea that certain conduct is censured and drawing the conclusion that human beings have "rights" not to be affected by such conduct. Thus, Islamic human rights include the "right" not to be made fun of or insulted by nicknames, which is obviously taken from the Qur'an 44:11, "Let not a folk deride a folk who may be better than they... neither defame one another, nor insult one another by nicknames." Other "rights" that have been derived from Islamic sources include the right of women not to be surprised by male family members of the household walking in on them unannounced and the "right" not to be tied up before being killed. In addition, one encounters a "right" not to have one's corpse mutilated, which seems to envisage that human rights protections should be extended to corpses, even though human rights concerns ordinarily presuppose that the rights claimant be living, not dead.

Indeed, when one thinks about the rights provision protection women from surprise intrusions, one realizes that, far from affording protection for freedoms, it contains implicit restrictions on women's rights. There is an assumption that the world is sexually segregated and that women stay at home in seclusion from men. So strict is this segregation meant to be that male family members should never intrude on women's quarters without giving women warning so that they can cover themselves in a suitably modest manner. Thus, the provision implies that even in the home there will be female seclusion and veiling, which in turn is connected with the woman's duty to avoid indecency. There is really nothing linking this supposed right of women not to be surprised by men of the family coming in unannounced with any principle of international human rights, only with traditional notions that women's obligations under the *shari'a* include the duties to stay segregated, secluded, and veiled.

In Islamic human rights schemes, there are provisions that guarantee the "right" not to be burned alive, the "right" to life—which turns out to be a right not to be murdered—and a woman's "right" to have her chastity respected and protected at all times. Although murder or rape does violate international human rights law if it is practiced as a matter of state policy, if no more than a criminal act by a private actor it is ordinarily left to domestic criminal legislation to impose a penalty. The Islamic "right" does not appear to be directed against state policy, only against the criminal. Furthermore, the woman's right to have her chastity respected is a very ambiguous one, since, in the context of the contemporary Middle East, the protection of women's chastity is often associated with regimes of sexual segregation and seclusion and female veiling, practices that can be justified on the grounds that they are necessary to protect women's chastity. So, the "rights" just discussed do not offer meaningful protections for individual freedoms, and at least one could be utilized to deprive women of freedoms.

A review of Islamic human rights schemes uncovers a pattern of borrowing substantive rights from international human rights documents while reducing the protections that they actually afford. This is accomplished by restricting the rights so that they can only be enjoyed within the limits of the *shari'a*, which are left unspecified. As a result, states decide what the scope of the affected rights should be. In this respect, the Islamic limitations on rights resemble the qualifications that have been placed on human rights in the African Charter on Human and Peoples' Rights, which have been decried as "claw-back clauses" that allow states "almost unbounded discretion" in using domestic legal standards to restrict internationally guaranteed human rights.

International law does not accept that fundamental human rights may be restricted—much less permanently curtailed—by reference to the requirements of any particular religion. International law does not provide any warrant for depriving Muslims of human rights by according primacy to Islamic criteria. Thus, relying on the *shari'a* to limit or dilute human rights means that the rights that are established under international law are being qualified by standards that are not recognized in international law as legitimate bases for curtailing rights.

Tradition and Laws. Celestine I. Nyamu, "How Should Human Rights and Development Respond to Cultural Legitimization of Gender Hierarchy in Developing Countries?" 41 Harv. Int'l L.J. 381 (2000).

Formal laws and cultural norms are modes of social control that play an important role in constructing social arrangements. Formal law may operate to give a natural and immutable appearance to dominant articulations of custom, and custom may be invoked to legitimize formal law. Attributing gender hierarchy to a vague notion of culture masks the role played by formal legal institutions in creating those conditions. A vague notion of culture provides a convenient scapegoat for government institutions and obscures the state's responsibility in redressing inequalities. A government can easily avoid addressing inequalities by claiming that it is powerless to alter social structures within the cultural sphere.

An example of government avoidance of responsibility for inequality can be seen in the framework adopted by some Anglophone African constitutions to accommodate cultural and religious pluralism. The Kenyan constitution, for example, exempts customary and religious laws in the areas of marriage, divorce, devolution of property on death, and other personal law matters from the anti-discrimination provision in section 82. In addition, any customary law limited to members of a particular race or tribe cannot be labeled discriminatory under the constitution.

Similar provisions are contained in the constitutions of Zimbabwe, Zambia, and Ghana. In Zimbabwe, the Supreme Court applied such a constitutional provision in a 1999 case and ruled that a Shona customary law barring a daughter from administering her deceased father's estate, solely on the basis of her sex, was not discriminatory. This Shona customary law was protected from constitutional scrutiny. In Kenya, a similar constitutional provision was applied to the highly publicized case of S.M. Otieno. The constitutional exception was invoked to justify the application of Luo customary burial law, denying a widow any role in deciding where her husband would be buried.*

These exceptions insulate practices carried out in accordance with customary or religious law from constitutional scrutiny. Aggrieved citizens within those religious or cultural communities are thus left without formal legal or constitutional remedies. Through these exemption provisions, the state facilitates the establishment and preservation of asymmetrical social arrangements by denying some citizens a voice in shaping social norms.

Proponents of gender equality must therefore challenge this systemic, state-sanctioned stifling of dissent and should explicitly endorse the participation of varied opinions and voices in the shaping and articulation of culture. A strategy that supports local efforts toward constitutional change promises more durable and far-reaching social reform than a campaign that calls for the abolition of specific cultural practices.

Having thus circumscribed a private sphere of cultural norms, governments use culture as the formal explanation for gender inequality. Kenya's national report to the Fourth United Nations Conference on Women (held in Beijing, China in 1995) illustrates this use of culture by the government: "Land title deeds were and are still issued to men and women without discrimination although due to cultural factors, men

---

* The case involved a burial dispute between a widow and her husband's clan. The widow wanted her husband buried in the Nairobi area, at the suburban home where their nuclear family lived. Her deceased husband's clan wanted him buried in Nyanza, Western Kenya at his parents' ancestral home. The only Kenyan law that addresses burial issues is the Public Health Act, which deals with the hygienic disposal of corpses. The Act contains no legal provision under which family members are entitled to control burial decisions. Therefore, despite the widow's objection, Luo customs on burial were applied and the husband was buried at his parents' ancestral home.

outnumber women." Under current practice, formal title is registered in the name of the head of household, who is presumed to be male. Even though no statutory requirement exists, government officials justify this practice as a reflection of community culture. It is not obvious, however, where culture ends and formal policy begins, particularly in the land titling exercise.* The cultural factors referred to in Kenya's national report to the Beijing conference, for instance, are as much a result of government action as of traditional social practice.

Unless the overlap between cultural norms (or the popular conceptions of these norms) and formal law and policy is acknowledged and analyzed, the government can exonerate itself by attributing any negative outcome to culture. Another tactic used by the Kenyan government further illustrates this scapegoating of culture. Before and during the 1994 African regional preparatory conference that preceded the Beijing conference, women's rights groups in Kenya publicized inheritance traditions that excluded girls as one example of discrimination against the girl-child. The Kenyan president seized upon this refrain and issued a directive that girls should receive a share of their fathers' property. The government, not otherwise known for its commitment to gender equality, was able to distance itself from the problem by placing the blame on recalcitrant cultural traditions that oppress women.** The women's rights groups had failed to analyze the close interaction between tradition and formal laws and regulations. The role played by formal institutions in producing these negative outcomes for girls was underplayed, thus making it possible for the government to position itself as blameless and as supportive of positive cultural change.

C. GENDER

Gender and Culture. Joel Richard Paul, "Cultural Resistance to Global Governance" 22 Mich. J. Int'l L. 1 (2000).

The international community has acknowledged the importance of gender equality, yet by continuing to defer to culture, it excludes women from the reach of public international law. The assumption that gender equality is culturally dependent is embedded in the discourse of gender equality.

---

* This convergence of culture and formal law disadvantages women in concrete ways. Ugandan author Lilian Ekirikubinza Tibatemwa observes that women experience adverse consequences due to the combination of negative customary attitudes and specific doctrines in English property law that bundle structure ownership with land ownership. This makes it difficult for women (in the context of inheritance) to claim entitlement to structures on land legally owned by their husbands. It is even more difficult to claim such entitlement when the legally recognized heir under customary law is not in the widow's immediate family. See Lilian Ekirikubinza Tibatemwa, *Property Rights, Institutional Credit and the Gender Question in Uganda*, 2 E. AFR. J. PEACE & HUM. RTS. 68, 70–71 (1995).

** The government did not, however, address the problematic national policy of land belonging to fathers and not to families. Moreover, this same government has exempted 12 Kenyan districts from the operation of the Law of Succession Act, which requires the universal provision of property for all children regardless of sex.

There are three responses to efforts to universalize women's rights. First, some Third World scholars accuse Western feminists of "essentializing" women. The anti-essentialist argument is often framed as a conflict between feminism and culture. Anti-essentialist arguments do not necessarily reject feminism or deny that gender equality may represent a universal value that transcends cultural boundaries. Some anti-essentialist arguments simply assert that gender equality should be viewed within a particular ethnic or national context. In other words, anti-essentialism tends to emphasize culture over gender. Some anti-essentialists may see this shift in emphasis as a pragmatic-political strategy to gain support for gender equality. Other may see it as a recognition of post-colonialism and an effort to differentiate local culture from dominant western culture. Implicitly, by focusing their critique on gender equality, anti-essentialists reinforce the idea that other rights—the right to contract, property, political participation, or legal process—do transcend borders without regard for culture. These rights may also be gendered in the sense that they primarily reference men, who are engaged in the public realm of commerce, politics, and law.

A second response is that feminists are imposing western liberal values on other societies without regard for historical and cultural differences. Some advocates for the Third World have rejected claims for gender equality as a universal human right as a form of cultural imperialism. Even some feminists express concern that women's rights may represent liberal western cultural biases:

In addition to these concerns for the inherent bias within international law against non-western cultures and women whatever their cultural background, the law generally also implies punishment and even forcible change. Even if one can inject a multicultural perspective and set of values into the law, how can mutual respect be maintained if the "losing" cultural value can be punished or even forced to change?

This argument appeals to the West's sense of moral responsibility for the history of colonialism. A refined version of this argument is that Third World objections to universal human rights norms offer a different universal norm, rather than denying any norm. When Islamic countries raise objections to women working with men, we could perceive those objections as presenting an alternative view of women's rights rather than as a denial of gender equality.

Ironically, by invoking culture in this connection, defenders of Third World countries are appropriating the same rhetoric once used to rationalize and legitimate colonialism. Whereas the Europeans referenced "high culture" as compensation for exploitation, subsequent generations of anthropologists have referenced Third World "culture" as a mark of underdevelopment and dependency. Why do we identify certain conduct as cultural? How we deploy the term itself reveals certain underlying value preferences. For example, by characterizing certain individual behavior, such as domestic violence, as cultural, we attribute certain bad acts to whole groups of people. We often label conduct as cultural when it is performed by a member of a racial or ethnic minority or a developing nation. When a member of the majority in the United States or Europe commits the same conduct, we typically blame the individual and not the culture. This labeling tends to exaggerate ethnic differences and supports the idea that white European culture is superior. Contrasting western liberalism with Third World culture reaffirms the existing status relations between the industrialized and developing states by implying that certain states are not sufficiently mature to assume responsibility for respecting women's rights.

Moreover, the cultural imperialism argument reifies certain historical and cultural distinctions and suggests that they should not be subject to foreign influence. This presumes that culture is static and bounded by the geography of sovereign states. One response to this argument is that national culture is an artificial social construct. Third World states are themselves the creation of western liberal ideology mapped onto the Third World. Imperialism produced Third World nationalism and sovereignty. The borders drawn by colonial powers do not determine the culture of Third World states. Family, tribe, village, religion, and commerce shape culture. These sources of culture cross and divide national borders. Which of these cultural influences is any more authentic than the views of women resisting gender inequality within Third World societies?

More ominously, by juxtaposing national culture against women's rights, Third World advocates subordinate Third World women to the private exercise of male privilege. Assertions of national culture may overlook sub-cultures or groups that do not willingly submit to the national culture.* By appealing to cultural generalizations in defense of Third World sovereignty, these advocates reinforce western stereotypes of Third World countries as patriarchal, intolerant and undemocratic. For example, the willingness to accept cultural justifications for the denial of women's rights in Islamic cultures may derive from western stereotyping of "orientalism."** Westerners reinforce negative stereotypes by explaining Third World cultural traditions in terms of the subordination of women. In so doing, the sympathetic westerner echoes the colonialist argument that pointed to the exploitation and abuse of Third World women as evidence of the backwardness of their colonies.

A third objection to a universal norm of gender equality is that cultural exceptions to international legal norms are no more or less suspect than domestic legal exceptions to international law. The objection here rests on the idea that since culture is indeterminate, we can

---

* The relationship between cultural claims and women's rights has also been evident in U.S. domestic law. Increasingly, cultural defenses have been brought successfully in criminal trials in which the victim was a woman. In particular, Asian–American men who have assaulted or killed Asian–American women have argued cultural defenses. The cultural defense operates to maintain the subordination of Asian–American women in their traditional culture.

** See generally Edward Said, Orientalism (1979). Professor Said shows how Europeans artificially constructed the category of "orientalism" in ways that subordinated cultural differences, denied history, and maintained European hegemony.

characterize the arguments raised by the United States against international legal norms as cultural just as we characterize the arguments of some Islamic states as cultural. For example, when Islamic countries object to extending certain rights to women based on the Koran, we regard that as cultural. Yet, if the United States objects to certain rights based on federalism concerns, we would characterize that objection as legal or constitutional. One scholar has suggested that there is no significant distinction between constitutional arguments against CEDAW [Convention on the Elimination of All Forms of Discrimination Against Women] made by the United States and cultural or religious arguments against the CEDAW made by some Islamic countries. In this view, both the Constitution and the Koran are sacred texts in their respective societies and both could be viewed as cultural. This argument collapses the distinction between law and culture. If law is indistinguishable from culture, then it makes no sense to talk about cultural exceptions to legal obligations.

In my view, this objection fails to acknowledge the real difference between cultural arguments and legal arguments. Of course, law is both a product and an instrument of culture, but it is distinguishable from culture. When an Islamic state argues that religious dogma justifies its treatment of women, it is asserting that the practice represents the teaching of the Prophet or of God. By their nature, religious obligations are immutable and are not subject to political processes. By contrast, legal arguments are asserting only that the political process requires this result. Legal outcomes are always subject to change either by statute, constitutional amendment, or judicial interpretation. Law is about a very specific discrete temporal process. Legal objections can be overcome by changing the law. Culture and religion do change over time, but they are much more difficult to change. No single event or process can transform a cultural or religious belief.

The difficulty of changing culture reflects another basic difference: culture is not readily identifiable. Within a society, there are many subcultures that intersect. An Islamic woman may feel one set of cultural norms are appropriate among her family, and a different set of norms are appropriate among friends, classmates, or co-workers. To privilege any one set of cultural norms is to subordinate some other set of norms. There is no single authoritative voice for interpreting culture. Islamic scholars disagree about what the Koran requires. The text might be authoritative and fixed, but legal structures provide for authoritative interpretation. When a constitutional obligation is raised to an international legal obligation, we can debate the legal arguments and eventually reach a consensus, change the Constitution, or receive an authoritative interpretation from a court of law.

In the final analysis, these three objections to the universality of gender equality—the anti-essentialist objection, the cultural imperialist objection, and the cultural indeterminacy objection—do not explain why gender norms are subject to cultural arguments while other human rights norms are accepted as universal.

Chapter 6

GROUP RIGHTS

Editors' introduction: *The Universal Declaration of Human Rights*, in one of its final articles, recognizes the right of people to participate fully in the "cultural life of the community." Indigenous groups and racial, ethnic and linguistic minorities, among others, claim the right to specialized protections necessary for the full enjoyment (and assured existence) of the cultural life of their communities. States are thus challenged by calls for cultural autonomy, racial and gender equality, self-determination, and even territorial secession, all potential routes toward full respect for group rights but also likely to threaten state authority. Group rights movements, and their attending human rights claims, contest both the ideal of universal norms (which assume a certain homogeneity, a "common humanity") and the territorial integrity of states themselves. Can international law guarantee a right to cultural preservation and still preserve the stability of the state system?

A. COLLECTIVE PARADIGMS

Indigenous Claims. Benedict Kingsbury, "Reconciling Five Competing Conceptual Structures of Indigenous Peoples' Claims in International and Comparative Law" 34 N.Y.U. J. Int'l L. & Pol. 189 (2001).

"Minorities"—or more often, a variant such as "national minorities"—has been utilized as a juridical category in international treaty law for several centuries and was promulgated actively and operationalized by post-World War I legal instruments and League of Nations institutions. After 1945, however, states looked to the lessons of Nazi Germany's irredentist use of disaffected German minorities in neighboring countries and to the imminent problems of nation-building in post-colonial states and became reluctant to establish international law standards focused specifically on minorities, preferring instead to build a general human rights program applicable to all individuals. Hence, there is a lack of minority rights clauses, beyond prohibitions of discrimination, in the 1948 Universal Declaration of Human Rights, the 1950 European Convention on Human Rights, and comparable regional instruments in the Americas and Africa. The body of international legal instruments focused specifically on "minorities" is thus an impoverished one. In the early 1990s, recognition of a need to face this deficiency resulted in the U.N. Declaration on Minorities (1992) and the Council of Europe Framework Convention for the Protection of National Minorities (1995); however, neither is very expansive, as many state governments have continued to be unwilling to support general normative provisions that may encourage group demands or inhibit national integration. Germany, for example, is willing to grant significant legal entitlements to some long-established groups within Germany, including the Danish and Sorb minorities, but much less to other minority groups. France continues to assert that there are no minorities in France to whom international law instruments on minorities should apply, although its internal legal practice is more nuanced, especially in favoring a degree of autonomy for Corsica. Algeria, Burundi, Madagascar, Senegal, Turkey, and Venezuela are among other states that have at times taken positions similar to that of France. Article 27 of the International Covenant on Civil and Political Rights, an instrument drafted in the early 1950s and adopted in 1966, thus remains the principal general minority rights treaty text of global application, and it is worded as an individual rights provision phrased with an aspiration to avoid encouraging the appearance of new minorities and seeking to impose only modest duties on states.*

Indigenous Right to Autonomy. Raidza Torres Wick Commentaries, "Commentaries on Raidza Torres, 'The Rights of Indigenous Populations: The Emerging International Norm'" (16 Yale J. Int'l L. 127, 1991), "Revisiting the Emerging International Norm on Indigenous Rights: Autonomy As an Option" 25 Yale J. Int'l L. 291 (2000).

One of the main objectives of the International Decade of the World's Indigenous Populations is adoption of a declaration on indigenous rights. There has been progress at the United Nations and the Organization of American States (OAS). In 1993, the U.N. Working Group on Indigenous Populations agreed on a draft declaration on indigenous rights (U.N. Draft Declaration), which the Sub–Commission on Prevention of Discrimination and Protection of Minorities submitted to the U.N. Commission on Human Rights in 1994. This declaration addresses cultural, economic and social, and land rights and, unlike International Labor Organization (ILO) Convention No. 169, establishes a comprehensive right to self-determination that, if read broadly, allows for independence. Further, the declaration calls upon states to take effective and appropriate measures to enforce it and asks the United Nations to take the necessary steps to facilitate its implementation.

In 1995, the U.N. Commission on Human Rights established an open-ended, intersessional working group to finalize the U.N. Draft

---

* Article 27 provides: "In those States in which ethnic, religious or linguistic minorities exist, persons belonging to such minorities shall not be denied the right, in community with the other members of their group, to enjoy their own culture, to profess and practise their own religion, or to use their own language."

Declaration. Indigenous advocacy groups and states participate in the working group sessions, which have been heated at times. The main point of disagreement remains the scope of self-determination rights. The OAS's efforts to adopt a declaration on indigenous rights have met with similar difficulties on the issue of self-determination, and indigenous groups have opposed aspects of the declaration adopted by the OAS's Inter-American Commission on Human Rights (the "OAS Draft Declaration"). Until this issue is resolved, it is unlikely that a final declaration will be issued.

The challenges in finalizing a declaration on indigenous rights—whether at the United Nations or the OAS—should not obscure the significant progress made towards the codification of a norm on indigenous rights. The fact that draft declarations are making their way through two top international organizations, and that the United Nations has made passage of such declaration a priority of the International Decade of the World's Indigenous Populations, underscores this progress. Further, states are modifying their behavior vis-à-vis indigenous populations in response to the norm.

For example, Ecuador's 1998 constitution specifically addresses the collective rights of indigenous populations and recognizes, inter alia, rights to their ancestral communal lands, cultural development, and economic and social development. Mexico has ratified the ILO Convention No. 169, and despite the government's concerns over the impact of indigenous claims on the unity of the Mexican state and sporadic armed confrontation, some indigenous villages in Chiapas have already organized themselves as autonomous communities. In 1992, the High Court in Australia issued its Mabo v. Queensland (No. 2) decision recognizing indigenous peoples' land rights and rejecting the concept of terra nullius. In New Zealand, the Waitangi Tribunal continues to review and adjudicate claims under the 1840 Treaty of Waitangi. Adoption of a final declaration on the rights of indigenous peoples by the United Nations should propel states to take further steps to incorporate indigenous rights into domestic laws and to provide for their implementation.*

In 1991, the emerging norm on indigenous peoples' rights consisted of four principal categories: cultural protections, land rights, economic and social welfare, and self-determination. These categories continue to form the core of the international norm on indigenous rights. There is general agreement among indigenous groups, international organizations, and states on the main aspects of the cultural and welfare rights of indigenous peoples.** Similarly, many states recognize indigenous peo-

---

* Despite the progress in the last ten years on indigenous rights, these rights are violated even in states that have recognized the indigenous norm. However, violation of a norm does not negate its existence.

** One emerging area of disagreement between states and indigenous groups is that of intellectual property rights. Indigenous groups are increasingly asking for rights in the development of medicines, science, and technology derived from their traditional knowledge and uses of flora and fauna. Under these claims, indigenous peoples may be entitled to compensation from companies that have developed technologies incorporating indigenous groups' resources, knowl-

ples' rights to develop their designated lands, although indigenous groups may express dissatisfaction with the land set aside for them by the state. Major disagreements between states and indigenous groups involve the scope of indigenous groups' right to self-determination and their potential to fracture a state's boundaries.

Self-determination claims may take different forms, ranging from independence to the power to determine local laws within a reservation. States are increasingly willing to grant limited self-rule to their indigenous peoples but have been reluctant to grant broad self-determination rights that, if fully exercised, would undermine the state's territorial integrity. The fragmentation of the Soviet Union and Yugoslavia has reminded states of their vulnerability to minority groups' self-determination claims and ethnic strife. Reflecting states' concerns, the OAS Draft Declaration recognizes indigenous peoples' right only to determine their political status (including autonomy and self-government), while the ILO Convention No. 169 is largely silent on this subject. Although some indigenous groups note that they do not seek independence, indigenous peoples' advocates have often insisted on a broad right to self-determination similar to that contained in the U.N. Draft Declaration.

There tends to be an inverse relationship between the definition of "indigenous peoples" and the scope of self-determination. A broader definition of the term "indigenous peoples" will bring more groups under the protection of a norm that recognizes a variety of individual and collective rights. Some of these rights—such as the right to land and self-determination—require that the state cede or share power, land and resources. If the right to self-determination in the U.N. Declaration (presently Draft Article 3) is left open-ended, or defined broadly to include the right of secession, states will perceive it as a threat to their territorial integrity. This perception will increase as the number of groups that qualify as indigenous peoples multiplies. There will be a growing concern that, at their most extreme, claims of indigenous rights will lead to political instability throughout the world by contributing to the balkanization of states, the proliferation of microstates lacking sufficient land or resources to support themselves adequately, and additional (non-indigenous) secessionist claims and armed conflict. In response to these concerns, states may seek to define self-determination narrowly in terms of limited control over specific "local" issues like resources and education, or worse yet, reject the indigenous norm altogether.

Definitions of indigenous peoples focus on their shared history of colonization and their distinct identity that reflects their "historical continuity with pre-invasion and pre-colonial societies." Self-identification plays a key role in whether a group is deemed an indigenous population. Geopolitical changes in the last decade, however, may sweep

edge of plants, or traditions. But most states' intellectual property laws do not recognize the claims of indigenous groups. Further, states are under pressure from corporations that are vulnerable to the intellectual property claims of indigenous peoples, but do not want to pay "royalties" to indigenous groups. Unsurprisingly, domestic governments have not been eager to implement these claims.

under this definition additional groups that had not previously gained media and international attention. For example, prior to the disintegration of Yugoslavia, Albanians in Kosovo were not generally mentioned in conjunction with indigenous peoples and their rights. Yet there are persuasive arguments that Albanians in Kosovo have a "historical continuity with pre-invasion" societies, and that, under Serbian rule, they represented a politically subordinate sector of society "determined to preserve, develop and transmit to future generations their ancestral territories, and their ethnic identity."

Are the Albanians in Kosovo "indigenous peoples"? Neither the U.N. Draft Declaration nor the OAS Draft Declaration provides a definition of the term "indigenous peoples," although the OAS declaration considers self-identification a key element in determining whether a group is indigenous. This lack of specificity would allow different states and advocacy groups to have differing views on what constitutes an indigenous group, resulting in conflict as to the scope of the indigenous norm. If a declaration on indigenous rights is to have practical meaning, it is essential that it contain a definition of the term "indigenous" that sufficiently limits the universe of groups that fall within its scope, and does not rely mainly on self-identification.

A clear definition of the term "indigenous people" should give states a greater level of comfort in recognizing indigenous groups' collective rights because the number of groups entitled to these rights will be narrowed. Further, this should create a more favorable environment for reaching a compromise on self-determination. If indigenous peoples are not seeking independence, states and indigenous groups should be able to reach a consensus on self-rule. States are already granting significant autonomy to indigenous groups. The goal should be to encourage rather than inhibit this behavior. Pressuring states to recognize an open-ended right to self-determination that could be used to justify secession will result in greater opposition to all indigenous rights and in the loss of important gains obtained in the past decade.

There ought to be a renewed focus on defining self-determination in terms of the broadest possible self-rule within the boundaries of a state. Autonomous communities such as Puerto Rico provide a model that can serve as a starting point for defining indigenous peoples' self-government. Limiting self-determination to internal self-rule for purposes of a declaration on indigenous rights need not mean that indigenous groups can never possess a right of secession. The U.N. Charter contains various references to the "principle of equal rights and self-determination of peoples." Similarly, the Universal Declaration of Human Rights notes that "the will of the people shall be the basis of the authority of government." Failure to restate these rights in the proposed declaration on indigenous rights will not extinguish them. The final U.N. declaration should simply note that any rights that indigenous peoples might have under other international instruments or in domestic law are not impaired or limited by the provisions of the declaration. This course of action should improve the likelihood that a declaration on indigenous rights will be adopted by the United Nations before the International Decade of the World's Indigenous Populations comes to an end.

Women's Rights. Rhoda E. Howard–Hassmann, Dueling Fates: Should The International Legal Regime Accept A Collective Or Individual Paradigm To Protect Women's Rights? Symposium Article: "(Dis)Embedded Women" 24 Mich. J. Int'l L. 227 (2002).

In some societies and among some communities, it is thought that to promote women's rights will undermine the religious group. This fear reflects reality. By virtue of their already being protected by individual human rights, women may well undermine tight collective membership in their religious groups. They may do so if they exercise their right freely to choose or to leave their religion. The right to apostasy, and the right to be an atheist, may remove a woman entirely not only from the legal (where there are State religions) but also from the normative or moral control of her religious group. Women may also undermine this tight collective membership if they exercise the right freely to choose whom they will marry. Thus, Ahmad Farraq in 1990 opposed article 16(1) of the Universal Declaration of Human Rights, which prescribes the right to marry "without any limitation due to race, nationality or religion," because he believed a Muslim woman should not marry a man who is not a Muslim.* Where religion and community are closely linked if not identical, marriage outside the religious group also removes women from the control of the social community.

One might suppose that any woman subject to normative or religious controls that deny her equality with men in her community will remove herself from that community so that she might enjoy her equal rights in the wider public sphere. But we know that this is not so.

Some women may independently and autonomously so value their religious membership that they will voluntarily subordinate themselves to its control, even in situations in which to do so contradicts the equal rights that as individuals they enjoy in the wider public sphere. For example, some Orthodox Jewish women voluntarily accept the principle that they may not divorce without a Get, a document signed by their husbands releasing them from their marriage. Some Catholic women vote for political parties that advocate restrictions on birth control and abortion, as in Poland since the end of communism.

Women may strive for greater equality within their religious groups, as do many Jewish or Catholic feminists. Nevertheless, because they value their religious membership so strongly, these women do not renounce Judaism or Catholicism, even as they continue to be subject to these religions' strictures of inequality between men and women. Even as they simultaneously and willingly partake in religious rituals that symbolize the subordination of women to men (such as the absence of women priests in Catholicism), they may prefer to stay within their

---

* Ahmad Farraq, "Human Rights and Liberties in Islam," in *Human Rights in a Pluralist World: Individuals and Collectivities* (Jan Berting et al. eds., 1990).

religious community, moving it through internal debate toward greater equality. Many Muslim, Christian, and Jewish women press for equality within their religious communities by referring to more liberal interpretations of religious texts, rather than renouncing their membership or denouncing their religions for their discriminatory teachings or practices.

Women who belong to religious groups that suffer discrimination, or that feel besieged because of their minority position in a certain country, are particularly unwilling to undermine their communities by making feminist demands. Thus, for many Jewish and Muslim women in North America, loyalty to their religio-ethnic communities supercedes their loyalty to the wider national group of women. Their primary interest is in keeping their community vibrant and close, not in asserting their feminist demands. They may be part of the statistical aggregate, but their sense of identity is not bound up with that aggregate. They are often more at home in the collectivity that is constituted by their religion, than in the physical group of women.

B. SELF–DETERMINATION

Territoriality. Lea Brilmayer, "Commentaries on Lea Brilmayer, 'Secession and Self–Determination: A Territorial Interpretation' (16 Yale J. Int'l L. 177, 1991), 'Secession and Self–Determination: One Decade Later' " 25 Yale J. Int'l L. 283 (2000).

There was little reason to think in 1990 that secession might turn out to be an important topic. Since *Secession and Self–Determination* was published in the *Yale Journal of International Law*, however, the Baltic states left the Soviet Union and the rest of the Soviet Union crumbled. Yugoslavia and Czechoslovakia fractured. Eritrea asserted its independence from Ethiopia after military success and then a democratic referendum. Quebec's separatist aspirations from Canada became front page news (along with the comparable aspirations of various of the indigenous peoples of Quebec). East Timor succeeded in its drive for independence. Prior to 1990, the only successful separatist movement had been in Pakistan, where East Pakistan had left to become Bangladesh. Other separatist movements, such as Biafra's war for independence, had failed completely.

The events of the last decade have by and large borne out the analysis offered in that article. The thesis there was that what makes a separatist movement's claim to independence convincing is the possession of an historical claim that its territory was wrongfully annexed. Secession, I argued, is correctly understood as an appropriate remedy for prior illegal annexation. This analysis was vindicated by the fact that rationales for the successful separatist movements of the 1990s were all articulated in the same terms.

In this respect, the new wave of secessions can be understood as analogous to the earlier wave of decolonizations in the 1950s and 1960s. That wave of decolonizations was powered by the modern acknowledgment that earlier colonial annexations had been morally indefensible. The 1990s showed that the principle that annexation of some other group's territory is wrongful is not limited to what was known as "salt water colonialism," meaning colonial empires that stretched overseas. Whether a conquered territory is treated as a colony or annexed to the central portion of an empire, its people have a right to fight for their freedom. In their fight for freedom, they are called "secessionists."*

The common characteristic of all strong cases for secession is a showing of illegal annexation. It was the historical record of illegal annexation that caused us to applaud the newfound independence of the Baltic states, of Eritrea, and of East Timor. Earlier theorists were incorrect in treating the key determinant to be homogeneity of the conquered people. What matters is not that it is "a people" who are seeking to be free. What matters is that this group—whether a homogeneous "people" or not—has a right to a particular parcel of land, a right that was wrongfully taken from them by a powerful neighbor.

It is important to ask how this obvious point might be overlooked. How could international lawyers and theorists have spent so many years assuming that the key point was ethnic, religious, or linguistic homogeneity rather than a history of wrongful annexation? When a group seeks to set up a new state on a particular piece of land, how could it not matter whether the group had a good territorial claim to the piece of land? In suggesting an answer to this question, I want to suggest that the failure to recognize this obvious point may be more general. The same odd blindness infects most Western discussions of "nationalism," to which similar misunderstandings pertain. It is caused by ignorance and by unwillingness to try to understand the moral claims of people with whom we do not identify—for reasons of differences of geographic location, race, religion, or culture.

In evaluating secessionist claims specifically, there are two different aspects of the claim on which one might focus. Traditionally, theorists had focused on the cohesiveness of the group asserting the claim—whether the group in question was a distinct "people" in the religious, linguistic, or ethnic sense. There is another issue at stake, however: the objective validity of the claim that the particular group espouses. Thus (as I argued ten years ago) the claim to a particular piece of territory will be more or less convincing depending on the existence (or nonexistence) of a historical claim to land. Regardless of the identity of the group making the claim, the claim itself might be more or less persuasive, depending on historical fact, legal reasoning, moral argumentation, and so forth.

---

* It is revealing that most "secessionists" reject the term. They typically claim that they are not seeking secession, but recognition of an independent state that existed all along. They argue that as the annexation of their territory was illegal, it was null and void. Thus they deny that they are trying to alter the existing territorial borders of the larger state. Instead, they claim, they are trying to preserve territorial borders as they always existed in the past.

Similarly, but more generally, nationalist claims potentially have two different aspects to investigate. One might focus on the identity of the group asserting the claim and find it morally significant that the claim in question is being asserted by a distinct national group (Poles, Armenians, Serbs, or East Timorese). Instead, however, one might ask whether the claim in question is objectively justified regardless of the nature of the group that asserts it. Claims that a particular national group is entitled to something are not necessarily dependent normatively on the fact that it is a national group that is making the claim. Indeed, I would argue, they typically do not.

The standard interpretation of nationalist claims is that they are saying: "My nation, right or wrong." The assumption is that nationalist claims are not based on anything more intelligent than a desire that one's nation prevail. But nationalists typically do not mean to be making such a claim. Instead, they are typically saying: "My nation, because it is in the right." Of course, there is always the chance that the person is wrong because his or her nation is actually not in the right. But this is no more true for claims made by nations than for claims made by individual people. The fact that a person is claiming something that he or she is not entitled to means that he or she is making an unwarranted claim. It does not mean that he or she is not attempting to rely on arguments about right and wrong.

The fact that a claim is being asserted on behalf of one's nation is not thought, in and of itself, to give one a justification for advancing the claim. The nationalist essentially admits that it is theoretically possible that the claim might be unjustified, even while he or she believes sincerely and deeply that the facts and argument on which the claim is based are in fact correct. The nationalist is not claiming that so long as he or she acts on behalf of his or her nation, no justification is needed. The nationalist simply feels that an adequate justification exists.

The erroneous interpretation of nationalist claims as being all of the sort "my nation, right or wrong" has two consequences. First, this misunderstanding obscures whatever real justification might exist (or be thought to exist by the national group) for the claim in question. The outside observer has no reason, or need, to take seriously the moral or legal argument that the nationalist wishes to advance. This misunderstanding thereby relieves the outside observer of any need to become acquainted with the facts or arguments of the parties to the dispute. Discussion in the outside world becomes a highly relativistic account of "what the Serbs want" or "what the Croats think they stand to gain." Once argument is reduced to this level, there can be no right and wrong. One nationalistic argument is as good or bad as any other.

Second, this misunderstanding gives nationalistic claims a pervasively negative connotation. Nationalist claims are bad because the essence of the claim is exclusionary. One wants something for one's own group, regardless of whether that group has any entitlement, and one's own group is defined in intrinsically ascriptive and illiberal terms. Nationalism smacks of racism, xenophobia, and bigotry.

With no genuine moral issue in sight—and with the atavistic reputation that "nationalism" has come to possess—the rest of the world dismisses real disputes, over serious matters, as "tribal" (if such disputes arise between black people) or "ethnic" (if they arise between whites). Regardless of where they arise, there is no need to take them seriously. They are bloody, primitive, and childlike. The West watches smugly.

Dismissing a position as "nationalistic" is essentially an ad hominem form of argument. The characterization distracts attention from the merits or demerits of the underlying claim. Dismissing claims to independence as "secessionist" is a particular application of this false and condescending logic. There truly are rights and wrongs in international relations, and the linguistic, ethnic, or religious homogeneity of the group asserting a claim has little, if anything, to do with whether a particular claim is right or wrong. The West takes seriously its own claims to what is right and what is wrong. It should take the claims of the rest of the world, and in particular the developing world, just as seriously.

Territorial Integrity. Paul C. Szasz, "The Irresistible Force of Self-Determination Meets the Impregnable Fortress of Territorial Integrity: A Cautionary Fairy Tale About Clashes in Kosovo and Elsewhere" 28 Ga. J. Int'l & Comp. L. 1 (1999).

Once upon a time, in a faraway world in which international law still mattered—remember this is just a fairy tale and that I am speaking of a very distant world—there was:

1. A force that many considered irresistible, called Self-Determination; and there was

2. A fortress that was advertised as impregnable, called the Territorial Integrity of States;

and these two fought many a brave battle for predominance; also participating in this conflict was:

3. A mischievous troll called the Uti Possidetis Principle—whose full name: "uti possidetis, ita possidetis," roughly translates as "[you may] keep what you had"—who sometimes reinforced Self-Determination by helping to put firm boundaries around newly created countries which could then claim Territorial Integrity, and sometimes reinforced the Territorial Integrity of States by hardening boundaries against the claims of Self-Determination; further there was

4. An evil wizard called Violence who was trying to attain international status and meanwhile sowed confusion among the other actors. When provoked he could become a giant whom no one could withstand; when allied with Self-Determination he was

often called Terrorism, and when allied with the Territorial Integrity of States he was sometimes called State–Terrorism; and, finally, as in any good fairy tale, there was

5. A white knight called International Law, who fought the wizard Violence, sometimes successfully, though rarely so when the wizard turned into a giant.

The present tale is about the interaction of all these actors and about their shifting alliances and conflicts in that faraway world. Each of them has a lengthy but somewhat checkered history:

Violence is the oldest, originating in the chaos before law emerged.

The Territorial Integrity of States is probably next in seniority, deriving from strivings for stability. It is recognized in UN Charter article 2(4), which upholds the Territorial Integrity of States against external military attacks, but not necessarily against subversion by Self–Determination.

International Law was born some 350 years ago in Westphalia at the end of the Thirty Years War.* Since then it has developed greatly and especially in the past half century has enjoyed a healthy adolescent growth spurt.

Self–Determination itself entered the stage at the end of the 18th century with the American and French Revolutions, one against external oppression and the other against internal. The Vienna Conference ending the Napoleonic wars sought to contain it, but in the 19th century it nevertheless manifested itself in the Balkans with the liberation of Greece, Serbia and Montenegro from the faltering Ottoman Empire, and in the decolonization of Latin America. During World War I both Lenin and Wilson proclaimed it—from different perspectives—but at the Paris Peace Conference it received only lip service as the Allied and Associated Powers re-arranged the map of Central Europe and the Balkans to suit their own misperceived interests. After World War II, Self–Determination was proclaimed in Articles 1(2) and 55 of the UN Charter—though not in the Chapters relating to nonself-governing or trust territories. Nevertheless, it became the intellectual engine of decolonization, a process now essentially completed. Most recently Self–Determination received a new lease on life—though subject to some constraints that I will mention—with the break-up of some of the post-WWI constructs: Czechoslovakia and the Soviet Union peacefully, and Yugoslavia violently.

Finally, the Uti Possidetis Principle apparently came into being with the decolonization of Latin America and later was observed in that of Africa. More recently it was cited as an apparent stand-in for the Territorial Integrity of States—as a justification for not allowing Croatia and Bosnia to be divided along ethnic lines, after these two new states had themselves been allowed to split off from Yugoslavia.

* [International law was born some 4000 years ago in ancient Mesopotamia.]—Eds.

So, who is stronger: Self–Determination or the Territorial Integrity of States? And on whose side is International Law?

International Law is largely made and practiced by states, that is by governments, and each government is bent on at least protecting its own Territorial Integrity. When the Territorial Integrity of a State is threatened anywhere in the world, other countries instinctively come to its defense. This is what has happened in respect of Cyprus, which has been effectively divided between a Northern (Turkish) sector and a Southern (Greek) one since 1974, when both sectors were ethnically cleansed; it is clear that the twenty percent Turks will not live in a state with a massive Greek majority, but nevertheless the international community is insisting there can be only one Cyprus—even if the United Nations must patrol the boundary between the two sectors indefinitely.

Let me now advance a proposition—which may be unpopular because it appears to legitimize Violence, or rather it openly assigns it a role in determining the conflict between Self–Determination and Territorial Integrity. My proposition is that when Terrorism becomes so strong that it can no longer be suppressed without an unacceptable level of State–Terrorism, then the state concerned has, either as a victim of Violence or as its perpetrator, lost the legitimacy that enables it to insist on its Territorial Integrity. Sometimes a State can avoid that fate by countering Terrorism not only by its own Violence, but also by other measures that deprive the terrorists of support and ultimately of legitimacy. In other words, Violence must be given its due, either by skillfully turning it aside or by formally yielding to it; it cannot just be disregarded because it is, almost by definition, not legitimate.

Let us now look at some alternative courses of action for the international community in situations where ethnic or other conflicts lead to Violence within a state:

1. The international community can refuse to intervene, even if a country is unable to control domestic Violence; if horrible massacres result, just shut off CNN, and close borders to the entry of refugees. But, in practice, these measures cannot be taken, as we learned in Rwanda and again in Kosovo.

2. The world community can also assist in suppressing Self–Determination in favor of Territorial Integrity—the course it is at present inclined to take. In Bosnia we see the results of that strategy: an indefinite, massive occupation, which still does not succeed in really reunifying the country and cannot help the displaced half of its population to return to their original homes. All of NATO's forces and all of NATO's men really can't put Yugoslavia/Kosovo together again!

3. Finally, the international community can tip the scale in favor of Self–Determination and against unconditional Territorial Integrity; if thereby new states are created it will, at the most, have to patrol their new mutual border—a much easier task than an occupation.

As to the economic viability of such state fragments, this should matter less and less in a more and more integrated region or world.

So, there it is. A pragmatic solution that may not be entirely morally pleasing, because it assigns such an important role to Violence in determining the outcome. And thus we see that this is not really a fairy tale. For in a fairy tale evil wizards are always defeated and destroyed, and the principal protagonists live together happily ever after. But the real world is not like that. It is an imperfect world in which unsatisfactory compromises must be made and ideals cannot always be maintained in their pristine purity. Nevertheless, knights must sally forth to right what wrongs they can and to protect the powerless as far as possible. And in doing so, they may find International Law as a useful ally, by no means invincible but hopefully steadily growing stronger.

These thoughts reflect my personal experiences during the past decade: first in participating in the successful liberation and attainment of independence of Namibia; then in a long, fruitless attempt to negotiate a constitution for Bosnia that would square the circle of creating a democratic state which a majority of its citizens do not want; and finally in trying to formulate a new constitution for Cyprus, in that the conundrum was essentially the same: how to create a functioning and democratic state, no matter how decentralized, that fully and permanently protects a suspicious minority against a large and unsympathetic majority. In these assignments I have learned both the limitations of international law and the satisfaction of pursuing it.

Autonomy and Minority Groups. Geoff Gilbert, "Autonomy and Minority Groups: A Right in International Law?" 35 Cornell Int'l L.J. 307 (2002).

For some groups, the autonomy to preserve their own culture will be the fullest extent of their self-determination, whereas for other groups it will extend to political autonomy through a federal State structure. In that sense, autonomy is a continuum, providing an appropriate degree of control to each group within society over its own affairs. International law accords this right to autonomy to groups within society through two guarantees: the right to self-determination and the right of members of ethnic, linguistic, and religious groups to enjoy their own culture. As the Permanent Court of International Justice noted in 1935, "There would be no true equality between a majority and a minority if the latter were deprived of its own institutions, and were consequently compelled to renounce that which constitutes the very essence of its being as a minority." Also, as the Human Rights Committee in Lovelace noted in 1981 with respect to Article 27: "The Committee recognizes the need to define the category of persons entitled to live on a reserve, for such purposes as ... protection of its resources and preservation of the identity of its people."

The confusion prevalent in discussions on these topics stems from the loose use of overlapping and undefined terminology. Autonomy is in one sense but one aspect of self-determination, but it is also much broader than a right solely of 'peoples' and extends to traditional minority rights. The confusion has been enhanced, though, by the inclusion of clauses dealing with autonomy, in the sense of regional or local self-government, in the more recent international instruments dealing with minority rights. The confusion is avoidable if one considers only the degree of control over its own affairs and the powers to achieve that end that the group requires, and one does not worry whether what is undoubtedly a minority group is also a "people." To take two examples, a religious group such as the Free Presbyterians in Scotland would not want territorial self-government, but, in satisfying Article 27 of the International Covenant on Civil and Political Rights (ICCPR), the State would necessarily permit it to run its own internal affairs and to hold property for its own purposes—in running the Church, it would be autonomous. On the other hand, some ethnic-national groups are recognizable and distinct from the dominant group within the State because of a difference of religion; in those cases, mere autonomy over church affairs would not properly meet the State's obligation to ensure the self-determination of all its peoples and, where appropriate, territorial self-government would be the true means whereby the group would achieve self-determination through being included in the democratic governance of the State. Furthermore, autonomy can meet the needs of an identifiable ethnic group that is not concentrated in one region of the State but is distributed in clusters. It is autonomy that spans both Articles 1 and 27 of the ICCPR, its implementation under each Article being appropriate not only to the particular right, but, more importantly, to the nature of the group, too. A right to autonomy, therefore, is both radical, since it applies to all groups in society, whether deemed peoples or minorities, and, at the same time, the logical consequence of two existing rights, the right of peoples to self-determination and the right of persons belonging to minorities to enjoy their own culture.

The right to autonomy is a right for the group to decide its own affairs, determined by reference to the nature of the group within the society. Although the degree of autonomy to be accorded will vary, there are, for the purposes of this paper, three facets to it—participation, culture, and financial matters.

Together, participatory, cultural, and financial autonomy, appropriate to the needs of the group, are the pre-eminent means of providing for the right to self-determination of non-colonial peoples and the rights of minorities within the State structure.

Secession and Self–Determination. Alfred P. Rubin, "Secession and Self–Determination: A Legal, Moral, and Political Analysis" 36 Stan. J Int'l L. 253 (2000).

Politically, it is undeniable that there are circumstances in which, correctly or not, a dissident group feels that the moral benefits of independence outweigh its detriments, or that the detriments fall on yet others whose well-being is not felt to be the responsibility of the acting group. Where there is a relative balance of forces (political, military, economic, and whatever other factors of power apply locally) the tensions can go on indefinitely. The receding "sovereign" is usually (but not always) reluctant to accept the secession as a fact.

Assume now that a secession has succeeded politically. To establish the moral framework for stability, it might be necessary to convince the populace of the seceding unit that a moral order as well as a political and legal order has been established. Revenge for real or imagined atrocities might be sought by both the new authorities and the old. Although political stability can be established by mere force, it is likely nowadays to lead to guerrilla attacks and endless reprisals. A pattern of unending reprisals is obviously inconsistent with stability. It would seem normally to be in the interest of the new sovereign to establish its moral position. There is, thus, a moral as well as a political calculation to be made in some cases to find a useful balance between the establishment of political stability by brute force and the establishment of that stability by the widespread acceptance of the new order as just. Indeed, it is not clear that either pattern, that of stability established by force and that of stability established by justice, can ever succeed in the long run without some intermixture. There are those who will never concede that any situation is just until all those in any way bound to a former oppressor are killed, expelled, or otherwise rendered helpless. There are others who will argue to the same ends on the ground of security or the overriding needs of stability as the basis for their conception of wise politics as well as justice. It is undeniable that in some societies, force is the glue that holds things together regardless of the considerations that others call justice. From this point of view, an internal situation might be stable but nobody would want to risk his/her capital or moral reputation on the society that bases its stability on force, whether in the interest of what the dominant members of that society consider justice or not. Furthermore, nobody would want to risk his/her capital or moral reputation dealing with or in a society that does not display some degree of legal and political stability. Again the problem is essentially not solvable in generalities.

On the other hand, it is predictable that economic and political stability, based on force or not, will encourage investment. In current international society, ways will usually be found to rationalize profitable economic dealing when that stability arises, regardless of the moral pain of those whose tender consciences prefer to deal only with or in societies that meet their standards of moral behavior. In general, it can be said that there will be a need for international dealing when a seceding province has established that its political situation meets the minimum demands of stability, and that third persons are interested in treating the now independent sovereign as if its legal order acted more or less independently of the legal order of the former metropole. In these circumstances, the international legal order must sooner or later accommodate itself to the new situation, with or without formal recognition.

From a legal point of view, the problem of transitional justice is one of determining which legal order governs the seceding entity. If the order of the receding metropolitan state determines justice in the seceding area, then the acts of the officials of the new state might be considered treasonous. If the order of the new state determines justice, then the acts of the soldiery of the receding metropole might equally be considered treasonous. If international law determines justice, then there is recognition of at least belligerency, which might well upset the receding sovereign because, as noted above, the receding sovereign typically denies that the matter involves two international entities. The simplest accommodation (and nobody could call it a "solution" or "resolution") is for third-party states to abstain from expressing any view until their own interests require attaching labels. This implies a regime characterized by the international law of belligerency and third-party neutrality.

The situation gets more complex when the third power has a role in administering at least part of the territory or population involved, as is the case with the forces of five NATO countries plus Russia in Kosovo at this time. The usual accommodation is for the authorities of the administering power(s) to determine the constitutional law of the place on the basis of their political interests and perceptions of politically significant facts, while the normal international law of belligerent occupation applies to the belligerent forces and nonbelligerent civilians. Under that model, the law of the receding metropole usually continues to apply to normal transactions among noncombatants; private property remains protected by law (although perhaps not very well protected in fact); murder and assault outside of combat remain murder and assault under the law of the receding metropole. The contract, tort, criminal, and other parts of private law are administered by whoever is in control of the levers of authority to administer the law. That control is normally determined not by law, but by the use of force and individuals' accommodations to it. Although justice has very little to do with the situation, in the interest of stability the administering power usually tries to administer rules of law that the private parties will accept as if just. That is not very different from the normal administration of justice in a stable society under its normal legal order.

A more complex question is that of reconciliation. Any major change in the constitutional order of any state is likely (although not necessarily) accompanied by bloodshed. Those losing authority or property usually fancy themselves in a defensive position and interpret the morality and law of self-defense to give them authority to commit whatever atrocities they consider useful to achieving their political goal of retaining either authority or property or both. The laws of war might purport to forbid at least some of those atrocities, but states have been notoriously reluctant to agree to the purview of any third party over the conduct of a struggle they consider internal to themselves. This is especially true if it involves the secession of a territory they regard as historically "theirs." Indeed, in all four of the 1949 Geneva Conventions relating to the protection of the victims of armed conflict, the major distinction in rules is based on the categorization of the conflict as an armed conflict "between two or more of the High Contracting Parties" (i.e., states), or an "armed conflict not of an international character occurring in the territory of one of the High Contracting Parties." The 1977 Protocols to those four conventions repeat this distinction: Protocol I relates only to international armed conflicts, Protocol II only to armed conflicts not of an international character occurring in the territory of one of the High Contracting Parties. Thus, although some rules have been agreed by positive law to restrict the atrocities committed by a defending government against some of its internal opponents or by some of those opponents against adherents of the defending government, there seems to be no jus standi in any other party to the Geneva Conventions or their Protocols to raise the issue as a matter of law.

This does not mean that the international community must remain silent in the face of atrocities. There are nongovernmental bodies, like the International Committee of the Red Cross and Amnesty International, whose public statements even in amicus legal briefs do not require legal standing in the sense used here, and forums like the U.N. General Assembly, at which such questions can be raised by governments regardless of their lack of standing. But they are not questions to be resolved by legal means. Instead, they are to be discussed as political or moral issues. It can even be suggested that one of the great successes of the Cold War was the conclusion of the 1975 Helsinki Accords under which the only colorably legal obligation any of the parties accepted was an obligation to discuss, at periodical meetings of the parties, progress made toward achieving the agreed goals of respect for the equal rights of peoples and their "right to self-determination." It might be noted that no provision was made for the representatives of those peoples to participate in the meetings, and, of course, no procedures were adopted for assuring that purported representatives had authority to speak for anybody but themselves as individuals. Yet, the ability of one country to call for open discussion of the practices of another in its internal difficulties did exert political pressure on all countries to observe their moral commitments and to live up to their stated aspirations.

Experience with the Helsinki Accords should point the way to the greatest influence that the nonlegal world can apply to those who commit atrocities: exposure and discussion coupled with municipal legislation or policy decisions. Exposure does not involve criminal trials or questions of standing. It might be institutionalized in municipal or international truth and reconciliation commissions, or it might remain in uninstitutionalized news media or other channels for exposure and truth. If nobody is willing to discuss and react to the exposure of an atrocity, then the conscience of mankind will have been tested and the purported atrocity held inconsequential. If the opinions of those who hold that the atrocity is more significant than the resulting benefit prove powerless to affect behavior, or if the detriment that flows from its punishment proves unable to influence the behavior of those who benefit from the atrocity, then the atrocity will remain uncompensated. In that case there need be no pretense of justice and the difficulties of reconciliation will be the practical result of this obduracy.

If, however, the winners of the struggle for authority truly want reconciliation, then exposure of all atrocities in the preceding struggle seems to be necessary. The moral remedies include isolation—losers and their friends (or simply those horrified by the reports of atrocities) refuse to deal with those whom they feel are responsible for the atrocities. Other remedies might include a sullen and unproductive population, continued murmurings and unquiet, and general difficulties in exercising authority without the expensive use of demoralizing force. At best, for those ordering or committing atrocities, an inability to leave their country might result. This result is often called the Waldheim solution—a former Secretary–General of the United Nations and President of Austria was effectively confined to his lovely country when he had reason to expect an old age of respect and honors abroad. This, despite the fact that Kurt Waldheim has never been convicted of anything by any tribunal, international or municipal.

If institutionalized, some weaknesses of the reconciliation process must be recognized. For example, it is patently impossible to isolate within their own communities those in a majority who have actually committed atrocities—Israelis who have killed Palestinians, Palestinians who have killed Israelis; Serbs who have killed Kosovar Albanians, Kosovar Albanians who have killed Serbs; and too many etceteras to contemplate. It is patently impossible, for example in Rwanda, for all those Tutsi who have killed Hutu, or all those Hutu who have killed Tutsi, to be isolated, thus, it is also impossible to exact retributive justice by punishment. In addition, as a practical matter, to expect a person to resume normal intercourse with a neighbor who has tortured or killed relatives of the first is probably unrealistic. And to apply legal or moral sanctions only to the leaders of those who commit atrocities (typically people who have ordered wicked things to be done but who have not killed or tortured anybody themselves) presumes a deterrent effect to those sanctions that has never been shown to work. In my opinion, only time can resolve the issues, and only exposure can allow time to do its healing. In the immediate aftermath of atrocities, no resolution is feasible and the only moral course seems to be to allow people to separate themselves into communities that refuse to deal with those each considers evil. From this point of view, it is possible to question the moral attitudes of the NATO powers in Kosovo, attempting to create a multi-ethnic community there on the model of the United States, Canada, and Australia, ignoring the difficulties faced by the attempts to encourage free movement of labor in Europe. From this point of view, reconciliation is the aim ultimately to be reached only by the people themselves involved, and aided by exposure of the atrocities on all sides until people become willing to face the evils done not only to their ancestors and kin, but by their ancestors and kin.

Legal secession, the creation of a new and independent legal order, is not a resolution of the moral problems. Moral secession, the retreat to the narrow community of like-minded fanatics within an existing legal order, seems a fitting, although only partial and not always feasible, resolution for the fanatics in our midst. That retreat need not be physical to be effective and, although only partial, is not necessarily effective in producing peace and stability. When the retreat to a community of fanatics is physical and accompanied by a legal secession, peace and stability are still not necessarily the outcome.

It would thus seem that despite various treaties, there is no positive law right to secession. The general multilateral treaty terms referring to national self-determination as a right represent agreement as to moral or political principle, not legal entitlement. It would also seem that as a matter of natural law, there is a moral entitlement to secession in some cases, but not in all. Generalities assuring such a right in the moral order either rest on values accepted a priori that are not necessarily shared by those to whom the argument is addressed, or rest on assumptions of value weighing about which reasonable people certainly differ. For example, if there is universal acceptance of a right to reasonable compensation for work done as well as to self-determination, and the price of self-determination is unemployment until a degree of economic stability is achieved, there are two inconsistent rights, and which right dominates will depend on the analyst's own preferences. Politically, an asserted right to secession represents the replacement of a dominant legislative body or class with another; and the receding body or class can be expected to defend its inherited or acquired status. From this point of view, the political right represents only a right to fight for a political goal. The fight involves death and destruction which raise moral problems and, if a legal status of belligerency is achieved, legal problems as well.

In all cases, it seems to be in the interest of the parties to any successful secession to aim at reconciliation. That itself is difficult since there can be no agreement as to the right in positive law. As to justice, that is a term in the moral order and definitions of justice are inconsistent. Therefore, justice cannot be done to universal satisfaction. Politically, the establishment of a stable legal order is probably essential for the establishment of a stable economic order, which is in turn probably essential for the establishment of a stable moral order. Thus it seems to be in the interest of all parties in cases of secession to find stability in whatever distribution of legislative and enforcement authority can be achieved that has some promise of stability. If feelings are high enough, stability might be impossible absent the use of draconian force, which is itself today probably destabilizing in the long run. In any case, absent draconian force, the surest ground rule for stability appears to be exposure of all relevant facts and freedom of movement. I am sorry to end on such a pessimistic note, but we are dealing with human beings and real feelings and convictions, so pessimism seems to be in order.

Chapter 7

HUMANITARIAN INTERVENTION

Editors' Introduction: Are states vulnerable to unauthorized humanitarian intervention and, if so, under what conditions? To an extent, the end of the Cold War de-politicized this question, allowing subsequent humanitarian crises to be considered more for their humanitarian consequences than as side effects of superpower turf war. Legal scholars could now speak in more than theoretical terms about state sovereignty as a *conditional* right, dependent on its treatment of its citizens and subject to external scrutiny. The conditions under which unauthorized humanitarian intervention is legally justified, and the implications for the evolving concept of sovereignty, are discussed in this Chapter.

Humanitarian Intervention. Fernando R. Tesón, *Humanitarian Intervention: An Inquiry into Law and Morality* (2005), excerpt.

Political institutions are justified only by reference to the rights and interests of individuals. International law is no exception. Sovereignty is therefore a *derivative* value, not an intrinsic value. The moral currency of the state wholly depends on its ability to serve the interests and protect the rights of individuals. If liberal institutions are morally justified, then they are appropriate for all persons regardless of history and tradition.

These propositions, however, still underdetermine the question of the legitimacy of humanitarian intervention. A critic can agree with the general views about sovereignty and human rights defended here and still maintain that armed force is never, or almost never, an appropriate remedy to end tyranny. Or she may say that humanitarian interventions can never be conducted permissibly by a state acting without proper authorization.

However, these principles should not be understood as strict necessary conditions for legitimacy. Rather, I suggest that they are principles in Ronald Dworkin's sense: if they apply, they *incline* our judgment toward approval of the intervention. They do not automatically determine legitimacy. Conversely, if the intervention does not satisfy any one principle, that is a *reason* against intervening, but it does not necessarily determine illegitimacy. For example, let us suppose that a government contemplates intervening to stop an ongoing genocide. Suppose the government deceives public opinion, or refuses to seek authorization. Those factors incline our judgment against legitimacy, but they do not force that judgment. We must weigh those factors against the urgency of saving lives in particular cases.

First principle. *Governments are, internationally and domestically, mere agents of the people. Consequently, their international rights derive from the rights and interests of the individuals who inhabit and constitute the state.*

International law historically emerged as a system of norms that governed the interaction of sovereign states. Perhaps the purpose of traditional international law was modest: to secure peace in a world populated by societies with few values in common. Viewed from that angle, international law's job is merely to secure a *modus vivendi* among sovereign states. But, of course, tyranny forces us to reconsider that vision. From a philosophical standpoint, states do not have the same moral status as individuals. Discourse about rights of states must be reduced to discourse about rights and interests of persons. Propositions about international rights of states can be translated into propositions about individual rights without loss of meaning. I submit that only representative nontyrannical governments have these international rights. This is the idea conveyed by the claim that state autonomy can only be predicated of governments that conform with appropriate principles of justice. The state's rights to political independence and territorial integrity, therefore, derive from the rights of individuals; governments do not have any independent or autonomous moral standing.

The liberal case for humanitarian intervention relies on principles of political and moral philosophy. Political philosophy is about justifying political power, and hence about justifying the state. Most liberal accounts of the state rely on social contract theory of some kind to explain and justify the state. Here I follow a Kantian account of the state. States are justified as institutions created by ethical agents, that is, by autonomous persons. The liberal state centrally includes a Constitution that defines the powers of governments in a manner consistent with respect for individual autonomy. On this view, the reason for creating and maintaining states and governments is precisely to ensure the protection of the rights of the individuals. Thus states and governments do not exist primarily to ensure order, but to secure natural rights. Accordingly, my defense of humanitarian intervention presupposes some form of social contract as the proper philosophical justification of the state. States and governments exist because individuals have consented, or would ideally consent, to transfer some of their rights in order to make social cooperation possible.

The theory of international law defended here (rights of states as derived from human rights) applies well beyond humanitarian intervention. All international rights of states are ultimately derived from the rights of individuals. Take the right of self-defense recognized in Article 51 of the U.N. Charter. Why is a war in self-defense morally justified? Under a human rights-based theory of international law, a war in self-defense is a war in defense of persons, that is, a war to protect the lives and property of the individuals attacked by the aggressor, and, where applicable, to defend the liberal Constitution itself. The government that reacts defensively is defending the rights of its own citizens against the aggressor. The use of force in self-defense, therefore, is also a use of force in defense of human rights. The corollary is surprising: *wars are justified only as defense of persons, their rights, and their freedom.* Self-defense is force used by a government to protect its own citizens, while humanitarian intervention is force used by a government to protect citizens of another state—to save strangers, as Nicholas Wheeler put it. There is no essential moral difference between the rights of citizens and those of foreigners, at least where basic human rights are at stake. Persons have rights as persons, not as citizens of particular states.

Second principle. *Tyrannical governments forfeit the protection afforded them by international law.*

An important consequence of the unified rationale for war discussed above is this: *tyrants do not have defensive rights against force aimed at them*—against humanitarian intervention. As I suggested above, the powers of government result from a consensual transfer by citizens of some of their rights. That vertical contract establishes the legitimate boundaries of government. A major purpose of states and governments is to protect and secure human rights, that is, rights that all persons have by virtue of personhood alone. Because sovereignty serves valuable human ends, those who assault them should not be allowed to shield themselves behind the sovereignty principle.

States and governments that are generally faithful to that original purpose are fully protected against foreign intervention—they hold against foreigners the rights of political independence and territorial integrity. To wage war against such states (except in self-defense) is a crime. But governments who turn against their citizens are on a different moral footing. By denying human rights they have forfeited the protection afforded them by international law. They are no longer justified qua governments, they no longer represent or are entitled to represent the citizens *vis-à-vis* the outside world, and therefore foreigners are not bound to respect them. Of course, there may still be decisive reasons not to act to depose tyrants, but sovereignty will not be one of them. Tyranny and anarchy cause the moral collapse of sovereignty.

Third principle. T*he fact that all persons have rights entails the following consequences for foreign policy. Governments have:*

(1) *The obligation to* respect *human rights at home and abroad;*

(2) *The obligation to* promote *respect for human rights globally;*

(3) *The* prima facie *obligation to* rescue *victims of tyranny or anarchy, if they can do so at a reasonable cost to themselves. This*

obligation analytically entails the permission *to rescue those victims—the right of humanitarian intervention.*

The liberal argument for humanitarian intervention has two components. The first is the quite obvious judgment that tyranny and anarchy are serious forms of injustice toward persons. The second is the judgment that, subject to important constraints, external intervention is (at least) morally permissible to end that injustice. The first part of the argument is uncontroversial. For the most part, critics of humanitarian intervention do not disagree with the judgment that the situations that (according to interventionists) call for intervention are morally abhorrent. The situations that trigger humanitarian intervention are, first, instances of severe tyranny such as (but not limited to) crimes against humanity, serious crime wars, mass murder, genocide, widespread torture, and second, instances of anarchy, the Hobbesian state of nature (war of all against all) caused by the collapse of social order. Rather, the disagreement between supporters and opponents of humanitarian intervention concerns the second part of the argument: interventionists claim that foreigners may help stop the injustices; non-interventionist claim they may not. The related claims that I make (that sovereignty is dependent on justice and that we have a right to assist victims of injustice) concern this second part of the argument. If a situation is morally abhorrent (as noninterventionists, I expect, will concede), then neither the sanctity of national borders nor a general prohibition against war should by themselves preclude humanitarian intervention.

The discussion here concerns *forcible* intervention to protect human rights—the threat or use of force for humanitarian purposes. However, the justification for the international protection of human rights is best analyzed as part of a *continuum* of international behavior. Most of the reasons that justify humanitarian intervention are extensions of the general reasons that justify interference in other states to help victims of grievous injustice. Interference and intervention in other societies to protect human rights are special cases of our duty to assist victims of injustice.

However, many people disagree that humanitarian intervention is part of a continuum: They treat war as a special case of violence, as a unique case, and not simply as a more violent and destructive form of human behavior that can nonetheless be sometimes justified. They do not regard war as part of a continuum of state action and do not agree with Clausewitz that war is the continuation of politics [*politik*] by other means. Intuitively, there is something particularly terrible, or awesome, about war. It is the ultimate form of human violence. That is why many people committed to human rights nonetheless oppose humanitarian intervention. To them, war is a crime, the most hideous form of destruction of human life, and so it cannot be right to support war, even for the benign purpose of saving lives. Good liberals should not support war in any of its forms.

I am, of course, in sympathy with that view. Who wouldn't be? If there is an obvious proposition in international ethics, it has to be that war is a terrible thing. Yet the deeply ingrained view that war is always immoral regardless of cause is mistaken. Sometimes it is morally permissible to fight; occasionally, fighting is even mandatory. The uncritical opposition to all wars begs the question about the justification of violence generally. Proponents of humanitarian intervention simply argue that humanitarian intervention in some instances (rare ones, to be sure) is morally justified, while agreeing, of course, that war is generally a bad thing. But it is worth noting that, with very few exceptions, critics of humanitarian intervention are *not* pacifists. They support the use of force in self-defense and (generally) in performance of actions duly authorized by the Security Council. So their hostility to humanitarian intervention cannot be grounded on a general rejection of war. They object to *this kind* of war, a war to protect human rights. They do not object to wars, say, in defense of territory.

This position sounds *ad hoc*, because many of the reasons to object to humanitarian intervention are reasons to object to other wars, such as defensive wars. The view also requires separate justifications for different kinds of wars. In contrast, the liberal argument offers a unified justification of war. War is justified if, and only if, it is in defense of persons (their lives and their freedoms). The duty (and, consequently, the permission) to rescue victims of tyranny follows, as Terry Nardin has argued, from common sense morality. The permission to use force in defense of others is anchored in the principle of beneficence, itself related to the idea of respect for persons. Henry Shue echoes the same sentiment: "the rest of us are not free merely to leave human beings to their fates when it is impossible for their basic rights to be protected by their national institutions." Outsiders (foreign persons, governments, international organizations) have a duty not only to respect those rights themselves but also to help ensure that governments respect them. Like justified revolutions, interventions are sometimes needed to secure a modicum of individual autonomy and dignity. Persons trapped in such situations deserve to be rescued, and sometimes the rescue can only be accomplished by force. The right to intervene thus stems from a general duty to assist victims of grievous injustice. We have a general duty to assist persons in grave danger if we can do it as reasonable cost to ourselves.

If this is true, we have, by definition, a *permission* to do so. Is humanitarian rescue a duty or a permission? The answer largely depends on an analysis of the costs of intervening. Once the myths associated with state sovereignty are set aside, the general principle is that we all have a duty to rescue victims of tyranny if we can do so at a low cost. If, on the other hand, the cost rises, the duty turns into a permission. We may, but do not have to, rescue victims of tyranny when doing so would be costly. The public outrage that followed the international community's inaction in Rwanda was in great part based on the sense that preventing the 1994 genocide there would have been relatively easy. On the other hand, much of the criticism of the war in Iraq (to the extent that it could be justified on humanitarian grounds) points to the high costs *for the intervenor.* Things are complicated by the fact, once again, that a state is not a person. When a government intervenes it sends *others* to fight. Unlike the typical case of an individual who contemplates rescuing someone in danger, a government does not internalize the costs of the intervention (except in the political sense, loss of support, and so on). So, in the case of humanitarian intervention, the question of cost should be approached by evaluating the burdens that the government that contemplates intervention is likely to impose on its own citizens.

Intervention: Legal Limits and Conditions. Written for this Handbook by Anthony D'Amato.

The question of whether any particular intervention is desirable, right, or just, is a matter for individual determination. But the question of its legality is up to customary international law. I have endeavored in the past, at the times of the Grenada, Panama, Nicaragua, and Kosovo interventions, to specify and defend legal conditions and limits on the legality of humanitarian interventions. My observations have appeared in journal articles, op-ed pieces, internet listserves, and internet blogs, too numerous to cite here. The following is a brief summary of the conclusions that I reached in those various forums based upon my study of the relevant customary international law:

BRIEF DEFINITION OF TERMS:

Intervention—a forceful military incursion limited in space and duration

Intervenor—the attacking state

Target state—the state that is attacked

Dangerous situation—the object of the intervention

INTERNATIONAL LIMITS AND CONDITIONS:

1. *There must exist a "dangerous situation" that objectively constitutes a clear and present danger to its citizens or to the world community.* The dangerous situation includes a military coup of a democratic government (Grenada), a tyranny (Iraq under Saddam Hussein), or the manufacture or stockpiling of weapons of mass destruction.

2. *The "dangerous situation" must be beyond the power of the citizens of the target state to remove.* Citizens are usually powerless to remove a tyrannical government. But there may be cases where a dictatorial government has the support of the people, such as Hitler's government in the 1930s. Despite the popular support, it was clear that the people were powerless to remove Hitler even if they had wanted to. Therefore a humanitarian intervention by foreign states to remove him would have met this second condition.

3. *Multilateral intervention must first be attempted.* Because of the veto in the Security Council, it may not be possible, for political reasons,

for any intervenor to obtain broad-based multilateral support for the intervention. Nevertheless, before proceeding unilaterally, the intervenor must in good faith ask all other nations to support the intervention.

4. *The intervention must not be aimed at either the territorial integrity or political independence of the target state.* Article 2(4) of the United Nations Charter prohibits the threat or use of force against the territorial integrity or political independence of a state. Research into diplomatic terminology shows that the term "territorial integrity" does not mean that a state's boundaries cannot be violated by foreign military incursion, but only that no part of the state may be annexed or otherwise taken away.* The "political independence" of a state would be violated if the intervenor exercises continuing control over its government or controls the target state's foreign policy. However, the intervenor may replace the target state's government if necessary to remove the dangerous situation that was the purpose of the intervention.

5. *The planned intervention may not proceed if it is reasonably estimated that the injuries and damage caused by the intervention will be greater than the evil to be prevented (the "dangerous situation").* This principle is akin to the war-crimes prohibition of the use of force beyond military necessity.

6. *The intervention must use sufficient military force to accomplish its objective.* This rule should not be confused with the quite different customary rule of "proportionality" that applies to the limits of forcible self-defense. Instead, the more general customary law prescription to minimize the loss of life applies here (as well as it applies to self-defense). Confusion about the notion of proportionality may have led the United States to use *too few* troops in its intervention in Panama in 1989, with the result that there were many civilian casualties. A larger military force may have made local opposition seem hopeless, thus saving lives on balance. From a jittery soldier's point of view, there is "safety in numbers."

8. *When the dangerous situation has been removed, the intervening state must withdraw active military forces and may only leave peacekeepers.* Were military forces to be left in place when the purpose of the intervention is achieved, then the intervention would be indistinguishable from a military take-over in violation of Article 2(4) of the Charter.

9. *The intervention terminates when all foreign military personnel including peacekeepers have been removed.*

10. *CONDITION SUBSEQUENT: If at any time before the intervention terminates the target state loses its territorial integrity or political independence, then the entire intervention is retroactively deemed to have violated international law.* In legal terminology, this condition subsequent "relates back" to the original intervention. Sometimes it is impos-

---

* See Anthony D'Amato, *International Law: Process and Prospect* 50 (2d ed. 1995) (covering the definitional derivation of "territorial integrity" and "political independence").

sible to tell whether an intervenor is acting in good faith. What appears to be a humanitarian intervention might in fact be a mask for aggression. Or even if it is not a mask, the intervenor may change its mind midway through the intervention and decide to annex part or all of the target state. If this occurs, then international law will deem the entire intervention to have been illegal *ab initio*.

The Kosovo Intervention. W. Michael Reisman, "NATO's Kosovo Intervention: Kosovo's Antinomies," 93 A.J.I.L. 860 (1999).

No lawyer, whatever his or her conclusion as to the lawfulness of NATO's action in Kosovo, can look back at the incident without disquiet. While some in our profession will strain to weave strands from various resolutions and *ex cathedra* statements of UN officials into a retrospective tapestry of authority (unintentionally contributing to bases for other claims and actions), all appreciate that NATO's action in Kosovo did not accord with the design of the United Nations Charter. The question is whether Kosovo comes under the "suicide pact" rule, the *exceptio* for that very small group of events that warrant or even require unilateral action when the legally designated institution or procedure proves unable to operate. That is a judgment that must be made in light of the law at stake, the facts and feasible alternatives at the moment of decision.

One can reasonably criticize many of the international actions and inactions during and after the dissolution of Yugoslavia and deplore the fact that some of those earlier international choices may have actually exacerbated ethnic tensions and conflicts. But decision makers must act on current facts, not on wishful if-onlys and wistful might-have-beens. The facts were alarming. As always, information was imperfect, but enough was available to indicate that bad things were happening, things chillingly reminiscent of some earlier as well as, lamentably, more recent events in this century; and it was reasonable to assume (and, to some, irresponsibly naive not to assume) that, given the people involved, worse things were in store. Economic sanctions and diplomacy were failing to dissuade the officials ordering and carrying out the bad things. In the post-Cold War world, responsible leaders properly turn to the Security Council. But the Security Council was paralyzed. Hence, the feasible options were to forgo formally lawful action under the Charter or to forgo the lives and human rights of the Kosovars. NATO states chose the first.

Military action is a blunt instrument and, no matter how careful operators are, some innocent people get killed or hurt. But the other instruments of strategy had failed, so it was either military action or self-righteous public hand-wringing with improbable (and, to most of the victims, probably irrelevant) assurances—even as the crimes continued to be committed—that someday their killers and rapists would be put on trial. When military force was brought into play, the ensemble of strategies that until then had failed, finally worked. That is not to say that NATO's action transformed Kosovo into a paradise. No reasonable person expected that it would. But it achieved its objective: Kosovars are back in their homes. Serb oppression has ceased and there is now an opportunity, which one hopes will not be squandered, to plan and implement a reconstruction program. Skilled diplomacy has incorporated Russia in the solution and in the peace-maintenance operation. There are, inevitably, new problems, some arguably created by the NATO action itself—that is the dialectical nature and continuous challenge of politics at every level—but what would the situation now be in Kosovo, and in human rights law, if the NATO states had concluded that, without Security Council authorization, they could not act?

Yet it is appropriate, indeed incumbent on international lawyers, to ask whether these events come under the "suicide pact" *exceptio* that would warrant action outside the UN procedure, with the costs to international law that such action often incurs. The answers to those questions all have a desperate inevitability to them.

—Were the human rights violations in Kosovo "bad" enough to warrant international concern? Different people have different thresholds of tolerance for other people's pain. Fortunately, an event on the scale of the Holocaust has not become the *minimum* requirement for the exercise of international concern.

—Why was the military instrument used to address the human rights violations in Kosovo? Because all the other instruments of policy had failed.

—Why was action undertaken without Security Council authorization? Because the authorization could not be secured.

—Why was there only an air campaign? Because it was the best of the feasible alternatives. The air campaign did not look chivalric and had its dramatic errors, but a ground campaign would have caused more collateral damage. Moreover, it would not have sustained the necessary domestic political support in the most critical NATO states. In any case, no rule requires a combatant otherwise in compliance with the law of armed conflict to choose a course of conduct that is more, rather than less, dangerous to itself.

—Why did the outcome not provide 100 percent improvements in the human rights situation? One might better ask whether it produced a significant improvement as compared to what would have happened if nothing had been done.

—Does the Kosovo intervention not set a bad precedent for the use of force without Security Council authorization? One may equally ask whether a better precedent would be that no one may do anything effective to stop the destruction or expulsion of the Kosovars of the future, if the Security Council proves unable to operate.

—Why was comparable action not taken in Rwanda?—to name only one recent case in which the world stood by and solemnly talked of future criminal prosecutions, while the criminals consummated their unspeakably wicked deeds. This would be a truly bizarre invocation of legal precedent. The proper question is whether Rwanda is to be taken as a precedent that limits future action or as a lesson of the type of international nonfeasance that should never again be allowed to occur.

None of us who are compelled to ask hard questions about the lawfulness of the Kosovo action is a consistent strict constructionist of the Charter. After all, who among us insists on a textual interpretation of Article 2(7)? But we all are stricter when it comes to reading Article 2(4), for no one wants a return to the world of classic international law in which states could resort to violence against each other at will.

Kosovo does not erode Article 2(4). Article 2(4) was changed by the contraction of Article 2(7), which, by effectively eliminating for serious human rights violations the defense of domestic jurisdiction, removed from the sphere of the "political independence" of a state the right to violate in grave fashion and with impunity the human rights of its inhabitants. But a treaty, such as the United Nations Charter, is an integrated conception; one cannot change part of it without making appropriate adjustments in other parts. Assigning a nearly exclusive right to use force to a Security Council, on which the five most powerful states of the world sit as permanent members, is a workable idea if the responsibility of that Council is restricted to resisting threats to and breaches of the peace and acts of aggression. These are fundamental and venerable postulates of international politics on which, for the time being, the permanent members can usually agree. But the assignment of exclusive power to the Council ceases to be workable if the writ of the United Nations is also extended to the protection of human rights, the international control of the essential techniques by which governments manage and control their people internally. On these matters, there are profound, possibly unbridgeable divides between the permanent members.

It is the installation in international law of the code of human rights that has created the antinomies of the Kosovo action, for international law now sets as an imperative objective a peremptory standard by which the behavior of governments is to be tested and, where necessary, restrained and sanctioned. This mandate ultimately requires the use of force, yet the far-reaching innovation of human rights does not, at the same time, adjust the inclusive enforcement mechanism so that it can implement the new objectives. Hence the *legal* imperative for the Kosovo action, the virtual impossibility of accomplishing it through the Security Council, and the simultaneous sense of relief, anomie and anxiety that the apparently successful action has generated.

The procedures for deciding and appraising the lawfulness of the Kosovo action were not those contemplated by the Charter. That is not good and, no matter how noble and urgent the outcome, it will not be good when it happens in the future. Yet, if the circumstances require, it should—it must—be done again! The practical question is whether Kosovo-like decisions that come under the "suicide pact" rule will be essentially uncontrolled actions taken by one or more powerful states in their own special interest—and truly violate the spirit of Article 2(4)—or whether they will be subjected to the discipline of international law standards and contribute to the major purposes of the United Nations Charter.

The Kosovo experience shows that they can be controlled. In addition to governments, the modern international legal process incorporates intergovernmental organizations, private entities, the mass media, non-governmental organizations and individuals; their members and representatives communicate through an international electronic nerve system and at all levels of international society, including the most formal diplomatic arenas. It is this modern, inclusive international process that promoted and demanded the international human rights code and, make no mistake, demanded and appraised every step of the Kosovo action as a necessary implementation of those rights. In this respect, Kosovo bears no likeness to previous examples of humanitarian intervention, which were, to varying degrees, for all their high rhetoric, instruments of policy of particular states, whose commitment to human rights was not always consistent or credible.

An unorganized decision process is neither as efficient nor as procedurally just as an organized and enlightened one. Hence law's ceaseless quest for organization and institutionalization. When human rights enforcement by military means is required, it should, indeed, be the responsibility of the Security Council acting under the Charter. But when the Council cannot act, the legal requirement continues to be to save lives, however one can and as quickly as one can, for each passing day, each passing hour, means more murders, rapes, mutilations and dismemberments—violations of human beings that no prosecution will expunge nor remedy repair.

Kosovo as Anticipatory Intervention. Jonathan I. Charney, "NATO's Kosovo Intervention: Anticipatory Humanitarian Intervention in Kosovo" 93 A.J.I.L. 834 (1999).

Neither of the permissible uses of force in international relations under the UN Charter—enforcement actions by the Security Council under Chapter VII and self-defense—provides a legal justification for the NATO action. The International Court of Justice acknowledged this problem (without purporting to decide the merits) in its decision refusing to grant the FRY's request for interim measures of protection.

Various scholars and diplomats have searched for exceptions to the UN Charter prohibition on the use of force, principally through liberal interpretations of the phrases "territorial integrity" and "inconsistent with the purposes of the Charter" contained in Article 2(4). But those arguments are unfounded. The use of force by bombing the territory of a state violates its territorial integrity regardless of the motivation. Furthermore, the first purpose of the Charter is "to save succeeding generations from the scourge of war" by "maintaining international peace and security." The protection of human rights is also among the primary purposes of the Charter but is subsidiary to the objective of limiting war and the use of force in international relations, as found in the express Charter prohibitions on the use of force. This interpretation is supported by the *travaux preparatoires* of the Charter. They establish that the phrases "territorial integrity" and "inconsistent with the purposes of the Charter" were added to Article 2(4) to close all potential loopholes in its prohibition on the use of force, rather than to open up new ones. Neither the use of force by regional organizations against nonconsenting states nor intervention to support domestic insurrections is permitted absent authorization by the Security Council or resort to self-defense. Any other uses of force that may have been legal under pre-Charter law ended when the Charter entered into force.

Despite the limitations in the text of the UN Charter, humanitarian intervention arguably provides a lawful foundation for the NATO actions. Unfortunately, humanitarian intervention is not an exception to the Charter prohibitions on the use of force. No reference to such a right is found in the Charter. The doctrine of "humanitarian intervention" is not well-defined and the evidence does not establish a rule of law permitting the use of force against a state in situations like that of Kosovo.

Most situations in which this theory is arguably applied actually involve actions by states to protect their citizens abroad from alleged mortal danger. Such intervention probably falls under the doctrine of self-defense. Examples include actions in the Congo, the Dominican Republic, Entebbe, Grenada and Panama. With the apparent sole exception of the Entebbe raid, however, many consider that the justifications given for those interventions were actually ruses to conceal the fact that they were conducted for other political objectives. This risk of abuse points to the need to adhere closely to the core Charter prohibitions on the use of force, even though it may be lawful to intervene to protect a state's own nationals. Other situations invoked as solidly supporting the theory of humanitarian intervention also fall short. For example, India intervened in East Pakistan allegedly to protect the ethnic Bengalis during the 1971 civil war in Pakistan. This action was condemned by a large majority in the UN General Assembly and India clearly had objectives other than merely humanitarian ones. The resolution adopted by the General Assembly in response to this incident makes clear that the international community opposed the doctrine. Intervention carried out apparently for humanitarian reasons has often been justified as a matter of law on the basis of an alleged request to intervene by the government of the state concerned, e.g., Czechoslovakia, the Dominican Republic, Grenada and Hungary. Not only were the requests of dubious legitimacy, but the humanitarian grounds put forward were designed to mask other political objectives. Some situations have involved the collapse of a state's effective government and intervention was allegedly undertaken to restore order, such as in Cambodia, the Congo, Liberia and Uganda. Again, other political interests have often animated the intervening states.

Finally, few, if any, interventions can be found in which the intervening states have expressly based their actions on the right of humanitarian intervention. In the absence of such a linkage by the intervening states, the actions can hardly serve as *opinio juris* in support of such a right.

Perhaps the Kosovo intervention sets a precedent for the development of new international law to protect human rights. After all, general international law may change through breach of the current law and the development of new state practice and *opinio juris* supporting the change. The Kosovo intervention, however, presents problems in this regard. In the *Nicaragua* case, the International Court of Justice found that, to challenge a rule of international law, the state practice relied upon must be clearly predicated on an alternative rule of law; but NATO has not justified its actions on the basis of a specific rule of law—even humanitarian intervention—new or old. Throughout the campaign, NATO offered no legal justification for it. Only in the recent suits against the intervening NATO states before the ICJ did the respondents begin to articulate legal justifications. Nevertheless, only Belgium even mentioned humanitarian intervention, and then merely as a possible legal justification.

Another obstacle to changing the existing international law is that the rule prohibiting the use of force is derived from the UN Charter. Charter law may very well not be subject to change by new general international law. By its terms, the UN Charter overrides all inconsistent treaties, regardless of the date of their entry into force. One would expect the same rule to apply to developments in general international law, especially since treaties supersede all but *jus cogens* norms. Furthermore, because the Charter restrictions on the use of force are themselves *jus cogens* norms, it would take a new norm of that quality to override them. The only clearly effective solution would be to amend the United Nations Charter on the basis of a norm of equal status.

One might argue, of course, that the doctrine of humanitarian intervention is merely a new and improved interpretation of the human rights provisions already in the Charter. This view might be supported by reference to the Vienna Convention on the Law of Treaties, which gives an agreement of treaty parties persuasive value in regard to its interpretation. But no such agreement of UN members can be shown.

Alternatively, one might argue that the international legal system has radically changed since the founding of the United Nations, resulting in the development of a right of humanitarian intervention. At the time the Charter entered into force, international law centered on state sovereignty. The independence of states, especially with respect to matters of domestic concern, was of foremost importance. New developments in international human rights law, particularly with regard to international crimes, authorize, if not require, all states to take action in the face of widespread grave violations of human rights amounting to such crimes. Thus, one might argue that contemporary public international law and a proper contemporary interpretation of the UN Charter permit pure humanitarian intervention without Chapter VII authorization by the Security Council or a situation of self-defense.

But has the law changed so radically? Does the international community wish to authorize individual states or groups of states, by themselves, to use force against a nonconsenting state in such situations? It is hard to find an international consensus to support this proposition, even among the NATO states. Certainly, it is not supported by widespread state practice and *opinio juris*. Past resolutions by the General Assembly that condemn specific interventions and other resolutions and declarations addressing broad subjects like intervention, the use of force, self-determination and human rights foreclose such actions, demonstrating international opposition to such a rule. Furthermore, the statutes of none of the existing or proposed international criminal tribunals—the Tribunals for Yugoslavia and Rwanda and the International Criminal Court—authorize such interventions. Accordingly, a doctrine of humanitarian intervention that would legitimate NATO's Kosovo actions cannot be found.

One might further ask whether, as a policy matter, international law should make humanitarian intervention legal. One could argue that this step is morally and ethically required. Public international law, as all law, should conform to the highest ideals. Humanitarian intervention would also protect human rights already encompassed by international law and the law of the Charter. This aspect is particularly important since the situations concerned may pose risks to international peace and security that might be stopped only by forcible intervention.

On the other hand, humanitarian intervention presents grave risks of abuse, as illustrated by virtually all of the past actions put forward in its support. Once established, such a right would be difficult to check, thwarting containment of those unacceptable risks. It is clear, therefore, that humanitarian intervention raises serious difficulties despite its noble objectives. That was the judgment of states participating in the San Francisco Conference when they negotiated the UN Charter after World War II and it remains unchanged.

Chapter 8

INTERNATIONAL CRIMINAL LAW

Editors' introduction: The relative length of this chapter attests to the profound expansion of international criminal law—not its creation, but its *application*—in the last dozen years. Over this time, heads of state have been stripped of their immunity, international tribunals have been set up, and the concept of extraterritorial jurisdiction has been given real meaning. As examined below, the period has seen a flurry of legal action against those who likely never imagined themselves facing charges and their accusers in a court of law. While the lessons of the law have come to bear in a nightmarish way for those previously deemed legally untouchable, many in the human rights and humanitarian law fields breathed a sigh of relief that laws which had been firmly established on the books were finally being used—not against low-level soldiers, but against those at the highest levels of the chain of command. While we are reminded that such defendants are entitled to equal protection of the law, we must nonetheless appreciate that the veil of sovereignty seems to have been lifted, making this an exciting time indeed for the field of international criminal law.

A. GENOCIDE

The Defendant Speaks. Opening statement of Accused Slobodan Milosevic, 15 February 2002. http://www.un.org/icty/transe54/020215IT.htm.

Now, I'm asking you, what kind of Tribunal can you talk about if you refuse to try people for all these crimes, the crimes committed by the leaders and governments and army of the NATO pact countries that I enumerated, that I quoted, on the territory of Yugoslavia. And you call yourself a war crimes Tribunal for crimes committed on the territory of Yugoslavia. Not even in the Security Council Resolution which set you up, although it was unlawful in taking that Resolution, but not even in that Resolution with respect to crimes in Yugoslavia are the Americans, French, or anybody else exempt. And nowhere is it written that those are the crimes that should be tried in Yugoslavia. And not only the ones that you say were committed by the Serbs.

So you yourselves have interpreted your competencies and authorities in terms of reference that you—that some perpetrators of crimes were exempt, but that you try only those who defend themselves from attackers in their homes, and you refuse to consider those attackers as being responsible and the true perpetrators. You keep repeating the fact that this is a trial of the side that defended itself. And thus you have defined yourself as the exponents of the side that perpetrated the crimes and as accomplices in crimes against somebody who defended themselves on their own territory.

You say that you are not trying Yugoslavia or Serbia but that you are trying me personally. However, I have put forward a series of arguments which you yourselves have put forward here. You have said that you are going to try everyone, but you tell me I am responsible by virtue of a chain of command, a command responsibility that exists in no laws. That means that the armed forces of Yugoslavia whom I commanded committed a crime in defending their country, in defending their people. So you are actually holding a trial of a whole country here, a country that stood up in defence against its attackers.

Saddam's opening statement here

SADDAM'S OPENING STATEMENT. Culled and organized by the editors from various reporters' notes taken on the first day of Saddam Hussein's appearance before the Iraqi High Criminal Court in Baghdad on October 19, 2005.

MR. HUSSEIN: I am the president of Iraq. I will not answer to this so-called court. [Opening a copy of the Koran and reading from it]: "In the name of God, the most gracious, the most merciful. Men said to them, "A great army is gathering against you," and frightened them. But it only increased their faith.

JUDGE RIZGAR MOHAMMED AMIN: Identify yourself by writing down your name.

MR. HUSSEIN: First of all, who are you and what are you?

JUDGE AMIN: The Iraqi criminal court.

MR. HUSSEIN: All of you are judges?

JUDGE AMIN [ignoring the question and asking Awad Bandar seated next to Hussein]: Identify yourself.

MR. BANDAR: I was robbed of my identity. The guards forced me to leave my headdress outside this courtroom. I demand that it be given back to me.

[Judge Amin orders that all the headdresses be brought into court. The defendants slowly put them on.]

JUDGE AMIN [to Mr. Hussein]: What is your name?

MR. HUSSEIN: I will not recognize this court's authority because it is a pawn of the American aggressors. This court is based on a falsehood. All things that arebased on a falsehood are false.

JUDGE AMIN: Is your name Saddam Hussein?

MR. HUSSEIN: I am not going to answer to this so-called court, out of respect for the truth and the will of the Iraqi people.

JUDGE AMIN: Shall I record you as pleading guilty?

MR. HUSSEIN: I've said what I've said, and I'm not guilty.

JUDGE AMIN: Are you Saddam Hussein?

MR. HUSSEIN: I can tell you are an Iraqi from your accent, and I'm sure you know who I am. My identity is as the president of the Republic of Iraq. And I ask, who are you, and what are you? Who are these judges?

JUDGE AMIN: Who are you?

MR. HUSSEIN: You know who I am. And you know I don't get tired.

JUDGE AMIN: These are formalities. We need to hear it from you. You are Saddam Hussein al-Majid, former president of Iraq, born 1937.

MR. HUSSEIN: I didn't say "former president," I said "President," and I have the constitutional rights according to the Constitution, among them immunity from prosecution. I reserve my constitutional rights as the president of Iraq. I don't recognize the body that has designated and authorized you, nor the aggression.

Defending a Person Accused of Genocide. Anthony D'Amato, "Defending a Person Charged with Genocide" 1 Chicago Journal of International Law 459 (2000).

I believe it is important for lawyers who may be thinking of serving as defense counsel at the ICTY* or other international criminal tribunals to know of some examples of the obstacles that can be placed in their path by the Office of the Registrar. At the outset of my representation of Dr. Kovacevic, I announced to the Registrar my intention to bring in co-counsel. I was flatly informed that the Registrar has discretion to approve or disapprove such a request. I did not contest the Registrar's power to pay or refuse to pay fees to my co-counsel. But the Registrar informed me that even if I paid for co-counsel out of my own pocket, they still had to approve the selection. I was told that this is what the rules require, and if anything is a conversation-killer in dealing with the Registrar it is when they invoke "the rules:" (These rules can defy all reason, such as the rule that requires all counsel to provide a photocopy of their actual law school diploma in order to practice in the Court.) When they do so, they do not genuflect and lift their eyes slowly toward the ceiling. But they convey that picture anyway.

If the Registrar makes it tough to get co-counsel, what follows is a compounding of troubles. I had invited some Northwestern Law students to come over for a few weeks in the summer to help me prepare the Kovacevic case for trial. I assigned one to become familiar with the topics of the voluminous documents already filed in the case and to be prepared to locate them when needed from a huge stack of three-ring binders. We had the binders spread out in the courtroom on several of the tables and chairs that were set aside for the defense attorneys. During the morning proceedings, this student was allowed to be inside the courtroom. But when the court recessed for lunch, the guards told her to leave. We had planned to use the lunch break together to prepare for the afternoon's arguments. Indeed, the Registrar personnel, the translators, and all the prosecutors and their assistants regularly used the courtroom during the lunch break. I was allowed to use it, but my assistant was not. The reason: "Security." This word is even holier than "the rules." I told the guard that my assistant would stay there with me because we were working on the case, and it would be impossible to move all the documents and ring binders to the small table in the defense counsel office without thoroughly rearranging them and setting us back considerably in our work. The guard argued with me, and I told him that unless he arrested me, my assistant and I were not moving.

* [In the International Criminal Tribunal for Yugoslavia, the author represented Dr. Milan Kovacevic, a Bosnian Serb anesthesiologist indicted for complicity in genocide and whose impending trial was the first at the ICTY under the charge of genocide—Eds.]

The guard left to call in reinforcements. Meanwhile another guard who had observed the situation told me that the sergeant in charge is new on the job, and that the sergeant who was usually there would have understood my need for workspace.

The Deputy Registrar then showed up with a contingent of guards who threatened my student, and she decided that it was wise to leave the courtroom. Respectfully and patiently, I explained to the Deputy Registrar that it was unfair to allow the prosecutors' assistants to use the courtroom during lunch break but not the assistants for the defense counsel. "The rules," he said, "do not provide for people who are not admitted to practice before this tribunal to be in the courtroom during the lunch break." Why? I asked. "Security," he said (and there was a virtual thunderbolt outside the building).

"Well," I protested, "you can look again inside her briefcase to see if there are any Molotov cocktails." (We both knew that my student, as well as every person in the building, had previously been searched carefully by the guards at the entrance gate.) That's not the point, he replied; the point is that a rule is a rule. True, a different head security officer might have interpreted it differently, but this one did not, and he was not necessarily wrong. I asked the Deputy Registrar what he was going to do about it. "As a favor to you," he said, "I won't do anything. Normally I'd write this incident up as a breach of your obligations to the tribunal, and you would receive a letter of reprimand from the court."

The foregoing account of the Registrar's mind-set is reflected to an extent in the rule-bindedness of the judges themselves. In the early days of the ICTY, various procedural rules were drafted by a committee of international experts. Naturally, though they thought they had done a brilliant job, in fact they failed to anticipate many of the problems that would come up. Unintended consequences then arose, but "a rule is a rule." Only the judges could ever permit a departure from the rules, and then, only after counsel had filed a motion, supporting briefs, asked for oral argument on the point, and made a convincing showing that an absurd rule was in fact absurd.

One example may illuminate the hassle—but also the ultimate fairness of the judicial proceedings. At the pretrial stage in my case, the prosecutor wanted to amend the indictment to include more counts against my client. The rules of the tribunal provided that, with respect to all indictments, the prosecutor submits the indictment to a reviewing judge who passes on their sufficiency and approves or disapproves them. The framers of the rules had in mind the initial indictment process, prior to the arrest of any person. But since the rule on its face applied to all indictments, the prosecutor figured that he could add new indictments to the Complaint in an ex parte proceeding before the reviewing judge. Without notice to me, he approached the reviewing judge (the judge who had initially approved the genocide indictment against Kovacevic and Drljaca), and she simply approved the added counts. At this point, Dr. Kovacevic was already in custody and I was already defending him. Yet the prosecutor resorted to this ex parte procedure because the rule seemed to authorize it. As soon as I received a copy of the Amended Indictment (listing a great many more counts against my client), I filed a motion in protest. A hearing was held before our pretrial panel (three judges). I argued as vigorously as I could that an ex parte procedure, once a person has been arrested and is represented by counsel, is fundamentally unfair. The prosecutor was seeking to change the entire nature of the case against my client without allowing me to object to the evidentiary sufficiency of the added indictments. The prejudice to my client, and to the reputation for fairness of the tribunal, was compromised by such a procedure, even if the rules of the tribunal appeared to allow for it. I argued that any rule that frustrates fundamental fairness should not be allowed to stand.

The tribunal took the motion under consideration. I went back to Chicago (where fortunately I had a semester's leave for research) and continued to work on the merits of the case from my office. Two months later, on my next trip to The Hague, I heard informally that the judges had met in plenary session and made several amendments to the rules of procedure. I went to the Registrar's office and obtained a copy of the changes. I discovered that the judges had amended the indictment rule so that once an accused person is in custody, an indictment cannot be amended on an ex parte basis. The rule was also made retroactive. So I discovered, in this totally informal way, that I had won my motion. But the panel never issued a decision on my motion. Indeed, the motion was now moot because the rule had been changed. Future counsel, faced with an amendment to the complaint against their clients, would simply assume that the rules always provided for representation by counsel if the prosecutor sought an amendment to the indictment. Although I was glad to have won even a silent victory, future counsel may be inhibited from challenging the rules of procedure assuming that such motions are never granted (the court simply changes the rule in closed session). Therefore it is important for defense counsel to know that rules can be challenged and that judges can be persuaded that a given rule is unfair. Unfortunately, because the tribunal hides in secrecy their reasons for changing a rule, the rules may appear over time to acquire an imperviousness that renders them virtually unchallengeable. This false history may operate as a deterrent to any defense attorney who might otherwise wish to challenge a rule. Perhaps these European tribunals are influenced by canon law, which traditionally is changed in secret meetings of the church hierarchy who then tell the world that the canon law has never been altered.

For counsel trained in the common law tradition, civil law courts such as the ICTY may seem to be unfair venues to defend clients accused of a crime. There is no doubt that the job is difficult. Yet the recent international criminal law tribunals have taken on a grave and historic responsibility for making hitherto immune state officials responsible for their criminal conduct. I left the ICTY with the same total commitment to its goals as when I first took on the Kovacevic case. Perhaps the foregoing comments may aid in improving the fairness and efficacy of the tribunal.

B. WAR CRIMES

The Prosecutor Speaks. Opening statement of Chief Prosecutor Carla Del Ponte, Trial of Slobodan Milosevic, ICTY, 12 February 2002. http://www.un.org/icty/transe54/020212IT.htm.

Today, as never before, we see international justice in action. Let us take a moment at the start of this trial to reflect upon the establishment of this Tribunal and its purpose. We should just pause to recall the daily scenes of grief and suffering that came to define armed conflict in the former Yugoslavia. The events themselves were notorious and a new term, "ethnic cleansing," came into common use in our language. Some of the incidents reveal an almost medieval savagery and the calculated cruelty that went far beyond the bounds of legitimate warfare. The international community was shocked to witness the vicious disintegration of a modern state, and the Security Council of the United Nations was quick to recognise the grave threat caused by the serious crimes it believed to have been committed. This Tribunal is one of the measures taken by the Security Council acting for all Member States of the United Nations to restore and maintain international peace and security. That is our purpose, and our unique contribution is to bring to justice the persons responsible for the worst crimes known to humankind.

The crime of genocide, crimes against humanity, and the other crimes within the jurisdiction of this Tribunal are not local affairs, and their prosecution may be beyond the capability of national courts. Crimes of the magnitude of those in the indictment before the Chamber affect all of us throughout the world. The law of this Tribunal—international humanitarian law—is the concern of people everywhere. These crimes touch every one of us, wherever we live, because they offend against our deepest principles of human rights and human dignity. The law is not a mere theory or an abstract concept. It is a living instrument that must protect our values and regulate civilised society. And for that we must be able to enforce the law when it is broken. This Tribunal, and this trial in particular, give the most powerful demonstration that no one is above the law or beyond the reach of international justice.

Defenses to War Crimes. Anthony D'Amato, "National Prosecutions for International Courts" in M. Cherif Bassiouni (ed.), *International Criminal Law: Enforcement* (1987), excerpt.

In focusing on violations of the laws of war, we should not forget that persons accused of war crimes have human rights too. Unquestioned is their right to a fair and public trial. In addition, international customary law has evolved certain other human rights of defendants that apply when they are prosecuted for war crimes:

1. *Superior Orders.* Under international customary law, a plea that the defendant was merely carrying out the orders of a military superior has rarely if ever been allowed as a defense to the commission of an international crime. At the same time, it has almost always been allowed in mitigation of punishment. The problem the defense counsel, therefore, is to introduce the fact of superior orders at the trial level so that it might be taken into account in the tribunal's assessment of the guilt of the accused, rather than postponing the question of superior orders to the post-trial assessment of punishment where its effectiveness will be diminished and where it would be routinely allowed anyway.

In the many trials in the Far East following the Second World War, one may read in the transcripts considerable discussion of the defendants' conduct in obeying the principles of the Empire and the Emperor and of loyalty to the generals in the field without often encountering the phrase "superior orders." What in effect happened was that counsel introduced the concept of superior orders without using the vocabulary, undoubtedly because the tribunals might have ruled such arguments out of order if they came labelled as "superior orders" arguments. This tactic clearly is an important one for the defense in any trial where superior could be a factor in assessing guilt.

The plea of superior orders would be far more difficult for a person accused of terrorism, due to the lack of a military command structure. A terrorist seems to be a person acting under his own volition, quite unlike a soldier in the field responding to his commander's orders. On the other hand, a terrorist, like a soldier is presumably acting not out of personal motives but for a general cause. The imperatives of that cause, couched in principles that obviously are important for the terrorist, might be assimilated to "superior orders." The problem for defense counsel is certainly more difficult here, because if counsel says that evidence concerning the imperatives of the cause is relevant as functionally analogous to "superior orders," the court may disallow the evidence on the theory that superior orders, even if proven, is not a defense.

Perhaps the most practical use of "superior orders" is at the plea-bargaining stage. It is clear that the Nuremberg and Far Eastern prosecutions did not descend to the level of the common soldier, presumably because the soldier was "only following orders." Prosecutors therefore must have taken superior orders into account in deciding whom to indict. At this level a potential defendant would do well to stress the conflict between obedience to orders and obedience to the general rules prohibiting international crimes, as it is a conflict that prosecutors might understand better than courts.

2. *Lack of Command Responsibility.* Command responsibility is the other side of the coin of superior orders. The military commander is held responsible, under international law, for the crimes of his subordinates if (a) he knew or had reason to know those activities, and (b) he was in a position to prevent or mitigate them.

Thus, if a defendant is charged with commission of an international crime not because of any of his acts. but because of his position as a commander or person in charge, his defenses under international customary law would have to fall under either (a) or (b) or both. Of these, (a) is far more difficult to sustain. A commander, by virtue of his position alone, is generally charged with knowing or having reason to know of the acts of his subordinates, unless those acts are sporadic and isolated. A court will generally not believe that any widespread pattern of war crimes would not be known to the commander; thus the court did not believe General Yamashita who said at his trial in the Philippines that he did not know of the commission of war crimes by his troops.

A defense under (b) has more promise. Here, the mere fact that the defendant was a commander is not enough for culpability. An inference should not be drawn under (b), as it was under (a), that a commander simply by virtue of his office could have prevented or inhibited the commission of war crimes or other international crimes by his subordinates. In the Far Eastern trial of Admiral Toyoda, although the admiral was charged with the command of 20,000 naval troops in Manila that committed atrocities against Filipino civilians, in fact it was shown that the real command lay in General Yamashita and not in Admiral Toyoda. The admiral was acquitted. The commission in Toyoda's case did not need to reach the issue of knowledge because it found a lack of control.

Sometimes a commander can show that he took steps to prevent or inhibit the commission of crimes by his subordinates. However, a mere "paper record" of orders not to commit crimes will not exonerate a commander who in fact tolerated or even approved of those activities. General Yamashita testified at his trial that he removed his Chief of Military Police because there were reports of abuses that reached his ears. On one level, this testimony hurt Yamashita because it constituted evidence that he knew about the abuses. On a second level, however, the testimony would have helped his case had there not be subsequent abuses by the military police, such as mass executions of prisoners, that occurred after the removal of the Chief of Military Police.

If there is evidence that a military commander actually ordered his subordinates to commit war crimes, and the subordinates committed those war crimes, may the commander nevertheless defend himself in court by arguing that his commands constituted unlawful orders of a superior, that his subordinates were under an international legal obligation to disobey those orders, and therefore the fact that he issued those orders cannot be enough to impute to him the (illegal) acts of his subordinates? So far as I know, this paradoxical-sounding defense has never been attempted.

In the case of terrorists who operate in peacetime and whose victims are innocent persons, a plea of lack of command responsibility on the part of a terrorist leader may be effective. The lack of a military organization may excuse a terrorist "commander" from liability on the theory of command responsibility. At the same time, however, such a commander would undoubtedly be prosecuted under a co-conspirator theory, in which case the prosecution would have to prove that the defendant aided and abetted the plan. This is a somewhat stronger test than command responsibility, and if it had been applicable in General Yamashita's case (it wasn't, because he was a military commander, not a peacetime terrorist), on the evidence available against Yamashita his case might have ended in acquittal.

3. *Tu Quoque.* There are occasions where a defendant may argue to the court that nationals of the prosecuting state have engaged in acts similar to those the defendant is charged with, but have not been prosecuted for them. To the extent that this tu quoque plea is saying that others have committed similar crimes, the prosecution can answer simply that such a fact is irrelevant to the present trial. "Prosecutorial discretion" may account for the lack of prosecutions in the other cases, but that does not mean that the present indictment should be dismissed.

Yet there is a strong sense of justice in the defense of tu quoque raised by Admiral Karl Donitz at Nuremberg that Admiral Chester Nimitz of the United States had waged unrestricted submarine warfare in the Pacific, refusing to pick up survivors. Since Donitz was charged with allowing shipwrecked survivors to drown, and for failure to carry out rescue missions, he could well question the impartiality of the proceedings against him. Donitz was eventually sentenced to ten years' imprisonment; the avoidance of a death sentence meant perhaps that his arguments carried some psychological weight.

In any event, a more precise version of tu quoque would be not that others have committed similar crimes, but rather the fact that others have committed similar acts without being prosecuted therefor signifies that the customary international law has changed to a point where such acts are no longer in practice regarded as criminal. The evidence of such a change in the customary law is, of course, the fact that others were not prosecuted for those acts but not that they should have been prosecuted! For example, although rescuing ship-wrecked survivors is itself a laudable goal and one that might very well be considered a duty under customary international law, conditions regarding submarines in the Second World War may have called for a contrary practice. A submarine that spends time rescuing survivors is vulnerable to air attack, for it is likely that the vessel that was hit radioed to the shore its latitude and longitude. (Indeed, revelations about "Enigma" that came out many years after World War II showed that, on many occasions, the Allies knew in advance of U-boat attacks against Allied ships through decoding of German radio communications, but did not strike immediately for fear of tipping off the enemy that their code had been cracked. One possible incident involved Donitz himself. After sinking the British vessel Laconia, he ordered naval commanders to provide aid to the shipwrecked sailors. British Liberator bombers soon showed up, however, and ignoring the victims in the water the bombers began to bomb the U-boats that had gathered to assist in the rescue operation.) Perhaps Admiral Chester

Nimitz in the Pacific theater did not rescue survivors because of the danger to his submarines, and hence one might question whether the pre-second world war norm of rescuing survivors remained intact during that war.

4. *Legitimacy of Reprisals.* A "reprisal" is an act that is illegal in itself, but arguably becomes legal because it is taken in retaliation for a prior illegal act by the other side. In recent years there have been many acts of "reprisal" in the Middle East, some limited and some extensive, but all said to be justified because of prior illegalities.

Although a reprisal is backward-looking in that it seeks its justification in a prior illegal act by the other side, its best legal support is mustered if it can be shown to have forward-looking consequences. In other words, a reprisal taken solely for the purpose of revenge is on extremely weak international grounds, whereas a reprisal that can be said to have a deterrent function is on a much more solid legal foundation. A defendant citing a "reprisal" justification for his violation of international criminal law should make sure that the reprisal is characterized, if it can be, in terms of deterrence and not as revenge.

An illustration of this point can be found in the trial of Hans Albin Rautner before a national tribunal of the Netherlands after the Second World War. Occupied Dutch citizens had engaged in acts of violence against German soldiers. German reprisals were then taken against Dutch citizens at random. The tribunal recognized that the occupying power had a right to answer violent resistance by retributive action, but found that Rautner's reprisals were taken for purposes of revenge and not as a deterrent. The conclusion was based on the fact that Rautner made no attempt to arrest the actual perpetrators of the resistance actions but rather killed hostages at random.

In addition, any defense of the legitimacy of reprisals would have to take into account the questions of military necessity and proportionality, which will now be considered.

5. *Military Necessity.* Many formulae have been advanced to describe the plea of military necessity, but it is my judgment that underlying all of them is a notion of cost-effectiveness. For example, assume there is a war where if one belligerent's capital city can be destroyed there will be capitulation. The other side could destroy the capital city immediately, but instead decides first to destroy one or more other major cities. Prolonging the war in this manner, with no justification, and at increased cost to both sides, would clearly violate military necessity.

Often examples of lack of military necessity serve to prove the underlying offense. Adolf Eichmann, in Budapest in 1945, diverted German troops from their task of defending the city against the approaching Russian army so that they might continue to carry out the program of genocide against Hungarian Jews. The murder of civilians was itself clearly a war crime; its criminal nature serves to be underlined by the fact that there was no possible justification of military necessity. A related example occurred during the atrocities committed under General Yamashita in the Philippines; scarce gasoline was used to burn the bodies of civilians. The murder of civilians was itself a war crime; the use of gasoline rations underscored the lack of military necessity.

Military necessity must either be disproved by the prosecution or proved by the defense. It is part of the prosecution's case to disprove when military necessity is named in the war-crime charge itself. Thus, one of the war crimes specified in the "Nuremberg principles" adopted by the United Nations General Assembly in 1950 is "wanton destruction of cities, towns or villages, or devastation not justified by military necessity." However, most of the time the plea of military necessity is raised by way of justification by the defendant.

The defendant need not prove strict cost-effectiveness. Considerable latitude is given to commanders in the field to judge what appeared to them at the time to be reasonable and prudent from a military standpoint. They are not required to abstain from an act because of its brutality or infliction of grave punishment upon the enemy if the act is justifiable from a military perspective and is not per se a war crime. The bombing of munitions factories is justifiable by military necessity even though many workers and their families will inevitably be killed. On the other hand, the concept of military necessity cannot be stretched so far as to include acts of brutality committed solely to terrorize the opponent. The American fire-bombing of Tokyo on March 10, 1945, for the most congested urban residential districts in the world, and numerous repeated bombings of other populated areas in the ensuing three months, can hardly be justified in terms of military necessity without scuttling all of the laws of war.

It is difficult to assess at this early stage whether an organization dedicated to overthrowing a government and using terrorist means, such as the Irish Republican Army in Northern Ireland, could employ a defense of military necessity in trials of some of its members. The question whether terrorism should come under the laws of war is at present hotly debated. In addition, there is a question whether the situation is one of "war." And apart from the name, is the I.R.A. a military organization? Despite all these theoretical difficulties, one might still draw a line between terrorist acts that might be justified by "military necessity" and those that have no possible claim to such a defense. Acts of sabotage against government military installations, for example, might conceivably fall under the rubric of military necessity, but random terrorist attacks upon civilians for the purpose of intimidating the population and calling attention to the goals of the terrorists are of an entirely different character. Perhaps "military necessity" might be a useful defense if a terrorist organization is directly attacked by a military unit, and fights back in self-defense. Even though the military unit will claim that it is only exercising a police function against common criminals, there is a possibility for an argument here that resistance is not criminal if it would have been justified by military necessity if the terrorist organization were in fact a belligerent.

The attempt to extrapolate from the international criminal law to situations involving terrorists is a difficult one, partially because the very label "terrorist" suggests someone who is not entitled to any defenses and ought to be summarily executed. But the same reaction was vetted in the early days of the establishment of war crimes, where it was generally felt that no act could be legally prohibited if directed against the hated enemy. Yet war crimes became established in international law precisely because of a more enlightened realization that without them wars would become more brutal for no good reason and that both sides would be the losers. Similarly, if the admittedly unjustifiable acts of terrorists could be channeled into areas not involving brutality for brutality's sake against innocent civilians, that might be a worthwhile benefit to justify the cost of giving terrorists some incipient rights under the customary laws of war.

6. *Proportionality.* Under the doctrine of proportionality, anticipated military advantage or antecedent provocation are assessed in terms of the costs of collateral civilian deaths and destruction of property. The concept is close to that of military necessity, but there is a difference. An illustration of the difference is the hypothetical case of a densely populated residential area containing in its midst a small legitimate military target such as an armory of a light-vehicle factory. Bombing the area, with great collateral damage to civilians, might be justified under military necessity but might run afoul of the requirement of proportionality. The latter doctrine conceivably could bar bombing of the military target entirely if the bombs used (for example, nuclear weapons) would create too much civilian destruction in proportion to the worth of the military target that is hit. A second example would be the laws governing reprisals, already considered above. There may be no military necessity at all in an act of reprisal, but even if there is not, the reprisal still must pass the proportionality test.

Proving disproportionality is normally part of the prosecution's case. However, if a particular court assigns the burden of proof to the defendant, the defendant should stress the costs and benefits as they reasonably appeared at the time of decision. Not only is second-guessing after the fact an unreasonable burden to place upon the defendant—amounting almost to a retroactive application of law—but more importantly, the laws of war are meant to deter unreasonable conduct while still allowing for the necessarily brutal task of subduing an enemy. An imbalance either way in the application of the laws of war can be counterproductive to their humanitarian origin.

7. *Other Defenses.* The defenses that have been covered here are those that may generally be asserted under international law when a person is accused of war crimes in an international or a national court. They stem not from the laws of the forum state, but rather from the same source that the forum state invokes in its indictment—international criminal law.

However, in national courts, many other defenses may exist under the particular laws of the forum state. The above enumeration and discussion of generally available defenses under customary international law should not be construed as pre-empting or replacing or otherwise diverting recourse to those defenses that are available in any criminal action under the laws of the forum state.

C. CRIMES AGAINST HUMANITY

Theory. David Luban, "A Theory of Crimes Against Humanity" 29 Yale J. Int'l L. 85 (2004).

"Humanity" refers to humankind—the set of individuals—not humanness. Under this interpretation, "crimes against humanity" suggests that the defining feature of these offenses is the party in interest. In law, some wrongs—chiefly civil wrongs, like torts—are thought to affect only the victims and their dependents. Other wrongs, inflicted on equally determinate victims, violate important community norms as well, and the community will seek to vindicate those norms independently of the victim. These wrongs are crimes, not torts or other civil breaches, and the community, not just the victims, has a distinct interest in punishment. If, for example, you punch me in the nose, I may sue you for damages, and the civil case will be named after the parties in interest: Me v. You. But, in addition, you may be prosecuted for assault and battery, and the criminal case will be titled State v. You, People v. You, or Crown v. You. The former case name reflects the fact that you have injured me, and that I am seeking recompense; the latter case names connote that by injuring me, you have committed an offense against the community. In the former, the parties in interest are you and I. In the latter, the interested parties are you and the state, the people, or the Crown. I may decide to drop my civil lawsuit against you, perhaps because we have settled out of court. But that will not matter to the state, which remains free to proceed with the assault prosecution despite our settlement because the state's interest in punishing the wrong differs fundamentally from my own interest. Viewed along these lines, the term "crimes against humanity" signifies that all humanity is the interested party and that humanity's interest may differ from the interests of the victims.

Crimes against humanity are committed by politically organized groups acting under color of policy. The Nuremberg Charter presupposed that crimes against humanity were committed by agents of a state. Article 6(c) requires that crimes against humanity be committed "in execution of or in connection with" crimes against peace and war crimes, both of which could be committed only by state actors, or by high-placed civilians embroiled with state actors. This state action requirement excludes, for example, "free lance" anti-Semites who decided to piggy-back on the Nazi lead and murder Jews on their own, as happened repeatedly in Romania, Latvia, and the Ukraine. Their crimes could be prosecuted as murder under domestic law, but not as crimes against humanity under international law. Indeed, the nexus to state acts was deemed necessary to bring the crimes into the purview of international law.

The Bosnian War led drafters to weaken the "state action" requirement because the Serb militias were unofficial and only loosely affiliated with the Yugoslav state. Thus, the Statute of the International Criminal Tribunal for the Former Yugoslavia (ICTY) requires only that crimes against humanity be committed "in armed conflict, whether international or internal in character." However, the armed conflict requirement still presupposes armies and government-like entities. The Tadic judgment, for example, refers to "entities exercising de facto control over a particular territory but without international recognition of formal status of a de jure state, or by a terrorist group or organization." Rwanda led to an additional weakening of the requirement because unaffiliated civilians committed much of the genocide, which had no direct connection with armed conflict, occurring as it did in areas of the country outside the battle zones of the civil war. Here, the state action requirement—broadened in Yugoslavia to include non-state but state-like actors—was broadened again. In place of the "armed conflict" requirement, the Statute of the International Criminal Tribunal for Rwanda (ICTR) requires only "a widespread or systematic attack against any civilian population on national, political, ethnic, racial or religious grounds." Finally, the Rome Statute for the International Criminal Court adopts nearly identical language but eliminates the requirement that the attack be on national, political, ethnic, racial or religious grounds. Offenses are crimes against humanity "when committed as part of a widespread or systematic attack directed against any civilian population, with knowledge of the attack." The Rome Statute also requires that the offenses flow from "a State or organizational policy."

In this way, the state action requirement has metamorphosed into a broader "widespread or systematic attack" element, linked with a state or organizational policy. What all these requirements have in common seems to be that crimes against humanity are crimes committed through political organization. Although perpetrated by individuals, they are not individual crimes. To count as a crime against humanity, the perpetrator's decision to commit the crime must be mediated by his participation in, and knowledge of, a widespread or systematic attack. We may summarize this feature as the requirement of organizational responsibility.

Crimes against humanity cut deep; they are the worst thing that human beings do to each other. Intuitively, they seem to violate humanness itself. The question is how.

What makes this question so pressing is that the very idea of "humanness itself," what Richard Rorty derisively calls "Man's Glassy Essence," seems deeply suspect. The Judaeo–Christian notion of man created in God's image, like the metaphysical concept of an immaterial, immortal soul, is too parochial and too contestable to anchor our intuitions about what makes humans special and gives us special value—all the more so if these intuitions are supposed to be shared across confessions and cultures. Indeed, it seems likely that any metaphysical theory of humanness will prove far more debatable than the intuitions it is supposed to anchor. For that reason, it would be a mistake to seek an answer to our question through metaphysical investigation. Instead, we should seek the idea in the same set of intuitions that informs the law of crimes against humanity. That is, we should seek the image of humanness reflected in the law.

Relation to War Crimes. William J. Fenrick, "Should Crimes Against Humanity Replace War Crimes?" 37 Colum. J. Transnat'l L. 767 (1999).

Traditionally, international humanitarian law has been divided into two major components: the law of Geneva, which is concerned with the protection of victims of war, and the law of the Hague, which is concerned with the conduct of hostilities. As a general statement, at any given moment in time, the law of Geneva is a much more elaborate body of law than the law of the Hague. States are much more willing to accept restrictions related to treatment of war victims than they are to accept restrictions related to effective modern weapons or methods of waging war. Similarly, states are willing to accept more detailed restrictions in the conduct of international armed conflict between, legally speaking, sovereign equals than in the conduct of internal armed conflicts where the warring factions are the established government and rebel groups which challenge the right of the government to exercise control over some or all of the state's territory. The most voluminous source of international humanitarian law is treaty law, although some of the law is still rooted in custom or, to a lesser degree, general principles of law.

International humanitarian law/law of war has had a long and useful history, primarily as a body of preventive law, setting standards for the conduct of armed forces. Violations of the law have rarely been prosecuted, although many cases were prosecuted after World War II, and a number of cases related to the conflicts in the territory of the former Yugoslavia and in Rwanda are being prosecuted before the ICTY, the ICTR and national courts. Traditionally, war crimes have been regarded as serious violations of the law applicable to international armed conflict. More recently, it appears to have become generally accepted that war crimes can also occur when serious violations of international humanitarian law are committed in internal armed conflict. This contemporary understanding is particularly significant as war crimes are generally regarded as international crimes that may be prosecuted on the basis of the universality principle. Under this principle, any state which has custody of the accused has the authority under international law to prosecute him or her.

As a general statement, war crimes are: (a) one of a list of acts generally prohibited by treaty but occasionally prohibited by customary law, and (b) committed during an armed conflict. Some acts are prohibited in international conflicts alone, some in internal conflicts alone, and some in all conflicts. The acts are committed (c) by a perpetrator linked to one side of the conflict, and (d) against a victim who is neutral or linked to the other side of the conflict.

As an application, where the grave breach provisions of the Geneva Conventions are concerned, the prohibited act must be: (a) listed as a grave breach in one of the four Geneva Conventions, (b) committed when Common Article 2 of the Geneva Conventions applies, that is, during an international armed conflict or during a few other situations, (c) committed by a perpetrator, civilian or military, linked to one side of the conflict, and (d) against persons or property protected under a Geneva Convention listing the prohibited act as a grave breach. For example, unlawful confinement is a grave breach of the Fourth (Civilians) Convention but not of the Third (Prisoners of War) Convention because prisoners of war are usually confined in camps.

In international conflicts, the victim groups are usually civilians linked to the other side or prisoners of war, although there are a few war crimes, such as the use of unlawful weapons, which can be committed against enemy combatants. The victim groups for war crimes committed in international conflicts would normally not include civilians on the perpetrator's own side. For example, during World War II, Polish Jews killed by German forces would have been regarded as victims of war crimes.

German Jews killed by Germans would not have been regarded as victims of war crimes and neither would Hungarian Jews because Hungary was an ally of Germany. For internal conflicts, as the concept of prisoner of war has no legal significance, the victim groups are "persons taking no active part in the hostilities, including members of armed forces who have laid down their arms and those placed hors de combat" (Common Article 3 of the Geneva Conventions) and "all persons who do not take a direct part or who have ceased to take part in hostilities" (Article 4 of Additional Protocol II).

As a general statement, although it is relatively easy to identify which types of acts constitute war crimes, it is often quite difficult to spell out the elements of individual offenses because substantial portions of international humanitarian law are expressed at a high level of abstraction or generality and because many offenses have rarely, if ever, been prosecuted in criminal courts. This problem is particularly apparent where the law of the Hague is concerned.

At the present time, crimes against humanity constitute a distinct and significant part of international criminal law, together with other international crimes to which universal jurisdiction applies, such as war crimes or piracy. International humanitarian law is a relatively voluminous body of law, at least where international conflicts are concerned, and, as it prohibits certain acts which constitute international crimes, it is related to international criminal law. Whether crimes against humanity should be regarded as a part of international humanitarian law is debatable, as crimes against humanity can occur in non-conflict situations. Because crimes against humanity also occur during conflicts, however, they must exist in a relationship with war crimes, including grave breaches of the 1949 Geneva Convention and of Additional Protocol I of 1977.

Professor Leslie Green has suggested that crimes against humanity should replace war crimes as the criminal law component of international humanitarian law, as this would circumvent the conflict classification problem. The most elaborate statement of crimes against humanity in a treaty text to date is that contained in Article 7 of the Rome Statute, and it is unlikely that utilization of the offenses enumerated therein would provide a complete substitute for war crimes.

A major difficulty and a major opportunity faced by the ICTY is caused by the complex nature of the conflict in the territory of the former Yugoslavia and by the fact that treaty-based international humanitarian law has evolved on two tracks as a result of the preferences of states. The ICTY must face the conflict classification issue in almost all of its decisions. It also has the opportunity to explore creative approaches to circumvent the conflict classification issue.

The Office of the Prosecutor (OTP) of the ICTY has itself tried a variety of ways to work around the problem of conflict classification. One device is to rely on what may be regarded as "common core" offenses which are prohibited in both international and internal conflicts. This approach was initially suggested by the ICTY Appeals Chamber in the Tadic Jurisdiction Decision, which suggested that the following rules apply to all conflicts regardless of classification:

a) the rules in Common Article 3 (paragraph 102);

b) the principles in UN General Assembly Resolution 2444 (paragraphs 110 and 112);

c) the principles in UN General Assembly Resolution 2675 (paragraphs 111 and 112).

If practicable, we prefer to root Article 3 (violations of laws or customs of war) charges in analogous provisions of separate treaties applicable to both international and internal conflicts. For example, both Article 51(2) of Additional Protocol I, which applies to international conflicts, and Article 13(2) of Additional Protocol II, which applies to internal conflicts, both prohibit attacking civilians. A charge rooted in both of these provisions applies regardless of conflict classification.

A second approach we in the OTP have used is in line with the suggestion of Professor Green; however, we have made some modifications. We have used crimes against humanity charges whenever it has been practicable to do so, including in connection with combat incidents. When we use crimes against humanity charges in relation to attacks, particularly in relation to killing at a distance, however, we also require proof that the casualties were caused as a result of an unlawful attack by law of the Hague criteria. Attacks which are directed against legitimate military objectives and which do not cause excessive incidental civilian casualties cannot be crimes against humanity because they do not meet the requirement that they be directed against the civilian population. Lawful, but regrettable, incidental, but not disproportionate, civilian casualties caused in the course of an attack directed against a legitimate military objective should not be converted into the victim group of a crime against humanity charge by creative recategorization.

This comment posed the question: should crimes against humanity replace war crimes? The answer is "not yet," because the content of the crimes against humanity concept is as yet too skeletal to provide a satisfactory replacement. The suggestion of Professor Green that identical rules should govern all conflicts is, however, meritorious, and elaboration of the crimes against humanity concept may provide a vehicle to reach that objective.

The Crime of Rape. Kate Nahapetian, "Selective Justice: Prosecuting Rape in the International Criminal Tribunals for the Former Yugoslavia and Rwanda" 14 Berkeley Women's L.J. 126 (1999).

Although rape has been categorized as a crime against humanity in past international declarations and has been prohibited in military codes as far back as 1385, it has only recently begun to gain more widespread recognition as a crime against humanity, a war crime, or a form of genocide.

For example, the world passively watched as over 200,000 Bengali women were raped by Pakistani soldiers in Bangladesh's war for independence in 1971. Between 1932 and the end of World War II, the Japanese Imperial Army raped and enslaved over 200,000 Korean, Filipino, and other Asian women, in addition to systematically raping Chinese women in Nanking. However, rape was not a focus of the International Military Tribunal for the Far East and only a few men were prosecuted for rape as a war crime. Similarly, the International Military Tribunal at Nuremberg did not prosecute nor charge anyone for rape as a war crime.

However, with the establishment of the International Tribunal for the former Yugoslavia (ICTY) in 1993, rape began to gain stature as a violation of international law. The statute governing this tribunal explicitly enumerated rape as a crime against humanity. In addition, the International Criminal Tribunal for Rwanda (ICTR), which was established by a United Nations resolution in 1994, includes rape as a crime against humanity, and enumerates rape and enforced prostitution as grave breaches of the Geneva Conventions.

The rapes of over 200,000 women in Asia went virtually unpunished after World War II. Today, men have been prosecuted by the ICTY for the rape of a single woman. In addition, the ICTR recently convicted a former mayor for his incitement of sexual violence against Tutsi women.

What has precipitated the international community to respond to such atrocities previously given only cursory consideration in the international military tribunals after World War II, but which have been the mainstay of almost every war since?

Prior to Yugoslavia and Rwanda, the world community saw rape as a tolerable and inevitable consequence of war. However, the rapes in the former Yugoslavia and Rwanda were viewed not as attacks against women, but campaigns to annihilate an ethnic group. For example, in the former Yugoslavia, Serbs raped not only as a form of terror, but also to actually impregnate Bosnian Muslim women with "Serb" children. Women were raped and detained until it was no longer legally possible to get an abortion. After being raped, women were told "You will now bear a Serb baby." In Rwanda, "the rape of Tutsi women was systematic and was perpetrated against all Tutsi women and solely against them. A Tutsi woman, married to a Hutu, testified before the Chamber that she was not raped because her ethnic background was unknown."*

The genocidal elements of these crimes commanded attention from the United Nations and other human rights organizations. As a result, rape and sexual violence were no longer seen through a gender prism as exclusively crimes against women. Instead, the violations were perceived as human rights violations, rather than as sexual assaults against individual women.

In addition to the sheer number of rapes and the close proximity to Europe, the rapes were particularly brazen. For example, women were enslaved in hotel rooms, houses, or apartments where soldiers would rape and torture them repeatedly for months. In one case, a fifteen year old girl was allegedly raped, tortured, and enslaved for eight months. During this time, she was continually gang-raped by countless men who later sold her to other soldiers. To allow such egregious and systematic violations of international law to go unpunished in Europe's backyard would have constituted a complete failure of international human rights law.

In 1993, the United Nations' Security Council adopted the statute of the ICTY giving the Tribunal jurisdiction to "prosecute persons responsible for serious violations of international humanitarian law" committed in the former Yugoslavia. Article 5(g) of the ICTY statute explicitly enumerates rape as a crime against humanity. Rape is not listed as a war crime or form of genocide, but it is implicitly prohibited under these provisions.

To date, the Tribunal has indicted and convicted several people on charges of rape as a war crime. The so-called Foca indictment, which has received much publicity, was the first ICTY indictment to deal specifically with rape and sexual assault. Submitted in June 1996, it charged eight Bosnian Serb police and military officers with the rape and sexual assault of at least fourteen Bosnian Muslim women in the town of Foca, in Southeastern Bosnia. The men were charged with detaining and enslaving women, some as young as twelve, in houses and apartments

---

* See United Nations, *Judgment in the Case Against Akayesu*, htpp://www.un.org/ictr/english/singledocs/jpa_summary.html.

that were run as brothels by paramilitary troops. These women—and girls—were subjected to almost constant rape, sexual assault, and torture: These crimes had a devastating impact on their lives.

The physical and psychological health of many female detainees seriously deteriorated as a result of these sexual assaults. Some of the women endured complete exhaustion, vaginal discharges, bladder problems and irregular menstrual bleedings. The detainees lived in constant fear. Some of the sexually abused women became suicidal. Others became indifferent as to what would happen to them and suffered from depression. Many women suffered permanent gynaecological harm due to the sexual assaults. All the women who were sexually assaulted suffered psychological and emotional harm; some remain traumatised.

In November 1998, the Tribunal convicted Hazim Delic, a Bosnian Muslim deputy commandant assigned to the Celebici prison camp, of two rapes and two murders and sentenced him to twenty years in prison. The court found Delic guilty of rape as torture and therefore guilty of a war crime in grave breach of the Geneva Conventions. Significantly, the trial chamber emphasized that "there can be no question that acts of rape may constitute torture under customary law."

One month later, on December 10, 1998, the Tribunal convicted a Bosnian Croat paramilitary chief, Anto Furundzija, of rape as a war crime for his involvement in the rape of a Bosnian Muslim woman. Furundzija's conviction, carrying a prison sentence of ten years, was the first war crime conviction based exclusively on rape. This case is also extraordinary because Furundzija was found guilty not because he committed the rape himself, but because he allowed it to occur under his command. The judge wrote, "In such situations the fellow perpetrator plays a role every bit as grave as the person who actually inflicts the pain and suffering." The judgment relied exclusively on the testimony of the woman, notwithstanding the defendant's claim that she suffered from post-traumatic stress disorder and therefore could not accurately remember the events.

Despite these few high profile convictions and indictments, the Tribunal, as a whole, has room for much improvement. Alarmingly, over 20,000 women were the victims of rape, but, as of January 12, 1999, only seventeen accused perpetrators were awaiting either arrest or the completion of their proceedings.

In contrast to its swift reaction to widespread rapes of Bosnian women in the former Yugoslavia, the international community was slow to respond to the systematic rape of women in Rwanda. Genocide and rape in Rwanda were reported a full year before the large-scale massacres of April 1994, yet no international action was taken. In March 1993, one human rights observer reported that, "women have been raped on a phenomenal scale by soldiers."* Yet it took the death of at least 500,000

---

* *The Government and Armed Forces Responsible for the Reign of Terror in Rwanda*, Canada Newswire, March 8, 1993.

Rwandans and the rape of hundreds of thousands of women before Rwanda was afforded a tribunal of its own.

The ICTR was established by the United Nations Security Council on November 8, 1994. It built upon the advances of the ICTY, permitting grave breaches of the Geneva Conventions to be prosecuted during internal conflicts. In addition, Article 4(e) of the statute explicitly enumerates rape and enforced prostitution as a grave breach of the Geneva Conventions, and Article 3(g) specifically lists rape as a crime against humanity.

Despite strengthened mechanisms to prosecute rape and evidence of widespread rape during the genocide, the Tribunal waited almost three years before it indicted anyone for a sexual violence crime. Within a year of the first indictment, however, the Tribunal handed down its historic decision against Jean Paul Akayesu, a former mayor, who was alleged to have rallied his troops with the cry, "don't ever ask again what a Tutsi woman tastes like." Akayesu was convicted of genocide for inciting rapes and sexual violence against women. The Tribunal also convicted him of crimes against humanity for these acts. The judgment explained that rape and sexual violence "constitute genocide in the same way as any other act as long as they were committed with the specific intent to destroy, in whole or in part, a particular group, targeted as such. These rapes resulted in physical and psychological destruction of Tutsi women, their families and their communities."

While the ICTY and the ICTR represent progress in the efforts to prosecute rape as a war crime, to date, prosecution under the current system of international law has been highly dependent on the whims of the political leaders of the most powerful nations including the United States and the nations of Western Europe. The ICTY and ICTR examples suggest that these leaders will not be galvanized to criminally prosecute the rape of women unless either the women are from a European country, or the situation is as extreme as it was in Rwanda.

The international community's inaction in the past may serve as an illustration of what is likely to happen in the future. For instance, Human Rights Watch reported that in 1993 many women from the Muslim minority of Rohingya in Burma were raped "after their husbands or fathers had been taken for forced labor. Sometimes the rapes occurred in the homes, other times the women were taken to a nearby military camp where they were sorted out by beauty. In some cases, the women were killed." The report also noted another neglected conflict in Somalia where:

> a staggering number of rapes, as well as abductions of women and forced marriages, have occurred during the civil war, particularly during the fighting of 1991–1992 but by no means confined to those years. Women who lack the protection of powerful clan structures or who belong to particularly vulnerable groups, such as ethnic minorities, are particularly at risk.

Like the women who lack a powerful "clan structure" in Somalia, minority women lack a state actor who is willing to pressure the international community to take action. The state actor who could speak for them is often the actual abuser. Therefore, women from disempowered minority groups, who are most often the victims of rape, are least capable of pressing their concerns. Bosnian Muslim women, formerly a minority within the country of Yugoslavia, were partly granted a voice when the newly formed state of Bosnia pressured the international community to hear their cases.

The recent rulings and convictions for rape as a form of genocide and as a war crime in both the ICTY and ICTR are reason to celebrate, but, as the system stands, the determination of who will receive this justice is a highly political matter. As Regan Ralph, Executive Director of the Human Rights Watch Women's Rights Project, explained, "Rape is a serious war crime like any other. That's always been true on paper, but now international courts are finally acting on it." There is still a danger, however, that what once was only a paper right will evolve into a privilege exercised only for a certain minority of women whom the world leaders deem worthy of receiving retribution. As a result, advocates for women must continue to press the international community to enforce international law and prosecute the rape of *all* women as a crime against humanity, a war crime, or a form of genocide.

D. UNIVERSAL JURISDICTION

Negative. Henry Kissinger, "The Pitfalls of Universal Jurisdiction" Foreign Affairs 86 (July/ August 2001).

In the aftermath of the Holocaust and the many atrocities committed since, major efforts have been made to find a judicial standard to deal with such catastrophes: the Nuremberg trials of 1945–46, the Universal Declaration of Human Rights of 1948, the genocide convention of 1948, and the antitorture convention of 1988. The Final Act of the Conference on Security and Cooperation in Europe, signed in Helsinki in 1975 by President Gerald Ford on behalf of the United States, obligated the 35 signatory nations to observe certain stated human rights, subjecting violators to the pressures by which foreign policy commitments are generally sustained. In the hands of courageous groups in Eastern Europe, the Final Act became one of several weapons by which communist rule was delegitimized and eventually undermined. In the 1990s, international tribunals to punish crimes committed in the former Yugoslavia and Rwanda, established ad hoc by the U.N. Security Council, have sought to provide a system of accountability for specific regions ravaged by arbitrary violence.

But none of these steps was conceived at the time as instituting a "universal jurisdiction." It is unlikely that any of the signatories of either the U.N. conventions or the Helsinki Final Act thought it possible that national judges would use them as a basis for extradition requests regarding alleged crimes committed outside their jurisdictions. The drafters almost certainly believed that they were stating general principles, not laws that would be enforced by national courts. For example, Eleanor Roosevelt, one of the drafters of the Universal Declaration of Human Rights, referred to it as a "common standard." As one of the negotiators of the Final Act of the Helsinki conference, I can affirm that the administration I represented considered it primarily a diplomatic weapon to use to thwart the communists' attempts to pressure the Soviet and captive peoples. Even with respect to binding undertakings such as the genocide convention, it was never thought that they would subject past and future leaders of one nation to prosecution by the national magistrates of another state where the violations had not occurred. Nor, until recently, was it argued that the various U.N. declarations subjected past and future leaders to the possibility of prosecution by national magistrates of third countries without either due process safeguards or institutional restraints.

Yet this is in essence the precedent that was set by the 1998 British detention of former Chilean President Augusto Pinochet as the result of an extradition request by a Spanish judge seeking to try Pinochet for crimes committed against Spaniards on Chilean soil.* For advocates of universal jurisdiction, that detention—lasting more than 16 months—was a landmark establishing a just principle. But any universal system should contain procedures not only to punish the wicked but also to constrain the righteous. It must not allow legal principles to be used as weapons to settle political scores. Questions such as these must therefore be answered: What legal norms are being applied? What are the rules of evidence? What safeguards exist for the defendant? And how will prosecutions affect other fundamental foreign policy objectives and interests?

The ideological supporters of universal jurisdiction also provide much of the intellectual compass for the emerging International Criminal Court. Their goal is to criminalize certain types of military and political actions and thereby bring about a more humane conduct of international relations. To the extent that the ICC replaces the claim of national judges to universal jurisdiction, it greatly improves the state of international law. And, in time, it may be possible to negotiate modifications of the present statute to make the ICC more compatible with U.S. constitutional practice. But in its present form of assigning the ultimate dilemmas of international politics to unelected jurists—and to an international judiciary at that—it represents such a fundamental change in U.S. constitutional practice that a full national debate and the full participation of Congress are imperative. Such a momentous revolution should not come about by tacit acquiescence in the decision of the House of Lords or by dealing with the ICC issue through a strategy of improving specific clauses rather than as a fundamental issue of principle.

The doctrine of universal jurisdiction is based on the proposition that the individuals or cases subject to it have been clearly identified. In

---

* [Pronounced Pin-o-shett—Eds.]

some instances, especially those based on Nuremberg precedents, the definition of who can be prosecuted in an international court and in what circumstances is self-evident. But many issues are much more vague and depend on an understanding of the historical and political context. It is this fuzziness that risks arbitrariness on the part of prosecutors and judges years after the event and that became apparent with respect to existing tribunals.

For example, can any leader of the United States or of another country be hauled before international tribunals established for other purposes? This is precisely what Amnesty International implied when, in the summer of 1999, it supported a "complaint" by a group of European and Canadian law professors to Louise Arbour, then the prosecutor of the International Criminal Tribunal for the Former Yugoslavia (ICTY). The complaint alleged that crimes against humanity had been committed during the NATO air campaign in Kosovo. Arbour ordered an internal staff review, thereby implying that she did have jurisdiction if such violations could, in fact, be demonstrated. Her successor, Carla Del Ponte, in the end declined to indict any NATO official because of a general inability "to pinpoint individual responsibilities," thereby implying anew that the court had jurisdiction over NATO and American leaders in the Balkans and would have issued an indictment had it been able to identify the particular leaders allegedly involved.

Most Americans would be amazed to learn that the ICTY, created at U.S. behest in 1993 to deal with Balkan war criminals, had asserted a right to investigate U.S. political and military leaders for allegedly criminal conduct—and for the indefinite future, since no statute of limitations applies. Though the ICTY prosecutor chose not to pursue the charge—on the ambiguous ground of an inability to collect evidence—some national prosecutor may wish later to take up the matter as a valid subject for universal jurisdiction.

The pressures to achieve the widest scope for the doctrine of universal jurisdiction were demonstrated as well by a suit before the European Court of Human Rights in June 2000 by families of Argentine sailors who died in the sinking of the Argentine cruiser *General Belgano* during the Falklands War. The concept of universal jurisdiction has moved from judging alleged political crimes against humanity to second-guessing, 18 years after the event, military operations in which neither civilians nor civilian targets were involved.

Distrusting national governments, many of the advocates of universal jurisdiction seek to place politicians under the supervision of magistrates and the judicial system. But prosecutorial discretion without accountability is precisely one of the flaws of the International Criminal Court. Definitions of the relevant crimes are vague and highly susceptible to politicized application. Defendants will not enjoy due process as understood in the United States. Any signatory state has the right to trigger an investigation. As the U.S. experience with the special prosecutors investigating the executive branch shows, such a procedure is likely to develop its own momentum without time limits and can turn into an instrument of political warfare. And the extraordinary attempt of the ICC to assert jurisdiction over Americans even in the absence of U.S. accession to the treaty has already triggered legislation in Congress to resist it.

The independent prosecutor of the ICC has the power to issue indictments, subject to review only by a panel of three judges. According to the Rome Statute, the Security Council has the right to quash any indictment. But since revoking an indictment is subject to the veto of any permanent Security Council member, and since the prosecutor is unlikely to issue an indictment without the backing of at least one permanent member of the Security Council, he or she has virtually unlimited discretion in practice. Another provision permits the country whose citizen is accused to take over the investigation and trial. But the ICC retains the ultimate authority on whether that function has been adequately exercised and, if it finds it has not, the ICC can reassert jurisdiction. While these procedures are taking place, which may take years, the accused will be under some restraint and certainly under grave public shadow.

The advocates of universal jurisdiction argue that the state is the basic cause of war and cannot be trusted to deliver justice. If law replaced politics, peace and justice would prevail. But even a cursory examination of history shows that there is no evidence to support such a theory. The role of the statesman is to choose the best option when seeking to advance peace and justice, realizing that there is frequently a tension between the two and that any reconciliation is likely to be partial. The choice, however, is not simply between universal and national jurisdictions.

The precedents set by international tribunals established to deal with situations where the enormity of the crime is evident and the local judicial system is clearly incapable of administering justice, as in the former Yugoslavia and Rwanda, have shown that it is possible to punish without removing from the process all political judgment and experience. In time, it may be possible to renegotiate the ICC statute to avoid its shortcomings and dangers. Until then, the United States should go no further toward a more formal system than one containing the following three provisions. First, the U.N. Security Council would create a Human Rights Commission or a special subcommittee to report whenever systematic human rights violations seem to warrant judicial action. Second, when the government under which the alleged crime occurred is not authentically representative, or where the domestic judicial system is incapable of sitting in judgment on the crime, the Security Council would set up an ad hoc international tribunal on the model of those of the former Yugoslavia or Rwanda. And third, the procedures for these international tribunals as well as the scope of the prosecution should be precisely defined by the Security Council, and the accused should be entitled to the due process safeguards accorded in common jurisdictions.

In this manner, internationally agreed procedures to deal with war crimes, genocide, or other crimes against humanity could become institutionalized. Furthermore, the one-sidedness of the current pursuit of universal jurisdiction would be avoided. This pursuit could threaten the very purpose for which the concept has been developed. In the end, an excessive reliance on universal jurisdiction may undermine the political will to sustain the humane norms of international behavior so necessary to temper the violent times in which we live.

Affirmative. Kenneth Roth, "The Case for Universal Jurisdiction" Foreign Affairs 150 (2001).

Kissinger's critique of universal jurisdiction has two principal targets: the soon-to-be-formed International Criminal Court and the exercise of universal jurisdiction by national courts. (Strictly speaking, the ICC will use not universal jurisdiction but, rather, a delegation of states' traditional power to try crimes committed on their own territory.) Kissinger claims that the crimes detailed in the ICC treaty are "vague and highly susceptible to politicized application." But the treaty's definition of war crimes closely resembles that found in the Pentagon's own military manuals and is derived from the widely ratified Geneva Conventions and their Additional Protocols adopted in 1977. Similarly, the ICC treaty's definition of genocide is borrowed directly from the Genocide Convention of 1948, which the United States and 131 other governments have ratified and pledged to uphold, including by prosecuting offenders. The definition of crimes against humanity is derived from the Nuremberg Charter, which, as Kissinger acknowledges, proscribes conduct that is "self-[evidently]" wrong.

Kissinger further asserts that the ICC prosecutor will have "discretion without accountability," going so far as to raise the specter of Independent Counsel Kenneth Starr and to decry "the tyranny of judges." In fact, the prosecutor can be removed for misconduct by a simple majority of the governments that ratify the ICC treaty, and a two-thirds vote can remove a judge. Because joining the court means giving it jurisdiction over crimes committed on the signatory's territory, the vast majority of member states will be democracies, not the abusive governments that self-protectively flock to U.N. human rights bodies, where membership bears no cost.

Kissinger criticizes the "extraordinary attempt of the ICC to assert jurisdiction over Americans even in the absence of U.S. accession to the treaty." But the United States itself asserts such jurisdiction over others' citizens when it prosecutes terrorists or drug traffickers, such as Panamanian dictator Manuel Noriega, without the consent of the suspect's government. Moreover, the ICC will assert such power only if an American commits a specified atrocity on the territory of a government that has joined the ICC and has thus delegated its prosecutorial authority to the court.

Kissinger claims that ICC defendants "will not enjoy due process as understood in the United States"—an apparent allusion to the lack of a jury trial in a court that will blend civil and common law traditions. But U.S. courts martial also do not provide trials by jury. Moreover, U.S. civilian courts routinely approve the constitutionality of extradition to countries that lack jury trials, so long as their courts otherwise observe basic due process. The ICC clearly will provide such due process, since its treaty requires adherence to the full complement of international fair-trial standards.

Of course, any court's regard for due process is only as good as the quality and temperament of its judges. The ICC's judges will be chosen by the governments that join the court, most of which, as noted, will be democracies. Even without ratifying the ICC treaty, the U.S. government could help shape a culture of respect for due process by quietly working with the court, as it has done successfully with the international war crimes tribunals for Rwanda and the former Yugoslavia. Regrettably, ICC opponents in Washington are pushing legislation—the misnamed American Servicemembers Protection Act—that would preclude such cooperation.

The experience of the Yugoslav and Rwandan tribunals, of which Kissinger speaks favorably, suggests that international jurists, when forced to decide the fate of a particular criminal suspect, do so with scrupulous regard for fair trial standards. Kissinger's only stated objection to these tribunals concerns the decision of the prosecutor of the tribunal for the former Yugoslavia to pursue a brief inquiry into how NATO conducted its air war against the new Yugoslavia—an inquiry that led her to exonerate NATO.

It should be noted, in addition, that the jurisdiction of the Yugoslav tribunal was set not by the prosecutor but by the U.N. Security Council, with U.S. consent. The Council chose to grant jurisdiction without prospective time limit, over serious human rights crimes within the territory of the former Yugoslavia committed by anyone—not just Serbs, Croats, and Bosnian Muslims. In light of that mandate, the prosecutor would have been derelict in her duties not to consider NATO's conduct; according to an extensive field investigation by Human Rights Watch, roughly half of the approximately 500 civilian deaths caused by NATO's bombs could be attributed to NATO's failure, albeit not criminal, to abide by international humanitarian law.

Kissinger claims that the ICC would violate the U.S. Constitution if it asserted jurisdiction over an American. But the court is unlikely to prosecute an American because the Rome treaty deprives the ICC of jurisdiction if, after the court gives required notice of its intention to examine a suspect, the suspect's government conducts its own good-faith investigation and, if appropriate, prosecution. It is the stated policy of the U.S. government to investigate and prosecute its own war criminals.

Moreover, the ICC's assertion of jurisdiction over an American for a crime committed abroad poses no greater constitutional problem than the routine practice under status-of-forces agreements of allowing foreign prosecution of American military personnel for crimes committed overseas, such as Japan's arrest in July of a U.S. Air Force sergeant for an alleged rape on Okinawa. An unconstitutional delegation of U.S. judicial power would arguably take place only if the United States ratified the ICC Treaty; then an American committed genocide, war crimes, or crimes against humanity on U.S. soil; and then U.S. authorities did not prosecute the offender. Yet that remote possibility would signal a constitutional crisis far graver than one spawned by an ICC prosecution.

National courts come under Kissinger's fire for selectively applying universal jurisdiction. He characterizes the extradition request by a Spanish judge seeking to try former Chilean President Augusto Pinochet for crimes against Spanish citizens on Chilean soil as singling out a "fashionably reviled man of the right." But Pinochet was sought not, as Kissinger writes, "because he led a coup d'etat against an elected leader" who was a favorite of the left. Rather, Pinochet was targeted because security forces under his command murdered and forcibly "disappeared" some 3,000 people and tortured thousands more.

Furthermore, in recent years national courts have exercised universal jurisdiction against a wide range of suspects: Bosnian war criminals, Rwandan *genocidaires*, Argentine torturers, and Chad's former dictator. It has come to the point where the main limit on national courts empowered to exercise universal jurisdiction is the availability of the defendant, not questions of ideology.

Kissinger also cites the Pinochet case to argue that international justice interferes with the choice by democratic governments to forgive rather than prosecute past offenders. In fact, Pinochet's imposition of a self-amnesty at the height of his dictatorship limited Chile's democratic options. Only after 16 months of detention in the United Kingdom diminished his power was Chilean democracy able to begin prosecution. Such imposed impunity is far more common than democratically chosen impunity.

Kissinger would have had a better case had prosecutors sought, for example, to overturn the compromise negotiated by South Africa's Nelson Mandela, widely recognized at the time as the legitimate representative of the victims of apartheid. Mandela agreed to grant abusers immunity from prosecution if they gave detailed testimony about their crimes. In an appropriate exercise of prosecutorial discretion, no prosecutor has challenged this arrangement, and no government would likely countenance such a challenge.

Kissinger legitimately worries that the nations exercising universal jurisdiction could include governments with less-entrenched traditions of due process than the United Kingdom's. But his fear of governments robotically extraditing suspects for sham or counterproductive trials is overblown. Governments regularly deny extradition to courts that are unable to ensure high standards of due process. And foreign ministries, including the U.S. State Department, routinely deny extradition requests for reasons of public policy.

If an American faced prosecution by an untrustworthy foreign court, the United States undoubtedly would apply pressure for his or her release. If that failed, however, it might prove useful to offer the prosecuting government the face-saving alternative of transferring the suspect to the ICC, with its extensive procedural protections, including deference to good-faith investigations and prosecutions by a suspect's own government. Unfortunately, the legislation being pushed by ICC opponents in Washington would preclude that option.

Until the ICC treaty is renegotiated to avoid what Kissinger sees as its "shortcomings and dangers," he recommends that the U.N. Security Council determine which cases warrant an international tribunal. That option was rejected during the Rome negotiations on the ICC because it would allow the Council's five permanent members, including Russia and China as well as the United States, to exempt their nationals and those of their allies by exercising their vetoes.

As a nation committed to human rights and the rule of law, the United States should be embracing an international system of justice, even if it means that Americans, like everyone else, might sometimes be scrutinized.

The Practice of States. M. Cherif Bassiouni, "Universal Jurisdiction for International Crimes: Historical Perspectives and Contemporary Practice" 42 Va. J. Int'l L. 81 (2001).

Universal jurisdiction has become the preferred technique by those seeking to prevent impunity for international crimes. While there is no doubt that it is a useful and, at times, necessary technique, it also has negative aspects. The exercise of universal jurisdiction is generally reserved for the most serious international crimes, such as war crimes, crimes against humanity, and genocide; however, there may be other international crimes for which an applicable treaty provides for such a jurisdictional basis, as in the case of terrorism.

Unbridled universal jurisdiction can cause disruptions in world order and deprivation of individual human rights when used in a politically motivated manner or for vexatious purposes. Even with the best of intentions, universal jurisdiction can be used imprudently, creating unnecessary frictions between states, potential abuses of legal processes, and undue harassment of individuals prosecuted or pursued for prosecution under this theory.

Universal jurisdiction must therefore be utilized in a cautious manner that minimizes possible negative consequences, while at the same time enabling it to achieve its useful purposes. It must also be harmonized with other jurisdictional theories. Furthermore, it should be noted that private international law has not yet developed rules or criteria of sufficient clarity to consider priorities in the exercise of criminal jurisdiction whenever more than one state claims jurisdiction.

Universal jurisdiction resembles a checkerboard. Some conventions recognize it and some national practices of states demonstrate its existence, but it is uneven and inconsistent. Most of all, the practice of states does not evidence its consistent or widespread application.

The confusion about universality is that it has at least five meanings:

(1) universality of condemnation for certain crimes;

(2) universal reach of national jurisdiction, which could be for the international crime for which there is universal condemnation, as well as others;

(3) extraterritorial reach of national jurisdiction (which may also merge with universal reach of national legislation);

(4) universal reach of international adjudicative bodies that may or may not rely on the theory of universal jurisdiction; and

(5) universal jurisdiction of national legal systems without any connection to the enforcing state other than the presence of the accused.

The diverse meanings attributed to universal jurisdiction have probably been among the reasons why confusion has surrounded its legal significance. Similarly, the diverse theories of extra-territorial jurisdiction that were applied by international and national judicial bodies have also contributed to this confusion. But the writings of scholars added to the confusion when they expressed in lex lata terms what may have been de lege ferenda or only expected desiderata.

What truly advanced the recognition and application of universal jurisdiction has been the acceptance of the maxim aut dedere aut judicare as an international civitas maxima. The duty to prosecute or extradite and, where appropriate, to punish persons accused of or convicted of international crimes, particularly jus cogens crimes because of their heinous nature and disruptive impact on peace and security, necessarily leads to the recognition of universal jurisdiction as a means of achieving the goals of aut dedere aut judicare.

The writings of scholars have driven the recognition of the theory of universal jurisdiction, particularly for jus cogens international crimes. These writings reflect idealistic universalistic views, as well as pragmatic policy perspectives.

The combination of international and national sources of law has produced a cumulative effect sufficient to warrant the recognition of universal jurisdiction for jus cogens crimes. Universal jurisdiction is the most effective method to deter and prevent international crimes by increasing the likelihood of prosecution and punishment of its perpetrators. This approach to international criminal accountability is also believed to be a factor in reducing impunity for the perpetrators of these crimes.

A dynamic interaction exists between: (1) international and national norms of international criminal law; (2) international and national processes for the enforcement of international criminal law; and (3) state and non-state actors' cooperation in the development of norms and processes and in their implementation. This dynamic interaction is breaking down traditional compartmentalization between international and national law. As a result, hybrid norms and processes have developed that include both international and national characteristics and incorporate the combined supportive roles of state and non-state actors in the development of norms and processes, as well as in their implementation. This dialectical relationship, which some call "complementarity," is, however, even more complex. It is an amorphous and changing process that is difficult to define, predict, or assess, other than to recognize that it is both growing and evolving. The fact that it is, in part, the product of contingent circumstantial and occasional factors does not diminish its continued growth.

The policy-based assumptions and goals of universal jurisdiction are that such a jurisdictional mechanism, when relied upon by a large number of states, can prevent, deter, punish, provide accountability, and reduce impunity for some international crimes, and that can enhance the prospects of justice and peace. Irrespective of the checkered nature of the recognition and application of universal jurisdiction in international and national law and practice, the policy arguments advanced in its favor, particularly in light of the historic record of impunity that has benefited so many of the perpetrators of these crimes for so long, support its application. But universal jurisdiction must not be allowed to become a wildfire, uncontrolled in its application and destructive of the international legal processes. If that were the case, it would produce conflicts of jurisdiction between states that have the potential to threaten world order, subject individuals to abuses of judicial processes, human rights violations, politically motivated harassment, and work denial of justice. In addition, there is the danger that universal jurisdiction may be perceived as hegemonistic jurisdiction exercised mainly by some Western powers against persons from developing nations.

To avoid these and other negative outcomes, while enhancing the positive outcomes of an orderly and effective application of universal jurisdiction, it is indispensable to arrive at norms regulating the resort by states and international adjudicating bodies to the application of this theory. At first, guidelines should be developed that in time may garner consensus among scholars and, ultimately, among governments. At that stage, an international convention should be elaborated so that these guidelines can become positive international law.

The history of contemporary international law is replete with examples of scholarly and NGO initiatives that have set in motion a process that ripened into conventional international law. The Princeton Project on Universal Jurisdiction is one of these instances, and hopefully it will result in an international convention on universal jurisdiction for jus cogens and other international crimes that includes jurisdictional priorities, provides rules for resolving conflicts of jurisdiction, and minimizes the exposure of individuals to multiple prosecutions, abuses of process, and denial of justice.

As the French philosopher Pascal once said, "Every custom has its origin in a single act," and in this case, there is ample evidence of many such acts. However, it is their cumulative effect which gives weight to the proposition that universal jurisdiction is part of customary international law. Nevertheless, the fact that there is a customary international law recognition of universal jurisdiction does not imply that it can be exercised with respect to all international crimes or that it can be exercised by all states without limitations. The question as to which crimes universal jurisdiction applies is still an unsettled question, though there is more generalized agreement that it includes piracy, slavery and slave-related practices, war crimes, crimes against humanity, genocide, and by convention, torture and some international terrorism crimes. In addition, customary international law has not yet settled the issue of whether there needs to be a nexus to the enforcing state, such as the presence of the accused on its territory. There are also other issues that remain unresolved, such as the temporal immunity of heads of states and diplomats, a number of issues pertaining to the rights of the individual to prevent vexatious and multiple prosecutions, as well as how to ensure due process and fairness in the course of proceedings based on universal jurisdiction. Consequently, it can be said that the recognition of universal jurisdiction in customary international law is in its first stage of evolution, and that it has to be followed by other stages needed to clarify the rights and obligations of states in the exercise of this form of extra-territorial jurisdiction in order to maximize the benefits of universal jurisdiction and eliminate its potential for abuses.

E. PROSECUTING HEADS OF STATE

The Pinochet Precedent. Mary Margaret Penrose, "It's Good to Be the King!: Prosecuting Heads of State and Former Heads of State Under International Law" 39 Colum. J. Transnat'l L. 193 (2000).

Many human rights activists and scholars have openly proclaimed that the Augusto Pinochet precedent is one of the most important advances since the Nuremberg Trials. Could we be approaching an era where kings might be subject to the same laws and regulations that govern their subjects? Could we actually be nearing a time when the Genocide Convention and the Torture Convention will deliver the protection and relief they promise? Are we reaching that point—long strived for by proponents of human rights—where law, in the form of criminal culpability, will triumph over politics?

Perhaps the greatest difficulty this author has experienced in accepting the Pinochet precedent is that those countries arguing most strongly for prosecution—Spain, Belgium, Switzerland, France and the United Kingdom—disingenuously relied on the force of international law (via resort to frequently unenforced treaties), morality, and the need to end impunity as reasons for acting against Pinochet. Moral authority does not provide a sufficient basis, standing alone, to support criminal prosecutions. Rather, as a world bound by legal precedents, procedures, and treaties that restrain state action, it would have been more prudent to recognize that the issue of prosecuting former and sitting heads of state is opaque at best.

State practice surely did not—and, arguably does not—support the Pinochet precedent. In fact, not even the state practice of the most ardent supporters of his prosecution has demonstrated a past willingness to prosecute heads of state. France continues to provide refuge to Duvalier. Senegal has determined that, despite its position as the first state to ratify the Rome Statute and despite the force of the Pinochet rulings, it does not have authority to prosecute acts of torture committed abroad.

Unlike the Pinochet precedent, which was observed loosely at best, the authority of the two U.N. ad hoc tribunals has been firmly established by Security Council Resolution and subsequent jurisprudence. Further, both tribunal statutes mandate individual state cooperation in the enforcement of criminal sentences. The former President of the ICTY, the Honorable Gabrielle Kirk McDonald, openly called for increased cooperation by nation-states in a speech at American University in 1998. Judge McDonald explained that "the nature of the modern State and its place in the international community means that it is they [the individual states] who are expected, in fact required, to provide the structural and systematic support necessary to sustain the Tribunal."

Despite the clarity of the statutory language and the continued acknowledgment that states are not adequately assisting with enforcement, only seven European States have agreed to render prison space to the ICTY. Only two African states have offered their assistance in receiving ICTR prisoners. Where, one must ask, are Belgium, Switzerland, France and the United Kingdom with respect to this international legal conundrum? And, where is the United States? Where is the force of moral authority that these countries so vehemently displayed when faced with the arrest and possible prosecution of Pinochet? Why is there not an equally supportive attitude displayed toward the prosecution of the war crimes committed in Yugoslavia and Rwanda?

The difficulty of moral authority is that it falters when the true "morality" of the position being asserted is unveiled. None of the Pinochet countries has fully met the requirements under either the ICTY or ICTR Statutes. Spain alone has agreed to accept ICTY prisoners (and only as recently as March 28, 2000, after proceedings against Pinochet were initiated). Is moral authority only an acceptable answer when the state pursuing the prosecution has been harmed, or has had citizens harmed, by the acts of the individuals being punished? And if so, do we not return immediately to "victor's justice," which permeated Nuremberg and the Tokyo Tribunal?

As we continue to seek a truly international solution to torture, genocide, and crimes against humanity, perhaps we should pause to consider state practice. State practice is a legitimate and well-established principle of international law. Current state practice indicates an increasing trend toward eradicating immunity. This trend is only just beginning to gain ground and still does not demonstrate with sufficient forcefulness that dictators—e.g., Pol Pot, Idi Amin, Mengistu Haile Mariam, "Baby Doc" Duvalier, Moammar Gadhafi, Alfredo Stroessner and Slobodan Milosevic*—will be subject to prosecution. In fact, state practice currently weighs more heavily on the side of Truth Commissions and Amnesties than on the side of criminal prosecutions.

The Pinochet Case. Michael Byers, "The Law and Politics of the Pinochet Case" 10 Duke J. Comp. & Int'l L. 415 (2000).

Politicians and publics tend to be very attached to traditional concepts of sovereignty and may feel greatly affronted by what—to international lawyers—are legitimate applications of widely accepted rules of international law. As a result, governments, and perhaps judges, will weigh the often ambiguous benefits of enforcing international criminal law in a specific case against the very real costs that may result to their country's political alliances, national security, and trade.

The Pinochet case raised precisely these issues. It taxed the imagination and understanding of more than twenty national judges, none of whom were specialists in international law, nor young enough to have studied international law when it was based on anything other than the traditional, state-centric model. The case also raised extremely sensitive political questions concerning the relationship between European powers and their former colonies and the appropriateness, rather than simply the legality, of interfering in the domestic affairs of states undergoing delicate transitions from authoritarianism to democracy. From the perspective of a changed geopolitical situation having new and perhaps far less dangerous imperatives than those that had previously prevailed, the Pinochet case called into question the wisdom of re-examining anti-communism actions taken during the Cold War. Lastly, the case threatened to damage an economic relationship of considerable importance, with British companies having invested heavily in Chile, and with Chile being an important market for the British arms industry.

The proceedings in the Pinochet case were thus significant in two inexorably intertwined respects, one primarily legal and the other primarily political. First, the proceedings posed, in the most direct terms, a choice between two competing visions of the international legal order. On the one hand, there was the international law of the past whereby a head of state could do what he wished and rely, for the rest of his life, on the fact that he was immune before the courts. On the other hand, there was the international law of the present and future, in which a former head of state was not immune from claims brought by, or in relation to,

---

* [Mr. Milosevic is now a defendant at the ICTY. See Section A of this chapter.—Eds.]

egregious wrongs perpetuated on innocent victims. Second, the proceedings were significant because they challenged judges and politicians in the United Kingdom to exercise the universal jurisdiction available to them in a high profile situation of considerable political sensitivity, where the politically expedient decision would—almost certainly—have been to set Pinochet free. The intertwined character of the law and the politics of the Pinochet case, and the way in which rules and legal institutions constrained the behavior of politicians and judges, may be best exposed through a chronological account of the arrest and subsequent proceedings.

Legal and political actors are motivated by a variety of often-conflicting factors and interests that include much more than a simple desire to "apply" the law. For example, the British government was clearly caught between an expressed desire to uphold international criminal law and protect human rights, and an unexpressed desire to avoid the political and economic risks associated with having such a controversial series of events unfold on British soil.

The Chilean and Spanish governments were caught in similar binds. According to some rumors, many members of the Chilean government were secretly pleased that Pinochet had been arrested overseas and thus removed from the domestic political scene. Indeed, there are those who attribute the victory of Socialist candidate Ricardo Lagos in the January 16, 2000 presidential election to Pinochet's absence from Chile. There is a sense that, thanks to the arrest, the country was finally able to close the chapter on the Pinochet years. The announcement, by President Lagos immediately after his election, that immunity from prosecution in Chile would no longer be accorded to Pinochet, is but one example of the positive effect that the situation has had on the development of Chilean democracy. Nevertheless, throughout the case, and especially during the hearings in Pinochet III, the Chilean government felt compelled, for domestic political reasons, to claim the sovereign right to have Pinochet tried in Chile, and not abroad.

The Spanish government clearly had mixed feelings about proceedings of this kind against the former leader of a former Spanish colony—and a country with which Spain maintains important cultural and economic links. These mixed feelings were perhaps most apparent when Spain decided against joining Belgium and the human rights organizations in challenging Jack Straw's decision not to release the medical report. However, like the British government, the Spanish government was constrained by the fact that the investigation and extradition request constituted a judicial and not a political process.

A variety of other actors added to the complex picture presented in the Pinochet case. First, there were the human rights organizations, whose efforts to apply and develop international criminal law were clearly in fulfillment of their own mandates, but who also benefited enormously—in terms of fundraising and membership—from their close involvement in such a high profile case. These organizations, with their transnational networks of activists and their connections with judicial authorities in different countries, were critical in bringing the various strands of the case together: of accused, of victims, of willing prosecutor, and of available jurisdiction. They had also been crucial in establishing some of the legal institutions that figured prominently in the case, most notably the Torture Convention. Second, there were the journalists and their employers, who saw the drama in the story and seized upon it to attract and maintain audience interest in what would otherwise have been a slow period for news. Lastly, something of a more disturbing—and much less noticeable—role was played by those transnational corporations who helped fund Pinochet's legal defense and whose involvement bore a striking resemblance to the role of other corporations (most notably ITT) in Pinochet's rise to power in 1973.

The existence and involvement of these multiple actors presents a complexity that challenges any attempt to understand the full dimensions of the Pinochet case. On the one hand, the complexity demonstrates that multiple factors were at work, that legal rules and institutions were only part of the picture, and that politics were also intrinsically involved. On the other hand, and contrary to what some might have assumed, the arrest and detention of Pinochet was not strictly about politics. Law and politics were interacting constantly throughout this period, constraining some actors, and empowering others. The constraining effects of the law were most apparent upon the governments of Chile and the United Kingdom, as well as upon the judges in Pinochet III.

In terms of empowerment, the law was of greatest assistance to Pinochet's individual victims, and to the human rights organizations that took up their cause—both on its own merits, and as a means of further developing the law. The significance of their success extends far beyond providing an essential sense of redress for Pinochet's victims. The development of international human rights and the more recent growth of an "international civil society" reflect an international system that is slowly but surely embracing the rule of law. Only in a world with generally accepted rules and institutions is there space for individuals and human rights groups to flourish, to challenge the prerogatives of state sovereignty (along with its cynical politics and reliance on military and economic power), with moral authority and the slow but sure evolution of binding rules and effective judicial processes.

[As of February 2005, a Chilean appeals court has upheld the indictment of General Pinochet over the disappearance of three dissidents during his military rule, unanimously rejecting an appeal by the defense that he was physically unfit to stand trial. So far a total of 119 persons have been identified as having been abducted and later killed in the 1975 secret operation. The appeals panel determined that security agents could not have carried out arrests and killings without Pinochet's approval, and the case appears headed to the Supreme Court.—Eds.]

F. THE INTERNATIONAL CRIMINAL COURT

Policy. David Scheffer, "U.S. Policy and the International Criminal Court" 32 Cornell Int'l L.J. 529 (1999).*

The theory of universal jurisdiction for genocide, crimes against humanity, and war crimes seized the imagination of many delegates negotiating the ICC Treaty. They appeared to believe that the ICC should be empowered to do what some national governments have done unilaterally, namely, to enact laws that empower their courts to prosecute any individuals, including non-nationals, who commit one or more of these crimes. Some governments have enacted such laws, which theoretically, but rarely in practice, make their courts arenas for international prosecutions. The problem for any national government seeking to exercise such universal jurisdiction is to exercise personal jurisdiction over the suspect. Without custody, or the prospect of it through an extradition proceeding, a national court's claim of universal jurisdiction is necessarily and rightly limited.

Admittedly, many recent international treaty regimes, including those directed at terrorism, have used universal jurisdiction as a means of enforcement. Under such a treaty, criminals involved in airplane hijacking, airplane bombings, and attacks on diplomats as internationally protected persons, can be tried in the courts of any treaty signatory, no matter the place of the offense or the nationality of the victim. The treaties against hostage-taking and torture also provide for universal jurisdiction, as the lawyers for General Augusto Pinochet have recently learned. However, the exercise of universal jurisdiction is limited to treaty parties. Additionally, use of universal jurisdiction in the operational law of war has been halting. The 1949 Geneva Conventions make use of it for grave breaches of the conventions, but these four conventions are limited to the deliberate mistreatment of civilians, prisoners of war, the wounded, and the ship wrecked. The Hague regulations and the laws and customs of war which establish the limits on war do not directly provide for universal jurisdiction. Protocol I of 1977 to the Geneva Conventions defines as a grave breach any disproportionate use of force, or the use of force in environmentally objectionable ways, but the United States and a number of other countries have not yet ratified Protocol I. Thus, the universal jurisdiction created by the Rome Conference would mean something new, at least for U.S. troops stationed abroad.

The ICC is designed as a treaty-based court with the unique power to prosecute and sentence individuals, but also to impose obligations of cooperation upon the contracting states. A fundamental principle of international treaty law is that only states that are party to a treaty should be bound by its terms. Yet Article 12 of the ICC Treaty reduces the need for ratification of the treaty by national governments by

---

* [The author was the Ambassador-at-Large for War Crime Issues from 1997–2000.—Eds.]

providing the ICC with jurisdiction over the nationals of a non-party state. Under Article 12, the ICC may exercise such jurisdiction over anyone, anywhere in the world, even in the absence of a referral by the Security Council, if either the state of the territory where the crime was committed or the state of nationality of the accused consents. Ironically, the Treaty exposes non-parties in ways that the parties themselves are not exposed.

Why is the United States so concerned about the status of non-party states under the ICC Treaty? Why not, as many have suggested, simply sign and ratify the Treaty and thus eliminate the problem of non-party status? First, fundamental principles of treaty law still matter and we are loath to ignore them with respect to any state's obligations vis-a-vis a treaty regime. While certain conduct is prohibited under customary international law and might be the object of universal jurisdiction by a national court, the establishment of, and a state's participation in, an international criminal court are not derived from custom but, rather, from the requirements of treaty law.

Second, even if the Clinton Administration were in a position to sign the Treaty, U.S. ratification could take many years and stretch beyond the date of entry into force of the Treaty. Thus, the United States could have non-party status under the ICC Treaty for a significant period of time. The crimes within the court's jurisdiction also go beyond those arguably covered by universal jurisdiction, and court decisions or future amendments could effectively create "new" and unacceptable crimes. Moreover, the ability to withdraw from the Treaty, should the court develop in unacceptable ways, would be negated as an effective protection.

Equally troubling are the implications of Article 12 for the future willingness of the United States and other governments to take significant risks to intervene in foreign lands in order to save human lives or to restore international or regional peace and security. The illogical consequence imposed by Article 12, particularly for non-parties to the Treaty, will be to limit severely those lawful, but highly controversial and inherently risky, interventions that the advocates of human rights and world peace so desperately seek from the United States and other military powers. There will be significant new legal and political risks in such interventions, which up to this point have been mostly shielded from politically motivated charges.

We clearly recognize the dilemma posed by the limitations of Article 12, namely that it will exclude from the court's jurisdiction strictly internal atrocities committed by non-consenting non-party states, absent a Security Council referral. On the one hand, we object to any presumption that sixty ratifications of the Treaty, and its entry into force, automatically exposes every individual everywhere in the world to the ICC's jurisdiction unless the Security Council exercises its Chapter VII powers. We always envisaged this Treaty regime's reach to grow as more states ratify it. However, we did not envisage the Security Council giving the court the ability to leap-frog over jurisdictional barriers. On the other hand, we are open to considering ways to address the most obvious manifestation of contemporary illegality, namely the self-inflicted atrocity by the rogue regime. The obvious procedure is the Security Council referral.

In Rome, the U.S. Delegation offered various proposals to correct the jurisdictional problem. The other permanent members of the Security Council joined us in a compromise formula during the last week of the Rome conference. One of our proposals was to exempt from the ICC's jurisdiction conduct that, in the absence of a Security Council referral, arises from the official actions of a non-party state acknowledged as such by that non-party. This would require a non-party state to acknowledge official responsibility for an atrocity in order to be exempted, an unlikely occurrence for those who usually commit genocide or other serious violations of international humanitarian law. In contrast, the United States would confirm as a matter of course its participation in international peacekeeping and enforcement actions. It is likely that there would be odious non-party regimes that would not blink at admitting genocide as an official state policy. However, that simply reflects the fact that the ICC cannot pretend to cover everyone everywhere under every circumstance if the Security Council fails to act. Regrettably, our proposed amendments to Article 12 were rejected on the premise that the proposed draft of the Treaty was so fragile that if any part were reopened, the conference would fall apart.

The final text of the Treaty includes the crime of aggression, albeit undefined until a Review Conference seven years after entry into force of the Treaty will determine the meaning of aggression. This political concession to the most persistent advocates of a crime of aggression without a consensus definition and without the linkage to a prior Security Council determination that an act of aggression has occurred, should concern all of us. The PrepCom is addressing the issue, however, and we hope it will proceed responsibly in the years ahead. If handled poorly, this issue alone could fatally compromise the ICC's future credibility.

I will not belabor the final hours of the conference except to say that it could have been done differently and the outcome might have been far more encouraging. While we firmly believe that the true intent of national governments cannot be that which now appears reflected in a few key provisions of the ICC Treaty, the political will remains within the Clinton Administration to support a treaty that is fairly and realistically constituted. We hope developments will unfold in the future so that the considerable support that the United States could bring to a properly constituted international criminal court can be realized.

Politics. Diane F. Orentlicher, "Politics by Other Means: The Law of the International Criminal Court" 32 Cornell Int'l L.J. 498 (1999).

As Ambassador Scheffer's remarks reflect, the U.S. government's principal criticism of the Rome Statute is that nationals of non-States

Parties can theoretically be prosecuted before the ICC. By virtue of Article 12 of the Statute, when an investigation has been triggered by either the Prosecutor or a State Party, the ICC can exercise jurisdiction only if at least one of the following States is a Party to the Rome Statute or has accepted the Court's jurisdiction with respect to the crime in question: 1) the State in whose territory the crime occurred, and 2) the State of which the accused is a national. Theoretically, then, a national of a non-State Party alleged to have committed a crime within the territorial jurisdiction of a State Party could be prosecuted before the Court.

In the view of the U.S. and Indian governments, this provision violates a basic rule of international law: a treaty may not impose obligations upon a non-State Party without its consent. But this argument is misplaced. Article 12 does not impose obligations upon non-States Parties. Rather, it establishes further preconditions to the exercise of jurisdiction that must be satisfied when the ICC's jurisdiction has been triggered either by the Prosecutor pursuant to Article 13(c) or by a State Party pursuant to Article 13(a). Non–Parties to the Rome Statute have no obligation to assist the ICC when it exercises jurisdiction pursuant to these provisions. In contrast, States Parties assume various obligations relating to the arrest and surrender of individuals indicted by the Prosecutor. Thus, while Article 12 has potential implications for nationals of non-States Parties, it does not impose corresponding obligations upon those States. The fact that the Rome Statute potentially enables the ICC to assert jurisdiction over nationals of non-States Parties does not in itself breach any principle of treaty law. It is well established that, once a group of States has created an international organization through a multilateral treaty, that organization possesses an objective legal personality even vis-à-vis States that are not parties to its constituent treaty. This principle is equally relevant to an international court established by multilateral treaty.

This point is by no means a mere technicality. It reflects the fundamental nature of the Court's jurisdiction. Empowered to exercise jurisdiction "over persons for the most serious crimes of international concern," the ICC was established to enforce a body of law whose very essence is its direct application to individuals—not States. The principle of individual responsibility was, of course, the central idea of Nuremberg, and is the foundation of the ICC's jurisdiction as well.*

This is not to say that international criminal law is impervious to the concerns of States with respect to prosecution of their nationals. Some treaties reflect those interests by recognizing that, as between the treaty Parties, primary or even exclusive jurisdiction over certain crimes lies with courts of the alleged perpetrators' State of nationality. For

---

* The Nuremberg Tribunal took pains to emphasize that those who commit "acts which are condemned as criminal by international law" do not enjoy the protection generally accorded persons acting on behalf of their States pursuant to "the doctrine of the sovereignty of the State." The Tribunal thus made clear that individuals who commit international crimes generally are not to be assimilated to their States, but rather stand directly before the bar of international justice.

example, Status of Forces Agreements frequently contain provisions vesting primary or exclusive jurisdiction over certain types of crimes allegedly committed abroad by servicemen deployed by States Parties in the courts of the defendants' State of nationality. In a similar vein, many extradition treaties include a provision to the effect that States Parties are not required to extradite their own nationals, though such treaties commonly require authorities to submit otherwise extraditable offenses to their own criminal justice system if they decline to extradite suspects on this ground.

It is simply incorrect, however, to suggest that the Rome Statute violates international treaty law by exposing nationals of non-adhering States to potential prosecution without the consent of their governments. Many bilateral extradition treaties and a growing roster of multilateral treaties allow or require States Parties to prosecute or extradite individuals alleged to have committed certain crimes, regardless of the nationality of the suspect and regardless of whether his or her State of nationality is a Party to the Treaty; the United States is a Party to a number of these treaties. For example, the Convention against Torture and Other Cruel, Inhuman or Degrading Treatment or Punishment (Torture Convention) requires each State Party to "take such measures as may be necessary to establish its jurisdiction over [torture and certain related offenses] in cases where the alleged offender is present in any territory under its jurisdiction and it does not extradite him...." The treaty imposes this obligation in addition to States Parties' duties to establish jurisdiction over acts of torture committed in their territorial jurisdiction or by their nationals. In effect, then, the Torture Convention establishes a system of mandatory universal jurisdiction that binds States Parties but potentially operates vis-à-vis nationals of non-States Parties.

Each of the four Geneva Conventions of 1949 establishes a similar system of mandatory universal jurisdiction. All four Conventions identify certain violations as "grave breaches" and impose upon each High Contracting Party "the obligation to search for persons alleged to have committed, or to have ordered to be committed, such grave breaches, and [to] bring such persons, regardless of their nationality, before its own courts" unless it hands those persons over for trial to another High Contracting Party.

The United States is also a Party to several anti-terrorism conventions that require each State Party either to prosecute or to extradite persons alleged to have committed defined offenses when those persons are present in its territory. Like similar provisions in the Torture Convention and the Geneva Conventions of 1949, the provisions in these treaties apply regardless of the nationality of the suspect or the site of the alleged crime.

Does this mean that States enjoy unfettered power to subject any individual to the jurisdiction of their own courts or to that of an international court merely by concluding a treaty between at least two of them? Of course not. But Article 12 vests the ICC with potential jurisdiction only under conditions clearly permitted by international law.

Chapter 9

TERRORISM

Editors' Introduction: To what extent and under what conditions can a state claim "unprecedented circumstances" before taking action that appears to stretch international rules nearly to the breaking point? The U.S.-led "war on terror," begun after the September 11 attacks but likely to last for many decades, poses such a challenge. "Terrorism" and "terrorist" are ill-defined terms in international law, and a state, operating on the principle that "we know it when we see it" is bound to come up against existing rules that were written for conventional, inter-state conflict. Terrorists are non-state actors who have weak affinity to states and their territorial jurisdictions. Looked at one way, the rules appear to need revision or risk being broken. Or is this an exaggerated argument? The readings probe the question of whether existing rules are fully relevant, or the extent to which they can be unilaterally reinterpreted, in the fight against terrorism. We are above all interested in what occurs when a powerful state deems the rules to be inadequate to confront the threat and begins to operate outside the established legal framework.

A. TERRORISM AND STATE RESPONSIBILITY

The War on Terror. *The National Security Strategy of the United States of America*, September 2002. http://www.whitehouse.gov/nsc/nss.htm/.

The United States of America is fighting a war against terrorists of global reach. The enemy is not a single political regime or person or religion or ideology. The enemy is terrorism—premeditated, politically motivated violence perpetrated against innocents.

In many regions, legitimate grievances prevent the emergence of a lasting peace. Such grievances deserve to be, and must be, addressed within a political process. But no cause justifies terror. The United States will make no concessions to terrorist demands and strike no deals with them. We make no distinction between terrorists and those who knowingly harbor or provide aid to them.

The struggle against global terrorism is different from any other war in our history. It will be fought on many fronts against a particularly elusive enemy over an extended period of time. Progress will come through the persistent accumulation of successes—some seen, some unseen.

Today our enemies have seen the results of what civilized nations can, and will, do against regimes that harbor, support, and use terrorism to achieve their political goals. Afghanistan has been liberated; coalition forces continue to hunt down the Taliban and Al-Qaida. But it is not only this battlefield on which we will engage terrorists. Thousands of trained terrorists remain at large with cells in North America, South America, Europe, Africa, the Middle East, and across Asia.

Our priority will be first to disrupt and destroy terrorist organizations of global reach and attack their leadership; command, control, and communications; material support; and finances. This will have a disabling effect upon the terrorists' ability to plan and operate.

We will continue to encourage our regional partners to take up a coordinated effort that isolates the terrorists. Once the regional campaign localizes the threat to a particular state, we will help ensure the state has the military, law enforcement, political, and financial tools necessary to finish the task.

Relation to Laws of War. Steven Ratner, "Jus ad Bellum and Jus in Bello After September 11" 96 A.J.I.L. 905 (October 2002).

The underlying legal rationale of the U.S. response to the events of September 11 was made clear the very night of the attacks. In a speech to the nation, President George W. Bush stated, "We will make no distinction between the terrorists who committed these acts and those who harbor them." Within days, the Bush administration stated that the latter category included, in the case of the Qaeda network suspected in the September 11 attacks, the government of Afghanistan. The president made a set of "demands" to the Taliban government in a speech to the U.S. Congress on September 20 and repeated: "From this day forward, any nation that continues to harbor or support terrorism will be regarded by the United States as a hostile regime."

Despite some apparent movement by elements within Afghanistan to encourage Osama bin Laden to leave, on October 7, 2001, U.S. and British air forces began attacking governmental (i.e., Taliban) and Qaeda strongholds in Afghanistan. That day, in a letter to the UN Security Council, the U.S. representative to the United Nations stated that the United States was asserting a right of self-defense against Afghanistan because of "the decision of the Taliban regime to allow the parts of Afghanistan that it controls to be used by this organization as a base of operation." Thus, the United States clearly staked its position on the right of a state that has been attacked by terrorists to respond in self-defense against any state "harboring" them.

Academic critics of the U.S. use of force have made numerous legal arguments. Although space does not permit discussing them all, several hinge on the legitimacy of self-defense against Afghanistan as a state in response to the actions of Al Qaeda there. These challenges raise questions as to (1) the appropriate interpretation of the Charter, in particular the definition of an "armed attack" in Article 51; (2) the requirements under customary international law of necessity and proportionality in reactions of self-defense; and (3) the customary law of state responsibility, in particular whether a state is liable for actions undertaken by those with a nexus to it, in this case the planning of terrorist acts by nonstate actors on its territory.

Numerous decision makers in the international legal process have addressed these questions. On the first issue, the General Assembly's 1974 Definition of Aggression, conceived as a guide to the Security Council in carrying out its functions under the Charter, offers a list of activities by armed forces that constitute aggression. Although the definition does not define "armed attack," it confirms governmental understandings that aggression includes a variety of actions, from cross-border attacks to attacks on naval ships, and then adds "the sending by or on behalf of a State of armed bands, groups, irregulars or mercenaries, which carry out acts of armed force against another State of such gravity as to amount to [the previously listed acts of aggression], or its substantial involvement therein." The International Court of Justice (ICJ) stated in *Nicaragua v. United States* that such sending of armed bands amounts to an armed attack only if "because of its scale and effects" it would be more than a "mere frontier incident" (or, as it later said, if it were "on a significant scale"), and famously rejected the notion that mere assistance to rebels was an armed attack triggering the right of self-defense. On the second issue, regarding necessity, the most frequently invoked pronouncement is the exchange of diplomatic correspondence from the 1837 *Caroline* incident, in which both the United States and the United Kingdom seemed to accept the idea that a state asserting self-defense must demonstrate its "necessity ... [as] instant, overwhelming, and leaving no choice of means, and no moment for deliberation." Scholars have already reached vastly different conclusions about the application of the *Caroline* to September 11 or terrorist attacks generally.

Regarding state responsibility for the conduct of nonstate actors, the *Nicaragua* Court held that the acts of the Nicaraguan contras could not per se be imputed to the United States because the latter had not issued specific instructions to them. In 1999 the appeals chamber of the International Criminal Tribunal for the Former Yugoslavia (ICTY) held in *Prosecutor v. Tadic* that the acts of the Bosnian Serb army could be imputed to Serbia because Serbia had exercised "overall control" over the former. And the International Law Commission (ILC) put forth its view of extant law—based on an exhaustive review of state practice—in its draft articles on responsibility of states for internationally wrongful acts of 2001. The draft articles regard a state as responsible "if the person or group of persons is in fact acting on the instructions of, or under the direction or control of, that State in carrying out the conduct"; "if the person or group of persons is in fact exercising elements of the governmental authority in the absence or default of the official authorities"; and "if and to the extent that the State acknowledges and adopts the conduct in question as its own."

Decision makers prescribing or interpreting international law in particular subject areas (or, in the ILC's terminology, those prescribing primary rules of state responsibility) have determined that states can also be responsible for acts of omission regarding nonstate actors. This form of state responsibility has been recognized in the various hijacking and sabotage conventions, which require states to extradite or prosecute offenders found on their soil; and by regional human rights courts interpreting treaties to require a state to exercise due diligence to prevent or punish violations of human dignity by private actors.

Whether or not the U.S. position on self-defense is consonant with the Charter scheme on armed attacks or the customary law limits regarding necessity (my own view is that it is), it seems clear, on the issue of state responsibility, that none of the tests cited above—those of the ICJ, the ICTY, or the ILC—supports the harboring theory of the United States. That position, stated by President Bush, effectively imputes responsibility based on the toleration of such acts by the government.* Of course, the actual evidence of Al Qaeda–Taliban links, much or most of which has not been revealed publicly, may demonstrate that toleration included active protection of the former by the latter, perhaps even rising to the level of ratification of Qaeda acts by the Taliban. Moreover, authoritative decision makers have endorsed, in both the state responsibility and the individual responsibility contexts, the broad notion of complicity, whereby one actor can be held responsible for aiding and abetting another in an illegal act, with knowledge of its actions. Yet complicity is not the same as imputation of direct responsibility.

Thus, these apparently authoritative pronouncements suggest that normally states would not hold another state responsible per se for the actions of nonstate actors on its territory absent proof of a connection closer than harboring, and certainly not to justify the use of force against that state in self-defense. My point is not whether these pronouncements are right or wrong. Indeed, the ICTY in *Tadic* found the ICJ mistaken in its limited view of state responsibility for the acts of foreign organized armed groups; and state practice may well support a wholly different view of imputation than that endorsed by the International Law Commission. The point is simply that the U.S. view, on its face, significantly differs from them.

Despite the divergence of the U.S. justification from these statements regarding state responsibility, most governments have reacted with support for it. On September 12 and 28, 2001, the Security Council, in its first resolutions on the events of September 11, "recognized the inherent right of individual or collective self-defence in accordance with

---

* It is barely worth a footnote to dismiss some academic perspectives that have suggested that the Bush doctrine implies that those states in which terrorists may act but which, despite bona fide law enforcement, are unable to prevent or punish those acts, are harboring terrorists. Although clearly the Bush proposal is vague at the margins, it has not endorsed such a view.

the Charter." On September 12, the North Atlantic Council, NATO's policymaking organ, stated that "if it is determined that this attack was directed from abroad against the United States, it shall be regarded as an action covered by Article 5 of the [1949] Washington Treaty," making an attack on one ally an attack on all, and invoked the "commitment to collective self-defence." On October 2, following classified briefings of its officials, the secretary general of NATO announced that the evidence linking Al Qaeda to September 11 provided the factual basis for invoking Article 5 of the Washington Treaty. On September 21, the Organization of American States adopted a resolution similarly "recognizing the inherent right of individual and collective self-defense in accordance with the [OAS and UN] Charters," and stating that "those responsible for aiding, supporting, or harboring the perpetrators of the September 11 attacks are equally complicit in these acts." (The choice of the phrase "complicit in," rather than "responsible for," suggests, however, that the OAS's members may have assumed a slightly different posture on state responsibility compared to the United States or NATO.)

Once the U.S. military campaign started, support from these quarters continued. Several NATO states offered logistical assistance to the United States; on October 16, an OAS committee of senior officials adopted a resolution stating that "the [U.S.] measures in the exercise of its inherent right of individual and collective self-defense have the full support of the states parties to the Rio Treaty." The United States also secured the permission of key central Asian states near Afghanistan to allow U.S. troops to operate there.

More important, beyond these perhaps predictable allies, official circles in other states were nearly unanimous in supporting or abstaining from criticism of the U.S. military campaign, although various private actors, from political parties to student groups to journalists to academics, protested the U.S. action. As academic critics of U.S. action have noted, only a handful of governments opposed the U.S. attacks. This opposition included strong condemnations by Iraq, Sudan, and North Korea, all of which essentially said that an attack on the people of Afghanistan for the acts of terrorists was unjustified, as well as more nuanced condemnations by the governments of Cuba, Malaysia, and Iran. Iran seemed more concerned about the evidentiary question of a link between Al Qaeda and the events of September 11 than the underlying principle that a state could be the target of self-defense merely by harboring terrorists. Its foreign minister stated: "Under the UN law [the United States has] the right to defend itself, but first those behind the attack should be identified and then punished. No evidence has been offered to show [bin Laden's] implication in the attack. If there is such evidence it should be offered to the people." Moreover, the same day as this statement, Iran also secretly made an offer to the United States to rescue any American aircrew that had to conduct an emergency landing in Iranian territory. Among international organizations, the Organization of the Islamic Conference, the Organization of African Unity, and the Association of Southeast Asian Nations all refrained from criticizing the U.S. use of force in its initial months despite ample opportunities to do so—including the passage of resolutions on terrorism.

Scholars may disagree on the meaning or effect of such acquiescence. I am not purporting to proclaim the definitive emergence of a clear new international rule. But my own view is to regard it as highly significant as an indication of contemporary expectations—suggesting something from tolerance to embrace of the U.S. legal position. The reactions of governments to a major episode in contemporary history suggest something about their views regarding the underlying legal norms that govern the relevant state of affairs. Others have sought to minimize the implications of these positions as based on some concept of nonlegal factors. But even such an orthodox attempt to isolate "legal" from "nonlegal" factors runs up against the difference between protest and nonprotest. If state B protests A's action, it might object to that conduct as either a legal or a policy (i.e., a nonlegal) matter; but the absence of protest—where state A's act is of a major, even constitutive nature, affecting all states—would strongly suggest that B endorsed, or at least did not object to, both the legal *and* the nonlegal bases for A's actions.

Lawful Responses. Davis Brown, "Use Of Force Against Terrorism After September 11th: State Responsibility, Self–Defense And Other Responses" 11 Cardozo J. Int'l & Comp. L. 1 (2003).

For the first time in post-Charter international law, states are now forced to reevaluate the long-standing notion that only a state has the capacity to commit an armed attack against another state (as opposed to merely attacking targets within or belonging to the state). If a non-state actor such as a terrorist organization commits aggression against a state, and the aggression is of sufficient scale and effect to amount to an armed attack, then the terrorist organization itself—notwithstanding its noncombatant status*—has committed an armed attack against the state. Under these circumstances the injured state may invoke the inherent right of self-defense to justify using force against that organization. It follows that if another state may be found originally or vicariously responsible for an armed attack by a terrorist organization, then that other state is considered to have committed the attack, just as if its own forces had done so. The injured state may then invoke the inherent right of self-defense against the responsible state.

When a terrorist organization is physically located within the territory of another state, which is not supporting it and not originally or vicariously responsible for the aggression, the inherent right of self-

---

* Irregular forces are lawful combatants if they: (1) are commanded by a person responsible for his subordinates; (2) wear a fixed distinctive emblem recognizable at a distance; (3) carry their arms openly; and (4) conduct their operations in accordance with the laws and customs of war. Because terrorists are not easily distinguishable from the population at large and do not carry their arms openly, they are unlawful combatants and their attacks, even if carried out on military targets, are criminal acts.

defense collides with two other fundamental principles of international law: sovereign equality of states and the renunciation of force in international relations. In international law, states have equal rights to enforce their laws within their borders. When a terrorist organization operates in a state illegally and without its sanction, that state has the primary right—and role—in preventing it from committing acts of terror and punishing it when it does. Indeed, customary international law imposes on states the duty to exercise due diligence to prevent their citizens, and non-citizen inhabitants, from committing wrongful acts which injure other states, as well as to punish them when they do. To use armed force against a terrorist organization in such a situation would not only violate the sovereignty of the other state, but also constitute an act of aggression against that state, and, if the aggression were of sufficient scale and effect, would even constitute an armed attack.

Such an attack would be lawful, however, if it satisfied one of three exceptions. The first exception is the consent of the state on whose territory the terrorists are located to another state's use of force against them. Under customary international law, as reaffirmed in the Nicaragua case, a state has the power to allow another state to use force on its territory and, once that consent is given, the latter may do so.*

The second exception is when the state inside which the terrorists operate is unwilling to prevent the use of its territory to launch attacks. This principle can be derived from the Definition of Aggression, which characterizes as aggression "the action of a State in allowing its territory, which it has placed at the disposal of another State, to be used by that other State for perpetrating an act of aggression against a third State." Similarly, when a state places its territory at the disposal of a non-state actor who subsequently commits aggression against another state, the injured state should have the right to respond against the non-state actor notwithstanding the sovereign status of the host state. This was the case with the Taliban's harboring of Al-Qaeda, placing Afghan territory at Al-Qaeda's disposal to carry out an armed attack against the U.S. If Afghanistan were not already vicariously responsible for the attack, then the use of force against Al-Qaeda would still be justifiable under this theory and would not infringe on the sovereignty of Afghanistan.

The third exception is when the state inside which the terrorists operate is unable to prevent its territory from being used to launch attacks. A hypothetical example would be if Al-Qaeda has established training camps in Somalia during the period when the country had no functioning government, or when the functioning government's military forces and law enforcement system were too weak to engage or expel an

---

* In a discussion of consent by the contras to U.S. intervention in Nicaragua, the ICJ wrote: "It is difficult to see what would remain of the principle of non-intervention in international law if intervention, which is already allowable at the request of the government of a State, were also to be allowed at the request of the opposition." Military And Paramilitary Activities In And Against Nicaragua (Nicar. v. U.S.) (merits), 1986 I.C.J. 14, 126 (June 27).

organization as well-financed as Al-Qaeda. Under normal circumstances, a state is not responsible to injured states for the unlawful acts of private persons within its territory, if the state has exercised due diligence to prevent and punish those acts. However, a state also has the inherent right of self-defense, including the defense of its nationals. Customary international law permits a state to use force to intervene in another state to protect its nationals: "It cannot be denied that at a certain point the interest of a State in exercising protection over its nationals and their property can take precedence over territorial sovereignty, despite the absence of any conventional provisions."* In such a scenario, the use of force against a terrorist organization does not translate into aggression against the state inside which the organization is located.

B. USE OF FORCE IN RESPONSE TO TERRORISM

War in Iraq. Mr. Dominique Galouzeau de Villepin, Minister for Foreign Affairs of France, speaking to the UN Security Council (14 February 2003).**

Here we are at the centre of the debate. What is at stake is our credibility and our sense of responsibility. Let us have the courage to see things plainly.

There are two options. The option of war might seem, on the face of it, to be the swifter. But let us not forget that, after the war is won, the peace must be built. And let us not delude ourselves: that will be long and difficult, because it will be necessary to preserve Iraq's unity and to restore stability in a lasting way in a country and a region harshly affected by the intrusion of force. In the light of that perspective, there is the alternative offered by inspections, which enable us to move forward, day by day, on the path of the effective and peaceful disarmament of Iraq. In the end, is that not the surer and the swifter choice?

No one can maintain today that the path of war will be shorter than the path of inspections; no one can maintain that it would lead to a safer, more just and more stable world. For war is always the outcome of failure. Could it be our sole recourse in the face of today's many challenges?

Therefore, let us give the United Nations inspectors the time that is necessary for their mission to succeed. But let us together be vigilant and ask Mr. Blix and Mr. El Baradei to report regularly to the Council. France, for its part, proposes another meeting at ministerial level, on 14 March, to assess the situation. Thus we would be able to judge the progress made and what remains to be accomplished.

---

* Beni–Madan, Rzini Claim, 2 R.I.A.A. 16 (1925), in D.W. Bowett, Self–Defence In International Law 9 (1958), at 87. Because this principle is part of the body of law on the inherent right of self-defense, the UN Charter does not supersede it.

** [The speech was given on 20 March 2003, 34 days before US forces began a military operations in Iraq, after which Mr. Villepin received applause, a rarity in the Security Council chamber.—Eds.]

In that context, the use of force is not justified at this time. There is an alternative to war: disarming Iraq through inspections. Moreover, premature recourse to the military option would be fraught with risks. The authority of our action rests today on the unity of the international community. Premature military intervention would call that unity into question, and that would remove its legitimacy and, in the long run, its effectiveness. Such intervention could have incalculable consequences for the stability of a scarred and fragile region. It would compound the sense of injustice, would aggravate tensions and would risk paving the way for other conflicts.

We all share the same priority: fighting terrorism mercilessly. That fight requires total determination; since the tragedy of 11 September 2001, it has been one of the main responsibilities of our peoples. And France, which has been struck hard several times by that terrible scourge, is wholly mobilized in this struggle.

Ten days ago, the United States Secretary of State, Mr. Powell, cited alleged links between Al-Qaeda and the Baghdad regime. Given the present state of our research and information, gathered in liaison with our allies, nothing enables us to establish such links. Moreover, we must assess that a disputed military action would have on that level. Would not such an intervention be likely to deepen divisions among societies, among cultures, among peoples—divisions that nurture terrorism?

France has always said that we do not exclude the possibility that, one day, we might have to resort to force if the inspectors' reports concluded that it was impossible for inspections to continue. Then the Council would have to take a decision, and its members would have to shoulder all of their responsibilities. In such a scenario, I want to recall here the questions that I stressed at our last debate, on 5 February, to which we must respond. To what degree do the nature and the extent of the threat justify immediate recourse to force? How do we ensure that the considerable risks of such an intervention can actually be kept under control?

Self-Defense. Michael J. Glennon, "Military Action Against Terrorists Under International Law: The Fog of Law: Self–Defense, Inherence, and Incoherence in Article 51 of the United Nations Charter" 25 Harvard J.L. & Pub. Pol'y 539 (2002).

The temptation always exists, upon discovering that "the law is an ass," to strain for ways of avoiding that conclusion, to argue that results so fundamentally incompatible with sound policy cannot possibly be correct. The lure to do so is especially strong in international law, where analytic tools have been dulled by decades of result-oriented commentary to the point where the distinction between *lex lata* and *lex ferenda*, between the law as it is and the law as one would like it to be, is often non-existent. Whole "schools" have arisen that implicitly conjoin the two. Predictably, Article 51 has not escaped efforts to rationalize international law's illogic. But its manifest failings do not justify an exercise to save Article 51 that requires buying into the same self-referential analytic methods that account for its incoherence. The reality is that Article 51 is grounded upon premises that neither accurately describe nor realistically prescribe state behavior. To ignore that dissonance ill serves efforts to develop a realistic, workable legalist order to govern the use of force. I suggest acknowledging the unhappy conclusion that these three corollaries* are part and parcel of Article 51, that each of these three corollaries prohibits or significantly constrains legitimate and reasonable actions that sensible states might take in their self-defense, and that none can guide responsible American policy-making in the war against terrorism.

The first corollary, in refusing a state the right to use force against a safe-harbor state following terrorist attacks launched from such a state, ignores the reality that the use of force against safe-harbor states may, in certain situations, be the only means available to a victim state to terminate the pernicious use of force against it—force that might, in every respect, represent the equivalent of state-sponsored force. In such circumstances there is, as the "Bush Doctrine" posits, no reason to distinguish between the two. The whole purpose of permitting a state to use force to defend itself from attack is to prevent massive injury. That injury is no less significant if private rather than public wrongdoers inflict it. In contemporary times, non-state actors are as capable of inflicting widespread injury as many state actors. If a host state is unable or unwilling to curtail harmful private conduct when that conduct originates from within the host state's territory, it makes no sense to insist that the victim state remain indifferent to such conduct, effectively sacrificing the integrity of its own territorial sovereignty for that of the host state. Similarly, it does not make sense to permit defensive force against the wrongdoer but not against the wrongdoer's host if the wrongdoer's capability to inflict harm depends upon the indifference of a host government that can curtail that harm simply by withdrawing its hospitality. Acts of omission in such circumstances shade into acts of commission, and aggrieved states should not be faulted for treating them the same.

The second corollary, in counseling that any use of force against such a safe-haven government is per se disproportionate, turns the principle of proportionality inside out. This corollary insists that *any* use of force against a safe-haven state, however restrained, is necessarily excessive in relation to *any* terrorist threat that might thereby be forestalled, however great. The proper application of the notion of

---

* They are not the only corollaries that have been urged to follow from Article 51. It has been contended, for example, that principles of necessity precluded the United States from acting against Afghanistan after a delay of three weeks because the American response did not meet criteria announced by Secretary of State Daniel Webster in the *Caroline* case. Britain, Webster wrote, was required to "show a necessity of self-defense, instant, overwhelming, leaving no choice of means, and no moment of deliberation." By this logic, use of force against Iraq following its invasion of Kuwait was also unlawful, inasmuch as that action was not commenced for some months afterwards, as was use of force against Japan following Pearl Harbor, which also was delayed by some months.

proportionality is directed at ensuring a sensible calibration of means to ends that will necessarily vary from one situation to the next, not at imposing a rigid test of per se invalidity that mandates a fixed conclusion even as facts vary. The mistaken application of this principle seems to flow from the supposition that use of force, being unlawful *ab initio* against a safe-haven state, necessarily renders that force excessive and therefore "disproportionate." But international law has long insisted upon the complete disjunction of *jus ad bellum* from *jus in bello*—i.e., upon keeping the rules concerning *when* force can be used completely separate from the rules concerning *what* force can be used. In traditional international jurisprudence, rules concerning how a war can be fought can, and must, be honored even though the war is fought for illicit ends, and wars fought for permissible ends still cannot be fought by illicit means. The plain illogic of this second corollary derives from conflating the two, from supposing that an impermissible object necessarily renders impermissible any amount of force employed in its pursuit. That conclusion cannot follow; if it did, the whole idea of proportionality would be rendered empty, with its standards met or defeated not by an independent measurement and assessment but by conclusions reached at the outset concerning the permissibility of the use of force.

The one advantage of the Court's ill-conceived treatment of proportionality is that it avoids an even more serious charge to which the principle lies open, namely, that proportionality is uselessly elastic in its capacity to justify any amount of force in any circumstance (or, on the other hand, to preclude any amount of force in any circumstance). But, at least in wartime, this crippling malleability is unavoidable. Waging war is bound to be disproportionate if the provocation is an isolated armed attack. To justify the vanquishing of Japan following Pearl Harbor, it was necessary either to regard the limits of proportionality as effectively waivable at the discretion of an aggrieved state that chooses to wage full-scale war, or to regard proportionality as permitting the wholesale destruction of enemy forces and occupation of its homeland in response to a manifestly lesser intrusion. Even the most elastic of principles would snap between the pull of these alternatives. But the analytic confusion is still greater. In wartime, the provocation is not simply an isolated armed attack. The provocation is an ongoing series of attacks that repeat in a retaliatory cycle that makes war a succession of deadly provocations. In this chain of attacks and counter-attacks, no answer possibly can be given to the question that underpins all proportionality analysis: proportional to *what*?

As though this were not enough, proportionality is at war with deterrence. Whereas proportionality counsels that harm returned should not exceed harm received, deterrence warns that harm returned *should* exceed harm received, for the greater the disproportionality, the greater the chance of avoiding harm to either party by avoiding conflict altogether. Tit-for-tat equivalence is a strategy ill-conceived for maintaining a comprehensive peace.

The third corollary, ruling out anticipatory self-defense, fights a losing battle with common sense. In its actions if not in its words, the United States rejected this corollary *de facto* throughout the Cold War by maintaining a launch-on-warning option in response to the threat of nuclear attack. Had the third corollary been in effect at the time of Pearl Harbor, it would have insisted that the United States wait until bombs actually fell before using defensive force. No rational decision-maker can be expected to exercise such restraint. And few have, as Israeli officials demonstrated when Israel destroyed an Iraqi nuclear plant in 1981 when it believed Iraq was manufacturing a nuclear device. Waiting for an aggressor to fire the first shot may be a fitting code for television westerns, but it is unrealistic for policy-makers entrusted with the solemn responsibility of safeguarding the well-being of their citizenry. If a state has developed the capability of inflicting substantial harm upon another, indicated explicitly or implicitly its willingness or intent to do so, and to all appearances is waiting only for the opportunity to strike, preemptive use of force is justified. Admittedly, that line is not bright. Mistakes may be made. It is better, however, that the price of those mistakes be paid by states that so posture themselves than by innocent states asked patiently to await slaughter.

It is easy to conclude that the problem with Article 51 is that the Article is simply "an inept piece of draftsmanship." But the problem is far more profound than a mere inability to come up with the right words. Form reflects substance. The problem is, again, that no consensus exists within the international community as to what constitutes "aggression," as failed efforts to define that term have revealed year after year. From the San Francisco conference that framed the U.N. Charter to the Rome conference that established the International Criminal Court, "aggression" has eluded the best-laid international efforts to define it. The few "successes" have been even greater failures. There is no point in trying to devise a legal-sounding formula for an exception if no agreement exists on the scope of the concept of "aggression" that lies at the heart of the general rule. Aggression and self-defense are opposite sides of the same coin. "This is our world," Paul Kahn has observed, "and speaking the language of law is not going to make it any different."

This article has therefore attempted merely to suggest what the rules are *not*, not what the rules *should be*. The rules are not what the U.N. Charter says they are. What the rules should be depends entirely upon what the rules *can* be. No rules will work that do not reflect underlying geopolitical realities. The use-of-force regime set out in the U.N. Charter failed because the Charter sought to impose rules that are out-of-sync with the way states actually behave. A new use-of-force regime that does work will have to rest far more firmly upon actual patterns of practice that reveal, with solid empirical evidence, what regulation of force is possible and what is not. Deontological rules that flow from imaginary *droits naturel* are doomed to failure. There is no use in telling ghost stories, Holmes said, to people who do not believe in ghosts.

At this point, the consensus within the international community on underlying values is not sufficient to sustain an authentic legalist regime that would subordinate the use of force to pre-agreed limits. One person's terrorist remains another's freedom fighter.* What is considered justified humanitarian intervention in one part of the world is a seen as a violation of state sovereignty in another. What is self-defense to one state is aggression, armed reprisal, armed attack, intervention, or forcible counter-measures to another. No advance in the art of legal drafting can bridge the enormous gulf that divides the international community over what constitutes acceptable use of force. Any linguistic formula that purported to do so would necessarily consist of a chain of endlessly contested weasel words. Perhaps that chasm will narrow as more active phases of the war against terrorism wind down. The conclusion of great conflicts of the past presented possibilities at Vienna, Versailles, and San Francisco to re-shape the contours of international legalist institutions. Even if no comprehensive re-integration or formal revision of the legalist order occurs, patterns of cooperation that develop in prosecuting the war on terrorism can still congeal gradually and incrementally into post-war legalist regimes. In the meantime, however, states will continue to judge for themselves what measure of force is required for their self-defense—action that is appropriate, it must always be borne in mind, not because defense is permitted by the U.N. Charter, but because defense is necessary for survival and survival is intrinsic in the very fact of statehood.

Preemption. Mary Ellen O'Connell *The Myth of Preemptive Self-Defense*, American Society of International Law Task Force on Terrorism (August 2002), http://www.asil.org/taskforce/oconnell.pdf.

The United States has consistently rejected preemptive self-defense for reasons of sound policy. This is not a right that the United States wants others to have. Glennon has argued that circumstances have changed and that Washington should reconsider the law. Yet as the examples of state practice show, international society and even the United States have found the standing rules adequate for dealing with the problems of terrorism, weapons of mass destruction and regimes such as that controlled by Saddam Hussein. Historically, the United States has argued against a right of preemptive self-defense because it has found the UN Charter rules to be in its interests as a matter of policy and prudence.

Clear rules limiting force support U.S. security and American values. The United States played a leading role in the adoption of the UN Charter, and since that time, the United States has been careful to make only those legal arguments relative to the use of force that it could accept in the hands of other states. Charter rules may restrain the

---

* Defining terrorism has proven no less intractable a task than defining aggression. In S.C. Res. 1373, the Security Council imposed broad requirements upon member states to prevent and suppress the financing of terrorism—without ever defining what constitutes "terrorism." S.C. Res. 1373, U.N. SCOR, 56th Sess., 4385th mtg., U.N. Doc. S/RES/1373 (2001), http://www.un.org/Docs/scres/2001/res1373e.pdf.

United States from time-to-time, but the benefit of restraining others, too, has been worth the cost. The United States can hardly wish to see an anarchic regime in which every state is entitled to initiate the use of force against its adversaries in preemptive self-defense.* Nor can the United States honor its fundamental values if it acts in disregard of prevailing legal principle. What Professor Henkin wrote in 1987, remains the case today:

> It is not in the interest of the United States to reconstrue the law of the Charter so as to dilute and confuse its normative prohibitions. In our decentralized international political system with primitive institutions and underdeveloped law enforcement machinery, it is important that Charter norms—which go to the heart of international order and implicate war and peace in the nuclear age—be clear, sharp, and comprehensive; as independent as possible of judgments of degree and of issues of fact; as invulnerable as can be to self-serving interpretations and to temptation to conceal, distort, or mischaracterize events. Extending the meaning of "armed attack" and of "self-defense," multiplying exceptions to the prohibition on the use of force and the occasions that would permit military intervention, would undermine the law of the Charter and the international order established in the wake of world war.**

Limits of Preemption. Richard N. Gardner, "Neither Bush nor the 'Jurisprudes'" 97 A.J.I.L. 585 (2003).

Defenders of the new Bush strategic doctrine have frequently cited the following statement made by President Kennedy when he announced the quarantine of Cuba during the Cuban missile crisis of 1962:

> We no longer live in a world where only the actual firing of weapons represents a sufficient challenge to a nation's security to constitute maximum peril. Nuclear weapons are so destructive and ballistic missiles are so swift, that any substantially increased possibility of their use or any sudden change in their deployment may well be regarded as a definite threat to peace.

It is significant, however, that the United States in the Cuban missile crisis did not use self-defense to justify its action in stopping foreign ships on the high seas in order to prevent the transfer to Cuba of Soviet missiles. I can provide some personal testimony on this episode, since I was serving at the time as deputy assistant secretary of state for international organization affairs and was asked by Secretary of State Dean Rusk to help in drafting Ambassador Adlai Stevenson's speech to the UN Security Council. Rusk made a point of asking that I consult with Abram Chayes, the State Department's legal adviser, and with Stephen Schwebel, the assistant legal adviser for UN Affairs, to develop

---

* Even allowing armed self-defense when an attack is "imminent" is a problematic rule, because "imminence" could mean any one of several things—an hour, day, week, year, or decade.

** Henkin, "Use of Force: Law and U.S. Policy," in *Might v. Rights, International Law and the Use of Force* (Louis Henkin et al. eds., 1989), p. 69.

a legal rationale for the U.S. action. The three of us quickly agreed that self-defense would not hold water as a legal argument. If the deployment of Soviet missiles in Cuba could justify an act of force by the United States in self-defense, the same right would have to be conceded to the Soviet Union in view of the presence of the U.S. missiles in Turkey, not to mention the continual movement around the Soviet periphery of U.S. B–52 bombers and nuclear-armed submarines.

The fact that the world had entered the nuclear age was not a good reason, in our view, to stretch the careful limits on preemption that had been set by Webster more than a century before. Accordingly, we sought to develop a different legal rationale based on the action of the Organization of American States in voting to endorse the Cuban quarantine. Admittedly, the OAS rationale was not entirely convincing, given the requirement in Article 53 of the UN Charter that no "enforcement action" can be undertaken by a regional organization without Security Council approval. But at least we had avoided opening up the "Pandora's box" of Article 51. To vary the metaphor, we felt that if we had to punch a hole in traditional legal restraints on the use of force, the hole should be as small as possible.

The considerations that led us to avoid enlarging the concept of preemptive self-defense in 1962 are just as valid today. The Bush doctrine, if it is intended to assert a right available to the United States alone, is obviously unacceptable. If it is intended to assert a new legal principle of general application, its implications are so ominous as to justify universal condemnation. For such a doctrine would legitimize preemptive attacks by Arab countries against Israel, by China against Taiwan, by India against Pakistan, and by North Korea against South Korea, to give some obvious examples. It would even serve to legitimize ex post facto Japan's attack on Pearl Harbor.

There is a famous saying that the law embodies "those wise restraints that make men free." International law can be seen as embodying those wise restraints on the use of force that safeguard the peace. Henry Kissinger, not known for his dedication to international law, put the matter succinctly in a column in the Washington Post on September 16, 2002:

> As the most powerful nation in the world, the United States has a special unilateral capacity to implement its convictions. But it also has a special obligation to justify its actions by principles that transcend the assertions of preponderant power. It cannot be in either the American national interest or the world's interest to develop principles that grant every nation an unfettered right of preemption against its own definition of threats to its security.

We would also do well to heed the cautionary note sounded by Justice Robert Jackson in *Korematsu* v. *United States*:

> A military order, however unconstitutional, is not apt to last longer than the military emergency. But once a judicial opinion rationalizes such an order to show that it conforms to the Constitution, or rather

rationalizes the Constitution to show that the Constitution sanctions such an order, the Court for all time has validated the principle. The principle then lies about like a loaded weapon ready for the hand of any authority that can bring forward a plausible claim of an urgent need.

By expanding the right of preemption against an *imminent* attack into a right of preventive war against *potentially* dangerous adversaries, the Bush administration has created a "loaded weapon" that can be used against the United States and against the general interest in a stable world order.

The new Bush doctrine is not only counterproductive, it is also unnecessary for the defense of U.S. interests. The administration has sought to justify the new doctrine because of the threat to the United States from Iraq, and more generally of the threat of suicidal terrorists possessing weapons of mass destruction. Neither of these justifications is convincing. The proper way to justify the United States use of force in Iraq was by reference to previous UN Security Council resolutions requiring Iraq's compliance with an intrusive UN inspection regime. Iraq had repeatedly been found by the Security Council to be in "material breach" of the disarmament requirements spelled out in Resolution 687, which laid down the conditions of the cease-fire that suspended hostilities in the Gulf War. Since Saddam Hussein was repeatedly found by the Security Council to be in "material breach" of the cease-fire terms, the United States and other UN members were once again free to act under the authority of Security Council Resolution 678, which authorized the use of force not only to liberate Kuwait but to "restore peace and security in the area." It was not unreasonable to claim that there could be no "peace and security" in the area unless there was effective verification that Iraq's weapons of mass destruction had been eliminated. The administration did eventually invoke this argument for the war with Iraq, but by the time it did so public opinion at home and abroad had come to view the Iraq war as the first application of the new "preventive war" doctrine.

The new Bush formulation was also unnecessary as a justification for U.S. military action in Afghanistan and against Al Qaeda generally. The UN Security Council and NATO both took decisions confirming that the events of September 11, 2001, constituted an "armed attack" on the United States, permitting the United States to claim its right of self-defense under Article 51. Moreover, in Resolution 1373, the Security Council imposed a legal requirement on all UN members to suppress Al Qaeda and other transnational terrorist groups. Read in the context of the long-recognized principle of international law that states must not permit their territory to be used for the purpose of launching attacks on other states, I believe the decisions of NATO and the United Nations provide a sufficient legal basis for military actions the United States needs to take to destroy terrorist groups operating in countries that do not carry out their legal obligations to suppress them. Thus the United

States can protect itself in this new age of suicidal terrorism and nuclear proliferation without resorting to the Bush doctrine.

If the new Bush preemption doctrine is neither necessary nor desirable, we should also reject the excessively narrow interpretation of the Charter by those "jurisprudes" who would permit the use of armed force only in the cases of self-defense against armed attack or of Security Council authorization. This narrow interpretation has already been modified by the practice of UN members. Notwithstanding the prohibition in Article 2(4) on the use of force against the "territorial integrity and political independence of any state," UN members have on numerous occasions used armed force to rescue their citizens and others on the territory of other countries when the territorial sovereign was unable or unwilling to assure their safety. In addition, the successful military campaign undertaken by NATO to put an end to ethnic cleansing in Kosovo, protested against by some UN members but not disowned by the Security Council, provides another example of a reinterpretation in practice of Article 2(4), this time to permit humanitarian intervention to stop genocide or a similar massive violation of human rights where the intervention has the sanction of a regional organization.

Nearly half a century ago Professor Arthur Lehman Goodhart, a distinguished American legal scholar at Oxford, asked "whether the limitation of force to self-defense against an armed attack is a reasonable and practical provision in a world in which the United Nations has not itself been able to carry out its duty to prevent threats of aggression and other breaches of the peace." He expressed doubts that the United Nations "can continue to be effective if it insists that so impractical a doctrine is an essential part of its existence."

Professor Goodhart's question is especially relevant today. Given the impracticability of amending the UN Charter, we must proceed carefully to encourage UN members to support modest reinterpretations of the law concerning the use of armed force—reinterpretations that stop short of opening a "Pandora's box" as the drastic formulation of a right of preventive war would do.

The Bush administration is right in asking that the traditional interpretation of international law be reexamined in the face of the new dangers of catastrophic terrorism, but is wrong in its proposed solution to the problem. In my view, the national interest of the United States and the general interest of the international community can best be served by a modest reinterpretation of the UN Charter along the following lines:

(1) Armed force may now be used by a UN member even without Security Council approval to destroy terrorist groups operating on the territory of other members when those other members fail to discharge their international law obligations to suppress them.

(2) Armed force may also be used to prevent a UN member from transferring weapons of mass destruction to terrorist groups.

(3) Article 51 continues to limit self-defense to cases of an actual or imminent armed attack in accordance with the *Caroline* doctrine, but self-defense can be extended to permit a state to rescue its citizens (and others) faced with a clear and present threat to their security.

(4) A right of "humanitarian intervention" permits military action by the United Nations or regional organizations to prevent genocide or similar massive human rights violations.

The United States needs to claim no more from international law than this. The rest of the world should concede no less.

Role of the Security Council. Ruth Wedgwood, "The Fall of Saddam Hussein: Security Council Mandates and Preemptive Self–Defense" 97 A.J.I.L. 576 (2003).

The September 11 terrorist attacks against the Pentagon and World Trade Center have changed the strategic responsibilities of democratic states. Deterrence and containment were the core doctrines of the Cold War. These do not translate easily to a brave new world of non-state terror networks. Part of the problem lies in the extraordinary destructive capability of chemical, biological, and nuclear weapons. But what is wholly new is the absence of credible disincentives against their use.

Thus, democratic governments may need to anticipate, rather than respond to, possible attacks. A terror network with unworldly motivations will give little thought to the costs of a "second strike" response. A rogue state that is utterly heedless of its people and has an undeveloped economy may not care about the potential collateral damage from a responsive military strike. The Taliban were not deterred by the threat of retaliatory action and continued to harbor Al Qaeda and Osama bin Laden in Afghanistan, even after the World Trade Center was bombed and the Security Council demanded their cooperation.

In addition, the ethical strictures of modern warfare eschew violence aimed at civilians, even in response to an unprovoked attack, and thus the asymmetry increases. One sees this moral hazard reflected in Protocol I to the 1949 Geneva Conventions, protecting civilians against reprisals but equally inviting asymmetric attack.

To a strategist, September 11 thus teaches that the keystone doctrines of the Cold War confrontation—namely, deterrence and containment—have ceased to be reliable. Rather, one must consider acting against terrorist *capability* before it is employed and, better yet, before it is acquired. The stated ambition of Al Qaeda to acquire fissile material and nuclear weapons, as well as biological and chemical arms, has reinforced this concern. A minimalist reading of the UN Charter's account of self-defense in Article 51—asking that one wait until an attack is launched before responding—may seem extremely ill-suited to these new circumstances. Phrases such as "a bolt from the blue" are now used in conversations from which they had long been retired.

The Security Council has had the prerogative of acting against destabilizing capability, at least where it does not interfere with a core guarantee of self-defense. The required notice to the Security Council of withdrawals from the Nuclear Non–Proliferation Treaty and the Biological Weapons Convention illustrate this point. Resolution 1373, adopted two weeks after the terrorist attacks, also fundamentally alters the standards of state responsibility, announcing that states will be held liable for any assistance to international terrorist groups. Going well beyond the standards of the *Nicaragua* and *Tadic* cases, the Council has decided that the failure to police the provision of logistics, finances, asylum, or materiel to an international terrorist group is delictual state conduct.

President Bush's *National Security Strategy* openly prefers that the thwarting of terrorist networks and potential state sponsors be handled through multilateral means. North Korea provides a case in point. Pyongyang startled the world community by admitting that it had deliberately breached the 1994 Framework Agreement, as well as the 1968 Nuclear Non–Proliferation Treaty. It claims to have two nuclear devices, admits that it has secretly processed enriched uranium, and brazenly broke the seals on eight thousand plutonium rods—escalating further by restarting the Yongbyon reactor and commencing the reprocessing of the rods. Most shockingly, North Korean negotiators at Chinese-hosted talks said to their American counterparts that Pyongyang was willing to sell fissile material or a nuclear device to any bidder. As much as war on the Korean peninsula, the latter threat is of extraordinary gravity—for Al Qaeda has expressed its continued interest in acquiring a nuclear device and its willingness to use any means against the West. In the face of military options that would cause great damage to civilian populations, the Bush administration has worked to involve China, Japan, and Russia, as well as South Korea, in negotiations with North Korea—in order to create the greatest chance of dissuading Kim Jong Il by peaceful means.

But the question remains whether a state can ever resort to the use of preventive force in unique cases—when intelligence is reliable and timing is sensitive, multilateral authorization is not practically available, and a state is sponsoring or hosting a network acquiring weapons of mass destruction. The national security white paper issued by George W. Bush is a political doctrine, not a legal exegesis, and as a declaratory doctrine may intimate more than it would deliver. However, the abstract answer to many strategists is yes—a given regime might have a record of conduct so irresponsible and links to terrorist groups so troubling that the acquisition of WMD capability amounts to an unreasonable danger that cannot be abided.

Preemptive self-defense should be broadly debated both in its strategic consequences and in its legal grounding. But we should not forget that the United Nations Charter system was born to a generation chastened by the consequences of collective passivity—the failure to counter the Fascist rearmament of Germany until a bolt truly came from the blue. The United Nations Charter is appropriately read, even now, as an attempt to overcome the failures of Woodrow Wilson's League of Nations and its covenant of inaction. The moniker of the United Nations stemmed from the Allies' wartime promise against making any separate peace with fascism and a contract to take timely action against aberrant state behavior that endangers human security. In a teleological understanding of the Charter, strengthened by commitments to human rights and democracy, defensive force may be necessary to counter the unpredictable violence of state and nonstate actors. This should inform the reading of Article 51 as much as the scope of Chapter VII.

Indeed, one may reread President John F. Kennedy's handling of the Cuban missile crisis in the same light—as a celebrated example of the prudent use of defensive force to prevent a dangerous change in capability. The introduction of nuclear weapons into Cuba, reducing Soviet launch time to seven minutes, would have destroyed any adequate interval for the assessment of nuclear warnings, imperiling American–Soviet stability and putting at risk thousands of innocent lives. The United States imposed a "defensive quarantine," blocking the movement of Soviet ships to Cuba and forcing Soviet submarines to surface. This action was not in response to an armed attack, within the central language of Article 51, or even in response to a concrete Soviet war plan, but in recognition of the danger of a sudden change in capability.

The United States bypassed the Security Council to avoid a Soviet veto, and took shelter in a "recommendation" of the Organization of American States. Law professors have enjoyed teaching the missile crisis ever since as a case study in casuistry—because the procedural rationales offered by the participating lawyers demonstrably did not work. Most notably, a recommendation by a regional organization such as the OAS was insufficient basis, in the classic view of the Charter, to warrant member states to go beyond the limits of Article 51 self-defense. Thus, one had to read Article 51 as permitting preemption of capability, or else consign the U.S. response to legal twilight. The U.S. defensive quarantine against the Soviet missiles was widely accepted as legitimate, yet can only be frankly described as an early and successful use of a doctrine of preventive force against a missile threat that presented a clear danger to nuclear stability.

In our own case, parts of the legal fabric may still be incomplete. The United States, for example, has held that the customary law of armed conflict forbids the first use of chemical weapons and the first or second use of biological weapons. But the United States has not previously suggested that customary law should reach further, to prohibit the development, acquisition, and possession of these weapons. Similarly, though the norms of the Nuclear Non–Proliferation Treaty forbid international transfers of nuclear materials for noncivilian purposes, the United States has not earlier claimed that customary law incorporates the same prohibition. Even treaty norms may need reassessment. For example, the evident attempt by Iran to develop nuclear weapons should highlight the dangers of the NPT itself—the Treaty's mandated sharing of nuclear technology for peaceful purposes innocently supposes that periodic international inspections will suffice to prevent the diversion of this adaptable technology to weapons programs.

There is a remarkable address by a former president of the American Society of International Law and former American secretary of state, prior to America's entry into the First World War. In 1914 Elihu Root reminded his fellow international lawyers that the United States could not enjoy a fortress security or always wait until the last moment to address international threats. "The right of self-protection may and frequently does extend in its effect beyond the limits of the territorial jurisdiction of the state exercising it," Root noted. And by necessity, he advised, a sovereign state may need to act alone, and does so "to protect itself by preventing a condition of affairs in which it will be too late to protect itself."

The challenges of asymmetric warfare, nonstate actors, and rogue regimes do not excuse any decision maker from the solemn duties of prudence, or from attempting to mobilize the resources of collective machinery. But they characterize situations requiring that the Charter system adapt itself to perilous changes in threat and capability, and that democratic states also work to that end.

C. PRISONER RIGHTS

The Torturer Speaks. Tom J. Farer, "The Torturer Speaks" from *The Grand Strategy of the United States in Latin America* by Tom J. Farer (1988), excerpt.

If a torturer were to defend his work, here is *what he might say:*

The world is at war, though the war is undeclared. Ferocious battles erupt, often unexpectedly, now in one country, now in another, often in several at once. Battles are won; others are lost. The war goes on. There are grounds neither for compromise nor pity. The stakes are too high for pity. Pity makes you weak. And there cannot be compromise because the antagonists hold utterly incompatible views about the ends of life and the organization of society.

We are defending a social order that has evolved over two millennia. We are defending the fundamental institutions of our civilization: the family, religion, private property, and the whole system of ordered liberty which they support and in turn supports them. The enemy, Marxists of one liturgy or another, are bent on destroying those institutions and abolishing liberty.

Because your societies are richer and more developed, because you have filled out all the empty spaces and imbued most citizens with respect for the civil order into which they are born, you can deal with the problem largely as an external threat. You do not need extraordinary measures. We are not so fortunate.

Your bleeding hearts talk as if we've butchered half of our population and the rest are starving to death. Then how, I ask you, is it that our towns and cities are awash with people, young people for whom we have no houses, no schools, and no jobs? Meanwhile the priests and other agitators, Marxists and their fellow-travelers, go around telling everyone he has a right to these things. The best of them are just irresponsible and dangerous fools throwing sparks onto tinder.

To build up the economy we need capital. To get the capital, we need social peace. To get that peace, we need to insulate the masses from the agitators. When the cancer of subversion has already penetrated into the healthy flesh of society, we have to cut out the cancerous tissue, quickly, before metastasis.

In societies like ours, ordinary measures don't work against clandestine groups. Torture does. You talk about us as if we were animals, subhuman, or you say we use these methods because we're not professionals, not well-trained. As if we invented torture. Were the Gestapo badly trained or the S.D. or other German units? Not on your life. But they knew that when you are dealing with organized political movements capable of energizing much larger groups if they go undetected, if you are dealing with such movements rather than isolated criminals, you need shortcuts, and you need to discourage those who have not yet committed themselves to the life of subversion.

You call us thugs and incompetents. Well, there's nothing unprofessional about the French security services; but they failed to root the terrorist cells out of the Casbah during the Algerian war. Then the paratroop units were sent, the elite of the whole French army, as fine a group of professional troops as exists. And they failed too, at first. Then they turned to torture, and when they finished, the Casbah was secure.

I admit that, as a matter of law, you have a point. Article 3 of the Geneva Conventions of 1949 does ban torture, while not preventing a government from executing its opponents during or after a civil war. All right; that's the law; but is this a morally compelling distinction? You could argue, you know, that torture has a far clearer military justification. The only justification for executing rebels at the end of a civil war or spies in time of peace is some very problematic idea about the long-term deterrent effect. But taking up the gun against the state is such a dangerous gamble to begin with. I doubt people do it unless they expect to win. With torture, on the other hand, you are seeking information directly related to reducing your casualties. The connection between this supposedly illegitimate means and the clearly legitimate end is much closer.

Moreover, society does not normally value freedom from prolonged pain more than it values life. In many of your states, capital punishment has been outlawed. But what is life imprisonment in conditions of maximum security other than torture? Even if a person prefers death, you won't let him have it. Just as your courts wouldn't allow a person in a state of acute pain and humiliating dependence to choose death. Indeed, you are prepared to force-feed a person to keep her alive.

Torture, summary execution, all the apparatus of terror is ugly, no doubt. And as a child of the enlightenment, I share with you a presumption against their use. But like all presumptions, it has exceptions. And we are not the only ones who have carved them out. You North Americans have done your part.

I remember a few years ago, on some anniversary of the atomic bombing of Hiroshima and Nagasaki, the survivors among those who had been involved in the decision to drop the bomb were asked whether they had repented. I can't remember one who admitted he had. Moreover, various eminent intellectuals who had not been involved were prepared with the wisdom of hindsight to defend the incineration of those two Japanese cities. Why? Because it saved lives. Classical utilitarianism: Maximize the sum total of happiness and minimize the pain.

The bomb was indiscriminate, a terror weapon, like torture and disappearance and mutilation and the other instruments we have found it useful to employ in times of grave national emergency. And who among you would not do the same in the right circumstances. Suppose you arrested a man a few days before Christmas who told you mockingly that he had planted a bomb in a department store which would go off in three hours. And suppose you were able to confirm that he had set off bombs in the past. So there was every reason to believe his claim. Maybe some among you would not have the stomach to torture the location of the bomb out of him. But how many would not feel the thrilling hope that there was someone willing to take on the job? As I said earlier, in North America and Europe, these extenuating circumstances don't yet arise very often. We are less fortunate in this respect.

Forcible Interrogation. Diane Marie Amann, "Guantánamo" 42 Colum. J. Transnat'l L. 263 (2004).

Within the framework of indefinite and unreviewed detention appears a most salient feature of detainees' daily existence—interrogation without assistance of counsel. Reports have surfaced of harsh methods, even of physical beatings. A photograph taken at the time of interrogation in Afghanistan showed American Taliban fighter John Walker Lindh strapped to a stretcher, naked except for a swaddling cloth and blindfold. Two detainees released in March 2003 from Bagram complained that they had been forced to remain for long periods in uncomfortable positions, had suffered sleep deprivation, and had observed enforced silence at all times save during interrogation. One said that he was questioned fifty-five out of sixty-five days; the other said that he underwent 230 interrogation sessions. Soldiers reportedly poured ice water on one as he stood nude, and insinuated that the dogs accompanying them might attack. The other described how authorities "conditioned" detainees before interrogation; for example, by staccato repetition of "Sit-Stand" commands. He said that one time he was ordered to count a pile of pebbles. When he reached fifty, he was told, " 'that is the number of years you will spend at Guantánamo if you refuse to talk.' " Their account jibed with other reports. Unnamed U.S. and European intelligence officials told reporters that the CIA indeed used such "stress and duress techniques," and further asserted that some captives had been handed over to countries "known to use mind-altering drugs." U.S. spokespersons declined to discuss specific cases, denied knowledge of "any torture or even physical abuse," and broadly maintained that all "enemy combatants" were being treated humanely. Responding to criticism from members of Congress and others, the Bush Administration in mid–2003 "pledged for the first time" not to subject detainees to torture or to cruel, inhuman, or degrading treatment. Yet on other occasions, U.S. officials admitted that detainees must submit to repeated interrogation outside the presence and absent the advice of attorneys, in settings likely to drain all will to resist. Before the District Court in Padilla, in fact, the government extolled prolonged incommunicado detention as essential to gathering intelligence in the post-September 11 campaign against terrorism.

Few propositions of law enjoy wider acceptance than the proscription against torture. Each of the four Geneva Conventions mandates humane treatment and prohibits, "at any time and in any place" the infliction of "cruel treatment and torture." International human rights law likewise admits no situation, not even the most dire emergency, that would justify torture to extract information. U.S. courts called on to interpret the law of nations thus have not hesitated to hold the ban against torture nonderogable. It is, after all, a bedrock principle of the U.S. legal tradition. The first codification of the law of armed conflict, undertaken by the United States during its Civil War, provided that "military necessity does not admit of torture to extort confessions," and a quarter-century later the Supreme Court made clear that to secure a confession through brutality violates the Constitution's due process guarantees.

Advocates of U.S. policy contended that conditions of interrogation, though hard on the psyche, do not constitute torture. That contention is not particularly germane. What will control in U.S. litigation is not whether the treatment may be labeled "torture," but whether it infringes the Constitution's guarantees of due process and freedom from unreasonable seizures. The contours of those guarantees, however, are unclear. For example, the Court has voiced concern about application of psychological pressure to persons in government custody, yet it has not rendered a definitive ruling on the point at which such pressure becomes unconstitutional. Just last term, all nine U.S. Supreme Court Justices did agree that abusive state conduct during interrogation may violate due process. But the case gave rise to six separate opinions, and the variety of views expressed and legal standards advanced underscored the uncertainty regarding the scope of permissible conduct. As with validity of unreviewed detention, therefore, study of external practice will aid resolution of these unsettled questions.

International instruments evince particular concern that states act humanely toward persons they have detained. Early scrutiny of methods used during questioning of such persons occurred in the landmark decision of the European Court of Human Rights in Ireland v. United Kingdom. In order to achieve "disorientation" or "sensory deprivation" of suspected terrorists, British agents had forced Irish interrogees to stand for hours spread-eagled against a wall, to endure loud noises, or to submit to interrogation wearing a dark-colored hood, sometimes having been denied food, drink, or sleep. The European Court held in 1978 that combined and prolonged use of these techniques "caused, if not actual bodily injury, at least intense physical and mental suffering and also led to acute psychiatric disturbances during interrogation"; therefore, Britain had violated, if not the European Convention's ban against torture, its equally nonderogable ban against inhuman and degrading treatment. The Inter–American Court of Human Rights embraced that decision in 1997, ruling in Loayza Tamayo that "incommunicado detention, being exhibited through the media wearing a degrading garment, solitary confinement in a tiny cell with no natural light, blows and maltreatment, including total immersion in water, intimidation with threats of further violence, a restrictive visiting schedule, all constitute forms of cruel, inhuman or degrading treatment." Although both regional courts shied from describing such mistreatment as "torture," the 1984 Convention Against Torture uses that precise term to include "any act by which severe pain or suffering, whether physical or mental, is intentionally inflicted on a person," by an official bent on gathering information. Congress followed this formulation in U.S. implementing legislation, so that an interrogator who uses or threatens to use "mind-altering substances or other procedures calculated to disrupt profoundly the senses or the personality" may be guilty of the federal crime of torture, punishable in some instances by death. The U.S. military itself has defined this conduct as "torture" subject to capital punishment by the special military commissions that some Guantánamo detainees soon may face.

Disturbingly obvious are the parallels between interrogation techniques that the European and Inter–American Courts condemned and the methods alleged to have been used against post-September 11 detainees. That such methods will cause mental anguish and disrupt the senses is no less certain in the latter instance than it was in the former. Reports of "mental derangement," of "sporadic hunger strikes" among Guantánamo detainees, and of nearly three dozen suicide attempts on account of "tensions and deep frustrations," are, sadly, to be expected. Under international norms that the United States has endorsed, a state may not interrogate a person harshly, particularly within the context of endless confinement designed to break the person's resolve not to answer questions. A fortiori, it may not hand the person over to another state that is likely to commit torture on its behalf. Former detainees, as well as intelligence officials at home and abroad, have said that the United States has done both. If these allegations should prove true, external norms suggest that the U.S. government may be responsible for torture or inhuman and degrading treatment. This conclusion would compel another; namely, that the policy of the U.S. executive violates the

Constitution's core guarantees against unreasonable seizure and deprivation of liberty without due process of law.

Terrorism and the Law. Thomas M. Franck, "Criminals, Combatants, or What? An Examination of the Role of Law in Responding to the Threat of Terror" 98 A.J.I.L. 686 (2004).

It is common ground among most lawyers versed in constitutional and international law that the differences between the modern threat of terrorism and more familiar attacks on the legal order by criminals and aggressors affect the inconvenience costs of adherence to the rule of law in both its "due process" and "prisoner of war" models. For several reasons the terrorist *defi* is different.

First, the "due process" model fails fully to take into account the magnitude of the challenge involved in convicting terrorists as criminals by demonstrating culpability beyond a reasonable doubt. The obstacles include not only the risk to the prosecution of revealing sources and methods, which is likely to be much greater than in an ordinary criminal trial, but also the limitations imposed by criminal law on means of obtaining evidence. Means commonly employed overseas in covert operations, unauthorized wiretaps, for example, may render their fruits inadmissible in domestic criminal proceedings. Moreover, prosecutors are likely to find it difficult to persuade witnesses to come forward to testify, given the heightened danger of retaliation.

Second, no one questions that the costs of releasing a potential terrorist are likely to be greater than those that ordinarily accrue in the event of an accused's discharge for lack of evidence or procedural error. The adage that it is better for a hundred guilty persons to go free than for one innocent person to be incarcerated takes on a different hue in the age of high-technology terror.

In the "prisoner of war" model, too, the normal balance of convenience that supports restraints on authority is skewed by the phenomenon of modern terrorism. The logic behind the Geneva Conventions, for example, is, first, that humane treatment of prisoners of war will encourage other combatants to surrender peaceably. Second, it is assumed that, when one party to a conflict treats its prisoners humanely, the other will reciprocate. Third, it is probably an unspoken conjecture that ordinary prisoners of war do not have much information that is likely, whether revealed or unrevealed, to have a great impact on the outcome of the conflict. Simply stating these underlying assumptions of the law of war is to suggest that they are not so evidently applicable to an international terrorist conspiracy like Al Qaeda. On the other hand, to whatever extent the underlying reasons for normative constraints may be less applicable, that will alter the balance of convenience between upholding and circumventing those constraints.

Thus, there is a rather broad area of often unacknowledged agreement between those who disagree vehemently about the U.S. government's legal posture toward its detainees at home and abroad. Where that agreement dissolves into disagreement is in the consequences drawn by each side. Yes, terrorism *is* different. But what should be the legal concomitant of that difference?

The Departments of Justice and Defense of the U.S. government appeared to have concluded that the differences justify the wholesale suspension of the rule of law, in both its domestic and international manifestations. In views expressed in internal legal memoranda and, more formally in arguments made to the Supreme Court in the recent *Hamdi* and Guantánamo cases, the Justice Department had argued that terrorism challenges the nation with something approximating a state of perpetual war, in which the sole ultimate determiner of military tactics and of captives' rights must, perforce, be the president in his constitutional capacity as commander in chief. As for international law, it was also said, treaties could never diminish the illimitable constitutional powers of the supreme commander in a life-or-death struggle. Even the Third and Fourth Geneva Conventions, strictly construed, were said not to protect detainees alleged to be members of Al Qaeda, persons who are neither conventional prisoners of war nor quite civilian criminals.

To many civil libertarians, this broad assertion of presidential powers looked like an instance of throwing out the rule-of-law baby with the bathwater of inconvenient limits on absolute governmental discretion.

Now, fortunately, the Supreme Court has intervened in this discourse, and done so firmly on the side of the rule of law. Even in wartime, Justice Sandra Day O'Connor has wisely cautioned, the president remains subject to checks and balances vested by the Constitution in the Congress and the courts.

That breaks the deadlock between the president's lawyers and the civil libertarians who, all along, had argued that new circumstances cannot alone invalidate the normative constraints imposed on government by constitutional, congressional, and international law. Yet, while the Supreme Court has cleared away the doubts about applicable substantive law, it has (quite properly) not addressed the procedural problems its decision will generate, as Article III judges strive to apply normal legal rules to detainees whose circumstances differ radically from the norm.

This seems an appropriate time for scholars to talk with government lawyers and those in the law and policymaking process in searching for adjustments in applicable domestic and international law. Such a search must begin with the assumption that terrorism, as currently practiced, does constitute a new phenomenon: one to which traditional constitutional and international legal constraints may not be wholly responsive. It must equally accept, however, that no adaptation of law—no matter how efficiently responsive to the challenges of a new phenomenon that is both part crime and part combat, yet different from each—should be made at the cost of abandoning the basic concepts of the rule of law that define us and differentiate us from our adversaries. The irreducible core of the rule of law is this: that those who execute the law must *never* be the sole and final arbiters of that law.

For example, it must be a credible adjudicative process that determines whether a person has been detained for probable cause and is being treated in accordance with legal limits on coercive interrogation. After the historic decisions in the *Hamdi* and Guantánamo cases, it will no longer do to address the petitions of persons held in hard, indefinite detention by having a presidential appointee make an occasional review of their status, how cooperative they have been, and whether they still pose a danger to the national interest. We will have to come up with something more akin to a judicial hearing, more in conformity with the rule of law.

Yet it must also be acknowledged that this new modus operandi will pose unwanted responsibilities and managerial strains on judges. The process will encounter evidentiary issues and questions of onus of proof that do not quite fit the criminal law paradigm. Problems of judicial architecture will arise: what sorts of courts ought to address the new issues that will develop, and with what jurisdictional thresholds and procedures?

Similarly, the applicable international legal framework for the treatment and protection of detainees needs to be rethought in the light of contemporary conflict with terrorist movements that do not quite fit the models incorporated into the Third and Fourth Geneva Conventions.

Judges, attorneys, prosecutors, members of Congress, and the military, aided by academic experts, need to begin, now, to address these matters. There has always been a large measure of agreement that terrorism poses a new set of challenges for the rule of law. Now that it seems to have become clear that the rule of law—in both its domestic and its international configurations—still applies, the next task is to make it more responsive to the onerous new circumstances in which it must operate.

Chapter 10

THE GLOBAL ENVIRONMENT

Editors' introduction: We are all rightfully concerned with the viability of our environment. Yet the very idea of nation-states maximizing their own interests can, in the aggregate, destroy global environmental values. The global environment is the quintessential case of the commons, the "we all sink or swim together" principle. How is international law reacting to the problem of ecosystemic degradation? Is the nation-state system doomed to self-destruction by the difficulty of self-control required for preserving the global environment? There is hardly any question in international law more serious than the ones taken up in this chapter.

A. THE STUDY OF ENVIRONMENTAL LAW

International Environmental Law. David A. Wirth, "Teaching and Research in International Environmental Law" 23 Harv. Envtl. L. Rev. 423 (1999).

Over the past decade and a half, there has been a dramatic increase in awareness of environmental threats that demand concerted international responses. As the public has come to appreciate the urgency of warnings from the scientific community about widespread species loss, dramatic depletion of the stratospheric ozone layer over Antarctica, and other troubling indicators of the poor state of our planet's environment, governments have begun to respond. Issues such as the integrity of the global climate, which attracted negligible interest among the public and policy makers as recently as the middle of the last decade, now command attention at the highest levels of government. For instance, global warming featured prominently on the agenda of the 1992 United Nations Conference on Environment and Development (UNCED), attended by more than a hundred heads of state and governments. The creation of the new position of Under Secretary for Global Affairs at the Department of State in 1993 reveals the extent to which international environmental concerns have been elevated within our own government.

As the demand for policy responses has increased, the international law of the environment has also developed at a furious pace. International agreements, such as the two major multilateral conventions on biological diversity and climate signed at UNCED, have been negotiated and adopted at a feverish clip in recent years. New non-binding instruments on a wide variety of subjects and in many forms continuously augment the authorities applicable in the field. Moreover, there are now more international fora in the field of environmental policy and law than ever before. The Office of the Legal Adviser at the State Department, which as recently as the mid–1980s had only one lawyer working exclusively on environmental issues, now boasts a staff complement of at least six attorneys who spend part of their time on environmental issues.

Against this background, international environmental law has begun to come into its own as an academic sub-discipline. At least four new law school texts on international environmental law have been published in the past five years, where previously there had been none. Approximately forty percent of law schools now offer a course on international environmental law. Two law schools, Colorado and Georgetown, have created student-edited journals devoted entirely to the discipline. International environmental law has become a recognized legal discipline. A number of prominent scholars specialize primarily or exclusively in the area and, accordingly, academic writing in the field is now abundant. Subspecialties are beginning to proliferate, as are even more highly specialized courses. A minimum of eight law schools have offered courses devoted exclusively to the emerging issue of trade and environment, and at least one institution, the Washington College of Law at American University, offers a masters degree with a specialization in international environmental law.

In recent years international environmental law has been coming into its own not only as a subject of classroom instruction, but also as a recognized discipline of scholarly inquiry. One indicator, the issue of the *Index to Legal Periodicals and Books* covering the period September 1996 to August 1997, lists seventy-five journal articles under the heading "International environmental law and practice." The analogous period for the year 1988–89, the first in which this entry appears in the service, contains forty-two entries, an increase of more than seventy-eight per cent in just eight years.

Lessons Learned. Joseph F.C. DiMento, "Lessons Learned" 19 UCLA J. Envtl. L. & Pol'y 281 (2000/2001).

It is notable that even the most experienced international law observers differ as to this most basic question for a legal regime. Should the law aim to solve clear quantified selected present day environmental health challenges, such as water born deaths, and focus resources on those? Should world leaders in international environmental policy strive to create a sense of crisis and/or cooperation so that national governments otherwise not motivated to act for environmental goals respond positively? Or is the law's most important work in the environmental sphere to identify possibly catastrophic future manifestations of degradation and focus efforts on these? Some experts think it sufficient to structure instruments to foster cooperative environmental problem solving, while others are not satisfied unless quantitative limits on globally degrading activities are set.

Some experienced negotiators ask whether other international environmental law observers are being too ambitious in articulating the goals of international environmental law. In seeking quantitative parameters for reductions, for example, they may be articulating an unreasonable target. Achieving cooperation among nation states may itself be enough at this stage of the movement toward international solutions. Thus, despite modest quantitative emissions limitations goals, some participants saw the Global Climate regime as impressively successful in bringing parties to discuss a problem that was not even recognized until recently. Furthermore these efforts stimulate individual nation states and private sector actions that aim to stabilize the global environment, independent of a treaty.

How is effectiveness of international environmental law to be measured?

Regardless of overall goals, analysts also have varying views as to how to assess whether the goals are being reached; quite different benchmarks of success are employed. Thus, the Global Climate change regime can be measured by reference to quantitative limits set for the target years at Kyoto; by quantitative limits actually achieved; by the mobilization of private efforts, including those of Multinational Corporations, to voluntarily limit emissions; by the dynamics and processes energized by the Conference of the Parties; by the stated and underlying rationale for climate stabilization concern (consistent with economic growth as usual or reflective of a fundamental shift in the underpinnings of the international law).

The number of actual cases successively prosecuted can measure effectiveness of the adoption of penal sanctions in international environmental law. Criminalization of an activity that degrades the international environment makes a symbolic statement that may promote deterrence. Even less "measurable" but critical to some is the philosophical recognition of the importance of global environmental stewardship.

B. ENVIRONMENTAL GOVERNANCE

State Responsibility. Nicholas A. Robinson, "Befogged Vision: International Environmental Governance a Decade After Rio" 27 Wm. & Mary Envtl. L. & Pol'y Rev. 299 (2002).

Environmental management has emerged as an important element of governance in practically every nation. This was not the case before the United Nations convened the 1972 Conference on the Human Environment ("Stockholm") in Stockholm. After Stockholm, nations learned to build environmental ministries and work across sectors nationally, and discovered how difficult it is to reshape entrenched national practices in order to curb pollution and conserve natural resources. With growing experience and knowledge, nations came to realize that no one government alone could safeguard the environment, and that international cooperation would need to be enhanced.

Twenty years after Stockholm, nations had developed their capacity to assess environmental conditions and realized that environmental conditions were deteriorating more extensively than had earlier been understood. As a result, in 1992 the United Nations convened the UN Conference on Environment and Development (UNCED) in Rio de Janeiro. Despite UNCED's extensive recommendations and the oversight of the UN Commission on Sustainable Development (UNCSD), established to follow up on those recommendations, momentum to organize the international community to cope with environmental problems subsequent to Rio flagged. In order to refocus international efforts to advance environmental governance, in 2002 the United Nations General Assembly convened the World Summit on Sustainable Development (WSSD) in Johannesburg. Improvement in the system of international environmental governance was one of the priority themes assigned to the WSSD.

Despite the widely acknowledged understanding that environmental conditions worldwide have deteriorated since UNCED in 1992, the WSSD failed to respond in any significant new way to these challenges. Although the nations gathered in Johannesburg made modest progress in addressing the need to encourage sustainable energy systems and achieved some consensus that the supply of potable water and sewage treatment must be a global priority, they could do little to make new policies. The WSSD nations made no decisions addressing the improvement of international institutional systems for managing environmental problems. This reluctance to strengthen the systems for enhancing international environmental governance constituted a retreat from the consensus that strengthening governance was a goal of the WSSD. The WSSD simply reaffirmed the governance systems already in place as of 1992 and urged the existing bodies to do their jobs more effectively.

Why did the issue of international environmental governance stall at the WSSD, and whither will these issues now tend? It may be premature to hazard answers to these queries, but answers must be sought because many of earth's natural systems—upon which human well-being depends—are eroding faster than solutions are being established to sustain them.

Many causes contributed to the impasse regarding international environmental governance at the WSSD. As scientists report increases in pollution, in desertification, in losses of habitat, and the like, it is apparent that earth's governments are failing to respect the fundamental human right to live and work in a healthy and balanced environment. This occurs despite moral and religious injunctions, common to every diverse cultural tradition, to respect nature.

Why do nations disregard these traditional duties and watch while the quality of the environment deteriorates? One reason is that world events have conspired to distract governments from making environmental stewardship a priority. Since UNCED in Rio in 1992, the Cold War ended. Countries with once centrally planned economies are rapidly converting to market economies, slowing the development of their internal environmental governance systems. Significant governmental resources have been invested in developing liberalized trade, establishing the World Trade Organization, and in coping with the unanticipated protests against "globalization." Since 2001, governments preoccupied with immediate concerns for combating terrorism appear to be incapable of simultaneously addressing the festering problems of environmental security for their people and resources. In short, after UNCED, other priorities intruded such that there was virtually no progress in advancing environmental governance.

Considering the WSSD's impasse from this historical perspective, it is not surprising that nations respond to more immediate political situations before attending to problems whose pressures are more remote. Perhaps it is too much to expect that governance systems could respond rapidly to threats that grow only incrementally and gradually, as is the case with most environmental problems. When addressing environmental problems, nations do not face an external enemy, for each society and economy contributes to its own problems. Moreover, given that the system of nation-states has a crowded traditional agenda, national leaders have only gradually taken on environmental threats. Throughout the post-UNCED decade, both international and national decision makers mostly continued to assume that the laws of nature would function "normally" to serve human society. Although fish populations collapsed in the wake of excessive fishing and other warning signs persisted, governments and their leaders continued to take the bounty of nature for granted.

Between the 1972 Stockholm Conference on the Human Environment and the 1992 UNCED in Rio de Janeiro, nations individually concentrated on adapting their national norms and standards to address environmental threats: national legislation established environmental rules; constitutions were amended to provide the right to a balanced environment; and treaties were negotiated and ratified to establish regional and international standards. The result was enactment of an increasingly complex set of legal norms in most sectors, from the village to the global commons. A legal matrix of rules now operates as a continuum of environmental management to guide state conduct, whether exercised by local authorities, national officials or United Nations entities, toward stewardship of natural resources.

At UNCED in 1992, national heads of state and their delegates formally acknowledged that assumptions about nature's cornucopia could no longer be made. A consensus had emerged that proactive management would be needed to sustain the air, water, and other natural resources upon which the human economy depended. However, it has proved easier for nations to agree that stewardship is needed than for them to decide how to work together to strengthen the mechanisms for exercising that stewardship. Upon returning home, relatively few heads of state gave environmental governance the importance that they announced in their decisions at UNCED.

After UNCED, environmental concerns competed with other issues. The Commission on Environmental Cooperation was established to ensure that environmental standards were a priority in association with the North American Free Trade Agreement. More widely, however, the foreign policies favoring liberalized world trade led to popular resistance against the World Trade Organization and the efforts to build new rounds of negotiations under the General Agreement on Tariffs and Trade. Debate raged against trends in economic or social "globalization," with street riots emerging for the World Trade Organization meetings in Seattle in 1999, and the Group of Eight Summit Meeting in Italy in 2001. Ultimately, the terrorist assault on the World Trade Center in New York City on September 11, 2001 triggered a restructuring of the foreign policy of the United States. Both trade and environment were eclipsed by concerns for the threat and reality of terrorism less than a year before the scheduled World Summit on Sustainable Development in 2002. In short, the Rio consensus in favor of new institutions became befogged with the passage of time, and the emergence of new pressing political challenges clouded the vision that had seemed so clear at UNCED.

Despite the formulation of national and international laws establishing norms for sustaining the environment, there has been only modest attention devoted to how best to improve the institutional systems by which these norms are to be applied, observed, and enforced. The annual negotiations undertaken by the UNCSD have yielded less and less agreement on the need for or type of environmental governance. Nations had been enacting their frameworks of environmental legislation nationally, but the diplomats knew little about these complicated regimes. While the process of enacting further norms will doubtless continue within countries, and current standards will be streamlined and enhanced, it is evident that more attention must be devoted at the international level in order to strengthen governing institutions capable of efficiently and effectively implementing those norms.

Strengthening State Compliance. Harold K. Jacobson and Edith Brown Weiss, "Assessing the Record and Designing Strategies to Engage Countries" in *Engaging Countries: Strengthening Compliance With International Environmental Accords* by Edith Brown Weiss, ed. (1998), excerpt.

Traditional behavior is related to a country's culture. Culture provides a context and springboard for what a country does. But countries' cultures are neither fixed nor static, nor are they always uncontested. Japan found it easy to comply with the obligations of the World Heritage Convention because it had traditionally cherished its cultural and natural sites; protection of them was deeply embedded in Japanese culture.

The United States had similar traditions with respect to the natural environment dating to the early 1900s.

Another crucial factor contributing to the variance among the performances of countries is administrative capacity. Countries that have stronger administrative capacities can do a better job. Hungary's compliance, especially with the Montreal Protocol [on substances that deplete the ozone layer] demonstrates this point. Administrative capacity is the result of several factors. Knowledge is a fundamental ingredient in implementation and compliance. Having educated and trained personnel is important. But such individuals must have adequate financial support and an appropriate legal mandate in order to be effective.

The Indian administrative service had numerous and well-trained personnel, but its financial resources were extremely limited, and thus its effectiveness was restricted. Administrative capacity depends upon having authority. Administrators whose mandate is narrower than their assigned responsibilities, or who are subject to capricious interference, cannot do as well as their training and skills would make possible. Administrative capacity also depends on having access to relevant information. However much administrative capacity a country has, corruption can blunt its effectiveness.

Administrative capacity also is relative; it must be measured against the demands placed upon it. Even the European Union, Japan, and the United States, which had strong administrative capacity, had difficulty enforcing the obligations of the Convention on International Trade in Endangered Species (CITES). Given the many points of entry to these political units, and the vast number of people and goods moving in and out of their territories, it would be beyond the capacity of these units to enforce complete control at their borders.

Administrative capacity correlates with total GNP and GNP per capita. Countries that have many resources in relative terms, either because they are large (e.g., Brazil, China, and India) or because they have high per capita incomes, have the resources to develop strong administrative capacities. Outside agencies also can help countries develop administrative capacity.

Beyond relative richness, economic factors are important, but rather indirectly. The political units in this study have widely varying per capita GNPs that have grown or declined at substantially different rates. Changes in GNP or the rate of growth of GNP had little discernible effect on implementation and compliance. Economic collapse and chaos, however, can and did have a profound effect. In Cameroon and Russia, compliance with CITES seems to have declined since the mid–1980s, and this seems to be directly attributable to the economic collapse and chaos. Limited government resources and rapid rates of inflation had an impact on the incentive structure of the individuals who must enforce the provisions of CITES, the customs inspectors. In some instances they were not paid. In others, they saw the value of their salaries decline precipitously. Conversely, the value of illicit trade in endangered species has increased. Under the circumstances, the apparent increase in illicit trade in endangered species is perhaps understandable.

How production is organized makes a difference. Under the Soviet Union, when the state was responsible for production, state enterprises both produced goods and monitored the environmental consequences of their activities. This system did not result in effective environmental protection. The state enterprises were more concerned with production goals than with environmental protection. In 1986, under the Gorbachev regime, an independent ministry was created with a mandate to be concerned about environmental issues, and this began to have an effect. But enforcing compliance became even more effective after more production was privatized. Governments seem to be better at regulating the activities of nongovernmental entities than they are at regulating activities under their own control. Separating responsibility for regulation and production appears to have advantages in terms of promoting compliance with international environmental accord obligations.

The extent to which and the ways in which a country is engaged in international trade are also important. The more a country engages in international trade that is not controlled by state authorities, the more opportunities there are for illicit trade. Russia's and Hungary's shifting from controlled international trade directed by a central plan to free international trade provides evidence of this. At the same time, the more a country is engaged in international trade and the more it relies on investment from abroad, the more subject it is to international pressures. China's engagement in the world economy in the 1980s provides evidence of how a country can feel that it has to conform to international environmental standards as part of belonging to the international economy.

Political systems and institutions have an effect on implementation and compliance, but again the effect is mixed and complex. Large countries have a much more complicated task of complying with the obligations of accords than do smaller ones. Federalism also causes complications. There are several levels of political authority in Brazil, China, the European Union, Russia, and the United States. The European Union, of course, is a special case because its authority was still in the process of being defined in the 1990s. In cases where activities with which the accord deals are widely dispersed, as in the World Heritage Convention, CITES, and the International Tropical Timber Agreement, multiple levels of political authority must be coordinated, which is not always an easy task.

Sometimes the authority of the central government, which accepts international obligations, does not reach deeply into local areas. The government in Beijing, for instance, had great difficulty controlling activities in southern and western China. The central authorities in New Delhi had little ability to control events in the Manas National Park. Brasília had difficulty securing compliance in Amazonia, where subjects of CITES and [the International Tropical Timber Agreement] are found.

Moreover, these large countries contain within their borders widely different ecological regions that require variation in the way administration is conducted. The extent of a country's borders also makes a difference. Countries that have long borders touching many countries have more difficulty controlling smuggling than those that do not.

As part of its reform, Russia attempted to decentralize authority. In the process of decentralization, the authority of Moscow over localities was weakened. This shift appears to have resulted in a decline in Russia's compliance with CITES. Whether this decline was the temporary result of an administrative restructuring or a longer-term change will be known only in the future. Political stalemate and chaos can bring about a noticeable decline in implementation and compliance. This seems to have been the case in Brazil, Cameroon, and Russia at various times.

There are many features of democratic governments that contribute to improved implementation and compliance. Democratic governments are normally more transparent than authoritarian governments, so interested citizens can more easily monitor what their governments are doing to implement and comply with accords. In democratic governments, it is possible for citizens to bring pressure to bear for improved implementation and compliance. Also, nongovernmental organizations generally have more freedom to operate under democratic governments. In addition, fully independent courts can be used by nongovernmental organizations and citizens to force governmental action.

At the same time, democratic governments are normally more responsive to public opinion than authoritarian governments. Public opinion is not always supportive of environmental concerns—indeed, the economy is usually the public's greatest concern. Democratic governments allow conflicts about environmental issues to flare.

Because of the balance of factors mentioned in the preceding paragraphs, democratic governments are more likely to do a better job of implementing and complying with international environmental accords than nondemocratic governments. This generalization does not always hold, however, and democratization does not necessarily lead automatically or quickly to improved compliance.

Democratization in Brazil and in Russia, however, seems to have contributed to improved compliance. Brazil's 1988 Constitution mentioned environmental issues, stated goals, and made commitments. Improved compliance in the Soviet Union could be attributed to the greater transparency in governmental processes that started with the reforms under Gorbachev and were continued after the collapse of the Soviet Union. The increased activities of such nongovernmental organizations as Greenpeace were particularly important to strengthening Russia's compliance.

The importance of nongovernmental organizations—TRAFFIC [a division of the World Wildlife Fund], Greenpeace, the Worldwide Fund for Nature, for example—has already been mentioned. They play a crucial role in implementation and compliance. They mobilize public opinion and set political agendas. They make information about problems available, sometimes information that governments do not have or would prefer to keep confidential. Often the information they make available is essential to monitoring. They bring pressure on governments directly and indirectly. Because many local and national nongovernmental organizations have connections with NGOs in other countries and with international NGOs, NGOs are a means of ensuring a uniformity of concern throughout the world. There are also significant transfers of funds among NGOs, so those in poorer countries may have surprisingly extensive resources at their disposal. NGOs have become an instrument for universalizing concern.

However, not all nongovernmental organizations necessarily assist compliance. Some NGOs have purposes that are anathema to enhanced compliance with environmental treaties.

A country's physical conditions, its history, its culture, and its behavior (tradition, legislation, and regulations) with respect to the activity involved prior to adhering to the treaty establish basic parameters that affect implementation and compliance. The economy, political institutions, and attitudes and values have an effect, but this is generally indirect. These factors operate through proximate variables. In our view the most important proximate variables are administrative capacity, leadership, nongovernmental organizations, and knowledge and information.

Reassessing State Consent. Daniel Bodansky, "The Legitimacy of International Governance: A Coming Challenge for International Environmental Law?" 93 A.J.I.L. 596 (1999).

Apart from a few regimes such as the International Whaling Convention and the Antarctic Treaty System, state consent and legality have until now provided a relatively firm foundation for international environmental law. But two developments are likely to undermine their ability to do so in the future. First, the coming generation of environmental problems will probably require more expeditious and flexible lawmaking approaches, which do not depend on consensus among states. Second, to the extent that international environmental law is beginning to have significant implications for non- or substate actors (who have not consented to it directly), rather than just for the relations among states, state consent may for them have little legitimating effect. As international environmental law continues to grow more like domestic environmental law, it will be held to the same standards of legitimacy, and its lack of transparency and accountability will become increasingly problematic.

International environmental law has developed primarily through the negotiation of treaties that bind consenting states to rules rather than governance structures. In practice, this has usually meant an effort to find consensus, since states are reluctant to take action against global problems such as climate change or ozone depletion unless everyone (or nearly everyone) is required to do so; unilateral action simply raises a country's costs, thereby injuring its competitiveness, without necessarily solving the problem, if others continue to pollute.

Consensus decision making, however, involves numerous, by now familiar, problems. Attempting to achieve consensus is time-consuming and difficult. Agreements tend to be inflexible, given the difficulties of gaining agreement on any changes. Moreover, agreements must either represent the least-common-denominator, and thus be weak, or must create different obligations for different states. In many cases, reaching agreement at all is impossible, so a consensus requirement in effect precludes collective action. For these reasons, among others, within domestic society, "the unanimity rule is recognized as incompatible with effective government."

International environmental law has employed a variety of mechanisms to circumvent the "slowest boat" phenomenon associated with consensus decision making and thereby make possible more robust international standard-setting. But, despite some successes, most notably the ozone regime, the consensus requirement puts international environmental law under a serious handicap. It is difficult enough to enact domestic legislation to control water or air pollution in a system of simple majority rule, particularly when decisions impose significant costs on identifiable segments of society. But imagine trying to adopt such rules through a consensus mechanism. Consensus decision making is even less likely to be able to address international problems such as climate change, where states have (or at least think they have) very different interests, where the costs may be extremely high, and where the regime may need to change rapidly as scientific understanding of the problem improves. Instead, successful international action will depend on the ability to require common action even in the absence of consensus among states—it will depend, that is, on some form of supranational authority.

Consider, for example, the ozone regime. Compared to climate change, the ozone problem is simple—the science is much better understood and, in most cases, replacement technologies exist at a reasonable cost. But even the ozone regime has found it desirable to provide for non-consensus decision making. The Montreal Protocol on Substances that Deplete the Ozone Layer states that, once a chemical is subject to control measures, those controls may be tightened ("adjusted") by a qualified majority vote. This decision-making rule does not simply prevent a minority from blocking action; it subjects the minority to the majority's will. Adjustments bind all parties to the Montreal Protocol, not just those that give specific consent. In this regard, the Montreal Protocol's adjustment procedure constitutes an embryonic legislative mechanism, rather than merely a contractual mechanism by which states voluntarily assume obligations.

Non-consensus decision-making mechanisms may be even more crucial with regard to compliance issues. The 1997 Kyoto Climate Change

Protocol, for example, calls for the establishment of a compliance mechanism to oversee implementation of the Protocol's commitments—in particular, the various mechanisms by which parties will be allowed to trade their allocations of greenhouse gas emissions. Some proposals envision a compliance body with broad authority to determine whether states are in compliance with their emissions commitments, and, if not, what the consequences should be (for example, buyer liability for trades of non-existent emissions allowances). But it is difficult to see how such a procedure could work by consensus.

The use of non-consensus mechanisms is, of course, furthest advanced in the European Union. To make possible stronger EU action, and to avoid deadlock, the European Union has progressively moved from unanimity to qualified majority voting in the Council of Ministers. Under the current voting rules, most decisions require only sixty-two of the eighty-seven total Council votes. Over time, more and more types of decisions have been made subject to this majority voting procedure.

In the field of international environmental law, proposals have already surfaced to establish new, more authoritative institutions, in order to address global problems such as climate change. In 1989, representatives of twenty-four countries, including such major powers as Germany, Japan, India and France, adopted the Declaration of the Hague, which endorsed "the principle of developing new institutional authority" involving non-unanimous decision making to address the climate change problem. More recently, New Zealand proposed in the United Nations the establishment of a global legislative body with the power to adopt environmental rules that bind all nations. Although the Hague Declaration is sometimes seen as a blind alley that has not led anywhere, what is striking is the adoption of the Declaration at all, not its lack of immediate results.

Are the existing foundations of international law sufficient to legitimate institutions with non-consensus decision-making authority? Certainly, legal legitimacy would not suffice. Legal legitimacy takes what might be called an internal perspective: particular directives are justified in terms of a regime's secondary rules about who can exercise authority, according to what procedures, and subject to what restrictions. But legal legitimacy does not address whether a regime's ongoing governance arrangements are themselves justified. The fact, for example, that Chapter VII of the UN Charter permits the Security Council to authorize the use of force in former Yugoslavia does not answer the more fundamental question of whether the Council's composition and decision-making mechanisms are legitimate. Similarly, enactment of an EU regulation in accordance with the EU treaties is not enough to ensure its legitimacy, since that depends also on whether the governance arrangements established by those treaties are legitimate. To answer those questions, we need to step outside of the UN Charter or the EU treaties and evaluate their provisions based on some external standard of legitimacy.

To some degree, general consent could provide a basis of legitimacy for non-consensus decision-making mechanisms. States could agree to such a mechanism in a treaty, as they have done in the Montreal Protocol, the UN Charter, and the European Union agreements. From the perspective of social contract theory, this general consent should give these regimes a strong claim to legitimacy—indeed, a stronger claim than many national governments, since these regimes are based on actual contracts to which each member state gave its express consent, rather than on a merely hypothetical social contract. So long as a regime stays within its constitutional limits (i.e., has legal legitimacy), then states that freely consented to a non-consensus decision-making process should be bound by the results.

The persisting questions about the legitimacy of the European Union and the Security Council, however, suggest that general consent may not be sufficient, in itself, to legitimate a general system of governance or its resulting rules. General consent involves a much more significant surrender of autonomy than specific consent—and thereby raises more serious concerns about legitimacy—since, in giving consent, a state does not know what particular constraints may be imposed on it in the future. For this reason, the notion of "the consent of the governed" has come to mean more in modern political theory than simply initial, general consent to governmental authority; it implies ongoing consent through democratic elections. It requires, as P. H. Partridge notes, that "governments are made perpetually responsive to the ideas and demands of the governed." Although general consent may be sufficient to legitimate a relatively limited decision-making mechanism such as the Montreal Protocol adjustment procedure, where the range of possible decisions is narrowly circumscribed and the issues have a significant technical component, when an institution must be able to respond to changing problems in changing ways, "any concept of consent is unlikely to have any significant application unless we conceive it as a process, as a relationship that must be constantly renewed and maintained." That is why the consent of EU member states to the EU treaties, or of UN member states to the UN Charter, has not laid to rest questions about the legitimacy of the European Council or the Security Council respectively. By the same token, general consent in unlikely to be sufficient to legitimate environmental institutions with broad decision-making powers, of the kind envisioned by the Hague Declaration.

The process of globalization has put mounting strains on the state system. Environmental problems are increasingly escaping the control of individual states and international institutions have often been too weak to step into the breach. The result has been a "decision-making deficit," an erosion in the ability of government to address environmental problems effectively. In the long run, overcoming this deficit will require stronger international institutions and decision-making mechanisms. But, as the case of the European Union illustrates, the stronger the institution, the greater the concern about its legitimacy. Unless the issue of legitimacy is addressed, it is likely to act as a drag on the development and effectiveness of international environmental regimes.

Many factors can contribute to or detract from a regime's legitimacy. Legitimacy is a matter not of all or nothing, but of more or less. Authority should be exercised in accordance with law and principle (legal legitimacy). The decision-making mechanisms should be transparent and give people an opportunity to participate (participatory legitimacy). Furthermore, decisions should be based on the best scientific expertise (expert legitimacy). But these are minimum conditions. They contribute to legitimacy (and their absence undermines it), but by themselves do not provide a firm basis for legitimacy. They do not address the central problem, which is how decisions should be made when consensus cannot be reached—by whom, using what voting rule, and with what safeguards.

Calls for global environmental institutions with binding decision-making powers are usually criticized as utopian. This is perhaps too mild a criticism. The term "utopian" carries the connotation of desirable; the criticism suggests that global institution with real power would be a good thing, if only states would agree. But this is by no means clear, given the lack of a strong theory of legitimacy. In the absence of a global community, the one compelling candidate, democracy, does not provide an answer. And, at the moment, we lack any persuasive alternative.

What we need, then, is further work on the problem of legitimacy. Given the continuing importance of state consent, an important question is whether and how the system of state consent might be reformed, in order to make it more effective in addressing environmental problems and more legitimate vis à vis individuals. Where relatively clear blocs of states exist, for example, constituency voting and double majority requirements might provide a viable alternative to consensus decision making. Already, the Council of the Global Environment Facility may make decisions by a 60 percent majority vote, so long as donor countries representing at least 60 percent of contributions concur. The premise seems to be that, although states do not, in general, have sufficient mutual trust to accept majority voting, they do have such trust in the other members of their own group (due, for example, to common history, culture, or interests). Such decision-making approaches warrant further exploration.

In addition, we need detailed case studies of the legitimacy of particular environmental regimes, in order to understand how such factors as public participation, scientific expertise, and consent work in particular contexts to help legitimate international governance. What conditions make these factors more or less effective in legitimating a regime? Which combinations of factors work best, and which ones less well? And even if we cannot develop a satisfactory positive theory of legitimacy, can we at least identify more precisely what to avoid, as well as the factors that help make an institution resilient to claims of illegitimacy?

Finally, as international environmental law increasingly influences (or even displaces) domestic law, further study is needed on the relationship between international and domestic policymaking. In particular, how can we make the international environmental policymaking process more democratic within countries—for example, through the active involvement of legislators and interest groups in the treaty-making process?

Unless some other basis of legitimacy can be found, the continuing centrality of state consent (which remains, by default, the principal source of legitimacy for international environmental law) is likely to limit the possibilities of international governance. When states have common interests, and the issues involved are relatively technical, states might agree to establish institutions with flexible, non-consensus decision-making procedures, as they have done in the ozone regime. In such cases, general consent confers legitimacy initially, and technical expertise helps maintain this legitimacy on a continuing basis. But this approach is unlikely to work for problems such as climate change, where states have a much wider range of interests, and the issues involved are highly political. This is a sobering conclusion, but one that clarifies the challenges that lie ahead for international environmental law.

A World Organization? Steve Charnovitz, "A World Environment Organization" 27 Colum. J. Envtl. L. 323 (2002).

One point is agreed to by all of the participants in the debate over environmental governance—current environmental policies are inadequate to address the ecological threats. Thus, the debate is not about the need for more concerted international action, but rather about the utility and practicality of a more centralized management structure for solving these problems. A World Environmental Organization (WEO) is needed for two reasons: First, many ecosystems continue to deteriorate and the human environment is under serious, uncontrolled threats. Second, the processes of international environmental governance need better coordination.

While human stewardship over the earth's environment may not be disastrous, serious environmental problems exist that are not being adequately managed under current institutions. In GEO–2000, UNEP concluded, "if present trends in population growth, economic growth and consumption patterns continue, the natural environment will be increasingly stressed."* The most serious problems include a massive loss of biodiversity, over-fishing, depleted freshwater supplies, and global warming.

At this time, there are two realistic organizational structures for a WEO vis-à-vis UNEP. The first is a WEO that adds new flanks to UNEP, with UNEP retaining its organizational identity. The second is a WEO

---

* U.N. Environment Programme, Overview: Global Environmental Outlook 2000 (1999), available at http://www.unep.org.

that incorporates UNEP entirely by dissolving it into the new organization.

This WEO could be created as a specialized agency pursuant to Article 59 of the U.N. Charter or could be a new type of agency more central to the U.N. The Governing Council of UNEP might become the Governing Council of the WEO, but otherwise UNEP would retain its current programs and location in Nairobi. The remaining components of the WEO could include some multi-lateral environmental agreements (MEAs) and other environmental programs.

The second option would be to establish a WEO that incorporates the UNEP, with the intention of dissolving UNEP into the new organization. This WEO could be created as a specialized agency pursuant to Article 59 of the U.N. Charter or could be a new type of agency more central to the U.N. The remaining components of the WEO could include some MEAs and other environmental programs. Under this option, one could locate the headquarters of the WEO in a location other than Nairobi. Some analysts say that the Nairobi location for UNEP sharply diminishes its effectiveness.

What would be the implications of one approach versus the other approach? At this level of generality, it is hard to say much definitively. Either organization could be well funded or poorly funded. For example, the transformation of the GATT to the WTO did not lead to a large increase in funding, initially. Either organization could attract MEAs or fail to. Either organization could promote and utilize science well. Either organization could carry out monitoring and reporting. Either organization could strengthen MEAs.

One difference may be predictable, however. The second option would provide for more reorganization and therefore stands a better chance of attaining greater program integration. Of course, putting issues within the same organization does not necessarily cause them to be integrated. For example, in seven years of operation, the WTO has done little to integrate consideration of goods and services.

I have indicated that a WEO could be a specialized agency or something else. What else? Under Article 22 of the U.N. Charter, the General Assembly may establish such subsidiary organs as it deems necessary. Thus, it would be possible for the General Assembly to establish a new hybrid organization for the environment with some of the autonomy of a specialized agency while still remaining at the center of the U.N. This could be justified on the grounds that environmental concerns are too intrinsic to the U.N.'s mission to be assigned to a "specialized" agency. The downside of this approach is that anything less than full status as a specialized agency would subject UNEP to the same bureaucratic discrimination that it now has in the U.N. system, where U.N. bureaucrats reportedly still call UNEP a "second rate" agency.

C. UNILATERAL ENVIRONMENTAL ACTION

Is Force Justified? Michael K. Murphy, "Achieving Economic Security with Swords as Ploughshares: The Modern Use of Force to Combat Environmental Degradation" 39 Va. J. Int'l L. 1181 (1999).

The laws of war have always permitted nations to use force in a manner consistent with contemporary rules. These norms permitting or forbidding the use of force have been in a constant flux, changing as the needs and structure of the international community evolve. For the predominant portion of written history, war decision law rested upon the just war doctrine, allowing nations to resort to war in order to serve their own perceived good ends. The theory of just war encompassed a wide spectrum of ideals that suited the international structure of the time, including Athenian theories of justice, religious "holy wars" and the Christian Just War Doctrine, and finally the secular natural law period, symbolized by Hugo Grotius. At the end of the sixteenth century, the international system underwent a metamorphosis that saw the rise of modern nation states and the emergence of the concept of sovereignty. Termed the positivist era, this new system emphasized the sovereign's right to use force as an instrument of foreign policy and to intervene whenever necessary to limit revolutionary forces.

The twentieth century has witnessed several shifts in the war decision law, or the jus ad bellum. The international community ended the positivist era with an attempt to restrict recourse to war after World War I in the League of Nations system.* After World War II, the community again attempted to create a system limiting the sovereign right to use force with the U.N. Charter system. The Charter system itself has not been static, nor should it be in the future. Political paradigm shifts in the international community and pressing problems facing the community have forced the Charter system to alter the norms permitting the use of force. One flash point that may force redefinition of the war decision law in the future is a growing emphasis on addressing threats to the environment and a suspicion that environmental disasters may require military intervention in the next century.

The world's changing environment and mankind's abuse of its resources have already involved the use of force in the recent past. On December 9, 1992, a small force of United States Marines landed on the beaches of Somalia to protect food and aid deliveries to combat the drought in the Africa rift region and bolster that nation's failing infrastructure. The United States entered the conflict in Somalia at its own behest, gaining United Nations ratification quickly after its offer of military assistance. The United Nations authorized a multinational force to use "all necessary means" to bring aid to the nation. A second

---

* The Covenant of the League of Nations imposed a duty upon states to arbitrate their differences before resorting to armed conflict. The parties of the Pact of Paris (the Kellogg–Briand Pact) further renounced war "as an instrument of national policy in their relations with one another" as a direct rejection of the positivist jus ad bellum.

incident involved the use of force by Canada to seize a Spanish fishing vessel on the high seas in 1995. Outraged by the European Union's continued over-fishing of high migratory stocks that threatened the economic viability of its eastern fishing industry, Canada used its naval forces to intimidate and ultimately capture a vessel on the high seas.

The above examples only highlight the possibility that military intervention may be necessary to protect vital national interests from serious environmental damage. Imagine the following scenario. Mexico constructs a nuclear reactor near the U.S. border that lacks proper financing, safeguards, or containment buildings in opposition to repeated protests of the American government. Could the U.S. use force to eliminate the reactor before it goes on-line? Alternatively, if the reactor suffered a Chernobyl-type incident and Mexico refused to notify or to accept help from the international community, could U.S. military forces react and intervene unilaterally to contain and combat further fallout damage? While the nuclear accident hypothetical is the most obvious example of environmental damage and may seem unlikely in today's present political climate, it is not hard to imagine other scenarios where a state may feel compelled to use military force to protect its own environment from destruction by other international actors. Intervention into an existing military conflict for the sole purpose of limiting damage to the environment caused by one of the combatants may represent another alternative scenario in favor of the use of force to enforce the laws of war.

The Security Council arguably would have the power to order military action to deal with environmental difficulties without the consent of the states involved under its Chapter VII powers. There is little controversy that the United Nations Security Council has the power to act in order to combat environmental threats to the peace that effect the international community. It is not certain, however, what right individual states have under the current jus ad bellum to resort to armed force to deal with environmental disasters or severe environmental violations by other states. Several commentators have mentioned the possibility of the unilateral use of force to address violations of international environmental law, but few have fully investigated the matter under the current jus ad bellum of the modern era.

A number of scholars have begun using the term "environmental security" to refer to a growing recognition that environmental concerns directly impact ideals of international security. In today's world, environmental disputes concerning scarce resources, pollution damage, or noncompliance with important multilateral treaty obligations pose growing threats to international security and directly impact individual states' security interests.

To date, assertions of self-defense in response to incursions short of an armed attack have involved the use of force for questionable underlying geopolitical motives. A claim of self-defense in order to protect a nation from serious harm resulting from environmental mismanagement by another state is totally different from previous state practice in the international community and may succeed where other, more political, claims of customary self-defense have failed.

First, the use of force to deal with serious environmental disasters does not appear to violate a strict reading of U.N. Charter Article 2(4). Since the use of force could be narrowly tailored to redress the environmental damage alone, the use of force would not be against the territorial integrity or political independence of any state. While forces may have to temporarily occupy portions of another state or seize delinquent fishing vessels, the level of force necessary to achieve limited goals may not violate the Charter's prohibition of force.

Secondly, the growing acceptance of environmental security and the emerging norms of environmental law may cushion any political fallout over armed intervention for self-defense purposes. As states recognize the threat that environmental violations can cause, they will be more willing to accept unilateral action to protect vital state interests with military force. India's conflict with Pakistan over refugees represents a valuable analogy to a state's use of force to combat environmental damage. In this case, Pakistan began a systematic persecution of the Hindu population of East Pakistan, causing an exodus to India of as many as ten million East Pakistanis in a nine-month period. Faced with the heavy economic and social burden of caring for the refugees, India invaded on December 5, 1971, and replaced Pakistani rule with a newly independent state. India faced no international outrage at its use of force and the Security Council took no action. The General Assembly passed a resolution that merely called for the end of violence, refusing to condemn India for its actions. There can be no doubt that India acted to protect its own self-interest, as well as save lives in East Pakistan, unilaterally without first receiving an armed attack. Faced with massive refugee pressures, India simply had no choice but to act. While technically its actions went against the U.N. Charter regime, the international community accepted the intervention as a legitimate use of the inherent right of self-defense.

Similarly, a state faced with tangible environmental damage may find it necessary to act to protect its own self-interests. If the Security Council fails to act, as it has many times in the past, a state cannot be forced to stand by idly and watch itself suffer harm because environmental devastation cannot be qualified under Article 51 as an armed attack. Serious environmental destruction, if not dealt with expeditiously, may result in consequences that mirror an armed attack, namely threat to life and serious property damage. In this respect, the values of the U.N. Charter are upheld by allowing a state to react to address the environment, an issue that is growing on every nation's current political agenda. Allowing a state to deal with environmental crises with military force comports with the spirit of the Charter and follows the customary rules surrounding the use of force.

In order for any use of force in self-defense to be legal, however, it must qualify under the Caroline test for necessity and proportionality. The opportunity for abuse of any recognized right to use force cannot be understated. A use of force to deal with environmental disasters must be strictly construed against the requirements of necessity and proportionality. Thus, the threat must be imminent and present the possibility of great harm. There must be no alternative to force in avoiding the threat. In addition, the response must be proportionate to the danger. It must be narrowly construed to deal only with the disaster both in location and timeliness. These requirements ensure that the principles of the Charter are respected, limiting force to situations as dangerous to a state as an armed attack.

For example, the Canadian use of force to deal with overfishing of migratory stocks must be considered an illegality under the current jus ad bellum of self-defense. While the destruction of Canadian economic welfare is certainly serious, the threat was not imminent. There was time to negotiate a settlement through peaceful means and other avenues open to Canada short of force. Further, any use of force that threatened greater destruction than the interest protected would fail the proportionality test. The self-defense must be a last resort and the force must be equivalent to the treat. Analysis of most environmental violations will likely mirror this conclusion. A nation that violates CFC emission standards in violation of the Montreal Protocol or a nation that violates the Convention on International Trade in Endangered Species of Wild Fauna and Flora ivory import quotas will obviously cause harm to the environment of some states, or all states. The harmed states, however, could never claim self-defense by using military means to enforce the violated norms, but would instead be relegated to utilizing the existing law of state responsibility to redress any harms. The recourse to force must be the last option available for survival and the harm threatened must be nearly equivalent logically, not legally, to an armed attack. Environmental obligations that deal with biodiversity, atmospheric protection, or other goals are too far-sighted and will never meet this standard. The threat or the harm does not hurt enough for the use of force.

On the other hand, a scenario similar to the Chernobyl hypothetical will likely give rise to the right of self-defense. A nation that suffers massive radiation or toxic pollution from another member of the international community who refuses to adequately deal with the situation can easily satisfy the Caroline standard. This pollution must be the result of a massive one-time accident to qualify under the necessity prong of the test. A slow build-up can be dealt with through other peaceful means of negotiation, mediation, or arbitration. An accident that releases large amounts of toxic or radioactive gas, however, meets the immediacy requirement. The military response must be aimed at bringing a quick end to the crisis and must not last longer than necessary. Any deviation from the strict requirement of proportionality would quickly turn the intervention into an illegal act of aggression. Therefore, military force may only be used in self-defense if the environmental crisis threatens a state with immediate harm on the same level as an armed attack, threatening life and widespread property damage. If the state is left with no other viable options, it may act to unilaterally protect its own environment.

Unilateral Environmental Action. Dan Bodansky, "What's So Bad about Unilateral Action to Protect the Environment?" Euro. J. Int'l L. 339 (2000).

Like many concepts, we tend to know unilateralism when we see it. The Canadian assertion of environmental jurisdiction over Arctic waters in 1970 and its arrest of a Spanish fishing vessel in 1995; the British bombing of the *Torrey Canyon* oil tanker in 1967; the United States trade restrictions on tuna and shrimp caught in ways that harm dolphins and sea turtles respectively—in all of these cases, one state proceeded independently, on its own authority, with minimal (if any) involvement by other nations. That is the nub of unilateralism.

Defining what makes unilateralism problematic, however, is more difficult. In most instances, states are entitled to act unilaterally. That is the essence of sovereignty. In demarcating the problem of "unilateralism," the issue is to define when a state's right to act as a sovereign—that is, to act unilaterally—is appropriate, and when it should yield to an international decision-making process.

The preference for international action to address environmental problems is easy to understand. When an environmental problem has sources in many countries, it is beyond the control of any single country and requires collective action to combat effectively. When it has effects that cross an international border, then multiple parties have a stake in the problem and therefore a legitimate claim to take part in the decision-making process. An even when both the causes and the effects of an environmental problem are confined to a single country, the increasing integration of the global economy makes different national standards potentially disruptive, and suggests the need for greater harmonization.

But, although all of these factors point to the desirability, in the long term, of multilateral approaches to address environmental problems, unilateral action can still serve important functions. First, unilateral action, or its threatened use, has often played a critical role in the development of international standards to protect the environment. In the evolution of the international regime to prevent oil pollution, for example, unilateral action helped catalyse international standard-setting at many key steps along the way. In 1967, for example, the bombing by Great Britain of the *Torrey Canyon* to protect its coastal waters from a massive oil spill led to negotiation of the 1969 Intervention Convention, which recognizes the right of coastal states to take unilateral measures "to prevent grave and imminent danger to their coastline" from oil pollution. Similarly, in the 1970s, the threat by the United States to impose unilaterally double-hull standards on oil tankers entering its ports spurred the international community to adopt the 1973 MARPOL Convention and its 1978 Protocol.

The seemingly paradoxical role of unilateral action in promoting multilateral standard-setting is not difficult to explain. It is a familiar phenomenon in the development of customary international law, where unilateral national actions, sometimes of doubtful legality, can stimulate similar actions by other states, leading to the emergence of a new customary norm. The development of the continental shelf doctrine and the exclusive economic zone, in response to unilateral extensions of national jurisdiction, are prominent examples of this lawmaking process. In the environmental realm, multilateral negotiations are particularly prone to bog down, and tend to gravitate to the least common denominator, given the increasing reliance on consensus decision making. In this context, the threat of unilateral national regulation, which other states wish to forestall, can be one of the principal motivations to develop international standards.

Finally, although international law often seems to contain a presumption in favor of multilateralism, it is good to remember that, in general, unilateral action (sovereignty) remains the norm in environmental policy and international action the exception, requiring special justification. This is the message contained in the principle of subsidiarity (or, in the United States, federalism): policies should be addressed at the lowest governmental level possible. Even in an increasingly interconnected world, not every environmental problem requires a collective response. Where possible, states should be allowed to pursue their own environmental values and policies. The problem is to draw the dividing line between issues that require a multilateral response, and those where states can properly act on their own. The GATT Uruguay Round agreements create a presumption in favor of multilateral product standards, in order to promote free trade, and require states to provide some scientific basis for stricter national laws. But, as the *Beef Hormones* case suggests, it remains to be seen whether this is a workable test for distinguishing between a valid exercise of sovereignty by a state in pursuing national environmental values, and an improper, unilateral deviation from the international norm. Determining which actions fall into which category is likely to occupy the attention of international environmental lawyers for years to come.

D. TRADE LINKAGES

Trade-Environmental Disputes. Kevin C. Kennedy, "The Illegality of Unilateral Trade Measures to Resolve Trade–Environment Disputes" 22 Wm. & Mary Envtl. L. & Pol'y Rev. 375 (1998).

World trade and foreign investment have grown dramatically in the post-war era. Levels of environmental degradation and natural resource depletion have increased as well during that period. Some observers consider trade liberalization and environmental degradation to be locked in a direct cause-effect relationship. Some commentators view this development with concern, while others, primarily environmentalists, view the poor fit between trade and environment with alarm. A few environmentalists have even demanded an end to free trade. They argue that with free trade comes economic growth, and with economic growth comes unacceptable levels of pollution. Because market mechanisms do not always take full account of environmental costs, some environmentalists argue, a legal climate that promotes unbridled free trade could contribute to the unrestricted, transborder movement of hazardous products and waste. The linkages and frictions, both legal and economic, between trade and the environment are undeniable. Admittedly, the fit of international trade law and international environmental law is not well tailored. Trade and environment policies have proceeded at times on diverging tracks, at times on parallel tracks, and at other times on the same track but headed on a collision course.

The United States and the other Members of the WTO have committed to a comprehensive international trade law regime under the auspices of which all trade-environment disputes are to be resolved in a multilateral/bilateral forum. The core GATT obligations not to discriminate against imports regardless of their origin, the obligation not to discriminate against imports vis-à-vis the domestic like product, and the commitment not to impose quotas on imports create a legal framework that ensures that trade in goods will not be impeded. Regardless of whether this legal regime now is deemed to be harmful to the environment, the inescapable fact is that the United States and the other WTO Members have made a legal commitment to these rules. Unilateralism has been forsworn.

Beyond these three core GATT obligations, the Uruguay Round Agreements dealing with sanitary and phytosanitary measures, technical measures, subsidies, and dispute resolution put a substantial amount of flesh on the bare bones of the core GATT commitments. The scope of these agreements is broad. They establish a comprehensive legal regime that regulates the imposition of border measures on the grounds of health, safety, and other environmental concerns. The binding dispute settlement mechanism established under the Dispute Settlement Understanding gives WTO Members an adequate forum for resolving trade-environment disputes bilaterally. Once again, unilateral responses to trade-environment disputes are rejected.

The GATT–WTO rules are deeply sensitive to the fact that a national regulation that is nominally for the protection of the environment may be pretextual, that is, it may be nothing more than a thinly disguised trade protectionist measure. The Stockholm Declaration does not directly address the question of the impact of environmental regulation on growth and international trade. The Rio Declaration does provide in three places a broad framework for harmonizing environmental and trade concerns, essentially giving trade issues primacy over environmental concerns in the event the two conflict. In Principles 11, 12, and 16, the Rio Declaration specifically warns that pursuing aggressive environmental policies may have a potentially adverse impact on international trade.

States should cooperate to promote a supportive and open international economic system that would lead to economic growth and sustainable development in all countries, to better address the problems of environmental degradation. Trade policy measures for environmental purposes should not constitute a means of arbitrary or unjustifiable discrimination or a disguised restriction on international trade. *Unilateral actions to deal with environmental challenges outside the jurisdiction of the importing country should be avoided.* Environmental measures addressing transboundary or global environmental problems should, as far as possible, be based on an international consensus.

If the Stockholm and Rio Declarations are reasonably accurate reflections of world opinion on the interrelationship of trade and the environment, then a consensus exists that economic growth should not be sacrificed or the open world trading system wrecked in the name of environmental protection. Both Declarations encourage states to reflect carefully before pursuing economic policies that could damage the environment. Conversely, both Declarations urge states to exercise restraint and avoid environmental policies that could damage the world trading system it took fifty painstaking years to build.

Chapter 11

ECONOMIC GLOBALIZATION

Editors' introduction: Most of the law that we study, whether international or national, deals with compensatory justice. The law ideally can "right a wrong," that is, restore the parties to the *ex ante* position that was in place before one of them violated the rights of the other. But there is another kind of justice, namely, distributive justice. This is a justice that the courts cannot handle. Yet it is of the utmost concern to the people of the world. Is it possible for international law to take on the supremely challenging project of opening the global economy to equal opportunity and reducing or eliminating the excesses of monopolistic practices or national hegemonic intrusions? As you read the excerpts in this chapter, keep in mind the recurrent question: "What can international law do to rectify the unjust imbalances in the standard of living of the world's differently situated persons?"

A. ECONOMIC GLOBALIZATION AND INTERNATIONAL LAW

The Changing Role of States. Alfred C. Aman, Jr., "The Globalizing State: A Future–Oriented Perspective on the Public/Private Distinction, Federalism, and Democracy" 31 Vand. J. Transnat'l L. 769 (1998).

Globalization refers to complex, dynamic legal and social processes that take place within an integrated whole, without regard to geographical boundaries. Globalization thus differs from international activities that occur between and among states, and it differs from multinational activities that occur in more than one nation-state. The area of integration involved might be the entire globe or it might be a region or portions of regions around the world. The major distinguishing characteristic of global activities is that the areas of integration are largely oblivious to state boundaries, and that the processes of globalization usually occur without or with little direct agency of the state. Due to the liberating effects of technology and the flow of capital around the world, private decisions involving production, finance, and investment increasingly occur without direct, individual state involvement. Transnational corporations decide where it is most cost-effective to locate various activities in the value chains connected with the production and marketing of goods and services. They may locate research and development in one country, component assembly in another, final assembly in yet another country, and distribution networks in yet another. They also decide how much to customize the globally conceived product for local markets.

These factors, of course, do not mean that states are no longer important or do not have influence upon aspects of global business activities or problems. It does mean that the role states play is substantially different than in the past: the global economic opportunities and problems that result from these financial, production, and investment networks are not centered in states or within any one state; nor can problems involving, for example, the environment or public health be solved by one state alone. Any one state's jurisdiction to deal with these issues is limited in such contexts. As a result, new bodies of global and international law are developing to address issues that are neither wholly domestic nor wholly international. The distribution of problems outside any one state heightens the need for states to share or delegate power and responsibility to other states and an increasing number of non-state transnational actors, actors that are more powerful than ever before.

This is especially true of transnational corporations. Their power is not a traditional form of state power derived from control over resources within a geographical territory. Rather, it is a kind of structural political power derived from being an important participant in economic decisions. Transnational corporations can indirectly wield economic power that has very substantial political consequences for individual states and the municipalities within those states. A decision to shift production from one part of the world to another can drastically affect the economy of a particular area. Even the threat to do so can affect local policymakers. Transnational corporations do not dictate public policy to the states, but the potential impact of their decisions facilitates the flow of power from states to markets, as do technologies and the integration and interdependence of increasingly global markets. This shift of power is reflected in the changing role of and impact upon domestic, state-centered law and politics.

Globalization does not necessarily mean the end or the diminution of law, especially if one takes into account the need for and the creation of new forms of global law. For example, transnational corporations have a distinct need for dispute resolution techniques that are not directly linked to any one country, and elaborate and important arbitration procedures have been developing to meet these needs. Similarly, human rights have been conceptualized in ways that transcend any one state's view of these issues, and local courts have applied the rulings of the European Court of Justice to dramatically change local law. Indeed, in a global world, legal pluralism is increasing, as is the capacity for and the actual growth of various forms of global law.

State-centered law still needs to deal with problems that arise wholly or primarily within its own territories. Criminal law issues, local property rights, zoning laws, and the like, are state-centered, though they are very much affected by the integrated global economy in which they operate. This is particularly true of social and economic regulation, be it health, safety, and the environment, or electric and natural gas rate-making. The failure to understand the links between seemingly local issues and the global economy within which they arise, however, can lead to a mismatch between the conceptualization of regulatory problems by state-centered politicians and policymakers, and transnational actors, who must take a global perspective on how they operate their businesses and what markets they seek to reach. National and local goals and legal objectives may be at odds with or irrelevant to the demands of a global market and the global competition faced by certain industries. An individual state's reaction to nationally perceived problems cannot create a level playing field for all who do business within its borders, since integrated global markets mean that a variety of other legal regimes are involved in such a company's processes. Cost comparisons must be made among various jurisdictions and the results of these comparisons often drive investment and manufacturing decisions.

More fundamentally, the structural make-up of web-like companies that transcend state, regional, and national boundaries makes a territorially-centered, hierarchical law more problematic than when businesses—even multinational businesses—were focused on a single locale. State-centered law, with its natural hierarchy of authority in the courts, coupled with its conceptual ability to categorize certain issues and problems in ways that create domestic law capable of consistent and fair application, can be at odds with business operations whose territories are unrelated to state borders, as well as the pace of economic and technological change in many global industries. Markets and the flexibility of market responses to problems often seem a more appropriate response to the problems faced by and opportunities presented to business entities that operate globally. This more fluid sense of place arises not only because transnational companies are capable of doing business simultaneously in various states, but because of wholly national entities that seek to export their products to various developing worldwide markets. Since more potential and real marketplaces are involved, more factors affecting economic conditions are in play, necessitating quicker reactions and changes on the part of even those companies whose facilities are located wholly within a particular state, but which seek to sell their products on a global basis.

Quite apart from the fact that certain kinds of business operations do not adhere to state boundaries as they once did, other kinds of human concerns are clearly beyond the organization of our national economies and are not susceptible to regulation by any one state. Environmental problems, for example, know no particular bounds, as most pollution travels freely across state and national borders. Problems such as acid rain, greenhouse gases, ozone depletion, and the like, require multiple parties to agree before law may provide any effective solutions. In short, a state cannot exercise effective authority alone when the problems it is trying to solve or the actors it wishes to regulate are not centered within the state's borders. To the extent that these issues are state-based, such a location usually is only temporary and easily shifted. Thus, the decrease in state-centered regulatory power is a result that flows primarily from the nature of global problems, the global reach of the technologies involved, and the relative mobility and freedom of the transnational actors to which the law would apply.

A New International Architecture. Saskia Sassen, "The State and Economic Globalization: Any Implications for International Law?" 1 Chi. J. Int'l L. 109 (2000).

The emergence of a mostly private international institutional order wherein the strategic agents are not the national governments of leading countries, but a variety of private actors, may well have the effect of reducing the scope and exclusivity of international law. Further, this new institutional order also has normative authority—a new normativity that is not embedded in what has been (and to some extent remains) the master normativity of modern times, raison d'etat. Here my question to international law experts is whether these new conditions can reduce the normative power of international law. This new normativity comes from the world of private power yet installs itself in the public realm and in so doing contributes to de-nationalizing what had historically been geared towards national state projects and goals. One of the marking features of this new institutional order is its capacity to privatize what was heretofore public and to de-nationalize what were once national resources and policy agendas. This capacity to privatize and de-nationalize is both a cause and a result of specific transformations of the national state, or more precisely, of some of its components.

My argument here is not that we are seeing the end of states but, rather, that states are not the only or the most important strategic agents in the new configuration. Second, states, including dominant states, have undergone profound transformations as they become the institutional home for the operation of some of the dynamics that are central to globalization. This raises a question about what is actually "national" in some of the institutional components of states linked to the implementation and regulation of economic globalization. The hypothesis here would be that some components of national institutions, even though formally national, are not national in the sense in which we have constructed the meaning of that term over the last hundred years. Here my question to international law experts is whether such a change will weaken or alter the organizational architecture for the implementation of international law insofar as the latter depends on the institutional apparatus of national states.

One of the roles of the state vis-à-vis today's global economy, unlike earlier phases of the world economy, has been to negotiate the intersection of national law and foreign actors—whether firms, markets, or supranational organizations. This condition makes the current phase distinctive in a number of ways. We have, on the one hand, the existence of an enormously elaborate body of law developed in good measure over the last hundred years which secures the exclusive territorial authority of national states to an extent not seen in earlier centuries, and on the other, the considerable institutionalizing, especially in the 1990s, of the "rights" of non-national firms, cross-border transactions, and supranational organizations. This sets up the conditions for a necessary engagement by national states in the process of globalization.

The emergent, often imposed, consensus in the community of states to further globalization has created a set of specific obligations on participating states. The state remains as the ultimate guarantor of the "rights" of global capital, in other words, the protection of contracts and property rights. Thus the state has incorporated the global project of its own shrinking role in regulating economic transactions. Firms operating transnationally want to ensure the functions traditionally exercised by the state in the national realm of the economy, notably guaranteeing property rights and contracts. The state here can be conceived of as representing a technical administrative capacity which cannot be replicated at this time by any other institutional arrangement; furthermore, this is a capacity backed by military power, with global power in the case of some states.

This guarantee of the rights of capital is embedded in a certain type of state, a certain conception of the rights of capital, and a certain type of international legal regime. It is largely embedded in the states of the most developed and most powerful countries in the world, in Western notions of contract and property rights, and in a new legal regime aimed at furthering economic globalization. The U.S. as the hegemonic power of this period has led/forced other states to adopt these obligations towards global capital. And, in so doing, it has strengthened the economic forces and private actors that can challenge its power. The state continues to play a crucial, though no longer exclusive, role in the production of legality around new forms of economic activity, but increasingly this role has fed the power of a new emerging structure.

From the angle of my research, we can list at least the following possible consequences for international law. First, the fact of a growth in cross-border activities and global actors operating outside the formal interstate system affects the competence and scope of international law. Second, the fact that this domain is increasingly being institutionalized and subjected to the development of private governance mechanisms affects the exclusivity of international law. Third, the fact of growing normative powers in this private domain affects the normative power of international law. Fourth, the state's participation in the re-regulation of its role in the economy and the incipient de-nationalization of particular institutional components of the state necessary to accommodate some of the new policies linked to globalization transform key aspects of the state and in so doing alter the organizational architecture for international law.

Holding Business Accountable. David Weissbrodt and Muria Kruger, "Norms on the Responsibilities of Transnational Corporations and Other Business Enterprises with Regard to Human Rights" 97 A.J.I.L. 901 (2003).

On August 13, 2003, the United Nations Sub–Commission on the Promotion and Protection of Human Rights approved the "Norms on the Responsibilities of Transnational Corporations and Other Business Enterprises with Regard to Human Rights" (Norms) in its Resolution 2003/16. The Norms represent a landmark step in holding businesses accountable for their human rights abuses and constitute a succinct, but comprehensive, restatement of the international legal principles applicable to businesses with regard to human rights, humanitarian law, international labor law, environmental law, consumer law, anticorruption law, and so forth.

Throughout the past half century, states and international organizations have continued to expand the codification of international human rights law protecting the rights of individuals against governmental violations. In parallel with increasing attention to the development of international criminal law as a response to war crimes, genocide, and other crimes against humanity, there has been growing attention to individual responsibility for grave human rights abuses. The creators of this ever-larger web of human rights obligations, however, failed to pay sufficient attention to some of the most powerful nonstate actors in the world, that is, transnational corporations and other business enterprises. With power should come responsibility, and international human rights law needs to focus adequately on these extremely potent international nonstate actors.

Transnational corporations evoke particular concern in relation to recent global trends because they are active in some of the most dynamic sectors of national economies, such as extractive industries, telecommunications, information technology, electronic consumer goods, footwear and apparel, transport, banking and finance, insurance, and securities trading. They bring new jobs, capital, and technology. Some corporations make real efforts to achieve international standards by improving working conditions and raising local living conditions. They certainly are capable of exerting a positive influence in fostering development.

Some transnational corporations, however, do not respect minimum international human rights standards and can thus be implicated in abuses such as employing child laborers, discriminating against certain groups of employees, failing to provide safe and healthy working conditions, attempting to repress independent trade unions, discouraging the right to bargain collectively, limiting the broad dissemination of appropriate technology and intellectual property, and dumping toxic wastes. Some of these abuses disproportionately affect developing countries, children, minorities, and women who work in unsafe and poorly paid production jobs, as well as indigenous communities and other vulnerable groups.

There is also increasing reason to believe that greater respect for human rights by companies leads to greater sustainability in emerging markets and better business performance. For example, observance of human rights aids businesses by protecting and maintaining their corporate reputation, and creating a stable and peaceful society in which they can prosper and attract the best and brightest employees. Moreover, consumers have demonstrated that they are willing to pay attention to standards and practices used by a business that observes human rights and may even boycott products that are produced in violation of human rights standards. Similarly, there is evidence that a growing proportion of investors is seeking to purchase shares in socially responsible companies. All in all, business enterprises have increased their power in the world. International, national, state, and local lawmakers are realizing that this power must be confronted, and that the human rights obligations of business enterprises, in particular, must be addressed.

Accordingly, the Norms help to establish a level playing field for competition. Clarifying their duties may actually benefit businesses, as a growing body of evidence is demonstrating that compliance with human rights standards enhances a company's bottom line. Consumers are often willing to take the human rights conduct of a business into account in making their purchasing decisions. Nowadays, businesses are also more likely to be exposed to liability for conduct that violates human rights standards. Clarification would help businesses to determine whether they should pursue a proposed course of conduct that might expose them to liability, consumer backlash, investor flight, and/or loss of the best and brightest employees. Some companies have already expressed support for the Norms and agreed to apply them in their own operations as a way of affirming their commitment to the Universal Declaration of Human Rights.

Further, the Norms can strengthen the will of governments to insist that businesses avoid human rights abuses. Governments faced with the economic power of large companies will be assisted by the Norms in identifying and thus applying the minimum international standards that relate to the conduct of such companies.

Implementation remains a key issue in the future development of these standards. While the Norms contain rudimentary mechanisms for implementation, the next task for the United Nations, states, businesses, and others will be to continue to search for and elaborate more effective methods of implementation.

B. WORLD TRADE ORGANIZATION

The WTO and International Law. Joost Pauwelyn, "The Role of Public International Law in the WTO: How Far Can We Go?" 95 A.J.I.L. 535 (2001).

With one possible exception, no academic author (or any WTO decision or document) disputes that WTO rules are part of the wider corpus of public international law. Like international environmental law and human rights law, WTO law is "just" a branch of public international law. To public international lawyers, my call in the April 2000 issue of this *Journal* for WTO rules to "be considered as creating international legal obligations that are part of public international law" is a truism. To many negotiators and other WTO experts in Geneva, however, it comes as a surprise. Not a single legal argument has been (or, in my view, can be) put forward in their support. The fact that many negotiators of the WTO treaty (in numerous countries representatives of a trade ministry de-linked from that of foreign affairs) did not *think* of public international law when drafting the WTO treaty is not a valid legal argument. At most, it amounts to an excuse for the WTO treaty not to have dealt more explicitly with the relationship between WTO rules and other rules of international law.

Stating that WTO rules are just a part of public international law is one thing. It is quite another to submit that there is nothing special about WTO rules. In many respects WTO rules are *lex specialis* as opposed to general international law. But contracting out of *some* rules of general international law (for example, as does the WTO dispute settlement mechanism vis-à-vis certain rules of general international law on state responsibility) does not mean that one has contracted out of *all* of them, nor a fortiori that WTO rules were created completely outside the system of international law. Much has been written about so-called self-contained regimes. However, all references to this notion concerned certain international legal regimes (in particular, those of diplomatic immunities, the European Community, and human rights treaties) that, in terms of their compliance mechanism or secondary rules, may somehow be self-contained, without any or only limited "fallback" on general international law. No one has spoken of self-contained regimes in the sense of treaty regimes that are completely isolated from all rules of general international law (including the law on treaties, judicial proceedings, and matters such as the use of force and human rights), let alone treaty regimes concluded completely outside the international legal system. As noted above, states, in their treaty relations, can contract out of one, more, or, in theory, all rules of general international law (other than those of *jus cogens*), but they cannot contract out of the system of international law. As soon as states contract with one another, they do so automatically and necessarily within the system of international law.

WTO rules are thus rules of international law that, in certain respects, constitute *lex specialis* vis-a-vis certain rules of general international law. However, this does not mean that WTO rules are *lex specialis* vis-à-vis all rules of international law. WTO rules regulate the trade relations between states (as well as separate customs territories). Nonetheless, in today's highly interdependent world, a great number, if not most, state regulations in one way or another affect trade flows between states. Hence, WTO rules, essentially aimed at liberalizing trade, have a potential impact on almost all other segments of society and law. For example, liberalizing trade may sometimes jeopardize respect for the environment or human rights. Equally, enforcing respect for human rights or environmental standards may sometimes require the imposition of trade barriers.

Moreover, trade restrictions are resorted to increasingly in pursuit of all kinds of nontrade objectives, ranging from respect for human rights and the environment to confirmation of territorial borders. Such resort creates a huge potential for interaction between WTO rules and other rules of international law, as WTO rules cut across almost all other rules of international law. It also means that in certain respects these "all-affecting" WTO rules are framework rules only or *lex generalis*. Indeed, the WTO forms a general and increasingly universal framework for all (or almost all) of the trade relations between states. Although GATT/WTO rules replaced a myriad of other bilateral and regional arrangements, they do allow for certain more detailed or further-reaching regional and bilateral arrangements, as well as a series of exceptions related to the environment and national security, among other things. In these respects, WTO trade liberalization rules are general or *lex generalis* permitting the continuation or creation of more focused or detailed rules of international law (such as certain rules on the environment, human rights, or the law of the sea, as well as on customs unions and free trade areas). In this sense, WTO rules are not the alpha and omega of all possible trade relations between states. Other, more detailed or special rules of international law (in terms of either subject matter or the number of states bound by them) continue to be highly relevant.

Much has been said so far on how to solve conflicts between rules of international law. A logically prior step, however, is to define when two rules actually contradict each other. International law recognizes a presumption against conflict. The presumption derives from the fact that all international law is created in the context of preexisting law, which continues to exist unless new law overturns it. The presumption is grounded on the absence of any inherent legal hierarchy between existing and new rules of international law (other than *jus cogens*). In the context of assessing whether two specific treaty norms are indeed in conflict, it means that states negotiating a new treaty will have the old treaty in mind and continue to abide by it unless explicit wording to the contrary shows the drafters' intention to deviate from it. Thus, it is assumed that the later rule builds on and follows what the earlier rule has said. In most cases, potential conflicts can be "interpreted away."

Imagine, for example, that a WTO rule imposes an obligation not to restrict certain trade flows, but a later non-WTO rule (say, an environmental convention) grants an explicit right to restrict trade. Under the strict definition of legal conflict, set out above, there would be no conflict. Indeed, complying with the WTO rule (not restricting trade flows) would not mean violating the later environmental rule. It would simply mean forgoing the right (to restrict trade) granted by the environmental rule. In the absence of a conflict, the *lex posterior* rule of Article 30 would not even be activated. Thus, the (stricter) WTO rule would simply apply over and above the new (more lenient) environmental rule, not as a result of conflict rules but as a result of the very definition of conflict. However, for the new environmental rule to have any effect, it should be recognized that in these circumstances as well there *is* conflict, namely, conflict between an obligation in the WTO and an explicit right granted elsewhere. Here, too, the later-in-time rule should prevail, in principle. If not, one would consistently elevate obligations in international law over and above rights in international law. Consequently, it must be possible for an explicit right to restrict trade, agreed upon by certain or all WTO members either in or outside the WTO, to overrule a WTO obligation of free trade.

The practical consequences of a defending party's ability to invoke, for example, a rule of customary law, or an environmental or human rights convention or bilateral treaty to which both disputing parties are bound, in its defense against a WTO claim, must be determined by the relevant conflict rules. These rules may be spelled out in the WTO treaty itself, the treaty from which the contradictory rule derives, or general international law. If the relevant conflict rule indicates that the WTO rule in question prevails over the conflicting norm of international law, the WTO rule must be applied (and the complainant wins). If, in contrast, the relevant conflict rule demonstrates that the other rule of international law overrides or even invalidates the WTO rule, then the WTO rule cannot be applied (and the defendant wins), irrespective of whether the WTO treaty itself includes an exception or justification for the measure at hand. The latter case, however, does not result in requiring the WTO panel to judicially enforce the other rule of international law (say, the contradictory environmental norm). A WTO panel can only enforce claims under WTO covered agreements. To be able to enforce these other rules, a WTO panel would need expanded jurisdiction. Recalling the two levels at which WTO covered agreements operate (the general level of the entire corpus of international law, and the more concrete level of WTO dispute settlement), we can conclude that what has been taken away or overruled at the first level can no longer be enforced at the second level (i.e., a WTO rule that has been terminated or overruled under international law can no longer be enforced in WTO dispute settlement). What WTO members themselves have taken out of WTO covered agreements at the first level cannot be put back by a WTO panel in the second level. For a panel to do so anyway would amount to (using the words of [Dispute Settlement Understanding] Articles 3.2 and 19.2) "adding" to obligations of the defendant that, pursuant to other rules of international law and the way they interact with WTO rules, no longer exist. If a panel follows the approach suggested here and disapplies the WTO rule in these circumstances, the panel would not be "diminishing" the rights of the complainant. Rather, the complaining WTO member would have done so by agreeing to the conflicting non-WTO rule in the first place. Thus, the WTO panel would not create law but merely give effect to law created elsewhere by the WTO member itself. On the other hand, for claims under these non-WTO rules to filter through to the second level of WTO dispute resolution, an express intention to expand the jurisdiction of WTO panels would be required.

Treaty Protocol. Sabrina Safrin, "Treaties in Collision? The Biosafety Protocol and the World Trade Organization Agreements" 96 A.J.I.L. 606 (2002).

On January 29, 2000, over 130 countries adopted the Cartagena Protocol on Biosafety to the Convention on Biological Diversity (Biosafety Protocol or Protocol). The Protocol establishes international procedures applicable to the transboundary movement of bioengineered living organisms (referred to in the Protocol as "living modified organisms," or "LMOs"). The adoption of the Protocol marked the close of over four years of intensive, contentious, and often emotional negotiations regarding the multibillion-dollar trade in bioengineered organisms.

Human beings have genetically modified plants and animals through domestication and controlled breeding for some ten thousand years with little controversy. Since 1973, however, modern biotechnology techniques have enabled the transfer of genes from one species to another unrelated species. For example, genes from a flounder known to survive in frigid waters have been transferred to tomatoes to make them resistant to frost; and genes from a natural soil bacterium (bacillus thuringiensis) have been transferred to potatoes and corn to make them resistant to certain insects.

These modern techniques and the products created by them have generated considerable debate. Some commentators have raised ethical and religious concerns that these techniques enable human beings to play God. Others have raised health concerns that genetic modifications might produce foods that trigger allergies. Still others have asserted that economic considerations argue against genetically modified crops because they might disrupt small-scale farming systems and encourage monoculture. Most important as regards the Biosafety Protocol, a multilateral environmental agreement, are environmental concerns that transgenic plants might transmit their genes to other crops or wild plants through pollen dispersal or may evolve into invasive species as their superior traits allow them to out-compete other plants. Thus, the objective of the Biosafety Protocol is to contribute to ensuring an adequate level of protection in the field of the safe transfer, handling and use of living modified organisms resulting from modern biotechnology that may have adverse effects on the conservation and sustainable use of biological diversity, taking also into account risks to human health, and specifically focusing on transboundary movements.

One of the most difficult and controversial issues that the negotiators of the Biosafety Protocol faced was how to deal with the relationship between the Protocol and other international agreements, particularly the General Agreement on Tariffs and Trade and associated agreements under the umbrella of the World Trade Organization such as the Agreement on the Application of Sanitary and Phytosanitary Measures and the Agreement on Technical Barriers to Trade (collectively, the WTO Agreements). At issue was whether the requirements of the Protocol would prevail if they should conflict with the requirements of the WTO Agreements. This question lies at the legal heart of the perceived conflict between trade globalization and environmental protection.

Under the rules of customary international law, which are reflected in this respect in the Vienna Convention on the Law of Treaties, in the event of an incompatibility between two successive agreements relating to the same subject matter, the requirements of the later agreement prevail. Where the later treaty includes only some of the parties to the earlier treaty, the later treaty prevails only with respect to those who are party to both agreements. Otherwise, the earlier agreement governs.

To date not a single multilateral environmental agreement or government action taken to implement such an agreement has been found to violate the WTO Agreements. Such formidable multilateral environmental agreements as the Convention on the International Trade in Endangered Species of 1973, the Montreal Protocol on Substances That Deplete the Ozone Layer (Montreal Protocol) of 1987, and the Basel Convention of 1989 preceded the Uruguay Trade Round of 1994 and the agreements that emerged from that round. As indicated in Article 30 of the Vienna Convention, the Uruguay Round agreements would prevail in the event of a conflict between them and the earlier environmental agreements. Despite considerable legal commentary on whether the trade provisions of these agreements violate WTO rules and concern that a challenge to such agreements could happen any day, no government has filed a complaint challenging such multilateral environmental agreements or actions taken by another government pursuant to such agreements. If anything, the operations of these trade-related multilateral environmental agreements appear remarkably unaffected by the later-in-time Uruguay Round agreements.

Ultimately, a WTO tribunal's decision on whether a country has violated its WTO obligations with respect to restrictions on the import of LMOs may depend on, and be tailored to, the facts of a particular case. Unlike the negotiators of the Protocol, who lived in a realm of hypotheticals, a WTO tribunal would have the benefit of a fact pattern before it. When the fact pattern indicates that a party's purported environmental or health decision or measure derives from a protectionist impulse or stems from cultural preferences rather than from bona fide health or environmental concerns, a WTO tribunal would be inclined to view such actions with suspicion and disfavor. When, however, a party bases its restriction on the import of an LMO on a scientifically grounded environmental or health concern, that restriction would presumably pass WTO muster.

International Law and Economic Inequality. Frank J. Garcia, "Trade and Inequality: Economic Justice and the Developing World" 21 Mich. J. Int'l L. 975 (2000).

Economic inequality among states continues to be a challenge for international trade law in the closing days of the 20th century and the opening of a new millennium. At the WTO's Third Ministerial Meeting in Seattle, Washington in the last month of 1999, developed country hopes for the grand inauguration of a multilateral "Millennium Round" were dashed by, among other protests, concerted resistance by developing countries to certain elements of the developed world's trade agenda. Representatives of the developing world voiced the sense that their concerns and participation were being marginalized, and that those already holding an unequal share of the world's natural and social resources continue to receive an unequal share of the gains from trade. Such opposition should have come as no surprise. Since the Uruguay Round was concluded in 1994, commentators have been evaluating the effects on developing countries of the Round and its progeny, the WTO, with mixed conclusions. Some argue that the WTO's dispute resolution system reflects a victory for the developing world because the system more fully subjects powerful developed countries to the rule of law in their international economic relations. Unfortunately, other aspects of the WTO agreements reveal costly concessions by developing countries, in areas such as agriculture, intellectual property and investment, in the hopes of securing compensating benefits in other areas. It is not clear that the gamble has paid off.

The same concerns hold true at a regional level. In our hemisphere, the neoliberal economic paradigm has resulted in profound trade-oriented domestic reforms by developing countries. U.S. hemispheric policy mirrors this "trade not aid" philosophy, both bilaterally and in the Free Trade Area of the Americas (FTAA) negotiations, thus placing trade, for good or ill, at the center of Latin America's development plans for the next several decades.

The problem of inequality between states is a problem in moral philosophy as well as trade law. Moral and political philosophy are concerned with the order we bring to our social relations, both on the level of individual decisions and relationships, and in terms of the basic structure of our social institutions. The problem of inequality in the distribution of wealth and resources is a basic, yet troublesome, aspect of social life which theorists have struggled with since the beginning of political thought. The problem can be analyzed in terms of the distribution of resources within states, or the distribution of resources between states. Within even quite wealthy states, the problem of distributive justice remains as pressing now as it ever was, with a continuing, pronounced gap between rich and poor persons.

The problem of inequality acquires an even greater significance across borders, because the gap between rich and poor states is far, far wider. Moreover, the sort of remedial programs implemented domestically by states to address inequality problems within their borders are quite underdeveloped at the international level. Finally, and perhaps most ominously, the impact of international trade on the fact of inequality is not neutral: the smaller economies characteristic of developing countries are uniquely vulnerable in trade because of such inequalities. In other words, international trade exacerbates existing problems in the distribution of resources, and creates new ones—the rich can get richer, and the poor poorer.

Since international trade seems destined to serve as the cornerstone of global economic and social policy, then developed and developing countries alike must be prepared to evaluate the structure and effects of international economic law in terms of its basic justice. If the developed world's economic relationship to the developing world is in fact governed by moral obligation, and not simply by the instrumental calculations of the moment, then there must be a normative framework within which to articulate the implications of this inequality. Within such a framework, basic doctrines and policies of international economic law can be designed and evaluated in terms of their effectiveness in discharging basic obligations of justice, thereby serving both the normative and pragmatic interests of the developed and the developing world alike.

C. LINKAGES: TRADE AND ...

Trade and Human Rights. Gabrielle Marceau, "WTO Dispute Settlement and Human Rights" 13 Euro. J. Int'l L. 753 (2002).

The relationship between the dispute settlement mechanism of the World Trade Organization and human rights law is only a small part of the wider issue of ethics and trade. The human rights aspects of trade actions cover a wide spectrum of moral, ethical, political, social and legal issues. Allegations of conflicts between, on the one hand, trade considerations and rules, and, on the other hand, respect for human rights, are regularly made. Some believe that WTO obligations somehow encourage, lead to, authorize or permit human rights violations, and that the WTO treaty should therefore be condemned. Others have argued that violators of human rights are necessarily also violators of WTO rules. Still others want to use human rights considerations to justify deviations from WTO market access rules or to make preferences and other advantages conditional on compliance with human rights. Some recall that WTO Members are liable for the human rights consequences of their trade actions. The inconsistent positions of states in human rights and trade fora are also often alleged. Many suggest that conflicts between systems of laws (trade and human rights) and therefore systems of values must ultimately be addressed as matters of policy through political arenas, and that dispute settlement, by itself, is unlikely to resolve the issues.

Unless otherwise prescribed, WTO provisions must evolve and be interpreted consistently with international law, including human rights law. It is suggested that a good faith interpretation of the relevant WTO and human rights provisions should lead to a reading of WTO law coherent with human rights law. The issue of whether WTO Members can invoke human rights law to refuse to comply with WTO obligations (including allegations of "conflicts" between WTO and other norms of international law) can only be adequately answered by examining the nature of the "WTO applicable law"—a specific subsystem of law—and the limited competence and jurisdiction of WTO adjudicating bodies.

International law recognizes *lex specialis* systems which provide a specific system of treaty control and remedies. It is doubtful that WTO Members wanted to make WTO remedies available for human rights enforcement.

Yet, even if their occurrence would be very rare, pure conflicts between WTO law and human rights, including *jus cogens*, are conceptually possible. In case of conflicts, WTO adjudicating bodies do not appear to have the competence either to reach any formal conclusion that a non-WTO norm has been violated, or to require any positive action pursuant to that treaty or any conclusion that would enforce a non-WTO norm over WTO provisions, as in doing so the WTO adjudicating bodies would effectively add to, diminish or amend the WTO "covered agreements." A distinction exists between the binding obligations of states (WTO Members)—for which states are at all times responsible—and the "applicable WTO law." "WTO applicable law" refers to the law binding on states, as WTO Members, which can be enforced (by effective remedies) by WTO adjudicating bodies which have been granted compulsory and exclusive jurisdiction over such WTO matters. A special focus is given to *jus cogens*. Arguably, because of its very nature, *jus cogens* would be part of all laws and thus would have direct effect in WTO law. The customary prohibition against any violation of *jus cogens* is such as to invalidate *ab initio* any violating provision, a legal reality that binds all states and all institutions. Situations of pure conflicts between WTO provisions and *jus cogens* are, however, difficult to conceive. In most, if not all, cases, the strong presumption against a violation of *jus cogens* will lead to an interpretation of WTO law which avoids such a violation. Some may argue that WTO panels and the Appellate Body do not have the capacity to determine the nullity of a WTO treaty provision for violation of *jus cogens*, as they only have the capacity to recommend that a national measure be brought into conformity with the covered agreements (although WTO provisions must be interpreted in taking into account relevant human rights law). In all cases, however, WTO Members in violation of human rights law remain subject to rules on state responsibility and liable for the consequences of that violation. In short, there is no perfect coherence between the human rights and WTO systems of law and jurisdiction.

Ethics and Trade. David W. Leebron, "The Boundaries of the WTO: Linkages" 96 A.J.I.L. 5 (2002).

Trade and the environment. Trade and workers' rights. Trade and competition policy. Trade and eighteen million tiny feet. It begins to resemble a question from an IQ test: which of the preceding pairs of issues does not fit? Increasingly, it seems there is no pairing with trade for which some argument cannot be made. The "trade and . . ." industry is booming.

The growth of the "trade and . . ." business derives from two converging forces. First, more issues are now regarded as trade related in the narrow sense that the norms governing those issues affect trade, or conversely, that changes in trade flows affect the realization of those norms. Second, an increasing number of substantive areas are the subject of international coordinated action or multilateral agreements. Even if conduct in such areas does not directly affect trade flows, the creation of formalized regimes governing them raises the question how such regimes should be related to the trade regime and whether, for example, trade sanctions should be employed to enforce nontrade policies and agreements. In three important areas—human rights, workers' rights, and environmental protection—claims are based in part on concerns for the welfare of those in other nations. Domestic measures alone cannot address such concerns, and means (short of war) are therefore sought to influence governments abroad.

These issues came to the fore in both official negotiations and street protests at the Third Ministerial Conference of the World Trade Organization held in Seattle in 1999. Many developed nations sought to link issues of environmental protection and labor standards to the trade negotiations, an effort that most developing nations vehemently opposed.

As regards substantive linkage claims, disagreement with their substance will usually be the principal reason for opposition. For example, one of the claims for linkage advanced by environmentalists and labor activists is that free trade encourages a "race to the bottom" in environmental and labor regulation. Free trade advocates, on the other hand, have disputed that basic claim, arguing that under free trade each nation will choose its own optimal policies. Linkage may be resisted simply on the ground that factual and theoretical assumptions on which the claim is based are wrong. Of course, even if the substantive claims for linkage are conceded to be valid, strategic considerations (as elaborated below) might still argue, on a national or global basis, against linkage.

Strategic claims for linkage cannot be disputed on the basis that there is an inadequate substantive relationship between the norms governing the two issue areas, as the claim is not based on any such relationship. Instead, opposition must be based on the costs and benefits, in terms of the expected result, of linking those areas.

Every linkage potentially raises strategic problems, whether or not the reason for the linkage is strategic. One reason for opposition is the self-interest of the participant. Put simply, a participant might perceive that the linkage will lead to a less favorable arrangement, taking the expected results on both issue areas into account and comparing the linked result with the unlinked result.

Even if all parties would benefit from the linkage, the skewness of those benefits might cause parties to engage in strategic behavior so as to redistribute the rewards. Some parties might seek to exploit the linkage, perhaps by making claims that they would not make in the absence of linkage. Assume, for example, that agriculture and intellectual property are the only two issues on the trade negotiation agenda, and that one country has virtually no interest in the agricultural negotiations but a very strong interest in the intellectual property negotiations. It will potentially be to that country's advantage to resist making concessions in the agricultural negotiations, even though it has no objection to them, in order to enhance its negotiating position in the intellectual property discussions. In this way, linkage potentially encourages strategic behavior.

Beyond such self-interested strategic considerations, the argument might sometimes be made that linkage will reduce the global benefits to be obtained from multilateral negotiations. First, linkage might undermine the ability of nations to reach a consensus on the agenda and the resolution of the issues. In many instances, the degree of consensus regarding the norms in the linked regimes will differ considerably. Linking highly divisive issues on which there is no point of agreement between the parties can potentially inhibit agreement on the entire group of linked issues, including those on which agreement would have been possible in the absence of the linked issues. In general, the greater the number of linked issues, and the more controversial those issues, the less likely it will be for an agreement to be reached. When, however, issues are controversial in the sense that most outcomes will have highly skewed distributional consequences, it may ease negotiations to link the issues to another controversial issue (assuming that distributional results are independent, and thus can be used together to reach an agreement that falls within the norm of negotiating reciprocity). Thus, one cannot argue as a general matter that strategic considerations militate for or against linkage; it will depend on the circumstances.

Second, linkage has the potential to undermine the normative framework for a particular regime or the degree of commitment to that regime. For example, inclusion of labor or environmental issues in the trade regime is likely more generally to lessen fidelity to the most-favored-nation clause, and could therefore more broadly subvert adherence to, and the definition of, the fundamental norms of that regime. Equally important, linkage or the expansion of the regime's scope might weaken the degree of commitment to the regime, in particular the enforcement mechanisms to which the parties are willing to agree. Thus, given the weak enforcement mechanisms agreed to for the International Labour Organization, the inclusion of labor issues within the WTO framework might be expected to result in lessening the comparatively strong dispute settlement and enforcement procedures now available for trade disputes. In short, linkage is just as likely to result in "ratcheting down" to a weaker regime as ratcheting up. This slippage might not occur at the time of linkage but later as a matter of practice.

Linking disparate issues into a single regime also poses the risk that the policy goals of one of the issue areas will predominate, so that the goals of one are effectively sacrificed to the other. This is a particular danger where diverse issue areas or distinct regimes are amalgamated into a single structure, and the institutional structure or bureaucratic players favor one set of policy goals over another. Again, this danger will vary according to the means chosen. Membership linkage tends not to pose this risk, although forcing states that are hostile to the linked regime to join in order to obtain the benefit of the other regime may create obstacles to the development of the linked regime. Sometimes the cost of turning plurilateral agreements into universal multilateral agreements is too great. For example, over time the parties to certain human rights agreements might be able to achieve more effective enforcement of those covenants and elaborate on the obligations concerned in greater detail. If, however, states basically hostile to the ideas underlying those covenants, or to their enforcement against nations, are forced to join so they can participate in the World Trade Organization, the result might be to prevent the human rights institutions from functioning effectively and developing further.

Third, and relatedly, linkage will sometimes create an additional source of regime instability. A linkage that suits the parties at one point in time may cease to suit them at another. Once regimes are linked, it may be that no regime can be stronger or more stable than the least stable of those regimes. Of course, linkage just as possibly may add stability not only to some regimes, but to all the linked regimes. The degree to which instability is transmitted may depend on the structure of the linkage. Relatively weak forms, such as membership and participatory linkage, will tend to isolate stronger regimes from the instability of the weaker ones. On the other hand, weaker forms of linkage will do little to stabilize inherently weak regimes.

These are some of the risks and costs associated with recognizing linkage claims. Linkage also presents some potential advantages in addition to the substantive merits of the linkage claim. International linkage may serve to forestall unilateral linkage that would seriously undermine the regime. For example, the United States might be persuaded to abandon some of its unilateral efforts to link trade to the environment if international economic organizations succeed in explicitly incorporating environmental considerations into their decisions and dispute settlement procedures. Cooperation with limited linkage will often be preferred to unilateralism (or bilateralism or regionalism) that incorporates a fuller measure of linkage. And as previously noted, linkage in some circumstances offers the potential to expand the means by which mutuality can be achieved, and thus enhances the ability to reach an agreement.

So where does this leave us? Space constraints do not permit a detailed analysis here, but I will venture a few tentative observations. The general presumption in the multilateral context appears to be that strategic linkage across regimes or issue areas that are not substantively related (in the sense set forth above) is unfair or counterproductive. This will not always be the case, but it leads most nations to resist it. Perhaps the fundamental problem boils down to the lack of consensus as to whether the linked issue ought to be the subject of an international agreement, or at least doubt as to whether a strong international regime is appropriate to the governance of that issue. That is, it seems inappropriate to use linkage to create pressure to reach an agreement on a subject on which few believe there should be a multilateral agreement at all. Where linkage is sought, it generally ought to be by weaker means that do not undermine the ability to reach agreements.

Substantive linkage, on the other hand, provokes an array of responses for both substantive and strategic reasons. Where it is strongly supported (as for linking labor and environmental issues with trade), such linkage can probably not be resisted altogether. Rather, the goal must be to choose the means of linkage that most effectively advance the policies sought to be linked (e.g., environmental and labor), without undermining the ability to reach agreement and make progress in the other regime. Interpretive linkage holds promise in this respect, and the WTO now seems in effect to have endorsed this approach. With regard to the role of environmental agreements and norms in the interpretation of GATT obligations, for example, the WTO dispute panels have basically done an about-face. They have moved from a wooden, formalistic approach that largely ignored the evolution of international environmental law, to one that tries in a nuanced way to incorporate this evolution into a dynamic interpretation of the GATT rules.

Carefully tailoring the modality of linkage to the substantive (or on occasion strategic) claims advanced for linkage will enable us to see that these are not all-or-nothing claims but, rather, steps in the evolution of a complex multilateral regulatory framework across a variety of issue areas. Linkage so pursued should not obstruct agreement; on the contrary, it should further enhance the coherence of that multilateral world and the legitimacy of its institutions.

In general, however, linkage ought not to substitute for attempts to formulate and improve the distinct international regimes that govern the linked areas. Regime borrowing and sanction linkage in particular tend to reflect frustration and disappointment with the borrowing regime (or nonregime) governing the issue area to be linked. In most such situations, linkage is a second-best solution. It would be preferable to develop the unsatisfactory regime independently.

Trade and Global Governance. Andrew T. Guzman, "Global Governance and the WTO" 45 Harv. Int'l L.J. 303 (2004).

One of the most salient critiques of the WTO is that it places trade values ahead of other concerns, including the environment, human rights, and labor. The prioritization of trade issues is not surprising in light of the fact that the WTO is a trade organization, staffed by trade specialists, and guided by agreements negotiated with an eye toward the trading regime. To be fair, it may not be accurate to say that the problem stems from the WTO's focus on trade issues. Rather, the problem exists because the organization is relatively powerful and effective. If, for example, an environmental organization were in place that enjoyed similar influence and success, there might be less concern about the WTO. In the absence of such an environmental organization, however, there is a perception that trade interests trump environmental interests.

What is missing, then, is a way to counter the WTO's trade interests with appropriate environmental interests, labor rights interests, etc., without undermining the strengths of the trading system. One common proposal is to build stronger specialized non-trade institutions such as a "World Environmental Organization" or a more effective International Labor Organization (ILO). Although creating such entities would not reduce the trade bias of the WTO, the notion presumably is that these organizations would have their own biases and the various international institutions would keep one another in check.

Growth in the number of institutions, however, has significant dangers. First, there is no guarantee that new organizations could be established with universal membership. Developing countries have no reason to join a powerful labor organization that might force them to improve local standards to the detriment of their economic well-being. Similarly, an effective international environmental organization may have little to offer developing states who are often prepared to accept lower environmental standards in exchange for economic growth. Membership in a Global Environmental Organization would also be reduced because non-members could free-ride on the environmental protections required of member states. Getting the consent of all or even most states for such organizations, then, may not be possible. Without universal membership there is no reason to think these institutions will prosper and be able to check the influence of the WTO.

Second, even if one could establish a universal organization dedicated to, for example, environmental concerns, it may never achieve the success and influence of the WTO. In fact, the ILO is an example of such an organization with respect to labor issues. Despite having a large membership and being the recognized center for cooperation on such issues, the ILO remains much less powerful than the WTO.

Third, if the ILO became more powerful, and if an influential international environmental organization came into being, it is not clear that the mere existence of such institutions would lead to a desirable balance among trade, environment, and labor concerns. New issue-oriented organizations bring attention to the relevant issues, but do little to address the more important question of how conflicting priorities should be managed. How should the trade goals of the WTO be reconciled with the environmental priorities of a World Environmental Organization? How should conflicts between these organizations be resolved? Stand-alone organizations are unable to answer these questions and would, therefore, leave many international regulatory problems unaddressed. By incorporating a range of issues into a single institution, it would be possible for negotiators, appointed by national governments, to get down to the critical business of balancing the benefits of trade against the values of other issues such as the environment or labor.

For all of these reasons, establishing separate, stand-alone organizations is less promising than the incorporation of the relevant issue areas within a single organization. The question then arises: what is the appropriate organization? Should a new one be created from scratch, or would it be better to adapt an existing institution to the needs of the international community?

The case for using a reformed WTO to house these issues is powerful. The WTO has already established itself as a strong and effective institution with a good record of state compliance. Furthermore, it has incorporated at least one non-trade issue: intellectual property. Its strength and its demonstrated ability to incorporate additional issues are evidence in favor of an expansion of the WTO. With appropriate adjustments to the WTO, it would be possible to take advantage of the institutional strength of the organization to avoid or overcome the challenges facing stand-alone institutions, and at the same time limit the reformed organization's trade bias. Restructuring the WTO as a set of departments, I would separate the reformed organization from its trade roots enough to provide a fair hearing for other important values. Trade would not disappear as a priority, but it would share the stage with other issues.

The nature of international regulation often makes it unrealistic to expect international cooperation in non-trade areas without some form of linkage. International agreements in areas such as competition policy, labor, and environment are much more likely when states are able to make concessions that cross issue areas. Separating the negotiation of trade from non-trade issues, and separating non-trade issues from one another, handicaps negotiation and is likely to frustrate agreements that could make all states better off. This leads to the straightforward but nevertheless underappreciated point that a forum should exist in which issues are grouped together at the negotiation stage to allow for suitable cross-issue transfers.

One of the many challenges facing international cooperation in areas such as the environment, human rights, labor, intellectual property, and competition policy is that states have divergent interests. States may disagree because they have different tastes and priorities, but they may also disagree because states with different economies and trade flows will have conflicting goals. The clearest example is in the area of intellectual property. Developed states have every reason to support a strong intellectual property regime because the vast majority of innovation takes place in those countries. In fact, in the presence of trade, the preferred international regime for a country that exports intellectual property is actually more protective of intellectual property rights than would be the case in an otherwise identical closed economy (i.e., one without international trade). An open economy that exports intellectual property puts more weight on the benefits of future innovation than does a closed economy, and puts less weight on the reduced consumer access to the technology. This is because the state does not care about consumers that are located abroad. Thus, some of the costs of stricter intellectual property rules are felt by foreigners, and these costs are ignored when the innovating country considers its preferred policy. Moreover, all of the increased profits that go to innovators as a result of greater protection of intellectual property are enjoyed by the innovating country, so those gains are included in the policy calculus. The innovating country, therefore, prefers stronger protection for intellectual property if it is an exporter of intellectual property than if it is a closed economy.

On the other side of trade in intellectual property are, of course, importers. They do not receive any of the benefits of increased profits when intellectual property protections are increased, but they do suffer when their citizens are unable to gain low-cost access to the property. These importing states will, therefore, prefer an international policy with relatively weak intellectual property protections.

As long as there are net importers and net exporters of intellectual property, this divergence will exist. Note that the positions of the states result from their respective trade flows in intellectual property, and not a lack of communication, differences of opinion with respect to the economics of intellectual property, or idiosyncratic preferences.

Because underlying economic interests cause states to have inconsistent policy preferences, any agreement changing the existing level of international intellectual property protection will benefit some states and hurt others. Unless they are compensated in some way, states that would be harmed by an agreement will refuse to consent to it. In principle, compensation could take any number of forms—from cash to concessions in another area of international relations. For that compensation to be offered and accepted, however, negotiators must be authorized to bargain over more than just intellectual property. Discussing intellectual property in a specialized forum such as the World Intellectual Property Organization (WIPO) is unlikely to lead to an agreement because negotiators cannot offer concessions in other areas.

Embedding negotiation of intellectual property in an organization that also oversees negotiation on other topics, however, opens the door to an exchange of concessions across issue areas. Indeed, this is what happened with intellectual property. Many prior attempts to negotiate an agreement through WIPO failed, but once the WTO took up the issue, an agreement was struck in which developing countries were offered compensation in the form of concessions relating to agricultural subsidies, market access for agricultural goods, and protection against unilateral sanctions by developed countries, especially the United States. These concessions simply could not have been negotiated through WIPO.

Strategic problems of this sort are also present in other non-trade areas. In competition policy, developed countries are home to the bulk of firms that operate in imperfectly competitive industries (where antitrust is an issue), and so they favor relatively weak international antitrust protections. Developing states, on the other hand, have reason to favor relatively strong protections since their consumers benefit from increased competition.* As with intellectual property, an international

---

* These preferences relate to the level of international enforcement that would be preferred by the states if there were a single, harmonized global policy. It offers an

agreement on antitrust seems unlikely unless the negotiations provide for transfer payments. Though there is support in the competition policy literature for a single, stand-alone forum for the negotiation of international antitrust, that literature does not explain how the forum could overcome the divergent interests of states. I have argued elsewhere that the WTO is the most promising forum for arranging the necessary transfers among states.

Similar analyses could be applied to environmental and labor issues. For example, an effort to reduce deforestation is likely to be very costly to Brazil, but to benefit many other states. In this example, Brazil has no incentive to accept a globally desirable policy because it bears a disproportionate share of the costs. If other states want such a policy, however, it may be possible to obtain it by offering Brazil concessions in other areas. They may offer concessions in other environmental areas (e.g., other states could commit to tougher emissions policies), but there is even greater opportunity for cooperation if concessions can come in other forms. For example, Brazil might be prepared to join an agreement on deforestation in exchange for trade concessions.

With respect to labor, developing countries have concerns that international labor standards will reduce the competitiveness of their labor-intensive industries. Based on these concerns, developing states have an incentive to resist many international labor agreements. Again, if these agreements are desirable from a global perspective, it may be possible to achieve them through the use of concessions in unrelated areas. For example, a particular labor rights agreement might be acceptable to developing states if developed states agree to reduce agricultural subsidies.

In general, then, an expanded WTO offers a promising forum in which to negotiate agreements on topics that require concessions to be made across issue areas. Each of the issue areas discussed in this Article would benefit if transfers could be structured to make agreement on value-increasing deals possible. Furthermore, as each issue area is brought into the WTO, it will become a potential source of concessions when agreement is sought in other areas, further increasing the choice set for negotiators. Thus, for example, developing countries might receive an agreement on international competition policy in exchange for concessions relating to labor. Expanding the set of issues within the organization expands the number of potential deals. Though such cross-issue negotiations can be cumbersome, they can also lead to agreements that could not otherwise be achieved.

explanation for why the United States has consistently resisted calls for international harmonization while developing states have expressed an interest in such cooperation.

Chapter 12

EMERGING ISSUE AREAS

Editors' introduction: Of the many explosive issues knocking at the door of international law are the four we deal with in this Chapter: the rights of the child, human health, biotechnology, and the internet. The issue-areas of today are the chapters in the international law textbooks of tomorrow. Yet the fact that international law addresses these issues is not the same thing as solving them. Behind international law is the political will that can make the law effective. And behind the political will is our moral consciousness. The chapters in this Handbook do not profess to teach morality. They assume it.

A. RIGHTS OF THE CHILD

Proposal for Cross–Country Adoption. Anthony D'Amato, "Cross–Country Adoption: A Call to Action" 73 Notre Dame L. Rev. 1239 (1998).

On the television show 20/20, in October 1990, Ted Koppel described conditions in one of Romania's fifty state run institutions for unwanted children: "Children here are filthy and unattended. They lie in their own waste, covered with flies. Young girls, their heads shaven, were kept in a giant cage like animals: wild-eyed, screaming, half-naked." The New York Times made a similar report on the home in Plataresti, Romania. One room contained twenty five children who wallowed in urine sodden diapers and bedding, two to a crib, without a toy. There was one attendant for every twenty children, but the attendants were untrained. Because light bulbs were not available on the market, the light bulbs were all stolen out of the nursery, so that every night the children had to manage in the dark. The Washington Post reported on Romanian "warehouses for children": "Food is sometimes served by throwing it on the floor. Staffers hardly know their charges' names, much less their medical problems." A visiting French medical team reported that the mortality rate among the children is very high: "They die of hunger, of very dirty environments, of nobody touching them and of never getting out of their beds."

Many of these children die; others stay in the foster factory until they are old enough to venture out on their own (perhaps as "street children"), and some are adopted. But nearly all are affected with reactive attachment disorder, a condition that impairs their ability to get along smoothly in society and to relate warmly to friends. They may have no ability at all to understand the concept of romantic love or to experience it in their own lives. The deepest aspects of appreciation for human culture may be permanently inaccessible to them.

If you visit some countries in Latin America you will become immediately aware of the street children. These are the ones who somehow managed to survive the warehouses for children, and now roam the streets in packs. In Bogotá, Colombia, there is an estimated 200,000 unwanted and abandoned street children. In Latin America as a whole, over forty million street children are estimated to be living on the streets. The situation may even be worse though statistics are not available in some countries in Africa and Southeast Asia.

Even so, the children who survive the foster factories are in a sense the lucky ones. Many more children die from lack of food and care. Worldwide, in every second of the day twelve children die. Although intercountry adoptions are possible, the annual total of intercountry adoptions in the United States saves less than 0.004% (four thousandths of one per cent) of the number of children that die.

A great many of the street children could have been adopted within the first year or two of their birth; a great many of the children who die throughout the world today could be adopted. The demand to adopt children, mostly in the developed countries, is huge. In the United States, adoption agencies are able to place children in only one out of twenty families wanting to adopt them. Many poor people who want children don't even apply to the adoption agencies, because the fees average about $13,000. In this area, Catholic Charities is doing a great job helping poor people adopt children, but for the most part only with respect to in-country adoption and not cross-country adoption. The demand to adopt children is increasing because of the dramatic increase in infertility among families in developed countries. There are approximately two million childless families in the United States today wishing to adopt a child; only a very small fraction will get their wish. And if we look at families who have one or more children, but would also like to adopt a child, we increase the number by several million more families in the United States alone.

In short, we have a tremendous surplus of unwanted children all over the world and an equally great unsatisfied demand for those children. If the world were fair and rational, every one of these children would immediately be placed in adoptive families.

But as moral agents, we cannot sit back and bemoan the unfairness and irrationality in the world. We have a moral obligation, whenever it is possible to do so, to make the world just a little less unfair and just a little less irrational. Let me suggest two courses of action.

The first has to do with the way that we, as lawyers, look at the problem of intercountry adoption. We, and the public generally, tend to view adoptions from the point of view of the adopting family. The adopting family wants a child; they are willing to go to some trouble and expense to get one; they complain when bureaucratic obstacles get in the way, but they accept those obstacles as "given" and try their best to get around them.

We are looking at the problem backwards. It's not a matter of the adoptive family's right to get a child, but rather it's a matter of the human right of a child to have a family. The matter was well expressed by Mercedes Rosario de Martinez, founder of Colombia's Foundation for the Adoption of Abandoned Children, who said, "We don't give a child to a family; we give a family to a child."

The Convention on the Rights of the Child does not in so many words proclaim the right of every child to be brought up in a family, but taken as a whole it may be read to support that proposition. Article 6 states that "every child has an inherent right to life," and places the obligation upon states to "ensure to the maximum extent possible the survival and development of the child." The development of the child is referred to in the Preamble to the Convention: "The child, for the full and harmonious development of his or her personality, should grow up in a family environment, in an atmosphere of happiness, love, and understanding."

If we read this Convention, as I do, as standing for the proposition that every child has a right to a family, we are not asking governments to do the impossible. We are not saying that any government that fails to place every unwanted child in a family is violating international law. Rather, the proposition is one of those "positive" human rights, like the right to life, food, clothing, shelter, and the right to work, that are best construed in today's world as requiring governments not to stand in the way of private initiatives that secure those rights. For example, if you send a food package to a foreign country where there is widespread starvation, any government official who intercepts that package and sells it for his or her personal profit (a situation which unfortunately happens more than occasionally) would be violating the human right to food of the starving people. Thus, although a government itself may not be required by present-day international law to provide every child with a family, it should not block or impede adoption initiatives in the private sector. In particular, a government should not block intercountry adoption.

The very idea of having governments handle intercountry adoption doesn't work, despite the facilitative Hague Convention of 1993 on intercountry adoption. What happened in the case of Romania is instructive. At first, many Americans, seeing the program on 20/20 and reading about it in the newspapers, immediately said, "I'll adopt one of those poor children." A number of Americans traveled to Romania, paid various bribes to various officials, and came home with a child. And then the Romanian government began to tighten up, to make it harder for the children to be put up for adoption. In this respect, it followed the pattern of Korea some years earlier. Many Americans adopted Korean children in the 1960s and early 1970s, and then Korea clamped down on the practice. Romania and Korea are typical examples of developing countries' experience with intercountry adoption. For a while they open the doors to let unwanted children be adopted abroad, and then they slam the doors shut. They seem to prefer leaving their unwanted children to die in the warehouses.

The blame lies squarely with the media. Although a free press is an integral part of democratic governance, intercountry adoption is one case in which the media makes it virtually impossible for governments to send children abroad for adoption. The pattern is discouragingly similar in every country like Romania. As soon as the media learns that local children are being sent abroad for adoption, headlines appear that the government is "exporting our precious human capital." Rumors of bribery and corruption become media stories; government officials are accused of lining their own pockets by selling helpless infants and children to "greedy, wealthy foreigners." Articles appear that the religion and cultural identity of these children will be wiped out by their transplantation into a totally different country with materialistic values. The children may be mistreated and abused by the adopting parents. The opposition party criticizes the government's childcare policy: they claim that by sending the children abroad the government is admitting its own failure to cope with the country's most precious resources.

Note the inherent inconsistency in the media's position. If the government reacts by spending more money checking the credentials and standards of the prospective adoptive parents, it must pass these additional expenses on to the adoptive parents. The result is that the price of adoption goes up, and the media then cites the high fees as "blood money" to line the pockets of the government officials.

In every instance, the government predictably responds by closing down, completely or almost completely, the practice of intercountry adoption. Does the media then follow up by looking into conditions in the warehouses and crowded foster homes? No; their concern for the interests of the children lasted only insofar as it sold newspapers and television advertisements. Once intercountry adoption is shut down, the media looks elsewhere for new stories. Unwanted children dying in warehouses is not "news."

Intercountry adoption is still possible today, but it costs about $20,000 per adoption. The money goes into the hands of intermediaries, lawyers, facilitators, bureaucrats, notaries, nondescript officials of all kinds, and usually a payment to the natural mother. In addition there are extensive travel costs and time-consuming bureaucratic obstacles. A large part of the problem is the notion that adopting parents are adopting a particular child. This leads to a waiting period, a time for administrative procedures for the recognition of foreign adoption orders for that specific child. The waiting time depends on the requirements of the country of origin, the type of legal order given to the parents when the child leaves the country of origin, the recognition or nonrecognition of these orders by the receiving country, and the requirements of the receiving country. Types of legal orders include guardianship or custody orders, and orders that grant legal adoption in the country of origin depending on whether certain conditions have been met in the receiving country. Necessary documents include proof of the official residence of the child, its citizenship, future social security rights, provision for its education, inheritance rights, and choice of name; costly court proceedings can be involved at any stage.

But the worst problem is baby-snatching. As the price of adoptable children goes up, so does the temptation of theft. A sidewalk thief can steal a purse and be lucky if it contains fifty dollars; if instead he steals an infant from its mother's arms or from a baby carriage, and runs with it to a waiting car, he can sell it to a dishonest adoption agency for at least a thousand dollars. In poor countries, this kind of evil economic incentive can lead to tragedy for natural parents and popular pressure for shutting down intercountry adoptions.

What can people of good will do about placing unwanted children in families that want to adopt them? An action proposal would have to contain these two fundamental elements:

1. Neither the sending nor the receiving state should have to do anything. (It is important to keep governments out of intercountry adoption, for reasons I have already stated.)

2. The total cost of adoption should be zero or close to zero. (This would take away the economic incentive for baby snatching, remove the opportunity for bribery and corruption, and eliminate media charges that human capital is being sold to foreigners.)

My proposal is for an Intercountry Adoption Agency to be set up in Vatican City, funded by private donations. Unwanted children would be taken to a Temporary Hospital run by the Intercountry Adoption Agency, where they would be medically examined and treated if necessary, and then be turned over to the new adoptive parents. Any available information on their parentage, including health status if known, particularly heritable conditions, should be provided to the child. If nothing is known about the parentage, the child should at least be provided with a description of his or her ethnic heritage, including language, customs, and religion so that he or she will never feel anonymous and may interest himself or herself in his heritage later if he or she desires.

Let me briefly expand on these suggestions.

The Vatican City is an ideal neutral territory, because the Holy See is not a "state" in the traditional sense but in fact it has diplomatic standing in the community of states. The Holy See sends and receives ambassadors and issues its own passports. It also signs and ratifies multilateral conventions, and was one of the earliest ratifiers of the Convention on the Rights of the Child.

Unwanted children would be taken from any country in the world to the Vatican by any priest, nun, minister, rabbi, or other religious official who has proper identification. All world airlines could be persuaded to allow any such person who is taking a child to the Vatican to travel for free.

A temporary hospital should be constructed on Vatican grounds, funded by private donations. The hospital would be staffed by volunteers. Doctors and nurses all over the world would be encouraged to donate one month's time to serving at the hospital, in return for which they receive nothing more than a Certificate of Good Service. Other hospital employees might donate part of their time or be compensated by endowment funds. I have no doubt that simply by announcing this program, people and charitable organizations and foundations all over the world will eagerly send in substantial contributions.

The Intercountry Adoption Agency should have a staff (volunteers and regular workers) which does all the paperwork, but especially concentrates on two tasks. The first is to receive letters (e-mail, telephone, fax all included) from prospective adopters and engage in correspondence with them to determine (through questionnaires) their capacity to take on and care for a child. Once an adoptive family satisfactorily completes the questionnaire, it should be placed on a waiting list. The family may want certain characteristics of the adoptee (age, ethnicity, religion, whatever), and these conditions would be satisfied. The complexity of these factors requires good computing equipment (again, I think any manufacturer would be glad to donate computers to this cause).

Prospective adopters should be dealt with on a first-come-first-served basis with the following important qualification. A country (State A) which gives up a child for intercountry adoption should receive a "credit" for that child which will entitle any other family within State A that may want to adopt a child to priority on the list at the Vatican. This "credit" will help defuse any claim that State A is engaged in a net export of its human capital. Instead, the government of State A may explain to its citizens that, for the time being, we may be sending unwanted children abroad (due to a temporary famine, a civil war, temporary overcrowding, and so on) but in the future, if circumstances warrant, we will be at the top of the list, on a child-per-child basis, to obtain children from abroad for any of our citizens who want to adopt them. There is no necessary net export of human capital; rather, we get a credit "in the bank" for every child we give up.

The second major function for the staff at the Intercountry Adoption Agency might be called the "annual report" function. All adoptive parents who take a child with them away from the Vatican must, as a precondition, sign a pledge to write an annual report on the welfare of the child, including the current address of the family. Then a staff member (perhaps student volunteers) will write back a "thank you" letter repeating the highlights of the annual report and expressing the hope that, if there are any observable deficiencies in the treatment of the child, the situation will be improved as soon as practicable.

There should not be any sanctions. The only requirement of the adoptive parents is to send in the annual report. Yet this report can have huge beneficial effects. It will demonstrate to the parents that the Intercountry Adoption Agency really cares about the child and is continually interested in the child's welfare. It will encourage the parents to redouble their efforts on behalf of the child, because no one wants to send in an annual report that is false or falls below a generally acceptable standard. Indeed, my model for this procedure is the successful annual reports filed at the United Nations by trusteeship countries and administering countries of dependent and semi-dependent territories in the period 1945–1970. As one who has read a substantial number of these reports, I can attest to the significant role they played in getting the administering country to improve its standard of care, very few countries wanted to be in a position of having to say, with the next year's report, that things had gotten worse in the interim since the last report. For a nonpunitive procedure, the system of annual reports must be counted as one of the most effective tools in hastening the move from colonialism to independence. I think the analogy is strong with respect to adoption. The adoptive parents are custodians of the child's welfare, and their job is to prepare the child for eventual independence as an adult.

Of course, this is only a sketch, a "prospectus." Many changes and improvements will happen if people of good will take on the responsibility of setting up this kind of procedure for intercountry adoption. There are very few things I can think of in this difficult world that would make a bigger difference to the quality of life, not just for the unwanted children and the new families that they will adopt, but for everyone connected in any way to the procedure, and indeed for humankind in general in seeing how an international system can step in and do an essential job that nation-states have been self-disabled from doing. The bottom line is the preciousness of human life.

Child Abduction. Carol S. Bruch, "Religious Law, Secular Practices, and Children's Human Rights in Child Abduction Cases Under the Hague Child Abduction Convention" 33 N.Y.U. J. Int'l L. & Pol. 49 (2000).

The [1980] Child Abduction Convention's second mechanism to protect human rights is set forth in Article 20:

> The return of the child ... may be refused if this would not be permitted by the fundamental principles of the requested State relating to the protection of human rights and fundamental freedoms.

It is worth noting that this provision does not presume a controlling international law. Instead, in the tradition of private international law conventions, it supplies a choice of law rule—in this case, application of the law of the state hearing the return petition (the refuge state).

What kinds of concerns, specifically, are likely to be raised in this context? Although it was promulgated only some years after the Child Abduction Convention, the 1989 U.N. Convention on the Rights of the Child is a contemporary statement of human rights topics that may express forum law.

Religious courts and religious laws raise specific issues, human rights concerns among them, that may prompt other countries to refuse a treaty relationship or may give the courts of States Parties pause about returning children. Some of these focus on gender-based custody, travel, and support rules. It is important to emphasize, however, that the substance of these laws varies considerably between countries. Although, for example, we often think of Islamic nations (or countries with large Muslim populations) as a homogenous group, in fact there have been reforms in the child custody laws of several of these countries, particularly in North Africa. One therefore cannot assume that tenets of the traditional Hanafi school on a particular subject are necessarily the law that controls in a particular country, even if the predominant religious community in that country is properly understood to follow the Hanafi school. At the same time, legal secularization in these societies should not necessarily allay all concerns; whatever the face of the legal text, the religious and cultural norms of any society affect a judge's custody decisions. A sophisticated appraisal will, accordingly, consider practices that are extant in the community as well as in the courtroom.

Human rights issues arise even more directly where custody laws have not been amended or secularized. Some of these relate to gender-based custodial rules, while others relate to less well known religious doctrines. A possible example can be found in a trial court decision from Barcelona that involved not Islamic, but Jewish law. The case raised human rights is-sues in the context of religious law, and the Spanish court relied on Article 20 in refusing to return a young boy to an-other State Party, Israel. The boy's mother had brought him to Spain for a visit with the father's consent, but they did not return to Israel as scheduled. A rabbinical court in Israel thereupon transferred custody of the son to the father, and the Barcelona court believed this was because the mother now held the status of a "disobedient wife" (*moredet*) and the rabbinical court had wished to punish her. On that understanding, the Spanish court ruled that returning the child to a place where its custody would be determined according to the mother's status without regard to the child's best interests would violate the child's human rights and fundamental freedoms under Spanish law, which requires that custody be deter-mined according to the child's best interests.

The judiciary also differs from country to country in ways that may be important. In Israel, for example, the rabbis and *qadis* who sit in their respective religious courts have no training in secular law and often lack the equivalent of a secular high school education. Whether these judges could be expected to interpret and apply the Child Abduction Convention in a manner acceptable to other countries might fairly be questioned. Israel mooted this question by placing venue for return petitions exclusively in the country's civil courts. Countries considering the accessions of other nations where clerics or only the religiously devout serve as judges, however, may wish to consider first, whether the acceding country's judiciary is likely to apply the Convention in a skilled and impartial fashion and second, who will decide custody matters on the merits following a child's return from abroad.

Most importantly, this inquiry should address the values that undergird these ultimate custody decisions. Even legal standards that sound identical may vary dramatically in application. A great many countries, for example, now award custody according to a child's best interests. Yet what U.S. parents, lawyers, and judges understand by that test may be very different from a "best interests" analysis on the part of religious or secular judges in other cultures.

The legal rules and court practices for children who are returned to Israel from the United States are instructive. In Israel, Muslim children always have their custody decided by Islamic religious courts; this rule applies to children returned under the Child Abduction Convention as well as those for whom custody issues arise in other contexts. Jewish children, in contrast, ordinarily have their custody determined by civil courts unless both parents agree to the jurisdiction of a Jewish religious court. There is, however, a doctrine of pendent jurisdiction in the rabbinical courts that sometimes authorizes non-consensual religious court jurisdiction for custody cases. This doctrine applies, inter alia, to divorce and related custody actions that are filed in good faith by a left-behind parent while the other parent and the couple's children are abroad. Accordingly, Jewish children who are returned to Israel under the Child Abduction Convention may have their custody determined in a religious court even if the abducting parent objects.

What will happen in these contests on the merits? Because we already have a treaty relationship with Israel, so far as that country is concerned, this question is relevant only in the context of possible Article 20 defenses on human rights grounds. As to other countries, however, there are indeed matters we need to know much more about before we decide to accept accessions. Not only religious laws require scrutiny. Some secular practices are deeply troubling, and difficulties for children are compounded when these traditions are confused (in the countries where they are practiced) with religious obligations. Whatever their origin, we are properly reluctant to return children to nations that observe legal rules or secular customs that give rise to concerns about human rights or fundamental freedoms.

Exit restrictions provide just one example. The law of Jordan, for example, says that a mother and child cannot leave without the consent of the father, although the converse rule does not apply. Other forms of automatic exit restrictions exist elsewhere.

Honor crimes, found among Islamic, Christian, and ethnic communities in a number of countries (including several in the Middle East), provide a second example. These are crimes by family members who kill daughters, wives, or other female relatives if they are believed to have engaged in behavior that harms the family's honor.

Female genital mutilation, another human rights concern, is widely practiced, primarily in Africa, but also in immigrant communities around the world. Recent law reform in many countries that aims to eradicate the problem has thus far had little impact on actual practice.

Slavery-like practices ranging from child labor to child marriage are of concern to the U.N.'s International Labor Organization, among others. These practices, those I have already mentioned, and others not listed here continue to threaten children's welfare and human rights in much of the world.

How should countries respond to this tragic reality? I argue that we ought to be cautious about accepting accessions. While some diplomats have applauded this view, others disagree. One U.S. State Department official, for example, reasons that this country should accept every accession without fail. He fears that not doing so could subject this country's government to unacceptable criticism if a child were abducted from the United States to a place with laws and practices quite antithetical to our own. Should that occur, he foresees a firestorm of media attention emphasizing that we could have chosen to enter a treaty relationship that would have required the child's return but did not.

My view is quite different. I am concerned not only for children from this country who are taken abroad. I worry also about the price we would pay for these agreements and about the welfare of the children we would be obliged to send back to these treaty partners if we accept their accessions. I ask again that we think seriously about accessions. If the U.S. government decides to accept all accessions as a matter of course, my closing plea is for guidance at the federal level concerning what standards and proof should control. This could be provided by a federal statute or, perhaps, by more malleable executive or regulatory means. The purpose would be to articulate specific grounds that justify an application of Article 20 in this country. If properly constructed, the federal mandate could establish the existence and gravity of certain conditions and authorize or endorse a presumption that a human rights danger exists in specific situations. These steps would ease the burden of proof on individuals while also encouraging consistent results at trial. Although I am otherwise reluctant to expand defenses to return under the Child Abduction Convention, I am profoundly opposed to sending children into unconscionable or palpably dangerous situations. I hope that, upon reflection, others will share my concerns and will act upon them.

B. HEALTH

Human Rights. Stephen P. Marks, "Health and Human Rights: The Expanding International Agenda," from Proceedings of the Ninety-Fifth Annual Meeting of the American Society of International Law 65 (April 4–7 2001).

The health and human rights (H&HR) approach includes, but is not limited to, the medical profession's commitment to human rights. The traditional role of doctors is to apply the knowledge of medical science to alleviate the suffering of their patients from disease and injury. In doing so, they may face tough ethical dilemmas in negotiating the patient-doctor relationship, dilemmas that sometimes but not always are also human rights issues (as with the right to privacy or nondiscrimination). Doctors have also been involved with clear violations of human rights, such as performing medical experiments on human subjects without their consent or ensuring that torture does not result in death until the victim reveals information. These abuses of medical ethics have been prohibited by human rights texts such as the Nuremberg Code and UN texts on treatment of detainees. The current trend is to introduce human rights language and patients' rights into medical ethics and to expand the concerns of the profession to a broader involvement in international human rights.

The human rights approach to health policies and health systems is to focus on availability, affordability, nondiscrimination, participation of the population in determining priorities in health, and appropriateness of the preventive and curative strategies, rather than on giving exclusive priority to the biomedical model. The H&HR approach also focuses on specific obligations of the state to respect, to protect, and to fulfill with regard to a wide range of health issues in order to determine how human rights accountability contributes to lessening vulnerability and increasing well-being.

Second only to HIV/AIDS, reproductive and sexual rights have been the object of H&HR research and advocacy in recent decades. The range of human rights issues in this field is broad and includes, of course, all forms of gender-based discrimination, sexual violence, freedom in deciding when and how often to give birth or to avoid or end pregnancy, safe pregnancy, elimination of discrimination based on sexual orientation, and emerging issues of assisted procreation. The basic human rights texts have been supplemented by a specialized convention on discrimination against women. Considerable advances in mainstreaming women's rights as human rights were made at the international conferences in Cairo (Population, 1992), Vienna (Human Rights, 1993), and Beijing (Women, 1995). One of the most instructive examples is female genital cutting (often called female genital mutilation), which affects two million girls every year. In 1996, WHO, the UN Children's Fund (UNICEF), and the UN Fund for Population Activities addressed this issue in a statement regarding harmful practices. They called for the intervention of the international community to change people's behavior, which the document affirms is possible "when they understand the hazards and indignity of harmful practices and when they realize that it is possible to give up harmful practices without giving up meaningful aspects of their culture."

HIV/AIDS. Miriam Maluwa, "Aids In National And International Law," from Proceedings of the Ninety–Sixth Annual Meeting of the American Society of International Law 322 (March 16, 2002).

It has been increasingly recognized that health and human rights are not conflicting goals but are interdependent and mutually reinforcing. Both share the common objective of promoting and protecting the dignity and well-being of all individuals.

Health is a fundamental human right indispensable for the exercise of other rights. Every human being is entitled to enjoy the highest attainable standard of health conducive to living a life in dignity. The right to health is closely related to and dependent upon the realization of other rights, including rights to food, housing, work, education, human dignity, life, nondiscrimination, equality, freedom from torture, privacy, access to information, and the freedoms of association, assembly, and movement. All these are part of the framework for the right to health.

HIV/AIDS is a health condition, one of the worst we are facing today. More than sixty million people have been infected with HIV, and more than twenty million have died. HIV is the leading cause of death in sub-Saharan Africa and is the fourth biggest killer worldwide. Life expectancy in sub-Saharan Africa is now forty-seven years; it would have been sixty-two without HIV. The statistics from around the world show that AIDS is not exclusive to any particular region.

A human rights framework is as central to the HIV/AIDS response as it is in responses to other health conditions. In the last few years, the success of HIV/AIDS interventions has been shown to be directly proportional to the degree to which human rights are promoted and protected. These realities, demonstrated time and again over the course of the epidemic, have made it clear that the protection and promotion of human rights must be an integral component of the response to HIV/AIDS.

The promotion and protection of human rights in general is crucial to the response because HIV/AIDS thrives upon and, in turn, worsens situations that are prone to human rights abuses. There are at least three interrelated ways to illustrate this.

(1) Due to HIV/AIDS-related stigma and consequent discrimination, the rights of those infected are frequently violated solely because of their actual or presumed HIV status. People are refused employment, education, health services, insurance, and the right to get married and live in a family. Some are even killed because of their seropositive status. For example, in 1998 a young community volunteer, Gugu Dlamini, was stoned and beaten to death by her neighbors in South Africa after she had spoken out openly on World AIDS Day about her HIV infection. Violation of human rights increases the negative impact of the epidemic because instead of people worrying about their infection, they also worry about the further loss of their rights.

(2) Promoting and protecting human rights is a way of addressing the underlying social, cultural, and economic conditions that make people vulnerable to HIV infection. However, some groups of people, such as women, children, men who have sex with men, sex workers, injection drug users, prisoners, refugees, and migrants, are unable to realize their rights. HIV/AIDS prevention and care are hindered, for

example, where women do not have the legal power to make choices in their lives and to refuse unwanted sex; where people are persecuted because of their sexual orientation; or where children cannot realize their rights to education and information.

(3) Promoting and protecting human rights provides a more supportive environment for a national response to AIDS, including targeted prevention and care programs. Freedoms of speech and association and the rights to education and information (including information about HIV transmission) are crucial for effective prevention and care by individuals and community-based groups. Freedom from discrimination makes people with HIV less fearful of disclosing their status and organizing themselves in associations to contribute to the response.

Because the AIDS epidemic was discovered after most of the international human rights instruments were already in place, it is important to mainstream HIV/AIDS-related issues into the human rights mechanisms. There is thus a need to review the human rights instruments to determine how they apply to HIV. It is pleasing that recently there has been a wealth of developments in this area. For example, in relation to the right to nondiscrimination, Resolution 1999/49 and Resolution 2001/51 adopted by the UN Commission on Human Rights state that the term "other status" in human rights provisions should be interpreted to cover health status, in particular HIV status. The Commission also calls upon states to review their laws and policies to ensure that there is conformity between national law and this particular interpretation of the term.

States must respect, protect, and fulfill human rights, including in the context of HIV/AIDS. Further, it is in the interest of every individual state and of the international community of states to ensure that their legal obligations in international trade, economics, and human rights agreements contribute to, or in the least do not impede, measures aimed at reversing the trend of the HIV epidemic. Further, action taken by states individually and as a community should provide to those infected adequate care, support, and treatment.

This is the backdrop that has spurred on the current debate on how, for example, the Agreement on Trade Related Aspects of Intellectual Property (TRIPS) affects the right to health. It has also spurred debate on the need for patent rights to be viewed in the context of other social interests, including the right to health and the right to enjoy the benefits of scientific progress.

This debate is particularly timely because 95 percent of the persons with HIV are in developing countries and they are severely deprived of drugs to treat pain and common infections, as well as the antiretroviral medicines that have been proven to greatly reduce morbidity and mortality among populations able to access them.

Medical Experimentation. Benjamin Mason Meier, "International Protection of Persons Undergoing Medical Experimentation: Protecting the Right of Informed Consent," 20 Berkeley J. Int'l L. 513 (2002).

The horrors of involuntary medical experimentation still exist today. The AIDS epidemic has driven desperate African nations to permit scientists to test experimental vaccines on uninformed and unwilling subjects.

With spiraling worldwide infection of HIV in the 1990s, certain members of the scientific community increasingly came to believe that the best way to impede a worldwide AIDS epidemic was through preventive vaccine development. In 1996, scientists in France and the United States determined that the use of Zidovudine (AZT) during the final twenty-six weeks of pregnancy could reduce by two-thirds the chances that a baby would be infected with HIV. However, that specific AZT regimen was found to be prohibitively expensive and complicated for health care systems in developing countries, where AIDS had been felt most acutely. To create a more efficacious means of treating AIDS patients in the developing world, studies attempted to find the minimum amount of AZT needed to block transmission of HIV from mother to child. Among these studies, the "short course" AZT trials tested the efficacy of oral AZT in preventing transmission of HIV from mother to child during pregnancy and childbirth.

The United States began testing short course AZT treatments in Africa in 1994, through which the Centers for Disease Control (CDC) and the National Institutes of Health (NIH) funded the testing of over 17,000 women. Half of these women received only a placebo.* Among the subjects, there was little understanding about the testing or the ethical issues surrounding it, the effectiveness and possible dangers of the vaccine, or the nature of a placebo. Howard French gave a detailed explanation of the consent procedure used with Siata Ouattara, a subject in the study:

> Minutes after [Ms. Ouattara] was informed for the first time that she carried the virus, [the] pregnant woman ... still visibly shaken by the news, was quickly walked through the details of the tests. ... In less than five minutes, in which the previously unknown concept of a placebo was briefly mentioned, the session was over, and Ms. Ouattara, unemployed and illiterate, had agreed to take part in the tests. Asked what had persuaded her to do so, she responded, "the medical care that they are promising me."**

According to Stanford Professor David Katzenstein, who was running AIDS vaccine trials in conjunction with the University of Zimbabwe, "researchers often treat potential volunteers like patients, which means deciding what is best for them and then 'telling them they are

---

* Aside from informed consent issues, critics have found the short course study additionally unethical based on the use of placebos in research where a proven life-saving regimen already existed. Carol Levine, Placebos and HIV Lessons Learned, Hastings Center Rep., Nov.–Dec. 1998, at 43–44.

** Howard French, AIDS Research in Africa: Juggling Risks and Hopes, N.Y. Times, Oct. 9, 1997, at A1.

going to give them a medicine.'" In fact, as noted by Peter Lamptey, a physician from Ghana and head of the AIDS Control and Prevention Program (AIDSCAP), "if you interviewed the people in the study, most wouldn't understand to what they had actually consented."

Although U.S. government agencies were conducting the testing, these experiments took place without regard for U.S. medical research standards, which require, inter alia, that patients be fully informed of all possible treatment options and that they receive, at a minimum, the prevailing standard of care. Some U.S. scientific experts quickly denounced the testing as unethical. Sidney Wolfe, director of the Public Citizen Health Research Group, decried the experiments as "unethical as any experiments we have ever seen since the end of the Second World War." Many critics further blasted the study as a racist exploitation of people of color, and based upon the U.S. experience, compared the short course trials in Africa to the Tuskegee syphilis studies.

In addition to conflicting with U.S. law, the AZT experiments took place in violation of international ethical standards. Pursuant to international standards, it is clear that the subjects were neither sufficiently informed nor did they freely consent. The Nuremberg Code guarantees that subjects "should be so situated as to be able to exercise free power of choice." However, the very nature of the subjects' life-threatening disease, their low education, the researchers' offers of payment, and the lack of alternate medical options denied these subjects the ability to make an informed choice, and therefore made any consent obtained from them purely "illusory." These experiments also took place in violation of the Helsinki Declaration's informed consent standards, specifically those which provide that "ethical standards applied [abroad] should be no less exacting than they would be in the case of research carried out in [the sponsoring] country."

The African short course AZT testing has ended. In early 1998, the CDC announced that it would no longer continue the short course AZT trials in developing countries, stating that experiments in Thailand had yielded sufficient data. However, although the short course AZT trials have ended, human experimentation in developing countries—African countries in particular—has continued. Entrepreneurial scientific corporations, whose financial interests often do not align with the interests of their research subjects, are expanding into new markets. With increased globalization of trade, scientific acceptance of foreign data, and greater attention paid by developed nations to the hazards posed by "emerging infections," studies in developing countries will be a major part of future research efforts.

C. BIOTECHNOLOGY

Human Genetics. Allyn L. Taylor, "Biotechnology, Human Rights, and Intellectual Property" American Society of International Law Proceedings (March 16, 2002).

I would ask everyone to consider what meaningful contribution international law can make to protecting human rights and public health in this era of genetic advances. What are the strengths and limitations of international law as a tool to protect human rights and public health? As a number of scholars have noted, a plethora of international texts, principally the International Bill of Human Rights, contain core axioms of international human rights law that apply broadly to the protection of global public health and human rights in regard to genetic science. However, most of the rights enumerated at the global level are highly general principles that are not specific to genetics and technology.

An important effort of the global community to address the human rights implications of genetic science through conventional international lawmaking has just begun. In December 2001, the UN General Assembly established an ad hoc working group of the Sixth Committee to consider an international instrument to ban the reproductive cloning of human beings. This initiative, which was sponsored by France and Germany, was motivated by public announcements from certain laboratories of impending attempts to begin reproductive cloning of humans. It is reported that the venue of the Sixth Committee was sought, in part, because the sponsors of the initiative believed that a convention narrowly tailored to prohibit human reproductive cloning could be achieved relatively expeditiously in the Legal Committee. The Ad Hoc Committee met at the end of February in its first of two scheduled sessions to elaborate a mandate for the proposed treaty. I attended this closed session on behalf of WHO, but most of what occurred has already been publicly reported. Most notably, controversy has already swelled at the first session. The majority of delegations that took the floor supported the original proposal of France and Germany to limit the convention to the reproductive cloning of human beings. However, a small but vocal minority of states supported extending the proposed prohibition to cover therapeutic cloning. One of their principal arguments is that therapeutic cloning and embryonic stem cell research involve the destruction of human life, since cloned embryos are destroyed in the process.

The controversy in the first session of the Ad Hoc Committee has the potential to significantly slow down and perhaps completely derail the codification effort. Those interested in the role of international law in regulating genetic science should carefully watch this current treaty initiative. It raises important questions about the capacity of the international community to respond to developments in technology and science rapidly and effectively. It also raises questions about the capacity of international law to effectively address global issues raised by scientific advances that closely border the politically explosive question of when life begins.

Genetic Manipulation. Stephen P. Marks, "Tying Prometheus Down: The International Law of Human Genetic Manipulation" 3 Chi. J. Int'l L. 115 (2002).

Revolutionary developments have periodically transformed the relationship between international law and public health, especially infectious disease control. The triumph of "germ theory" in the late nineteenth century triggered the establishment of a great body of international law on public health issues. Sanitary-reform movements and the later development of vaccines and antibiotics gave states and international health organizations powerful new weapons in the global battle against infectious diseases. The latest revolutions have, however, been more sinister for global infectious disease control—the HIV/AIDS pandemic, emerging and re-emerging infectious diseases, and the rise of anti-microbial resistance. These and other developments simultaneously raise the profile of international law and create great uncertainty about international law's contribution to global infectious disease control. To this parade of public health horribles we now must add bioterrorism.

A central concern is with those methods that some fear will threaten human existence as we know it because, in this view, the genome of future generations will undergo unpredictable mutations and thus alter human nature itself. Others see in this technology the promise of improving human well-being by eliminating life-threatening diseases and enhancing the quality of life and the capacities of human beings. The Human Genome Project has fueled perceptions that genetic manipulation can result in either the improvement of human lives or uncontrollable mutation and economic exploitation. International law cannot resolve this tension between hope for, and fear of, advances in biotechnology and genetics, but it is already deeply engaged in the issue through international trade and intellectual property law, human rights law, and specific instruments relating to biomedicine. International legal regulation is required either to protect humans from potential harm—an interest all governments share—or to protect proprietary or financial interests of significance to international commerce—a concern of governments supportive of the business interests of individuals or corporations under their jurisdiction. What international law there is in this field appears to respond to these two sets of often conflicting concerns.

Developments in biotechnology involving modification of the genetic structure of human beings have attracted the attention of ethicists and legislators at the national level in Europe and North America, but much less so in developing countries for the obvious reason that both research and the potential application of such technology are beyond the means of a majority of countries in the political South. The three principal instruments of international law that address human genetic manipulation all result from initiatives by European states, namely the Universal Declaration on the Human Genome and Human Rights, the Convention for the Protection of Human Rights and Dignity of the Human Being with Regard to the Application of Biology and Medicine, and the Additional Protocol on the Prohibition of Cloning Human Beings. A fourth instrument, in preparation, is the Franco-German proposal to the United Nations for an International Convention Against Reproductive Cloning of Human Beings. These instruments are based on several assumptions underlying the current thinking on this subject in Europe, where the principal instruments have been drafted. Other conflicting assumptions are more common in the United States, although these geographical distinctions have many exceptions.

The impetus for the existing instruments in international law comes primarily from Europe (which Canada often joins) and reflects assumptions about the essence of human existence and the welfare function of the state. The European perspective focuses primarily on three areas of serious concern, some of which are shared by many groups in the United States and elsewhere: preservation of nature; protection from economic exploitation; and prudence in the face of uncertainty.

Certain considerations reflecting different, more utilitarian philosophical assumptions tend to be raised in the United States and draw upon neoliberal economic preferences. These considerations favor the freedom of individuals to select the technology that will improve their lives regardless of social consequences, and the freedom of individuals and corporations to pursue financial gain through exploitation of new technologies.

The predominant attitudes reflect a fundamental division of opinion between seeing human life in terms of its intrinsic value, or in terms of its utilitarian value. A gene is either life itself or a useful piece of kit. The divergent perspectives appear to combine both philosophical and economic considerations, essentialist with a penchant for the welfare state, on the one hand, and utilitarian with a neoliberal accent, on the other.

The preceding discussion should have made evident the tension that exists between two principles of international law, each with underlying philosophical assumptions. The first is the restrictive principle, which draws support from a half century of development of international human rights law, to which proponents of the position that the human species must be preserved appeal in order to place such technology beyond the pale. The opposing principle is the permissive principle, supported by international trade and intellectual property law, and justified by ideas of free markets, free trade, freedom of scientific research, and freedom of choice of consumers. This perspective calls for minimal limitations on the developing and marketing of technologies of human genetic manipulation. At the governmental level, the Franco–German initiative at the UN is expected to result in a convention banning reproductive human cloning by 2003. In addition, the Commission on Human Rights has requested that the Secretary-General draw up proposals on proper coordination of activities and thinking on bioethics throughout the United Nations system, and consider establishing a working group of independent experts, which would consider the possible follow-up to the Universal Declaration on the Human Genome and Human Rights. The Commission drew the attention of Governments to the importance of research on the human genome and its applications for the improvement of the health of individuals and mankind as a whole, to the need to safeguard the rights of the individual and his/her dignity, as well as his/her identity and unity, and to the need to protect the confidentiality of genetic data concerning a named person.

The non-governmental initiatives are unlikely to advance unless they join forces with the European initiative at the UN. If the eventual treaty appeals to a large number of states, it may be because it will not satisfy either the essentialist/welfare state or the utilitarian/neoliberal camp and will not constrain governments beyond what they have already accepted. At the same time, the convergence of the political left and right, as well as the religious and secular advocates on the issue of human cloning, may bring enough pressure for the United States to join the treaty. Scholars, scientists, and science fiction writers have predicted for generations that advanced genetic and medical technology could modify the genetic make-up of humans as a means of alleviating human suffering and improving the quality of life. Progress in reproductive health technology has already allowed thousands of people to make choices affecting the genetic heritage of their offspring. Embryonic stem cell research holds out hope for other advances. At the same time, the prospects for altering inheritable genes through human reproductive cloning and germline gene therapy have raised fears that such tampering with the gene pool would result in profound and irreparable harm to human existence. The most authoritative consultative bodies, such as those convened by the World Health Organization and the now defunct National Bioethics Advisory Commission, have acknowledged that it is premature to regulate beyond a moratorium on human cloning. In the meantime, specific issues that call for the application of international law will be settled by reconciling human rights and intellectual property law. The latter is supported by the dominant neoliberal paradigm, while the former builds on an international regime of human dignity. Although, as this article argues, international human rights law does not go as far as the species preservation advocates sometimes claim, where it does provide guidance, it should prevail in case of conflict with the international trade or intellectual property regimes. This conclusion is supported both by positive law and by elementary moral considerations.

Bioterrorism and Public Health. David P. Fidler, "Bioterrorism, Public Health, and International Law" 3 Chi. J. Int'l L. 7 (2002).

The September 11th terrorist attacks sparked legislative action in the United States for new anti-terrorism measures giving law enforcement officials the power to prevent and punish terrorist activities. These new law enforcement powers created concern about how much civil rights and liberties protected by constitutional and international law would suffer to improve "homeland security." The anthrax attacks exacerbate this tension between homeland security and the protection of civil liberties because they represent a new development in the fight against terrorism. In addition, the anthrax attacks create human rights concerns particular to public health that deserve attention. Discourse on bioterrorism has addressed the need to balance effective public health responses in emergencies with individual rights and liberties. Public health officials recognize that they may need to infringe on individual rights in order to control effectively an outbreak caused by bioterrorism. The powers public health officials need in the context of bioterrorism range from the moderate (for example, access to private medical records to track an outbreak) to the draconian (for example, quarantine of populations). Potential infringements on individual rights increase if terrorists use a pathogen that is communicable from person to person. Fortunately, anthrax is not communicable in this way which means that the anthrax attacks did not result in major governmental infringements on individual rights.

The anthrax attacks illustrate, however, the importance of the framework established in international law for infringing on civil and political rights to protect public health. Regional and international treaties on civil and political rights recognized the need for public health to have the power to override individual rights in order to deal with infectious diseases long before bioterrorism concerns emerged. What the treaties on civil and political rights establish, however, is a framework that public health authorities need to follow in order to ensure that individual rights and liberties are infringed only when necessary and in the least restrictive way possible.

International law on civil and political rights disciplines public health power in four ways: (1) the public health authority being exercised must be prescribed by law; (2) the authority must be applied in a non-discriminatory manner; (3) due process of law must be accorded before an individual's rights are infringed, unless an emergency situation exists, and then due process should be accorded as soon as possible after infringement; and (4) the infringement of rights must be necessary from both a scientific and a public health standpoint, and the infringement must be the least restrictive possible under the circumstances. In the twentieth century, the exercise of public health powers that infringe individual rights faded in developed countries as public health and healthcare systems improved. Bioterrorism raises the possibility that these powers must be dusted off and used in ways that again encroach on individual civil and political rights. The treaty disciplines outlined above have not been prominent in either public health or international human rights law in the last fifty years. The anthrax attacks, and the specter of bioterrorism involving highly communicable pathogens such as smallpox, place the tension between effective public health responses to infectious disease emergencies and civil rights and liberties high on the agenda of public health, constitutional law, and international law.

D. INTERNET

National Regulation. Sanjay S. Mody, "National Cyberspace Regulation: Unbundling the Concept of Jurisdiction" 37 Stan. J. Int'l L. 365 (2001).

Simply declaring that the Internet constitutes a distinct "cybersovereignty" does not make it so. As A. Michael Froomkin observes, "We do not find concepts such as 'telephonespace' or 'autospace' helpful, and for good reason; cyberspace too is not a place, but only a metaphor—often an unhelpful one." Thus, notwithstanding the fact that the Internet is a unique technological phenomenon, its real-world effects bring cyberspace participants within the realm of geographically based law. Put another way, conventional, transnational legal doctrine, which vests in the state primary authority for regulating land-based activity, carries over effortlessly into cyberspace.

The critics' first objection is that a state may not lawfully regulate cyberspace transmissions taking place beyond its territorial borders. While the critics do not dispute a state's broad authority to regulate activity on its own territory, they argue that a state may not extend its substantive laws to activity happening abroad. On this territorialist view, a state's geographical borders define the permissible scope of its rulemaking authority.

Over the past century, however, a state's jurisdiction to prescribe has become much more expansive. Although territoriality remains the "most pervasive and basic principle" for prescriptive jurisdiction under transnational law, it no longer constitutes the solitary principle. A few years after the American Banana decision, the Permanent Court of International Justice (PCIJ) introduced the idea that a state's regulatory authority may extend under certain circumstances to extraterritorial activity. In The Case of the S.S. Lotus, the Court held that the state of Turkey could apply its criminal laws to any foreigner who committed an offense abroad to the prejudice of Turkey or a Turkish subject, provided the foreigner was arrested within Turkish territory. In contrast to the strict territorial approach expounded by the U. S. Supreme Court in The Apollon and American Banana, the Lotus Court adopted a less rigid view of a state's jurisdiction to prescribe:

> Far from laying down a general prohibition to the effect that States may not extend the application of their laws and the jurisdiction of their courts to persons, property and acts outside their territory, [transnational law] leaves them in this respect a wide measure of discretion which is only limited in certain cases by prohibitive rules; as regards other cases, every State remains free to adopt the principle which it regards as best and most suitable.

Most importantly for present purposes, the PCIJ for the first time recognized local effects as a legitimate basis for prescriptive jurisdiction:

> No argument has come to the knowledge of the Court from which it could be deduced that States recognize themselves to be under an obligation towards each other only to have regard to the place where the author of the offence happens to be at the time of the offence. On the contrary, it is certain that the courts of many countries, even of countries which have given their criminal legislation a strictly territorial character, interpret criminal law in the sense that offences, the authors of which at the moment of commission are in the territory of another State, are nevertheless to be regarded as having

been committed in the national territory, if one of the constituent elements of the offence, and more especially its effects, have taken place there.

Under the "effects" principle (the so called objective territoriality approach), a state may prescribe rules for "conduct outside its territory that has or is intended to have substantial effect within its territory." As such, the principle reduces—but does not sever—the congruence between a state's territorial borders and its rulemaking authority: "jurisdiction [under the effects principle] continues to be tied to place, but [is] measured by a more complex relationship with the defendant than simply the location of his body." This "demise of hermetic territorialism" reflects an evolution in transnational jurisdictional doctrine toward a richer conception of territorial sovereignty. Whereas the strict territoriality principle confines a state's rulemaking authority to activity taking place entirely within its borders, the effects principle expands that authority to include activity occurring beyond its borders but causing local effects. The effects principle thus "constitutes an expanded conception of territorial sovereignty, not a rejection of the conception."

In summary, the fact that harmful activity takes place extraterritorially does not disqualify a state from regulating that activity under transnational law. Local effects, as much as local causes, are sufficient grounds for a state to exercise its regulatory prerogative. It follows that states may prescribe rules for cyberspace transmissions causing local harms, even when the sources of those transmissions—the content providers—are located across national borders. Consequently, the critics' first objection to national regulation does not pass muster.

The critics' second objection is that national cyberspace regulation raises a notice problem. In particular, they point out that the architecture of cyberspace prevents a content provider from knowing ex ante where precisely its transmissions will cause local harms. As a result, a content provider cannot ascertain beforehand which states' laws its transmissions will violate. Unlike the physical world, cyberspace does not contain "signposts that provide warning [to a content provider that it] will be required, after crossing, to abide by different rules."*

But the fact that national cyberspace regulation ineluctably leads to a lack-of-notice problem, even if descriptively accurate, n85 does not violate modern jurisdictional doctrine. First of all, the fact that more than one state exercises regulatory authority over a given activity does not by itself render such authority illegitimate. Surely this sort of "all-leads-to-nothing" proposition—i.e., the fact that all states in principle might be able to regulate a harmful activity means that no one state in fact should—flies in the face of historical state practice. Jack Goldsmith argues, for instance, that a state's regulation of pollution arriving from

---

* David R. Johnson & David Post, Law and Borders—The Rise of Law in Cyberspace, 48 Stan. L. Rev. (1996) at 1370.

an adjacent state does not become problematic simply because a third state (or, for that matter, a hundredth state) also decides to exercise rulemaking authority over the pollution source. As discussed above, a state may lawfully prescribe rules for activity originating outside its boundaries if that activity causes material local harms. The prospect that multiple national regulations will produce a legal "Tower of Babel" has no bearing on a state's prerogative, in principle, to regulate the conduct in question.

More fundamentally, the critics' argument wrongly imports a notice requirement for prescriptive jurisdiction. It is true that the Restatement (Third) of Foreign Relations Laws 403, lists as factors to be considered in exercising prescriptive jurisdiction "the extent to which the activity takes place within the territory, or has substantial, direct, and foreseeable effect upon or in the territory." But, international law does not in fact require a state to satisfy a reasonableness standard in exercising prescriptive jurisdiction.

In summary, the critics' objection that national cyberspace regulation leads to insufficient notice is unconvincing. In cyberspace, as in the real world, an extraterritorial activity causing local harms is not exempt from local regulations because the harm-producing actor is not aware of local governing law. A content provider might lack advance notice of which state (or states) will regulate its transmissions, but the lack of notice alone does not render illegitimate the exercise of prescriptive jurisdiction. Lastly, even presuming that a notice requirement exists under transnational law, it is highly unlikely that national cyberspace regulation would in practice violate such a requirement.

The critics' third objection is that national cyberspace regulation produces impermissible spillover effects. This objection subsumes two separate, but closely related, claims. First, the critics argue that because cyberspace transmissions appear simultaneously in every state, each prescribing its own rules, a content provider fearful of incurring liability will have to modify its transmissions to satisfy the law of the most restrictive state. A multi-jurisdictional regulatory system that subjects content providers to any and all states' laws thus causes a sort of overregulation: One state's comparatively stricter regulation deprives other states' residents of the benefits of, for them, lawful content. Second, critics argue that one state's unilateral regulation of cyberspace transmissions interferes with other states' sovereign authority to regulate their domestic affairs. Therefore, constituents in the nonregulating (or, more precisely, noneffectively regulating) states lack exit from, or voice in, the de facto governing law. National cyberspace regulation, the critics allege, raises serious questions of legitimacy by permitting government officials to establish on-line content standards for users to whom the officials themselves are not accountable. They thus protest a single state's power to enfeeble other states' regulatory efforts; in effect, to establish rules for the entire international system.

The critics' spillover argument is flawed for several reasons. First, the legitimacy of a state's exercise of prescriptive jurisdiction has never been held to turn on a measurement of its spillover effects. A state's regulation of extraterritorial activity causing local harms does not become invalid simply because the regulation has adverse consequences for other states. After all, countless laws have such spillover effects: when the United Kingdom applies its relatively strict libel laws to U.S. media corporations; when the United States applies its antitrust laws to British reinsurance companies; or when Canada applies its anti-fraud laws to the foreign-based operator of a telephone solicitation scheme. Moreover, these laws cause spillover effects, in varying degrees, in states beyond the one in which the regulated entity is located: forcing the creation of a less scintillating publication; giving up the benefits of a monopoly's synergies; or losing the trickle-down effects of currency obtained through fraudulent activity. Plainly, it is uncontroversial under transnational law for State A to apply its substantive laws to the acts of a company based in State B, no matter the impact of those laws on State C (or D or E …). The critics do not put forward compelling reasons why laws governing cyberspace merit distinctive treatment. In short, national cyberspace regulation might produce more wide-ranging and immediate spillover effects than "real-world" regulation, but these effects are different in degree, not in kind.

Furthermore, if spillover minimization were a criterion of legitimacy, practically no national regulation—whether governing conduct inside or outside a state's real-world borders—could be deemed legitimate. As several commentators have noted, it is almost impossible in an increasingly interdependent world for a state to apply its laws without producing spillover effects in other states. Given the unavoidability of spillover effects, it makes little sense for spillover minimization to serve as a criterion of legitimacy for a state's exercise of prescriptive jurisdiction. "It cannot be the case that a state is prohibited from engaging in any actions that produce changes in another state, because virtually … everything that one state does has impacts on the others."*

In summary, states enact laws producing spillover effects all the time, yet spillover effects do not imperil the legitimacy of those laws. Moreover, nothing about national cyberspace regulation qualifies it for distinct treatment, jurisdictionally speaking, from regulation of good old-fashioned, real-world activity. Consequently, the fact that one state's regulation of cyberspace transmissions might affect their availability or cost elsewhere is not relevant for the purpose of measuring the legitimacy of the regulation.

Unilateral Regulation. Jack Goldsmith, "Unilateral Regulation of the Internet: A Modest Defence" 11 Euro. J. Int'l L. 135 (2000).

Various harmonization strategies are being employed to address the challenges of regulating the Internet. Consider a few examples. Several

---

* Lea Brilmayer, *Justifying International Acts* (1989), p. 107.

recent treaties and related multinational edicts have strengthened digital content owners' right to control the distribution and presentation of their property online. These harmonization efforts grow out of an international copyright regime that is over one hundred years old. The G8 economic powers have recently begun to coordinate regulatory efforts concerning Internet-related crimes in five areas: paedophilia and sexual exploitation; drug-trafficking; money laundering; electronic fraud, such as theft of credit-card numbers, and computerized piracy; and industrial and state espionage. These initiatives mirror similar efforts to redress similar regulatory leakage problems in real-space contexts such as environmental policy, banking and insurance supervision, and antitrust regulation. Several international organizations have drafted model laws and guidelines to facilitate Internet commerce and related digital certification issues. There are scores of other international efforts in a variety of Internet-related contexts.

Harmonization strategies such as these are clearly an important response to the jurisdictional difficulties of Internet regulation. If successful, these strategies can reduce or even eliminate the costs of regulatory conflict. But public harmonization is not a panacea. It is useful to recall, in this regard, that there are good reasons for regulatory difference among nations. Nations have different regulatory commitments because of, among other things, differences in endowment, technological capacities, and preferences. A primary virtue of decentralized lawmaking by nation states (as opposed to uniform international rules) is that it allows populations to implement policies that reflect these differences. This in a nutshell is the theory that informs, among other things, the concept of national sovereignty, the European principle of subsidiarity, the American conception of federalism, and the economic concept of comparative advantage. In addition to these "substantive" differences among nations, there is "procedural" value in having decisions made at the smallest possible political unit.

These substantive and procedural values are diminished by international harmonization. They are costs to be weighed in the balance when considering the virtues of harmonization, especially since some harmonization efforts reflect coercion by powerful nations rather than truly fair or efficient regulatory improvements. In addition, these considerations suggest why harmonization is often not easy to achieve. When regulatory differences reflects important local values, harmonization is so hard because of (among other things) domestic political opposition. This is why so many international regulatory regimes are littered with (usually ill-defined) mandatory or local public policy exceptions. This fact should give harmonization's champions pause when addressing national differences in the Internet context.

It is difficult to generalize about when harmonization of Internet-related regulations will be successful, for the Internet covers a broad range of regulatory concerns. We can probably expect relatively robust harmonization in those contexts—like criminal law enforcement and perhaps consumer fraud—where nations' interests converge and the gains from cooperation are high. We are likely to see soft harmonization of contested national regulatory regimes before we see hard harmonization. Harmonization is also likely in coordination situations—such as the communication protocols that define the Internet—where every nation has an incentive to adhere to adopted standard. The particular standards adopted of course have distributional consequences, which usually mean that powerful nations determine their content; but after the standard is adopted, all nations have incentives to adhere to it. This type of coordination situation, it must be admitted, is not likely to be present when contested social values are in issue.

In many other situations, harmonization will either be undesirable or impossible to achieve. In these situations unilateral regulation will remain the primary method of public regulation.

Sovereignty and Internet Regulation. Julien Mailland, "Freedom of Speech, the Internet, and the Costs of Control: The French Example" 33 N.Y.U. J. Int'l L. & Pol. 1179 (2001).

In several French cases, internet sites have been deemed traditional press publications by definition. The Law on the Press of 1881 defines a press publication as "any service using a written mode of thought-communication, available to the public in general or to categories of public." French courts have embraced internet sits under this definition based on the public diffusion criterion. The relevant effect of this interpretation has been that the internet is not a law-free space, as some had initially contended.

Having established that French law applies to the novel medium of the internet, French courts turned to the question of jurisdiction. In the *Faurisson* case, the court reviewed the prosecution of a revisionist website edited in French and hosted in the United States. The defendant contended that the court had no jurisdiction over the matter since the publication had been created abroad, where the server was located. The court, however, recognized that the defendant's theory in effect would permit French authors to escape the reach of content obligations imposed by French law because it is technically impossible to prevent anyone with internet access from uploading materials to a foreign server. The court claimed jurisdiction over the matter under the reasoning that "activities [on the internet] are at the same time here and elsewhere, and, for a judge, declining jurisdiction amounts to admitting that he has no power to put an end to an activity that is blatantly illegal." The Faurisson court referred to Article 113–2 of the French criminal code, which deems a crime to be committed on the Republic's territory as long as one of its elements takes place in the territory. With regard to press publications, the court held that the crime is deemed to be committed wherever the writings are diffused or the broadcasts received. Territorial jurisdiction and applicability of French law, the court concluded, extended to the website, which, while hosted abroad, had been viewed within territorial limits.

A similar "effects" rationale was applied to exercise jurisdictional control over Yahoo!, Inc. The US company was prosecuted in a French court for displaying Nazi items on its auction pages and for hosting several xenophobic pages on Geocities, Yahoo's free webpage hosting service, in contravention of Article R 645–2 of the French criminal code. The court based its decision to exercise territorial jurisdiction on Article 46 of the New Code of Civil Procedure, which grants territorial jurisdiction to the court sitting in the jurisdiction in which the prejudice is suffered. In this case, the judge declared that the Paris Tribunal had jurisdiction over the case because the prejudice ("the offense to the country's collective memory") had been suffered in France.

The *Faurisson* and *Yahoo!* decisions reflected the French judiciary's attempt at legitimizing the application of state censorship regulations to the internet. However, it is unlikely that judiciary efforts along these lines will restrict the free flow of unlawful material to countries trying to control it. First, the *Yahoo!* court's assumptions regarding the technical possibility of identifying an estimated 90% of users are incorrect. As the French tribunal acknowledged, viewers may be able to bypass any screening devises Yahoo! Employs either by registering with a foreign ISP or by connecting through sites using a local ISP that will prevent the server from identifying the IP address of the user.

Second, it is doubtful whether the *Faurisson* and *Yahoo!* decisions could be enforced in the United States. Yahoo! recently has filed a declaratory action requesting a US court to declare that the French judgment is unenforceable in the United States. In order for a foreign judgment to be enforced in another sovereign's jurisdiction, it requires *exequatur* from local judges. Traditionally, however, a local judge will enforce a foreign judgment only if the ground for such judgment does not violate patently the fundamental legal principles and social norms of the country where enforcement is sought. In the *Yahoo!* case, it likely will be difficult for France to enforce its judgment in the country whose laws offer the utmost protection with regard to political speech.

The French courts grounded their territorial jurisdiction and their decision to apply French law solely on the fact that the speech at stake could be accessed from France and thus could cause harm to French residents. Because they did not spell out any other criteria, such as the intent of the site's publisher as to the audience it tried to reach, the courts have taken, as one of the lawyers in the *Faurisson* case remarked, "a universal, borderless, jurisdiction" with regard to territoriality.

The first issue created by the Nazi cases relates to international law and the (dis)respect of other countries' sovereignty. By sovereignty, I mean the ability of a country both to create and to enforce its own rules. It is especially shocking that the judge in *Yahoo!* Declared that the US company would "satisfy an ethical and moral requirement shared by all democratic societies" if it suppressed all Nazi-related pages from its servers. It is clear from US case law and jurisprudence that protecting the freedom of expression, even the expression of hatred, is a widely shared value in the United States. By denying this fact, well-known given the number of articles on the topic published in the European press for the past few years, the French judge showed a high level of disregard for the right of other nations to have different views, a right which flows from their sovereign characters.

The second unfortunate consequence of the French approach is that it might lead to serious limitations on the ability of French residents to access foreign sources of information. Because France regulates information production and distribution so extensively and imposes so many restrictions on the content of speech, virtually every page on the internet has the potential to violate a French rule. It is therefore possible that if France keeps on the track it is on today, a number of US hosts and search engines will try to block access by French residents to their services in order to avoid the accessing of pages that could violate *any* French law, from the most famous, the Law on the Press of 1881, to the most obscure, Article L 630 of the Public Health Code which prohibits the utterance of favorable comments about narcotics. The same reasoning is applicable to sites in all foreign countries, not just in the United States.

The third problem is that, from an international perspective, France has set a very bad precedent on the international scene. This in turn could have a negative global effect on respect for both the principles of sovereignty and the freedom of speech.

If France considers the protection of its "internal public order" to be strong enough an interest to justify taking coercive measures against foreign entities that do not direct their publications specifically towards France, then there is no reason to think that other countries will not reach the same conclusion for themselves. Again, from the international law point of view, all "internal public orders" are equal, and in principle, there should be no difference between those of France and those of other countries, even when these countries are less respectful of civil liberties than France. The French approach gives every other country a justification for taking coercive measures on foreign entities.

Chapter 13

INTERNATIONAL LAW TOMORROW

Editors' introduction: What common values undergird international law, and how can a values-based law system guide the future? The sweeping transformations of international law described in Chapter One and examined throughout this Handbook open new horizons for all fields of international law. These developments, and the related process of globalization, present a new challenge, one that has broad, normative dimensions. If there is a "common humanity," and if that humanity is today faced with complex global issues that cannot be managed adequately by narrow state-based interests, then is it not imperative to move beyond sovereignty and toward a common purpose? International law has a clear role to play in developing the components of a workable vision. We give the final word to two authors who call for a new ethos, one that accounts for the expanding needs of a common humanity.

Rethinking Common Values. Sissela Bok, "Rethinking Common Values," in Ken Booth and Time Dunne (eds.), *Worlds in Collision: Terror and the Future of Global Order* (2002), excerpt.

In September 2000, world leaders assembled at the United Nations in New York for a Millennium Summit. The presidents, prime ministers and other representatives of over 150 states who had come together concluded by signing a sonorous United Nations Millennium Declaration, setting forth and expansive set of common values. Among these were freedom, equality, solidarity, tolerance, respect for nature and shared responsibility—in other words, ideals that have conspicuously *never* been held in common by all or even most societies at any time in history.

Among the signatories were leaders of some of the most oppressive and aggressive regimes on earth; yet they, too, agreed to uphold the Declaration's panoply of values and to combat violence, terror and crime. Likewise, representatives of the states discriminating most severely against women were at one with the rest in claiming to resolve to ensure that (by 2015) children everywhere, boys and girls alike, will be able to complete a full course of primary schooling, and that boys and girls will have equal access to education.

The Millennium Declaration never rang more hollow than after the September 11 attacks the following year, offering harrowing evidence that the values so ringingly proclaimed, including the rejection of terror, are not nearly universal. The conclusion seems inevitable: any view which asserts that values such as those enumerated in the Declaration are universal is simply erroneous; it represents a mistaking of what many long to see as universal for what is all too obviously the case.

Skepticism in the face of such rhetoric about common values is surely needed. But indiscriminate skepticism has dangers all its own. It can lead those disenchanted by inflated claims about common values to swing over to imagining that societies in fact share no values whatsoever, and in turn to fatalistic acceptance of dismal projections. In this regard, too, the aftermath of the September 11 attacks proved instructive. True, they received no unanimous condemnation and evoked, instead, rejoicing by some and measured approval by others; but the vast outpouring of sympathy for the victims from so many countries was striking, as was the horror widely expressed at the transgression of the most fundamental moral requirements of respect for innocent life.

What might these moral requirements be? And might the ways in which they have been thought to be common to human societies have to be rethought in the aftermath of the attacks? In my book *Common Values*, I pointed to accumulating historical and anthropological research showing that the claim that societies share no values whatsoever is erroneous. No community can survive long without some limited set of internal constraints on violence, deceit and fraud, and some positive duties of mutual care and reciprocity along with rudimentary standards and procedures and standards for what is fair and just. These basic values are indispensable to human coexistence, though far from sufficient, at every level of personal and working life and of family, community, national and international relations.

These values have surely also been violated within all societies, even as they have often been held not to apply to outsiders and enemies at all. Any community—no matter how small or disorganized, no matter how hostile toward outsiders, no matter how cramped its perception of what constitutes childcare, say, or torture—requires at least rudimentary forms of nurturing and of internal curbs on violence, deceit and betrayal in order to survive.

The danger of ignoring the existence of shared but limited values takes many forms. It becomes easier to dismiss all talk about values as mere rhetoric, without making distinctions between vacuous invocations of vast lists of ideals and efforts to protect basic human rights. Such an attitude can facilitate, in turn, passivity in the face of atrocities, on the grounds that there can be no meaningful discourse about shared values or even understandings across cultural and linguistic boundaries. And many who dismiss the existence of shared values fall prey to unquestioning acceptance of erroneous prognostications and in turn to insufficiently carefully calibrated responses to stark violations of the most basic among these values.

Once we can conceive of these values as being so widely shared, we have a basis for dialogue and debate about how to extend them beyond the narrowest confines. These values can also offer criteria and a broadly comprehensible language for critique of existing practices. Within societies, they can buttress arguments against leaving out certain groups when it comes to fundamental forms of respect. Across societal boundaries, taking these values seriously can support arguments that they should hold everywhere; and that cross-cultural critique is fully justified when it comes to political or religious practices such as torture, slavery, terrorism or human sacrifice, as well as to doctrines that endorse such practices.

Is World Order in Decline? Richard A. Falk, from *The Declining World Order: America's Imperial Geopolitics* (2004), excerpt.

Contrary to widespread claims in the west, there is no empirical basis for the argument that the economic performance of a country is necessarily tied to constitutional democracy and human rights. Several countries in the Asia/Pacific region, most significantly China, have combined an outstanding macroeconomic record with harsh authoritarian rule. Globalization-from-above is not an assured vehicle for the achievement of Western-style constitution democracy, including the protection of individual and group rights. But democracy, as such, is the essence of a meaningful form of political action on the part of global civil society, especially to the extent that such action, even when radical in its goals, refrains from and repudiates violent means. In this regard, there is an emergent, as yet implicit, convergence of ends and means on the part of several distinct tendencies in civil society: these include issue-oriented movements, nonviolent democracy movements, and the emergence of governmental elites that minimize their links to geopolitical structures. This convergence presents several intriguing opportunities for coalition building and a greater ideological coherence among the various institutions and interest groups seeking to achieve a responsible global capitalism. Against this background, normative democracy seems like an attractive umbrella for theorizing, not dogmatically, but to exhibit affinities.

Normative democracy adopts a comprehensive view of the fundamental ideas associated with the secular modern state. Security is conceived in extending to environmental protection and to the defense of economic viability. Human rights are conceived as encompassing the social and economic rights of individuals, as well as such collective rights as the right to development, the right to peace, and the right of self-determination. Democracy is conceived as extending beyond constitutional and free, periodic elections to include an array of other assurances that governance is oriented toward human well-being and ecological sustainability, and that citizens have access to the various arenas of decision making.

The elements of normative democracy can be enumerated, but their content and behavioral applications will require amplification and adaptation in varied, specific settings. This enumeration reflects the dominant orientations and outlook of the political actors that make up the constructivist category of a substantive profile of normative democracy. This enumeration is not a wish list, but rather is descriptive and explanatory of an embedded consensus with respect to political reform. The elements of this consensus are as follows:

1. *Consent of citizenry:* Some periodic indication that the permanent population of the relevant community is represented by the institutions of governance, which confer legitimacy through the expression of freely expressed consent in the context of meaningful choice. Elections are the established modalities for territorial communities to confer legitimacy on government, but referenda and rights of petition and recall may be more appropriate for other types of political community, especially those of regional or global scope. Direct democracy may be most meaningful for the governance of local political activity.

2. *Rule of law:* All modes of governance should be subject to the discipline of the law as a way of imposing effective limits on authority and of assuring some form of checks and balances as between legislative, executive, judicial, and administrative processes. An independent and respected judiciary plays an indispensable role in fulfilling expectations about a rule-governed society that is also responsive to considerations of equity and justice. Also, there is a need for sensitivity to the normative claims of civil initiatives associated with codes of conduct, conference declarations, and societal institutions (for instance, the Permanent Peoples Tribunal in Rome).

3. *Human rights:* Taking account of differing cultural, economic, and political settings and priorities, the establishment of mechanisms for the impartial and effective implementation of human rights by global, regional, state, and transnational civil sources of authority. Human rights are conceived by references to the elements of human dignity. They encompass economic, social, and cultural rights, as well as civil and political rights, with a concern for both individual and collective conceptions of rights, emphasizing tolerance toward difference and fundamental community sentiments, and sensitivity to valued legacies of the past and the life prospects of future generations.

4. *Participation:* Effective and meaningful modes of participation in the political life of the society, centered upon the process of government, but extending to all forms of social governance, including the workplace and home. Participation may be direct or indirect, that is, representational, but it enables the expression of views and influence upon the process of decision making on the basis of an ideal of equality of access. Creativity is needed

to find methods in addition to elections through which to ensure full participation.

5. *Accountability:* Implying the existence of suitable mechanisms for challenging the exercise of authority by those occupying official positions at the level of the state, but also with respect to the functioning of the market and of international institutions. Establishing an international criminal court in 2002 provided one mechanism for assuring accountability by those in powerful positions who have been traditionally treated as exempt from the rule of law, provided the reach of this institution is respected by the powerful actors in world society, which is now only a distant prospect.

6. *Public goods:* A restored social agenda that corrects the growing imbalance, varying in seriousness from country to country, between private and public goods. Such an imbalance exists with respect to relieving poverty and improving health, education, housing, the conservation of scarce resources, and basic human needs, but also in relation to support for environmental protection, regulation of economic globalization, innovative cultural activity, and infrastructural development for governance at the regional and global levels. In these regards, a gradual depoliticalization of funding, either by a use or transaction tax imposed on financial flows, global air travel, or some form of reliable and equitable means to fund public goods of local, national, regional, and global scope is worth serious consideration.

7. *Transparency:* An openness with respect to knowledge and information that builds trust between the institutions of governance and the citizenry at various levels of social interaction. In effect, establishing the right to information as an aspect of constitutionalism, including a strong bias against public sector secrecy and covert operations, and criminalizing government lies such as the sort revealed in connection with CIA lies about alleged "UFO sightings" so as protect the secrecy of U.S. Air Force spy missions. Internationally, transparency is particularly important with respect to military expenditures and arms transfers. The priority given to counterterrorist activities of the government provides a sweepingly dangerous rationalization for governmental secrecy, especially in the wake of September 11 anxieties.

8. *Nonviolence:* Underpinning globalization-from-below and the promotion of substantive democracy is a conditional commitment to nonviolent politics and conflict resolution. Such a commitment does not nullify all rights of self-defense as protected in international law, strictly and narrowly construed. Nor does it necessarily invalidate a limited recourse to violence by oppressed peoples when peaceful methods to achieve change and rights have been frustrated and met with repressive responses. However, this ethos of nonviolence clearly imposes on governments an

obligation to renounce weaponry of mass destruction and to negotiate actively phased disarmament arrangements. It also demands commitments dedicated to demilitarizing approaches to peace and security at all levels of social interaction, including peace and security at the level of city and neighborhood.

†